Brothers and Sisters in Medieval European Literature

YORK MEDIEVAL PRESS

York Medieval Press is published by the University of York's Centre for Medieval Studies in association with Boydell & Brewer Limited. Our objective is the promotion of innovative scholarship and fresh criticism on medieval culture. We have a special commitment to interdisciplinary study, in line with the Centre's belief that the future of Medieval Studies lies in those areas in which its major constituent disciplines at once inform and challenge each other.

Editorial Board (2019)

Professor Peter Biller (Dept of History): General Editor
Professor T. Ayers (Dept of History of Art)
Dr Henry Bainton (Dept of English and Related Literature)
Dr J. W. Binns (Dept of English and Related Literature)
Dr K. P. Clarke (Dept of English and Related Literature)
Dr K. F. Giles (Dept of Archaeology)
Dr Holly James-Maddocks (Dept of English and Related Literature)
Dr Harry Munt (Dept of History)
Professor W. Mark Ormrod (Dept of History)
Professor Sarah Rees Jones (Dept of History): Director, Centre for Medieval Studies
Dr L. J. Sackville (Dept of History)
Dr Hanna Vorholt (Dept of History of Art)
Professor J. G. Wogan-Browne (English Faculty, Fordham University)

Consultant on Manuscript Publications

Professor Linne Mooney (Dept of English and Related Literature)

All enquiries of an editorial kind, including suggestions for monographs and essay collections, should be addressed to: The Academic Editor, York Medieval Press, Department of History, University of York, Heslington, York, YO10 5DD (E-mail: pete.biller@york.ac.uk)

Details of other York Medieval Press volumes are available from Boydell & Brewer Ltd.

Brothers and Sisters
in Medieval European Literature

Carolyne Larrington

THE UNIVERSITY *of York*

YORK MEDIEVAL PRESS

© Carolyne Larrington 2015

All Rights Reserved. Except as permitted under current legislation no part of this work may be photocopied, stored in a retrieval system, published, performed in public, adapted, broadcast, transmitted, recorded or reproduced in any form or by any means, without the prior permission of the copyright owner

The right of Carolyne Larrington to be identified as the author of this work has been asserted in accordance with sections 77 and 78 of the Copyright, Designs and Patents Act 1988

First published 2015
Paperback edition 2019

A York Medieval Press publication
in association with The Boydell Press
an imprint of Boydell & Brewer Ltd
PO Box 9, Woodbridge, Suffolk IP12 3DF, UK
and of Boydell & Brewer Inc.
668 Mt Hope Avenue, Rochester, NY 14620–2731, USA
website: www.boydellandbrewer.com

ISBN 978 1 903153 62 8 hardback
ISBN 978 1 903153 85 7 paperback

A CIP catalogue record for this book is available
from the British Library

The publisher has no responsibility for the continued existence or accuracy of URLs for external or third-party internet websites referred to in this book, and does not guarantee that any content on such websites is, or will remain, accurate or appropriate

Typeset by Word and Page, Chester

For my brother David Larrington,
and for Christina Brandenburg

CONTENTS

Acknowledgements	ix
Abbreviations	x
Introduction	1
1. The Medieval Sibling in History	17
2. 'Berr er hverr á bakinu nema sér bróður eigi': Fraternal Love and Loyalty	46
3. 'Io v'ho cara quanto sorella si dee avere': Sisters, and their Brothers	76
4. 'Næs þæt andæges nið': Fraternal Hatreds	104
5. 'Te souviegne de ce que je suis ta seur': Sisters and Hostility	129
6. 'The king's dochter gaes wi child to her brither': Sibling Incest	155
7. 'So wil ich dir ce wibe mine swester gebn': When Siblings Marry	181
8. 'Trewethes togider that gun plight': Fictive Siblings	208
Conclusion	235
Bibliography	239
Index	261

ACKNOWLEDGEMENTS

The number of people who have expressed interest in my siblings project over the years, who have suggested sibling stories, made sibling observations or answered my sibling questions, is enormous. And I am sorry for any omissions in the list that follows. Thanks in particular are due to: Frank Romany and Roger Lindsay for psychoanalytical and psychological leads; Elizabeth Archibald, Frank Brandsma and Kate McClune for Arthurian suggestions; Judy Quinn, David Clark, Jóhanna Friðriksdóttir, Guðrún Nordal, Ármann Jakobsson and Jo Shortt Butler for Norse siblings; Judith Jesch for runic material; Katharine Earnshaw, Gervase Rosser and Cyril Edwards for translation help; Alex Feldman for a chance reference to the *Gesta Romanorum*; Ceridwen Lloyd-Morgan for Welsh conversations; Tom Lambert for late Anglo–Saxon sworn-brothers, and John Pitcher for much miscellaneous advice over many years. Nigel Palmer, Keith Busby, Helen Cooper, Will Sweet have all, in different ways, made productive and helpful suggestions. I should also acknowledge the helpful comments made by anonymous publishers' readers, and the many valuable suggestions, particularly those relating to the thorny area of medieval demography, offered by Pete Biller for York Medieval Press. Caroline Palmer has been encouraging and enthusiastic about the project. Thanks too to Tim Bourns for help with the index.

Thanks are due also to many conference, lecture and seminar organizers, among whom are Steve Mitchell at Harvard, the CCASNAC team of 2010, Richard North, Jessica Stoll, and the audiences, students and conversation partners who have listened to me talk about and who have talked themselves about siblings and inlaws over the years. St John's College granted me a year of sabbatical leave to work on the early stages of this project, and I am grateful for the College's continuing support of my research.

This book is dedicated to my own sibling, my brother David, and to my former affine Tina Brandenburg.

ABBREVIATIONS

DNB	*Oxford Dictionary of National Biography* (online resource)
EETS	Early English Text Society
ES	Extra Series
FSN	*Fornaldarsögur Norðurlanda*, ed. Guðni Jónsson, 4 vols. (Reykjavík, 1954)
ÍF	Íslenzk fornrit
L-G	*Lancelot-Grail: The Old French Arthurian Vulgate and Post-Vulgate in Translation*, ed. N. J. Lacy *et al.* 5 vols (New York, 1993–6)
MGH	Monumenta Germaniae Historica
OS	Ordinary Series
PL	*Patrologia Latina*, ed. Migne (online resource)
Saxo, *GD*	Saxo Grammaticus, *Gesta Danorum*, online at: http://www2.kb.dk/elib/lit/dan/saxo/lat/or.dsr/index.htm
Saxo, *HD*	Saxo Grammaticus, *History of the Danes*, ed. H. Ellis-Davidson, trans. P. Fisher (Cambridge, 1998)
SS	Special Series

All translations are my own unless otherwise indicated.

INTRODUCTION

Why Siblings?

Sibling studies are the poor neglected stepchild of the history of the Western family. Interest in vertical relationships, in lineage and genealogies and in inter-generational strife has directed scholarly attention away from lateral ties, while Freudian paradigms have foregrounded mother–child bonds and the Oedipal acting-out of sons against fathers. The bond between brothers and sisters is, however, the relationship which lasts longest of all, from birth or shortly afterwards until death supervenes. From the beginning of the millennium historians of the family and literary scholars have been investigating sibling relationships in the post-medieval period, uncovering the social conditions which shape the sibling relationship and drilling down into the more abundant evidence of sibling emotions found in different kinds of post-medieval source.[1] Only in the last ten years, particularly in France, have historians embarked on detailed analysis of medieval sibling relations.[2] There has been even less investigation of brothers and sisters in the imaginative literature of the Middle Ages: it is this gap which this book aims to address.

The medieval family was, in many respects, as diverse in its formation as the modern family with its blends of half-, step-, full, adoptive and foster-children.[3] Parental mortality rates, remarriages and expansion of the family group to increase the availability of labour were all factors that contributed to complex family structures and created distinctions amongst the cohort of siblings who regarded one another as brother or sister. Leonore Davidoff suggests that nowadays the individual is less likely to have a full brother or sister than at any time in earlier history, thanks to the prevalence of marital breakdown, new

---

[1] See L. Davidoff, *Thicker than Water: Siblings and their Relations 1780–1920* (Oxford, 2012); *Sibling Relations and the Transformations of European Kinship 1300–1900*, ed. C. Johnson and D. W. Sabean (Oxford and New York, 2011); *Sibling Relations and Gender in the Early Modern World: Sisters, Brothers and Others*, ed. N. J. Miller and N. Yavneh (Aldershot, 2006); V. Sanders, *The Brother–Sister Culture in Nineteenth-Century Literature: from Austen to Woolf* (Basingstoke, 2002).

[2] For example, I. Réal, *Vies de saints, vie de famille: représentation et système de la parenté dans le royaume mérovingien [481–751] d'après les sources hagiographiques* (Turnhout, 2001); D. Lett, *Frères et sœurs: histoire d'un lien* (Paris, 2009), the special journal issue, *Frères et sœurs – Ethnographie d'un lien de parenté*, Médiévales 54 (2008), ed. D. Lett, *Frères et sœurs: les liens adelphiques dans l'Occident antique et médiéval*, ed. S. Cassagnes-Brouquet and M. Yvernault (Turnhout, 2007), and *La parenté déchirée: les luttes intrafamiliales au Moyen Âge*, ed. M. Aurell (Turnhout, 2010).

[3] See R. Edwards, L. Hadfield et al., *Who is a Sister and a Brother? Biological and Social Ties* (London, 2005).

household formation and innovations in reproductive technology.[4] Nevertheless, in the modern West 80 per cent of individuals do have a sibling: siblings who live much longer than their medieval counterparts, where child mortality ran at around 50 per cent. The modern sibling relationship can persist over seventy or more years: a truly life-long bond. Especially in childhood, sibling relationships are crucially formative of individual identity; behaviour is learned from peers as much as from parents, especially when older siblings assume care-taking roles, and innate personality traits are emphasized by the drive for differentiation from one's brothers and sisters. Sibling position is thus as important a constituent of identity as vertical lineage. As the historian Michael Roper observes:

> Too often, what goes missing from linguistic analyses is an adequate sense of the material: . . . of human experience formed through emotional relationships with others; and of that experience as involving a perpetual process of managing emotional impulses, both conscious and unconscious, within the self and in relation to others.[5]

Investigation of our cultural past invites us to attend to how siblings think and feel, and how this bears on their behaviour, and the cultural norms which are reinforced or interrogated by the actions of sibling individuals.

In the modern period, the management of emotional impulses can be uncovered in a variety of personal literary forms: in letters, journals, autobiographies and interviews. In earlier periods, emotion and its links to experience and to subjectivity must be excavated via all sorts of writing: from legal documents to sermons, sagas and romance. If we want to develop a more complex picture of medieval brothers and sisters within the families that shaped their identities, we must probe into literary depictions of siblinghood: for it is these which most fully demonstrate how, as Roper argues, 'the assimilation of cultural codes . . . [are] a matter of negotiation involving an active subject'.[6] How siblings behave to one another is strongly inflected both by gender and by social class; processes of social change reconfigure sibling interactions. Thus Boccaccio chronicles how, within a mercantile urban environment, the fact that the family business is run from home exposes a young girl to an unsuitable sexual partner, to the chagrin of her brothers.[7] The aristocratic sibling group, by contrast, both in the early and later medieval periods kept girls under close supervision and was thus better able to regulate sisterly sexuality. While some historical records and folk-tales fitfully illuminate the lives of siblings from the peasant classes,

---

[4] Davidoff, *Thicker than Water*, pp. 1–2.
[5] M. Roper, 'Slipping out of View: Subjectivity and Emotion in Gender History', *History Workshop Journal* 59 (2005), 57–72 (p. 62).
[6] Ibid., pp. 66–7.
[7] Giovanni Boccaccio, *Decameron* (IV.3), cited from: http://www.brown.edu/Departments/Italian_Studies/dweb/texts/DecShowText.php?myID=novo405&lang=it; *Decameron*, trans. G. Waldman (Oxford, 1993), pp. 283–6.

it is predominantly the lives of aristocratic and, later, gentry and mercantile brothers and sisters which are the focus of high-culture literary texts.

Analysis of medieval siblinghood must of course rest on a thoroughly contextualized and historicized understanding of changing social conditions within and beyond the medieval family, and make use of all available sources. The literature of the Middle Ages often attends very closely to the relationship of brother and sister, laying bare sibling behaviours in their most dramatic forms as models to emulate, admire or avoid, and it opens up multiple perspectives on the sibling emotions – love, hate, rivalry, desire, nurturance and ambivalence – which underlie its narratives. The ways in which medieval people thought and felt, and the interaction of cognitive and emotional processes that generates the actions underpinning medieval stories, have become a major focus of recent research. While the 'emotional turn' originated among historians, the proposition that literary texts make a crucial contribution to our understanding of the history of medieval emotion has gained ground.[8] In an early intervention in the field, I foregrounded the value of contemporary psychological theory in making sense of emotion, and its componential relationships with cognition and action, in medieval literary texts.[9] This book develops that argument in relation to the imaginative treatment of sibling and quasi-sibling relationships. Psychological (and to a lesser extent) psychoanalytic theories are grounded in the biological, embodied nature of human beings and thus they propose the existence of emotional and cognitive continuities through historical time. There is a powerful consonance between our own unofficial understanding of sibling bonds – the stories we still tell ourselves about brothers and sisters, the sibling stories of the past, and contemporary psychological and psychoanalytic formulations of sibling dynamics.

The 'sibling turn', which has come about in psychoanalysis and in developmental and cross-cultural psychology in recent years, yields different kinds of insight into sibling stories. It draws attention both to continuities and dissonances between modern understandings of the sibling and the ways in which the relationship was framed in the medieval period. Such approaches must be intelligently applied: it is debatable how far the particular claims of psychoanalysis to observe universal structures in the human psyche across

[8] There is a growing literature on methodologies for understanding emotion in both history and literature: see for example U. Frevert, *Emotions in History – Lost and Found* (Budapest and New York, 2011); the EMMA website: http://emma.hypotheses.org and its associated publications, such as *Le sujet des émotions au moyen âge*, ed. P. Nagy and D. Boquet (Paris, 2009) and *La chair des émotions*, *Médiévales* 61 (2011), ed. D. Boquet, P. Nagy and L. Moulinier-Brogi. P. C. Hogan's two important books, *The Mind and its Stories* (Cambridge, 2009), and *What Literature Teaches us about Emotion* (Cambridge, 2011), do not specifically treat medieval literature texts, but they make a compelling case for the value of literary texts for understanding emotions in the past.
[9] C. Larrington, 'Some Recent Developments in the Psychology of Emotion and their Relevance to the Study of the Medieval Period', *Early Medieval Europe* 10 (2001), 251–6.

very different social and cultural conditions can be profitably applied to a premodern self. Nor is it clear that the highly varied cultural conditions of, for example, Oceania, can bear comparison in many respects with medieval European societies. Nevertheless, psychoanalytic practitioners, developmental and cross-cultural psychologists, and anthropologists all offer theoretical insights into childhood– and adult–sibling relations which find productive resonance in medieval texts. Medieval writers also found models for and discussion of sibling ethics in the Bible and in theological writings. Below I outline some of the contributions of these modern disciplines to the sibling thinking in this book, followed by a summary of the principal brother–sister themes of medieval theology.

Psychoanalytic Theory and the Sibling

The psychoanalyst Juliet Mitchell's work has foregrounded and expanded the post-Freudian implications of sibling interaction. Freud had relatively little to say on the subject, beyond noting sibling rivalry, both as a general phenomenon and a personal experience, Mitchell argues.[10] He recognized that his adult friendships, in particular with the Berlin ear, nose and throat surgeon Wilhelm Fliess, were generally predicated on the ambivalences of the sibling relationship, noting his desire for 'an intimate friend and a hostile enemy', and that sometimes these roles would 'come together in a single individual'.[11] In his early correspondence with Fliess, Freud foregrounded the crucial importance of sibling relations, but by the time he came to elaborate the Oedipus complex, he seemed to have left sibling relations behind; desire and violence were attributed to the castration complex rather than to the tensions of siblinghood. Although there are a few early references to brothers and sisters in his work, such as the striking observation 'In none of my women patients . . . have I failed to come upon this dream of the death of a brother or sister, which tallies with an increase in hostility', Freud does not theorize sibling rivalry in any detail.[12] Nevertheless, he was well aware of sibling hatred as a contributing factor in neurosis; he records the repeated request of his patient Little Hans, as reported by Hans's father, that his mother should drown his baby sister in the bath.[13]

In the last decades, attention has turned from the Freudian triangle of father–

---

[10] See J. Mitchell, *Mad Men and Medusas: Reclaiming Hysteria and the Effects of Sibling Relations on the Human Condition* (Harmondsworth, 2000) and *Siblings: Sex and Violence* (Cambridge, 2003). S. Sherwin-White, 'Freud on Brothers and Sisters: A Neglected Topic', *Journal of Child Psychotherapy* 33 (2007), 4–20, demonstrates that Freud engaged both more closely and more widely with sibling issues than Mitchell credits.

[11] S. Freud, *On the Interpretation of Dreams*, Standard Edition vols 4 and 5 (London, 1953), p. 483.

[12] Freud, *Interpretation of Dreams*, p. 253.

[13] See Mitchell, *Mad Men*, p. 81; also M. Rustin, 'Taking Account of Siblings – A View from Child Psychotherapy', *Journal of Child Psychotherapy* 33 (2007), 21–35.

Introduction

mother–baby to focus on the intricate web of sibling bonds. Juliet Mitchell's two books have broken this new ground: they compellingly redirect attention to the sibling, not simply by identifying childhood trauma, but in charting continuing sibling effects in adult life. In *Mad Men and Medusas* (1999) Mitchell argues that the sibling bonds forged in the nursery lay the groundwork for other lateral or peer relationships, including those with spouses and with in-laws. In *Siblings: Sex and Violence* (2003), Mitchell pays particular attention to gender, making clear that passionate love, desire (the 'polymorphous perversity' of infant sexuality) and violent hostility can be attributed to the sister as well as the brother. Identifying 'the three faces of the sister who both cares for and destroys: the lateral would-be murderer, the nurse and the lawgiver' (recurrent aspects of the sister in the texts considered in this book), she investigates the roles available to sisters in literature as well as in life.[14] Mitchell offers three central conclusions about the sibling relationship. First, she charts the intensity and ambivalences of sibling relationship: 'the adored sibling, who is loved with all the urgency of the child's narcissism is also loathed as its replacement'.[15] Second, she emphasizes the persistence of conflicted sibling relationships into adulthood. Third, she illuminates how sibling ambivalences are projected on to spouses, affines and peers, noting that 'in a world where siblings . . . flourish, we can see their importance not only in themselves but for all lateral relationships'.[16] As the first social relationship is the sibling one, it sets the pattern for other social relations. Ego-development takes place as a result of interaction with peers rather than with parents; that struggle for identity differentiation is revisited when the sibling marries and a new brother- or sister-in-law is added to the sibling cohort.

Gender is particularly salient in the early years. While the birth of the younger sibling makes the boy fear that he has lost the power he was able to wield as 'His Majesty the Baby', according to Mitchell, a girl 'dreads feeling confirmed in her weakness and lack of social value'.[17] This fear of displacement is not limited to same-sex sibling pairs; cross-sex siblings are equally traumatized by the arrival of a new baby. Reflecting on the Antigone myth, Luce Irigaray assesses the brother–sister relationship as reciprocal only insofar as it stimulates the fear of mutual annihilation, 'Et chacun(e) bientôt reconnaîtra qu'en son égal(e) était aussi bien son pire ennemi, sa négation, sa mort' ('And each will soon realize that his or her equal is also his or her worst enemy, negation, and death').[18] More positively, Irigaray also identifies a recurrent role for sisters

---

[14] Mitchell, *Siblings*, p. 57. Antigone, as we shall see, is a frequent focus for discussion of normative sisterly loyalties (see pp. 95–7, 153 below).
[15] Ibid., p. 10.
[16] Ibid., p. 225. See also T. Apter, *The Sister Knot* (New York and London, 2007), p. 179.
[17] Mitchell, *Siblings*, p. 71.
[18] L. Irigaray, 'L'éternelle ironie de la communauté', in *Speculum de l'autre femme* (Paris, 1974), pp. 266–81 (p. 276); 'The Eternal Irony of the Community', in *Speculum of the Other Woman*, trans. G. Gill (Ithaca NY, 1985), pp. 214–26 (p. 222). See chapter three, pp. 90–2.

as their brothers' memory-keepers; as we shall see, sisters often arrogate to themselves the mission of creating and maintaining a saintly brother's cult.[19] Mitchell herself tentatively discusses the political oppression of women by their brothers as originating in sibling trauma.[20] 'Fratriarchy', the oppression of women by their brothers, has been identified chiefly as a post-Enlightenment phenomenon, as a move which extends concepts of equality and fraternity to one gender only.[21] Yet long before the eighteenth century, and consequent upon high adult mortality rates, medieval brothers habitually wielded as much power over their sisters as their fathers did. Marrying off a sister could absorb family assets in the provision of a dowry, or augment them through the payment of a bride-price. The family hoped to benefit from exchanging a woman with another family, bringing their interests into closer alliance and creating homosocial bonds between male coevals.

Ambivalences towards the sibling, feelings in which 'sibling sex and death ... are intricately entwined', must be resolved; the child must forge an individual identity for him- or herself, a task of psychological differentiation entrenched in deep-rooted concepts of sameness and difference.[22] Psychoanalysts regard this work as potentially traumatic, 'but in most cases these experiences will be healed and the dread and shock will turn into hate and love, rivalry and friendship'; the child will learn to acknowledge that there is room for the next in line.[23] 'Borderwork': the establishment of the boundaries of identity, the deliberate selection of different roles or personality traits to distinguish oneself from one's siblings, is crucial to identity formation. And so siblings choose, consciously or unconsciously, to carve out different paths through life. Brothers and sisters exist in an eternally present relationship, patrolling the boundaries of sameness and difference with respect to one another, while childhood behavioural patterns persist or recur throughout the lifespan. From a psychoanalytic perspective, the Western nuclear family generates historically unchanging psychological structures of hostility and affection, of anxiety and ambivalence.[24] The sibling's task in developing his or her identity is to learn to assimilate these feelings, to accommodate the 'next in line' and, pre-eminently, to find ways of negotiating the principles of differentiation and substitutability both on an internal psychological level and as aspects of social existence.

---

[19] See below, p. 92.
[20] Mitchell, *Siblings*, p. 71.
[21] See J. F. MacCannell, *The Regime of the Brother: After the Patriarchy* (London, 1991); C. Pateman, *The Disorder of Women: Democracy, Feminism and Political Theory* (Cambridge, 1989), pp. 33–53, for fraternal oppression as an underinvestigated aspect of patriarchy.
[22] Mitchell, *Siblings*, p. 29.
[23] Ibid., p. 48; p. 190.
[24] See chapter one, p. 22, for demographic evidence suggesting that medieval households tended to contain two generations at most; the multi-generational medieval household is, as a consequence of low life-expectancy, particularly in plague-years, not borne out by the data.

Introduction

Developmental Psychology and Siblings

Psychologists turned their attention to childhood sibling relations from the 1970s onwards, probing the ways in which older children react to the arrival of a new baby and in which sibling alliances shift and reform during later childhood and adolescence. Judy Dunn and her associates' research has confirmed the extreme and conflicted nature of sibling emotion among toddlers and teens; as one mother astutely commented to investigators, 'It comes down to love and hate, doesn't it?'[25] The toddler reacts to the arrival of the new sibling with rage and jealousy, 'feeling[s] of envy, primitive and horrible', but also with intense love, interest and loyalty.[26] The sibling is the first person to whom the child relates as a social being, with whom it works out how to play, how to negotiate the sharing of possessions, and how to relate to the parents; it forms shifting and strategic alliances with all members of the sibling group. Ambivalence is inherent from the outset in psychological characterizations of the sibling relationship.

Longitudinal studies trace how sibling bonds develop over an entire lifetime; these of course require around seventy years of sustained research, and so are significantly fewer in number. Although they lay different emphases on the emotions and behaviours of siblings from those foregrounded in psychoanalytical models, psychologists broadly agree that paradoxical drives and emotions – love and hate, rivalry and loyalty, nurturing and the desire for autonomy – continue to characterize the sibling bond through different life stages. Stephen Bank and Michael Kahn observe that while 'loyalty is a major theme or dimension of sibling relationships', it coexists with 'rivalry, conflict and competition' across the life-span.[27] Adult siblings still struggle to define themselves against their other siblings, repeatedly having to assert 'I am me, I am not you'. Meanwhile, others inside or outside the family may regard siblings as interchangeable: if one sibling is unwilling or unable to undertake a commitment regarded as a benefit for the whole family, such as taking over the family business, caring for an elderly – or younger – relative, or, in some cultures, entering into a marriage alliance, another sibling may be regarded as an acceptable substitute, irrespective of the individual's own views of the matter. The work of the sibling, particularly one of the same sex, is to differentiate him- or herself from the rest of the sibling group. This may be achieved through complementarity: promoting traits and developing identities which overlap minimally with other siblings' spheres of interest. Deidentification is divisive, a deliberate choice to be as unlike other siblings as possible. This strategy can

---

[25] J. Dunn and C. Kendrick, ed., *Siblings: Love, Envy and Understanding* (London, 1982), p. 208.

[26] Dunn and Kendrick, ed. *Siblings*; Apter, *Sister Knot*, p. 6 ; S. Bank and M. Kahn, 'Intense Sibling Loyalties', in *Sibling Relationships: Their Nature and Significance across the Lifespan*, ed. M. Lamb and B. Sutton-Smith (Hillsdale NJ and London, 1982), pp. 251–67.

[27] Bank and Kahn, 'Intense Sibling Loyalties', p. 251; cf. I. A. Connidis, 'Siblings as Friends in Later Life', *American Behavioural Scientist* 33 (1989), 81–93.

generate as much conflict as the rivalry caused by making identical life-choices; understood as rejection of all that the other sibling(s) stand for, it provokes extreme hostility. Counter-identification, a differentiation strategy which lies between complementarity and deidentification, often mediates competition successfully; the borderline so keenly patrolled by siblings is less likely to be infringed when counter-identities have been negotiated.[28]

'The continuing existence of a blood tie is taken as indicative of the continuing existence of a social relationship between the siblings', notes Graham Allen.[29] The sibling cannot opt out of his or her siblinghood, within neither medieval nor modern culture. Unlike friends, a sibling is a sibling for life: severance of the relationship is problematic.[30] Siblings can be mobilized when needed, turned to in times of crisis; yoked together by biological and legal genealogy, the family functions as a moral unit and, at the same time, a network of social relationships, each of which constrains and structures other relationships.[31] As in the medieval period, modern Western society maintains distinctions between full, half-, step-, adoptive and fictive siblings. Children do not necessarily live in the same household as their biological siblings; they may live with half- or step-siblings. Today's blended families raise similar questions about the relevance 'of culture, language, interpretation and subjectivity to constructing definitions, and social and emotional experiences, of who is a sibling, rather than a self-evident, biological or legal, state'.[32] Powerful affective bonds, both positively and negatively inflected, exist between half- or step-siblings, even when, in the medieval past, they enjoyed very different legal statuses and varying inheritance prospects.

Sibling roles vary over the course of medieval and modern lifetimes; yet the developmental patterns for contemporary siblings are markedly similar to those of medieval brothers and sisters. Sibling caretaking tends to be informal, delegated by the parents on a temporary basis, often to the oldest sister; essential social skills and values are transmitted from older to younger child.[33] Coalitions and conspiracies are formed among siblings in order to deal with parents; children mediate between parents and other siblings, explaining

---

[28] See C. J. Moser, R. Jones et al., 'The Impact of the Sibling in Clinical Practice: Transference and Countertransference Dynamics', *Psychotherapy: Theory, Research, Practice, Training* 42 (2005), 267–78; M. Charles, 'Sibling Mysteries: Enactment of Unconscious Fears and Fantasies', *Psychoanalytic Review* 86 (1999), 877–901, and S. Bank and M. Kahn, *The Sibling Bond* (New York, 1982), pp. 104–11.

[29] G. Allen, 'Sibling Solidarity', *Journal of Marriage and the Family* 39 (1977), 177–84 (p. 179).

[30] T. R. Lee, J. A. Mancini and J. W. Maxwell, 'Sibling Relationships in Adulthood: Contact Patterns and Motivations', *Journal of Marriage and Family* 52 (1990), 431–40.

[31] Allen, 'Sibling Solidarity', p. 180.

[32] Edwards et al., *Who is a Sister and a Brother?*, p. 3.

[33] See V. G. Cicirelli, 'Sibling Relationships in Adulthood: A Life Span Perspective', in *Aging in the 1980s*, ed. L. W. Poon (Washington DC, 1980), pp. 455–62, and A. Goetting, 'The Developmental Tasks of Siblingship over the Life Cycle', *Journal of Marriage and Family* 48 (1986), 703–14.

Introduction

and translating behaviour.[34] '[S]ibling rivalry . . . a type of conflict arising out of competition for parental rewards' persists concurrently with sibling solidarity.[35] While this pattern is set in childhood, as long as the parents are alive their offspring are likely at some level to compete amongst themselves. They may, however, avoid conflict by deliberately choosing *not* to compete, by selecting behavioural traits and making life choices which maximize the contrasts between them. Such differentiation 'need not always be negative in affect'; it fosters the development of different self-concepts, crucial to successful individualization and identity formation.[36] Adolescence tends to lead to a weakening of sibling bonds: age difference becomes particularly salient as an older sibling resents the younger's attempts to tag along. A sibling's marriage can lead to closer ties and improved relationships as new roles as husband, wife and in-law are explored; intimacy after marriage very often depends on how well one sibling gets on with a sibling's spouse.[37] Although the formation of the new married couple can close off sibling relationships for a time, once the married sibling has children and the roles of uncle and aunt become available, new claims are made on the unmarried siblings and family conduits reopen.[38] When a marriage ends, divorce or widowhood frequently reactivates emotional and supportive ties between siblings.[39] Sibling rivalry dissipates with age and geographical distance as brothers and sisters find different roles for themselves and for each other.[40] The death of the parents – whether early in the child's life, leaving a sibling group vulnerably dependent on others or on each other, or late, when adults must agree to negotiate the division of the parental legacy – remains a crisis point in family relations.[41] Dissent exacerbates tensions between siblings when arrangements for ageing parents have to be made.[42] More harmoniously, elderly siblings share reminiscences, validating one another's perceptions of the past, of their selves and of society and they act as one another's memory-keepers.[43]

---

[34] Goetting, 'Developmental Tasks', pp. 705–6.; cf. Bank and Kahn, *The Sibling Bond*, pp. 322–4.
[35] Lee, Mancini and Maxwell, 'Sibling Relationships in Adulthood', p. 433.
[36] H. S. Mosatche, E. M. Brady and M. R. Noberini, 'A Retrospective Lifetime Study of the Closest Sibling Relationship', *The Journal of Psychology* 113 (1983), 237–43 (p. 241).
[37] Allen, 'Sibling Solidarity', p. 181; I. A. Connidis, 'Life Transitions and the Adult Sibling Tie', *Journal of Marriage and the Family* 54 (1992), 972–82.
[38] See Connidis, 'Life Transitions'.
[39] Ibid., p. 973.
[40] Allen, 'Sibling Solidarity', p. 180.
[41] Goetting, 'Developmental Tasks', pp. 707–8.
[42] Compare Geoffrey of Monmouth's account of Leir and his daughters Gornorilla, Regau and Cordeilla when the king's extreme old age produces a crisis in the sisters' relationships: Geoffrey of Monmouth, *The History of the Kings of Britain: An Edition and Translation of* De gestis Britonum, ed. N. Wright, trans. M. D. Reeve (Woodbridge, 2007), ch. 31.
[43] Goetting, 'Developmental Tasks', p. 710, and cf. V. G. Cicirelli, 'Feelings of Attachment to Siblings and Well-Being in Later Life', *Psychology and Aging* 4 (1989), 211–16.

Psychologists regard birth order as highly significant both in terms of social roles and individual personality development. A biologically given fact – being older, younger or middle – becomes culturally elaborated.[44] While social convention often reifies the normative power and ability of the elder brother, folk-narratives correspondingly compensate for the elder's advantages, particularly under primogeniture. The youngest brother is endowed with qualities of courage and resourcefulness; these allow him to succeed despite lacking the social position and skills of his older sibling.[45] These popular stories address situations when there is a lack of fit between the ideological and actual characteristics of the older brother; those who are structurally marginal – younger brothers, younger sisters – possess 'cleverness, visionary insight, audacity, irresponsibility and social and geographical mobility [which] go[es] beyond what is ordinarily prescribed and tolerated'.[46]

'Studying the course of sibling relationships over time highlights the continuity of the family of origin' concludes Ingrid Connidis, 'focusing our attention on the process and effects of adding and losing members and subsystems. This affirms the systemic nature of families, characterized by interdependence, reciprocity, conflict, feedback, and readjustment.'[47] Medieval, like modern, birth families endow children with identities and rights that persist even after marriage and the formation of new family systems entail new obligations and affective ties. Medieval sibling narratives, as we shall see, focus particularly on the effects of adding and losing members: whether through the murder of a brother or the marriage of a sister, reaction to the new situation highlights exactly the issues of reciprocity and conflict Connidis identifies.

Siblings in Culture

'Siblings always *matter*. How siblings should relate to each other, what to call them, and what resources they are to have and share is important to all cultures. These matters are not left culturally undefined', notes Thomas Weisner.[48] Cross-cultural psychologists study how brothers and sisters interact and signify within different cultures, observing external socially determined processes rather than internal psychological motivations. Such observations, when drawn from non-industrialized cultures, frequently yield insights into family organization

---

[44] B. Sutton-Smith and B. G. Rosenberg, *The Sibling* (New York, 1970); M. Jackson, 'Ambivalence and the Last-Born: Birth-Order Position in Convention and Myth', *Man* 13 (1978), 341–61 (p. 341).
[45] Jackson, 'Ambivalence', pp. 346–51.
[46] Ibid., p. 349.
[47] Connidis, 'Life Transitions', p. 981.
[48] T. S. Weisner, 'Comparing Sibling Relationships across Cultures', in *Sibling Interaction across Cultures; Theoretical and Methodological Issues*, ed. P. G. Zukow (New York, 1989), pp. 11–25.

Introduction

in medieval Europe.[49] Sibling caretaking in non-industrialized societies tends to be institutionalized. 'Older siblings feed and comfort babies, keep younger siblings out of mischief and discipline them, assign various household and gardening chores to them and generally supervise their behavior', comments Victor Cicirelli, evoking the patterns evident in medieval sources dealing with siblings in peasant households.[50] The parents' time is thus freed for work while the siblings learn the skills they may need in case of family catastrophe; they become intimately involved in socializing and training the young.[51] This role is not without risk; sibling caretaking in medieval societies might end in disaster. Younger children often died through the carelessness of their older siblings, sometimes to be revived by the intercession of a saint, but, more often than not, to be registered as victims in coroners' rolls.

Siblings become more salient to their brothers and sisters at different stages of the life-span. Often social interaction occurs only within same-sex groups, and brothers and sisters occupy complementary social roles. In Oceania, for example, the brother is regarded as the sister's protector and the sister as her brother's spiritual mentor: parallel ideas of reciprocity can be found between saintly sibling pairs in the medieval Church.[52] While sisters are typically close, brothers tend to display more rivalry, especially where the oldest is empowered to make decisions on behalf of the whole group: similar affective patterns occur in medieval Europe. Brothers begin to take an interest in their sisters when the time comes for them to marry. In South Asia brothers often defer their own marriages until they have provided their sister's dowry through labour, a pattern not dissimilar to the dowry culture of late-medieval Italy. Brothers are also obliged to police the welfare of a married sister and her children; if a marriage ends, the sister may return to the brother's home or seek his protection. Brothers find themselves allied in economic or survival activities, tending to be more rivalrous where they work or fight side by side. Seniority entails authority; the eldest brother either shares or takes over the power of the patriarch and his younger siblings are mandated to obey; often the older sister takes on the role of mediator between the older brother and his disaffected siblings.[53]

Relationships between brothers, sisters and their affines have been central to anthropological analyses of kinship after Claude Lévi-Strauss: bonds within and between groups are mediated by the 'exchange of women'. Even more than fathers, brothers make or break marriage negotiations and alliances.[54] Analysis of sibling relationships thus becomes subordinated to the question of whose

---

[49] V. G. Cicirelli, 'Sibling Relationships in Cross-Cultural Perspective', *Journal of Marriage and the Family* 56 (1994), 7–20.
[50] Ibid., p. 9, here with reference to the Kwara'ae of the Solomon Islands.
[51] Weisner, 'Comparing Sibling Relationships', pp. 16–17.
[52] F. J. Griffiths, 'Siblings and the Sexes within the Medieval Religious Life', *Church History* 77 (2008), 26–53.
[53] Cicirelli, 'Sibling Relationships in Cross-Cultural Perspective'.
[54] C. Lévi-Strauss, *The Elementary Structures of Kinship*, trans. R. Harle Bell and J. R. von Sturmer, and R. Needham (London, 1969), p. 50.

sister a man will marry, resulting in an emphasis on in-law relations which chimes with the anxieties about affinal bonds evident in medieval literature and discussed in chapter seven below. The social and cultural importance of brothers-in-law is flagged up by the response of the Samoan Arapesh tribe, questioned by Margaret Mead about the possibilities of brother–sister incest. Echoing Augustine's view of the desirabilty of exogamy, they apparently retorted, 'Don't you realize that if you marry another man's sister, and another man marries your sister, you will have at least two brothers-in law, while if you marry your own sister you will have none? With whom will you hunt, with whom will you garden, whom will you go to visit?'[55] The brother-in-law relationship is the most fractious in medieval literature, a site of creatively dramatic tensions of loyalty, erotic attraction and strategic interests. The imperative to marry the sister outside the group – indeed according to ecclesiastical law, well outside the extended kinship: beyond the sixth degree of relatedness – multiplies the possibilities of affinal solidarities and fractures. Their apprehension of their common destiny, facing 'the hard fate of exiles, theoretically for ever, in foreign households, often different in language and customs', as Lévi-Strauss observes, creates solidarity among sisters.[56] While the assumption that the woman loses her rights and responsibilities within her birth family on her marriage, that she does indeed share 'the hard fate of exiles', has informed much analysis of Western medieval social customs – as chapter one will show – a sister's actual emotional ties to her brothers and her birth family vary significantly by social class and by geographical region. Feminist responses to the 'exchange of women' principle have noted the lack of agency ascribed to the sister in Lévi-Strauss's analysis (see for example the influential critiques by Sherry Ortner and Gayle Rubin).[57] In medieval, as in non-industrial, cultures, sisters are often able to work strategically to manage sibling and affinal relationships. As Jack Goody argues, 'exchange of women' is in fact an exchange of 'rights in women', and the woman too receives certain rights – to food, medical care, sexual attention – even if the exchange is unequal. Wives do not cease to be members of their natal lineages and certain rights continue to subsist to them. As we shall see in chapter one, although the exercise of these rights may depend heavily on geographical proximity, they nevertheless do not cease to exist simply because a married sister has moved away.[58]

---

[55] Ibid., p. 485, citing M. Mead, *Sex and Temperament in Three Primitive Societies* (New York, 1935), p. 84. See Augustine, *De civitate Dei* XV.15; http://www.thelatinlibrary.com/augustine/civ15.shtml.

[56] Lévi-Strauss, *Elementary Structures of Kinship*, p. 306.

[57] S. B. Ortner, 'Is Female to Male as Nature is to Culture?', in *Women, Culture and Society*, ed. M. Z. Rosaldo and L. Lamphere (Stanford CA, 1974), pp. 68–87; G. Rubin, 'The Traffic in Women: Notes on the "Political Economy" of Sex', in *Toward an Anthropology*, ed. Reiter, pp. 157–210; S. B. Ortner and H. Whitehead, 'Introduction: Accounting for Sexual Meanings', in *Sexual Meanings: The Cultural Construction of Gender and Sexuality*, ed. S. B. Ortner and H. Whitehead (Cambridge, 1981), pp. 1–27.

[58] J. Goody, 'The Labyrinth of Kinship', *New Left Review* 36 (2005), 127–39 (p. 131).

Introduction

Siblings in Christianity

The theories discussed above invite careful comparison between modern Western sibling experience, contemporary findings for non-industrial societies, and the family narratives preserved in medieval texts. Also available to medieval authors who wanted to consider sibling relations were a broad range of theoretical models, patterns and analogies. To the learned social strata, classical literature (usually transmitted through Latin) offered such examples as the fraternal strife which led to the fall of Thebes (considered in chapter four), the complex family relations in Ovid's *Metamorphoses*, or the conflict of Romulus and Remus at the foundation of Rome. More widely known and discussed, no doubt, were the Bible's authoritative gamut of sibling behaviours and emotions. Genesis emphasizes recurrent patterns of competition and rivalry between pairs or larger groups of brothers. From the primal murder of Abel by Cain (Genesis 4) and Abraham's willingness to dismiss Ishmael and his mother in favour of the late-born Isaac (Genesis 21), to Jacob's swindling his brother Esau out of their father's blessing (Genesis 25, 27), the envy of Joseph's brothers for their father's favourite and Joseph's forgiveness and protection for those same brothers (37, 42–5), Genesis consistently shows one brother as chosen and one as lacking in favour, both in the eyes of his parents and in the sight of God. Laban tries to pretend that his daughters Leah and Rachel are interchangeable, but Jacob labours seven extra years to secure the sister on whom his heart is set; those same sisters compete fiercely with one another in childbearing (Genesis 29–30). Exodus models a more cooperative fraternal relationship: Moses and Aaron stake out distinctive roles as political leader and priest respectively when they lead the children of Israel to the promised land. Later Old Testament books illustrate the powerful 'better-than-brother' relationship of David and Jonathan (I Samuel 18) and the incest of Amnon and Thamar (II Samuel 13). With wonderful concision and vividness the New Testament presents the Prodigal Son's elder brother's resentment (Luke 15), the annoyance of Martha at her sister Mary's avoidance of housework (Luke 10) and the hope of both sisters that Jesus might restore their brother Lazarus to life (John 11). These stories provided templates for medieval thinking about normative sibling behaviour: love and loyalty were expected, envy and disloyalty feared and reproved. Christian teaching in sermons, Bible commentaries, pictorial depictions of biblical story in stained-glass or tapestry, or in the dramatization of key episodes from the Old and New Testaments in mystery-play cycles reinforced social beliefs about sibling solidarity and the dangers of sibling rivalry.

Official Christian ideology demands the rejection of the biological family in favour of Christian kinship. This tenet is drawn from Luke 14. 26: 'If any man come to me, and hate not his father, and mother, and wife, and children, and brethren, and sisters, yea, and his own life also, he cannot be my disciple'. The logic of Christ's demand belongs to the days of the early Church, when families might genuinely be split by competing religious beliefs (providing the material of many early Christian martyrdom stories). In the early-medieval period, the family was recognized as an important vector of conversion; the outright rejection of kin ties was generally regarded as unnecessary once societies had become fundamentally Christian.[59] The Church regarded all men and women as brothers and sisters, reiterating the importance of the sibling relationship as the lifelong model for peer relations. Sibling bonds thus provided the fundamental metaphor for the ideal organization of social groups, whether in the monastery and convent or in chivalric orders; *pseudo-parentés* distinct from actual, often troubling, family ties were thus created.[60] The cross-sex sibling bond was regarded as a key model for right gender relations in early Christian thinking: brother and sister represented an ideal model for married couples. If a husband is able – as Clement of Alexandria was one of the earliest Church Fathers to urge – to overcome and control his sexual desire for his wife, then the marital relationship will become as God would wish it: like that of brother and sister, as innocent as Adam and Eve were before the Fall.[61] More than a millennium later, Chaucer's Parson recommends: 'Man sholde loven hys wyf by / Discrecioun, paciently and atemprely; and / Thanne is she as though it were his suster'; a similar sentiment is voiced in his 'Merchant's Tale'.[62] In the later-medieval period, exempla were promulgated which warned that a sister might embody at best distraction, at worst temptation for her brother.[63] Jean Gerson, chancellor of the University of Paris in the early fifteenth century, confessed that visits from his sisters induced troubling sexual fantasies in him.[64] Normal cross-sex sibling affection thus falls victim to pervasive Church misogyny.

While the proper functioning of sibling relations came to be regarded as central to the good order of medieval society, the perversion of sibling ties was imagined as a threat not only to the family, but to the whole social fabric. Didier

---

[59] The choice to join a monastic order could entail a sundering of family ties, understood by other family members as a betrayal; see A. Barbero, *Un santo in famiglia: vocazione religiosa e resistenze sociale nell'agiografia latine medievale* (Torino, 1991), p. 217.

[60] D. Lett, 'Les frères et les sœurs, "parents pauvres" de la parenté', *Médiévales* 54 (2008), 5–12 (p. 9).

[61] See E. Pagels, *Adam, Eve and the Serpent* (Harmondsworth, 1990), p. 30 for discussion of Clement of Alexandria.

[62] Geoffrey Chaucer, 'The Parson's Tale', in *The Riverside Chaucer*, ed. L. D. Benson (Oxford, 1988), line 861, p. 318, and note, p. 963; cf. also 'The Merchant's Tale', line 1454, p. 156. L. Patterson, in 'The "Parson's Tale" and the Quitting of the "Canterbury Tales"', *Traditio* 34 (1978), 331–80, notes that this framing of marital chastity represents Chaucer's own addition to his source in both passages (pp. 365–6).

[63] *Index exemplorum*, ed. F. C. Tubach (Helsinki, 1969), no. 4424, p. 337, in which a woman begs her brother, a monk, to come to see her after many years of separation. He visits, accompanied by two fellow-monks, but tells her that, because she is a woman, they can never meet again.

[64] B. P. McGuire, 'Late Medieval Care and Control of Women: Jean Gerson and his Sisters', *Revue d'histoire ecclésiastique* 92 (1997), 5–37 (p. 33, n. 98) and B. P. McGuire, 'Jean Gerson and the End of Spiritual Friendship: Dilemmas of Conscience', *Friendship in Medieval Europe*, ed. J. Haseldine (Stroud, 1999), pp. 229–50. See also F. Ledwige, 'Relations de famille dans la correspondance de Gerson', *Revue historique* 271 (1984), 3–23.

Introduction

Lett observes how extreme sibling behaviour tropes social breakdown: 'Les deux principaux dangers qui menacent les frères et les sœurs, et partant, mettent en péril la societé toute entière: le fratricide et l'inceste' ('the two principal dangers which threaten brothers and sisters, and beyond, putting the whole of society in danger [are]: fratricide and incest').[65] Incest and kin-murder are indeed symptomatic of the onset of apocalypse in the medieval imagination. In the Old Norse mythological poem *Vǫluspá*, composed around the year 1000, the onset of *ragna rǫk*, the end of the world, is signalled by the disruption of sibling relations:

> Brœðr muno beriaz   oc at bǫnum verðaz,
> muno systrungar   sifiom spilla;
> hart er í heimi,   hórdómr mikill.

('Brother will fight brother and be his slayer, / cousins will violate the bond of kinship;/ hard it is in the world, there is much adultery'.)[66]

So too, Boccaccio relates how in plague-ridden fourteenth-century Florence normal sibling love and caretaking evaporated:

> era con sí fatto spavento questa tribulazione entrata ne' petti degli uomini e delle donne, che l'un fratello l'altro abbandonava . . . e la sorella il fratello e spesse volte la donna il suo marito.

('men and women alike were possessed by such a visceral terror of this scourge that a man would desert his own brother . . . a sister her brother, and often a wife her husband').[67]

Whether as portent of catastrophe or as symptom of disaster, the fragmentation of sibling relationships figures social breakdown, heralding worse calamities as to come.

Summary

Although sibling murder and sexual transgression tend to occur – or to be documented as occurring – only in exceptional circumstances, both in modern and medieval culture, the sibling emotions which give rise to such extremes are, in Lévi-Strauss's phrase, 'good to think with'. Sibling interaction is not

---

[65] Lett, 'Les frères et les sœurs', p. 10.
[66] *Vǫluspá* st. 45, in *Edda: Die Lieder des Codex Regius*, ed. G. Neckel and H. Kuhn, 4th edn (Heidelberg, 1962); *The Poetic Edda*, trans. C. Larrington (Oxford, 2014). This and other examples of the trope may derive in part from Matthew 10. 21 which warns the Apostles of the difficulty of their mission: 'and the brother shall deliver up the brother to death, and the father the child: and the children shall rise up against their parents, and cause them to be put to death'.
[67] *Decameron*, Introduction; Boccaccio, *Decameron*, trans. Waldman, p. 10.

only about itself; siblinghood's social centrality allows writers to engage both with major literary themes and with urgent historical questions: with feud and reconciliation, with faith, morality and ethics, and with the justice of inheritance and marriage settlements. Medieval sibling narratives gesture towards the social and psychological pressures operating within and upon the medieval family; they highlight the anxieties and satisfactions which may not be so easily read out of other kinds of texts. 'It is ironic that laymen more than family experts acknowledge the importance of the sibling bond, and that artists more than researchers have succeeded in capturing its essence', suggested Jane H. Pfouts as the 'sibling turn' was beginning to manifest itself in social-science research.[68] Jack Goody writes that although the 'emotional tone and reciprocal rights characterizing such critical relationships' are seldom manifest in documents related to inheritance, 'the plots of many plays and novels make the point in a more dramatic way than is available to the historian and the social scientist'.[69] Literary narratives thicken and nuance our understanding of the sibling web, bringing together the historical specificity of medieval social practices and enduring – even universal – psychological patterns of thinking, feeling and acting.

The following chapters explore precisely that 'essence of the sibling bond', 'the emotional tone and the reciprocal rights of siblings', which Pfouts and Goody identify as most clearly visible in works of the imagination. They make use of the psychoanalytical and psychological concepts outlined above to bring into focus the specific and the universal, the outlandish and the familiar in brother–sister relationships. Chapter one analyses what can provisionally be claimed for historical sibling bonds in the medieval period. The two chapters which follow focus on love and loyalty: chapter two investigates fraternal solidarity and affection, while chapter three uncovers the particular dimensions of sisters' love for their siblings. Chapter four begins with the primal story of Cain and Abel, unpacking the horror of fratricide and the causes of fraternal hatred; chapter five fleshes out hostility between sisters, and conflict between sisters and brothers. Incest, that most unsettling of transgressions, is the subject of chapter six. Chapter seven deals with in-law relationships, investigating how sibling emotions spill over into relationships with affines, underpinning and threatening in-law alliances. The final chapter's examination of fictive sibling bonds – foster- and sworn-siblinghood – shows how a better-than-brother relationship, transcending the ambivalences of the blood-tie, becomes possible with a freely chosen friend. The conclusion draws together the thematic principles which guide sibling interactions in the medieval Imaginary, identifying recurrent sibling crises across a full range of genres and contextualizing the profoundly experienced emotional responses and distinctive behaviours which generate sibling drama.

---

[68] J. H. Pfouts, 'The Sibling Relationship: A Forgotten Dimension', *Social Work* 21 (1976), 200–4 (p. 200).
[69] J. Goody, *Family and Inheritance: Rural Society in Western Europe, 1200–1800*, ed. J. Goody, J. Thirsk and E. P. Thompson (Cambridge, 1978), p. 1.

1

The Medieval Sibling in History

Introduction

It is still too early to write the history of the medieval sibling, a history of the kind that has, in recent years, been written of medieval marriage and of the medieval family. The expanding field of the history of childhood has largely been shaped by an earlier historiography which saw as its primary challenge a correction of the views of Ariès, Stone and deMause. These historians argued that medieval parents did not make a strong emotional investment in their children: a detachment thought to be rooted in the high mortality rates for infants and young children. Attentive analysis of parent–child relations were the primary means of refuting these arguments, and thus vertical relationships came to be privileged, while sibling or lateral relations have been comparatively overlooked.[1] Other medieval historians have examined in close detail the documentary evidence in archives and have pored over marriage contracts and wills to uncover the patterns in dowry and inheritance customs across medieval Europe, again focusing largely on parent–child relationships. Piecing together primary and secondary material from archival evidence, individual microstudies, such as the work of Herlihy and Klapisch-Zuber for late-medieval Tuscany, or the investigations of the Carolingian polyptych evidence for tenth-century France, scholars have now found it possible to write the history of the family in its vertical relationships, and the history of medieval marriage across Europe.[2] The sources for writing histories of lateral relationships exist in the same archives and document collections, and in other sources as yet unexamined, but these have not yet come under sustained scrutiny. Some welcome beginnings have been made; for example, Isabelle Réal's research on Frankish society in the sixth to ninth centuries, and the work of Didier Lett and those French scholars who

---

[1] See B. Hanawalt, 'Medievalists and the Study of Childhood', *Speculum* 77 (2002), 440–60, for a full discussion of these arguments and their refutation.

[2] D. Herlihy, *Medieval and Renaissance Pistoia: The Social History of an Italian Town, 1200–1430* (New Haven and London, 1967); D. Herlihy with C. Klapisch-Zuber, *Tuscans and their Families: A Study of the Florentine Catasto of 1427* (New Haven and London, 1985); P. Toubert, 'The Carolingian Moment (Eighth–Tenth Century)', in *A History of the Family*, ed. A. Burguière *et al*. I: 379–406; *To Have and to Hold: Marrying and its Documentation in Western Christendom, 400–1600*, ed. P. L. Reynolds and J. Witte jr (Cambridge, 2007); *Medieval Families: Perspectives on Marriage, Household, and Children*, ed. C. Neel (Toronto, 2004).

have followed him in close interrogation of sibling relations through a range of case studies.³ However, until medieval European archival material has been analysed at the micro level with sibling questions in mind, the larger narrative, *qua* history, of brothers and sisters will remain occluded.

Yet sibling relations *are* traceable where legal documents exist, for example when brothers determine their sisters' marriage arrangements, or when the eldest brother receives homage from his younger brothers for property they hold in fief from him. Memorial runestones communicate the family relationships which obtained between those who commissioned them and those who are commemorated. Chronicles and other historical writings recount the behaviour of royal and aristocratic sibling groups; saints' lives, canonization materials and coroners' records furnish valuable insights into more ordinary families and their day-to-day activities, or discuss the consequences when actual kinship is replaced or overlaid by spiritual siblingship. Exemplary material used in sermons or other religious writing provides a glimpse of normative sibling relations: brothers rebuke sisters for their vanity; sisters take feckless brothers into their homes; brothers try to influence brothers' choice of career, while sisters compete for academic success. As Ronald Finucane argues, in reference to depositions about miracles, 'While the "miraculous" core may be unbelievable, the incidental or circumstantial details – the *nonessentials* [his italics], as far as most witnesses ... and parents were concerned when reporting these cases are of primary importance'.⁴ Siblings can be glimpsed getting on with their lives in the interstices of texts whose ostensible subject is something quite different.

This chapter will trace some of the evidence for the nature of medieval sibling relationships across the lifespan, drawing on the kinds of historical sources listed above. What follows is an overview of the factors that influenced sibling experience, organized across the lifespan, interspersed with snapshots of siblings in accounts drawn from historical or quasi-historical sources from medieval Europe (defined as roughly 500–1500).

Individual medieval families and social organization in different parts of Europe varied just as much as modern Western families. Full sibs, step and half-sibs, foster-siblings and adopted children, legitimate and illegitimate siblings might grow up together and maintain close relationships in later life, though the high childhood mortality rate would cull around a third of those born. The rights and responsibilities of brothers and sisters varied substantially between those parts of southern Europe where the common law had developed from the *lex Romana* and the areas of northern Europe which had not come under Roman rule and which had developed indigenous law codes. Additionally, marriage patterns in northwest and southern Europe contrast markedly with one another over the period. In the south, girls were very soon married after puberty; in

---

[3] Réal, *Vies de saints, vie de famille*; Lett, *Frères et sœurs: histoire d'un lien*, and the special journal issue *Frères et sœurs – Ethnographie d'un lien, Médiévales* 54 (2008), ed. D. Lett.

[4] R. Finucane, *The Rescue of the Innocents: Endangered Children in Medieval Miracles* (Basingstoke, 1997), p. 3.

the northwest a good number of women remained unmarried until the ages of twenty-five to thirty, and a significant number never married at all.[5] This deep-rooted difference between women's lives across Europe affected sisters and their brothers; legal responsibility for a young woman remained with father or brothers before she was married. Variations in dowry versus bride-price customs and, above all, in inheritance systems had a significant impact on sibling relationships. 'The sibling bond is a connection between the selves at both the public and the intimate levels; it is a "fitting together" of two people's identities', Bank and Kahn observe, and, as we shall see, while historical documents allow access most readily to the public sibling self, literary texts furnish the best evidence for the intimate sibling self.[6] Towards the end of the medieval period, increasing lay literacy permits a kind of personal writing not usual in earlier centuries. Here sibling emotions are alluded to, even occasionally laid bare, in German *Hausbücher* or Italian *ricordanze*. And, as Finucane's argument (above) suggests, other kinds of medieval writing allow glimpses of sibling feelings, which, if they cannot be regarded as 'real', nevertheless appear to be regarded as normative by the texts' authors.

Siblings in Childhood

As parents and psychologists know, the birth of a new sibling is not necessarily welcomed by existing children.[7] The *vita* of the eleventh-century monastic leader and reformer Peter Damian (b. 1007), composed by John of Lodi, who had obviously heard details of his subject's childhood at first hand, vividly demonstrates the antipathy of an older brother to the latest arrival. When his mother gave birth to Peter, his adolescent sibling complained that she had added yet another mouth to their overcrowded household, further diminishing what was already likely to be a meagre inheritance.

> Proh pudor! ecce jam tanti sumus quod in hac domo vix capimur, et quam male sibi congruunt haeredum turba et haereditas angusta!

> ('Oh shame! Look: we are already such a great number in this house, that we are barely contained, and how badly suited to each other are this throng of heirs and scanty inheritance!')[8]

---

[5] See P. J. P. Goldberg, *Women, Work and Life Cycle in a Medieval Economy: Women in York and Yorkshire c. 1300–1520* (Oxford, 1992); R. M. Smith, 'Some Reflections on the Evidence for the Origins of the "European Marriage Pattern" in England', *The Sociological Review* 28 (1980), 74–112 and R. M. Smith, 'Hypothèses sur la nuptialité en Angleterre aux XIIIe–XIIVe siècles', *Annales: Histoire, Sciences Sociales* 38 (1983), 107–36.
[6] Bank and Kahn, *Sibling Bond*, p. 13.
[7] Dunn and Kendrick, *Siblings*; Apter, *Sister Knot*, p. 6.
[8] *PL* 144, col. 115B. Thanks to Katharine Earnshaw and Pete Biller for this translation.

Consequently Peter's mother refused to suckle her last-born, almost bringing about his death; only when another woman took over the baby's care did she relent. Later, the orphaned Peter was entrusted to the care of this same brother, who treated him cruelly. Barefoot and dressed in rags, he was beaten and fed on slops fit only for pigs. When he was about twelve, another brother rescued him from his misery and educated him; in gratitude Peter adopted this brother's name: Damian. Peter also writes of visiting a much-loved sister on her deathbed; he recounts how traumatic he found crossing the threshold of the family home. Peter's persecution by one sibling and rescue by another neatly exemplifies the ambivalence inherent in fraternal relations, while his reaction to the visit home shows how childhood sibling experience continues to be processed in adulthood.[9] Such full accounts of young sibling emotion and behaviour are rare in medieval sources.

As Peter Damian's biography shows, the last-born child could find itself in a most perilous position. More likely to face orphanhood at a vulnerable age, its future would be shaped by the extent to which its siblings protected or abused it. If, like Damian, caregiving siblings helped orphans to gain an education, this not only benefitted their development as individuals but also empowered them to record their experiences.[10] The last-born might also be – or imagine itself to be – a particular favourite. Guibert de Nogent (c. 1064–1125) noted with pride that his mother 'showed me greater love and brought me up in greater distinction' than his other siblings.[11] Guibert relates a vision granted to his mother which showed his already-dead father in hellish torment, punished for fathering an illegitimate child that had died without baptism.[12] To mitigate her husband's suffering, Guibert's mother decided to take in an orphan child. Well-behaved by day, but apparently possessed by the devil at night, the infant wailed unceasingly. Guibert suggests that the devil was trying to undo his mother's good works in provoking the child to howl, but he also sounds a clear note of satisfaction that this last child was a trial to his mother rather than his rival for her affections.[13] The fostering must have occurred before Guibert left home at the age of twelve; although he writes many years later, his anxiety about being replaced in his mother's affections is palpable.[14]

[9] M. M. McLaughlin, 'Survivors and Surrogates: Children and Parents from the Ninth to the Thirteenth Centuries', in *Medieval Families*, ed. Neel, pp. 20–124.

[10] Mosatche, Brady and Noberini, 'Retrospective Lifetime Study', p. 241.

[11] Guibert de Nogent, *Autobiographie*, ed. and trans. E. R. Labande (Paris, 1981); see also J. Benton, *Self and Society in Medieval France: The Memoirs of Abbot Guibert of Nogent (1064?–c. 1125)* (New York and Evanston, 1970).

[12] Guibert's mother also saw one of her own children in the fiery pit: in Guibert's view his brother amply deserved this fate for his habit of taking the Lord's name in vain: Guibert, *Autobiographie*, ed. Labande, I.38, pp. 148–53; the brother is identified, pp. 152–3. Benton, *Self and Society*: the vision, pp. 92–5; the brother, p. 95.

[13] Guibert, *Autobiographie*, ed. Labande, I.38, pp. 154–9; Benton, *Self and Society*, pp. 96–7.

[14] See G. Duby, *The Knight, the Lady and the Priest: The Making of Modern Marriage in Medieval France*, trans. B. Bray (Harmondsworth, 1985), pp. 140–7, for discussion of

How large were medieval European sibling groups? Modern demographic historians rightly warn us that almost no quantifiable evidence survives. 'The medievalist must . . . regard all population "statistics" with suspicion', Goldberg notes.[15] In the generalizations about demography which follow, then, this warning must be borne constantly in mind. Coming from an earlier generation of historical demographers (he was born in 1900), the pioneering student of medieval demography, Josiah Russell, once calculated that an average of six children would be born into the typical European family around the year 1000. On average, he suggested, four of them, two boys and two girls, would reach the age of twenty.[16] Laurent Macé's analysis of thirteenth-century Provence indicates that 30–40 per cent of children would have lost one or both parents before reaching adulthood; like Peter Damian, younger children would be thrown back on the kindness of their siblings.[17] Using such sparse data as is available, such 'heroic' demographic speculations can be taken to point to fairly stable childhood mortality rates over the thousand years of the medieval period, at 200–300 deaths per 1000 within the first year of life, while 50 per cent of children would die before their fifth birthday. Most medieval adults then would have experienced the trauma of losing a sibling in childhood; such bereavements leave surprisingly little trace in historical, autobiographical or literary writing.[18] The high frequency of sibling losses in the medieval family raises an important psychological/psychoanalytical question: what happens to repressed childhood sibling grief, both on the personal and the cultural level?[19]

Medieval naming practice seems to have permitted the christening of a number of siblings with the same name. Macé notes that, in the lineage of the lords of Montpellier in the twelfth century, the first two males of each generation were invariably named Guilhem, while other male children tend to be given names which chime with the *Gui*-element.[20] Such consistent naming practice seems to support the idea of 'an heir and a spare' in these aristocratic families. Elsewhere, for example in post-Conquest England, the occurrence of the same names within sibling groups indicates both the restricted pool of available names and, as Barbara Hanawalt suggests, the tendency of parents to baptize

---

Guibert of Nogent, in particular pp. 145–6 on the vision and its consequences.

[15] P. J. P. Goldberg, *Medieval England: A Social History 1250–1550* (London, 2004), p. 71, and see also chapter six, 'Counting Heads'.

[16] J. C. Russell, *Medieval Demography: Essays by Josiah C. Russell*, with preface by D. Herlihy (New York, 1987), p. 117. See the affectionate characterization of Russell in the review of these essays by Joel T. Rosenthal, *American Historical Review* 94 (1989), 741–2.

[17] L. Macé, 'Les frères au sein du lignage : la logique du lien adelphique chez les seigneurs de Montepellier (XIe siècle)', in *Frères et sœurs*, ed. Cassagnes-Brouquet and Yvernault, pp. 127–36 (p. 129).

[18] S. Shahar, *Childhood in the Middle Ages* (London, 1990), p. 149. Some breaches of the silence surrounding childhood sibling loss are discussed later in this chapter, pp. 39–40.

[19] Some tentative answers to this question are discussed in chapters two and three.

[20] Macé, 'Les frères au sein du lignage', p. 134.

children after their godparents.[21] Negotiating sibling roles and identities with a sib whose name one shared must have complicated the important psychological tasks of acceptance and differentiation; the identical names would compound the fear of displacement by the new arrival.[22]

Psychologists regard birth order as an important factor in shaping siblings' personalities and behaviour, but medieval infant mortality rates meant that birth order was much less stable.[23] Oldest and youngest children would retain their positions if they survived, but intervening children could find themselves moving up in rank order as their brothers and sisters died. Sibling roles, and sibling views of themselves, might change radically in childhood and young adulthood.[24] To be the oldest child, whether the oldest brother, expected to inherit, the oldest sister, expected to marry first, or to be a younger sibling, whose role within the family might be less clearly defined, is crucial in determining sibling destinies, particularly under primo- or ultimogeniture inheritance systems.[25]

The size of sibling groups in childhood was highly variable; in late-medieval Florence, women would begin to reproduce early and continue to produce closely spaced children.[26] In late-fourteenth-century Lynn in Norfolk, Margery Kempe gave birth to fourteen children, though only one son is mentioned in his adulthood.[27] Where couples had to wait for the death of a parent to gain the resources to set up independently, later marriage was common.[28] This entailed the birth of fewer children: the father's death was likely to supervene before the mother's childbearing years were over. She in turn might marry again and produce half-siblings for her first children. The contraceptive effect of breastfeeding normally provided a spacing of around two to two and a half years between births. Age gaps between surviving groups could be much larger than in modern families: by the time the youngest children in a sibling

---

[21] B. Hanawalt, *The Ties that Bound: Peasant Families in Medieval England* (New York and Oxford, 1986), p. 174.
[22] Mitchell, *Siblings*, p. 29.
[23] See for example, the work of Alfred Adler, collected in *The Individual Psychology of Alfred Adler*, ed. H. L. Ansbacher and R. R. Ansbacher (New York, 1956); Sutton-Smith and Rosenberg, *The Sibling*; and importantly F. Sulloway, *Born to Rebel* (London, 1996). See also M. Mitterauer and R. Rieder, *The European Family: Patriarchy to Partnership from the Middle Ages to the Present* (Oxford, 1982), p. 67.
[24] Lett, *Frères et Sœurs*, pp. 61, 64.
[25] See the popular, but still insightful, book by F. Klagsbrun, *Mixed Feelings: Love, Hate, Rivalry and Reconciliation between Brothers and Sisters* (New York, 1992), pp. 40–79.
[26] There is not space here to expand on the very technical speculations of demographic historian Richard Smith (see n. 5 above). To summarize his findings, the early age of marriage for women in southern Europe, shortly after puberty, tended to raise family fertility levels, while the later age of marriage in northwestern Europe tended to depress them.
[27] *The Book of Margery Kempe*, ed. B. Windeatt (Harlow, 2000), p. 235.
[28] Such as in pre-plague Halesowen in the English Midlands: see Z. Razi, *Life, Marriage and Death in a Medieval Parish: Economy, Society, and Demography in Halesowen* (Cambridge, 1980).

group arrived the eldest members might have left home.[29] Siblings who are not reared together tend not to form such intense emotional bonds as siblings in the modern family, where, as Bank and Kahn observe, 'High accessibility during the developmentally formative years is the ... accompaniment of an influential sibling relationship'.[30] Medieval parents needed to be both fortunate and fecund if they were to rear children in circumstances which encouraged strong emotional ties. Henry III of England (1207–72) and Eleanor of Provence, who had four children in six years, made arrangements for them to be reared together in a separate household in order to promote sibling solidarity amongst their offspring.[31] In late-medieval Italy, Didier Lett notes, as a result of early marriage, long childbearing years and the patriarch's remarriages, a man's grandsons might be older than his youngest son by his new wife.[32] Nevertheless, the absolute importance of age differences can be exaggerated: the sibling experience differs significantly even within the same family.[33] For 'no two siblings have the same parents or the same family backgrounds', as Francine Klagbrun notes: the inexperienced first-time mother and father will have acquired some parenting skills by the time subsequent children are born.[34]

Families could take steps to decrease sibling distance. Putting the newborn child out to a wetnurse meant that late-medieval Florentine noblewomen could conceive children at shorter intervals. Poorer families spaced their offspring by continuing to breastfeed for longer – or they might reap some economic benefit by nursing a noble child.[35] In peasant families in particular, siblings would often care for one another while the parents were working. Setting very young children to watch their younger brothers or sisters frequently resulted in catastrophe, whether recorded in canonization depositions and miracle collections, or, more sombrely, coroners' rolls.[36] In the *Vita Wulfstani*, for example, a child playing with his older brothers in an orchard falls down a well.[37] On another occasion, a mother went to winnow, leaving her three-year-old to look after a one-year-old in the bath; the baby drowned.[38] These stories

[29] Mitterauer and Rieder, *European Family*, p. 52.
[30] Bank and Kahn, *The Sibling Bond*, p. 10.
[31] M. Howell, *Eleanor of Provence: Queenship in Thirteenth-Century England* (Oxford, 1998), p. 45; J. C. Parsons, '"Que nos in infancia lactauit". The Impact of Childhood Caregivers on Plantagenet Family Relationships in the Thirteenth and Early Fourteenth Century', in *Women, Marriage, and Family in Medieval Christendom*, ed. Rousseau and Rosenthal, pp. 289–324, especially pp. 293–300.
[32] D. Lett, 'Adult Brothers and Juvenile Uncles: Generations and Age Differences in Families at the End of the Middle Ages', *History of the Family* 6 (2001), 391–400.
[33] R. Plomin and D. Daniels, 'Why are Children in the Same Family so Different from One Another?', *International Journal of Epidemiology* 40.3 (2011), 563–82.
[34] Klagsbrun, *Mixed Feelings*, p. 21.
[35] H. Bresc, 'Europe: Town and Country (Thirteenth–Fifteenth Century)', in *A History of the Family*, ed. Burguière et al., I: 430–66 (p. 457).
[36] Shahar, *Childhood*, p. 243.
[37] Ibid., p. 142.
[38] D. Alexandre-Bidon and D. Lett, *Children of the Middle Ages: Fifth–Fifteenth Centuries*

end in the miraculous revival of the dead infants; other anecdotes end less happily.[39] In 1369, John Cok, aged five, was in charge of his baby brother when the infant's cradle (placed near the hearth for warmth) caught fire and the baby died; in another case a three-year-old who went out to play in the yard also failed to stop her infant sister's cradle from catching fire.[40] Siblings' quasi-parental responsibility for their juniors was not always disastrous: in London in 1307, seven-year-old Gilbert was first to notice that his toddler brother John had ended up feet-first in a water-butt.[41] Again saintly intervention revived him.

How surviving children might feel about the loss of their brothers and sisters may be glimpsed tangentially in miracle depositions. Marquet, aged twelve, lived with his sister and his brother, five-year-old Peter. When Peter died of fever after some days of illness, Marquet and his sister went to bed and wept for a long time before they fell asleep, the scribe notes. Happily, by the time they awoke, Peter had been revived by virtue of an appeal to St Louis.[42] In noble families, where children did not take practical care of one another, sibling affection could be just as strong. The biography of William Marshal (c. 1146–1219) records how, when he was five or six, William's father gave him as a hostage to King Stephen to guarantee a truce. The king expected John Marshal to surrender his castle, but, apparently reckless of his son's life, John reprovisioned it and continued to defy the king. Although the little boy was threatened with execution, he was eventually returned to his parents, where his first question, his biographer noted, was about his mother and his sisters. When William left home a few years later to be fostered by his mother's cousin in Normandy, his sisters wept at his departure.[43] William's biographer thought it important to mention (or to invent) the affectionate relationship between William and his sisters; in contrast, little warmth is ascribed to the bond between William and his father.

Brothers and sisters are recorded as supporting one another when one was in trouble. In the canonization documents for Thomas Becket a touching story is told of little Beatrice, who mislaid a piece of cheese which her mother had asked her to look after. Hugo, the brother closest to her in age, helped his anxious sister to search for it; he suggested praying to Thomas Becket for

---

(Notre Dame IN, 1999), p. 65; Finucane, *Rescue of the Innocents*, pp. 144–6.

[39] Finucane notes that medieval people were not especially skilled at determining whether or not death had occurred; many miraculous restorations to life could be ascribed to a child awakening from unconsciousness or coma.

[40] N. Orme, *Medieval Children* (New Haven and London, 2001), p. 100; Hanawalt, *Ties that Bound*, p. 174.

[41] Finucane, *Rescue of the Innocents*, pp. 105–6.

[42] Ibid., pp. 69–70.

[43] G. Duby, *William Marshal: The Flower of Chivalry* (London, 1986), pp. 65, 68; D. Crouch, 'Marshal, William (I), Fourth Earl of Pembroke (c. 1146–1219)', *DNB*, Oxford University Press, 2004; online edn, May 2007, http://ezproxy.ouls.ox.ac.uk:2117/view/article/18126, accessed 30 Dec 2011.

aid. The saint appeared to both siblings in their dreams to reveal the cheese's whereabouts (in an old butter-churn). Lett notes that the double appearance of a saint to petitioners tends to indicate a close relationship between the two witnesses.[44] Younger brothers sometimes worked for their elder brothers. A lad named Robert began counting the animals in the pasture that he was guarding for his brother, fell asleep on the job and lost his memory for two days. Medieval belief regarded falling asleep outside as hazardous, laying the sleeper open to attack from the noonday demon, though Robert's dramatic amnesia may equally have been a punishment for his idleness. Invoking Simon de Montfort restored his lost memory.[45]

Parents expected that young siblings would help and support one. The anxious Carolingian mother Dhuoda, who composed an educational manual for her son William in the 840s, reminds him of his duty to care for his younger brother Bernard: 'insinuare, nutrire, amare, ac de bono in melius provocare ne pigeas, caro enim et frater tuus est' ('take pains to be close to him, to nourish him, to love him, and to stir him from good to better. . . . He is your flesh and your brother').[46] Siblings, particularly those of the same sex, would often be educated together; this could lead to rivalry in the schoolroom. King Alfred's biographer Asser tells how the future king's mother Osburh showed him and his older brothers a book of poetry composed in Old English and promised it to the child who could first 'learn' it. Alfred indeed gained the book through his assiduous memorization, but since he took the book to his teacher to study it, his brothers probably had little chance to compete with him.[47] When personal letters begin to be preserved, minor but telling details about everyday sibling interactions emerge. A letter written in 1474 from one of the Norfolk Paston brothers, John Paston II, sent to another brother, informs him that their younger brother Walter, then aged about fifteen, has received a copy of the well-known story collection, *The Seven Sages*, sent him by the letter-writer.[48] Increasing rates of lay literacy in England from the fourteenth century onward made it easier for brothers and sisters from gentry and bourgeois families to keep in touch by letter; long-distance communication was no longer the prerogative of the aristocratic classes who could afford to retain personal messengers.

[44] Lett, *Frères et Sœurs*, pp. 158–60.
[45] C. Valente, 'Children of Revolt: Children's Lives in the Age of Simon de Montfort', in *Essays on Medieval Childhood*, ed. J. Rosenthal (Donington, 2007), pp. 91–107 (p. 103).
[46] K. Cherewatuk, 'Speculum Matris: Duoda's Manual', *Florilegium* 10 (1988–91), 49–64 (p. 58). For more on Dhuoda, see J. Marchand, 'Dhuoda: The Frankish Mother', in *Medieval Women Writers*, ed. K. M. Wilson (Manchester, 1984), pp. 1–29. See also I. Réal, 'Représentations et pratiques des relations fraternelles dans la société franque du haut Moyen Age (VIe–IXe siècles)', in *Frères et Sœurs*, ed. Cassagnes-Brouquet and Yvernault, pp. 73–93 (p. 75).
[47] *Alfred the Great: Asser's Life of King Alfred and Other Contemporary Sources*, ed. and trans. S. Keynes and M. Lapidge (Harmondsworth, 1984), p. 75.
[48] Orme, *Medieval Children*, p. 281; *Paston Letters and Papers of the Fifteenth century*, ed. N. Davis, 2 vols (Oxford, 1971–6), I: 576.

Young siblings often shared a bed. While this practice fostered closeness, it also permitted sexual experimentation. In his *Instructions for Parish Priests* the preacher John Mirk (fl. *c.* 1382–*c.* 1414) warns that boys and girls should no longer share a bed once they are seven years old, 'Leste they by-twynne hem brede / The lykynge of that fowle dede'.[49] Clear evidence for incest is hard to locate, however: Kathryn Gravdal argues that some infanticide trial records and pardon letters speak to the results of concealed sibling sexual activity.[50] As chapter six will show, the sister's pregnancy usually precipitates the final crisis in incestuous relationships, culminating in the death of mother and child or the baby's abandonment. Although canon law is more interested in policing questions of marriage and consanguinity, early penitentials systematically recommended penalties for incest: the seventh-century *Canons of Theodore* give a guideline penance of fifteen years for relations between brother and sister, and the same punishment for brother–brother sexual activity.[51]

Inheritance Issues

'What seems fundamental is the notion that different forms of property arrangements shape in an intimate fashion the total fabric of the family', observes David Sabean.[52] During the eleventh and twelfth centuries, the European family tended to move from a partible inheritance system (sharing property equally between children, or between male heirs), to a 'winner takes all' system of primo- or ultimogeniture (inheritance by the last born). Primogeniture became widespread in France between 1020 and 1060, but its obvious benefit of keeping the family land together generated unwelcome consequences.[53]

> Firstly it was likely to provoke rivalry among fraternal co-heirs (and their wives, if any); it could break up the family unit, with the younger brothers going off to seek their fortunes ... Secondly, the tendency to allow only the eldest son to marry in order to avert such rivalries – at least in the next generation – could bring about an abrupt and unintended extinction of the family line.[54]

Limited land supply and increasing numbers of bequests away from the family

---

[49] Orme, *Medieval Children*, p. 103; John Mirk, *Instructions for Parish Priests*, ed. G. Kristensson, Lund Studies in English (Lund, 1974), lines 216–21
[50] K. Gravdal, 'Confessing Incest: Legal Erasures and Literary Celebrations in Medieval France', in *Medieval Families*, ed. Neel, pp. 329–46.
[51] Ibid., pp. 330–1
[52] D. Sabean, 'Kinship and Property in Western Europe before 1800', in *Family and Inheritance: Rural Society in Western Europe*, ed. J. Goody *et al.* (Cambridge, 1976), pp. 96–111 (p. 111).
[53] Duby, *The Knight, the Lady*, p. 93.
[54] R. Fossier, 'The Feudal Era (Eleventh–Thirteenth Century)', in *A History of the Family*, ed. Burguière *et al.*, I: 407–29 (pp. 418–19).

to the Church restricted prospects for any but the heir. Jane Beitscher analyses conditions in the French Limousin area in the ninth to eleventh centuries 'where the mad scramble for fiefs never let up'.[55] Here, 'Brothers could have joined forces but they were too busy fighting over the same piece of pie. Brothers stole from each other and killed each other. . . . Parents contributed indirectly to blatant acts of violence by setting sons against each other.'[56] As a consequence of the 'mad scramble', the feudal system flourished in eleventh- and twelfth-century France; young men weighed bonds of service against bonds of blood, and went off elsewhere to make their fortunes. Quite often they joined the household of their maternal uncle, strengthening that particular bond.[57] Crusading, taking service with a close relative, or finding an available heiress were career options taken up by younger brothers in the eleventh to thirteenth centuries; such choices are, as we shall see in chapters two and four, clearly reflected in legend and romance.

The threat to sibling solidarity represented by strict primogeniture led to the development of strategies to temper or modify its effects. Noble French families began to find ways for younger sons to marry; a parage system, in which inheritance could be shared between brothers with the eldest inheriting the main seat, was dominant by the end of the twelfth century.[58] In twelfth-century England at least, such an arrangement had already been adopted between sisters when male heirs were lacking.[59] After the mid-fourteenth-century onset of the plague, primogeniture was often abandoned: the European population collapse meant that land became more plentiful and available. English peasant families tried to settle as many children as possible with enough property to marry.[60] Elsewhere in Europe, particularly in farming communities, different kinds of inheritance patterns evolved, striving to balance sibling interests with the preservation of the core estate.[61] Flexible inheritance systems evolved in response to late-medieval crises: 'living together, possessing [land] together, working together, the family clans acted together in the face of epidemics, climate instability and even the onset of a new sort of servitude which characterizes the period', comments Nicolas Carrier.[62] In mountainous regions, where cultivable land was at a premium, the *frèreche* system allowed a cooperative system of

---

[55] J. Beitscher, '"As the twig is bent . . .": Children and their Parents in an Aristocratic Society', *Journal of Medieval History* 9 (1976), 181–91 (p. 185).
[56] Ibid., pp. 189–90.
[57] Duby, *The Knight, the Lady*, p. 105. Relations between uncles and nephews are discussed in chapter seven.
[58] Ibid., pp. 91–2 finds forms of parage emerging from 1064 onwards; for parage as generally in force, see p. 276.
[59] S. L. Waugh, *The Lordship of England: Royal Wardships and Marriages in English Society and Politics, 1217–1327* (Princeton, 1988), p. 16.
[60] Razi, *Life, Marriage and Death*, pp. 50–5; 135–6.
[61] Bresc, 'Europe: Town and Country', p. 444.
[62] N. Carrier, 'Patrimoine et conflits dans les familles paysannes des Alpes occidentales au temps du "remembrement lignager" (XIIIe–XVe siècles)', in *La parenté déchirée*, ed. Aurell, pp. 129–45, here p. 129. Cf. Lett, *Frères et sœurs*, pp. 113–16.

land-use. Siblings held the land and the main farm in common, although they usually maintained separate households, or at least separate kitchens. At the death of the patriarch the land had to be divided and quarrels might ensue, though, as Carrier notes for Savoy in the thirteenth to fifteenth centuries, relatively few fraternal suits came to court.[63] In Austria, younger siblings would move with their parents when they retired and passed the farm on to a newly married eldest son; where ultimogeniture was the rule the older siblings might remain in the family house as servants.[64] Changes in demographic and economic conditions thus have a marked impact on modes of sibling relations over the medieval millennium.

In fifteenth-century England the continued ranking of brothers in their fathers' wills meant that they held differing interests in the family estate, business or other enterprise. If brothers worked together, as Joel Rosenthal argues, it was 'apt to be on some new project, some bond or enterprise forged in their generation, rather than on an inherited one . . . If we should not infer hostility, we should also be reluctant to make an *a priori* assumption about equality or cooperation. "Different roads" was probably the route most chosen.'[65]

The development of mercantile activity opened up possibilities for new kinds of career-making. In fifteenth-century Augsburg Lucas Rem records in the family *Hausbuch* how, after working for the Welser trading company, he and his brothers broke away to set up their own enterprise.[66] As eldest, Lucas expected to exercise authority and to elicit obedience from his younger brothers. These in turn sought ways of achieving autonomy and self-assertion within the company and one, much to Lucas's annoyance, secretly began to work for Welser again to escape his brother's authority.[67]

Inheritance law inflects sibling relationships in adulthood; the father's death or the division of fraternal goods can precipitate a crisis which creates discord and violence. In fourteenth-century Italy, a miracle attributed to the saint Lucchesio of Poggibonsi revived a man who had been murdered by his brother in a conflict over division of goods.[68] Strife over property was not limited to brothers; the quarrel between sisters over inheritance becomes, as we shall see in chapter five, a distinct literary topos. Nor does partibility guarantee sibling harmony, for one sibling can refuse to cede the other siblings' share. An eighth-century life of St Sauve recounts an incident in which two sisters

---

[63] Carrier, 'Patrimoine et conflits', pp. 143–4. Examples include a brother selling off a vineyard of which he owned only a half and another seizing all of a harvest which was meant to be held in common.

[64] Mitterauer and Rieder, *The European Family*, pp. 55–6.

[65] J. Rosenthal, *Patriarchy and Families of Privilege in Fifteenth-Century England* (Philadelphia, 1991), p. 111.

[66] A.-M. Certin, 'Relations professionnelles et relations fraternelles d'après le journal de Lucas Rem, Marchand d'Augsbourg (1481–1542)', *Médiévales* 54 (2008), 83–98.

[67] Ibid., p. 96.

[68] M. Goodich, 'Sexuality, Family, and the Supernatural in the Fourteenth Century', in *Medieval Families*, ed. Neel, pp. 302–28 (p. 317).

complain to the French king Charles Martel that their brother has snatched their share of their inheritance. The king orders him to return the misappropriated legacy, but he refuses. When he swears on the saint's tomb to his right to the whole inheritance, the recalcitrant brother bursts open: his guts fall out, and blood spurts from eyes, ears and mouth. Like the king and the saint, the text too finds in favour of the sisters.[69]

The widespread adoption of some form of primogeniture across much of Europe from the eleventh century onwards meant that brothers often took Rosenthal's 'different roads'.[70] Deliberate separation and distance is notable in many medieval fraternal relationships; competition could be avoided by choosing separate spheres of operation. Such different roles may have their origins in varying temperaments and non-shared environments in childhood, but, as Klagsbrun observes, 'they are also an expression of the need of each to be different from the other, to have an identity and space of his own'.[71] An early-fifteenth-century account of the Venetian Tocco brothers shows the two men, very close in age, working in close cooperation with one another, but in markedly complementary roles.[72] The son of the governor of the Ionian islands, Carlo became despot of Epirus, a title held from the emperor of Byzantium, while his younger brother Leonardo was Carlo's right-hand man and commanding officer, undertaking delicate diplomatic missions as well as military expeditions on his brother's behalf.[73] A military career, as we shall see in chapter two, might lead to the acquisition of new estates, enabling younger brothers to marry and expand dynastic interests in the next generation.[74]

Siblings in the Religious Life

Brother–sister pairs often vowed themselves together to the religious life. From the earliest days of eastern monasticism, double houses were often founded by religious sibling pairs, a practice which persisted when monasticism moved westwards.[75] So strong does this sibling tradition appear to have been in the early-medieval period that, when Pope Gregory the Great came to write the *vita* of Benedict of Nursia (*c*. 480–543), he may have invented St Scholastica as his

---

[69] Réal, 'Représentations et pratiques', pp. 85–6.
[70] Rosenthal, *Patriarchy*, p. 111.
[71] Klagsbrun, *Mixed Feelings*, p. 32.
[72] N. Zecevic, 'Brotherly Love and Brotherly Service: On the Relationship between Carlo and Leonardo Tocco', in *Love, Marriage, and Family Ties in the Later Middle Ages*, ed. I. Davis, M. Müller and S. Jones (Turnhout, 2003), pp. 143–56. Complementarity is an important psychological strategy in managing sibling relations; see Bank and Kahn, *The Sibling Bond*, pp. 62–4.
[73] Zecevic, 'Brotherly Love', p. 144.
[74] Compare the models of successful fraternal bride- and kingdom-acquisition in *Mélusine*, pp. 52–3 below.
[75] F. J. Griffiths, 'Siblings and the Sexes'.

protagonist's sister. '[C]arefully prescribed contact with a holy woman – ideally a sister – had become an important element in the spiritual portfolio of a holy man', argues Fiona Griffiths.[76] Scholastica and Benedict provide an ideal model for male–female spiritual friendships, an intimacy enabled by the sibling bond. Showing the saint as friendly to women, without courting suspicions of sexual scandal, broadened Benedict's appeal.[77] The biographer of the Anglo-Saxon saint Guthlac (673–714) recounts how the hermit-saint had many siblings and foster-siblings, but his sister Pega, leading an eremitical life elsewhere in the Fens, was spiritually closest to him.[78] Pega's powerful emotional reaction to her brother's death is discussed in chapter three.

Later in the medieval period brothers are recorded as offering their religious sisters both practical and spiritual support. The German nun and visionary Elisabeth of Schönau (1129–65) was joined by her brother Ekbert at the double monastery of Schönau; Ekbert acted as his sister's secretary, recording her visionary experiences. Ælred of Rievaulx wrote a spiritual guide for his anchoress sister; Christina of Markyate was encouraged by her monk-brother Gregory; Hildegard of Bingen's brother Hugo served as provost at her Rupertsberg foundation.[79] 'In each case', Griffiths notes, 'the brother provided care for his sister, founding a monastery for her, serving as her priest or as provost of her community, or writing letters or other texts to guide her in the religious life.'[80]

Whole sibling groups might freely choose a religious vocation, despite having good prospects in the world. St Bernard of Clairvaux (1090–1153) was joined at his foundation by his widowed father and all six of his brothers. Bernard thus avoided the normally essential requirement for entry into monastic life: separation from his earthly kindred. Instead he converted his carnal brothers into spiritual brothers by mapping the family relationship onto the spiritual one.[81] Under pressure from her brother, Bernard's married sister Humbeline also took the veil, joining her former sister-in-law Élisabeth at the nearby Benedictine foundation of Jully, and succeeding her as abbess.[82]

After the tenth-century Benedictine revival, the double religious house gradually disappeared and religious siblings could no longer live in close

---

[76] Ibid., p. 37.
[77] S. Hollis, *Anglo-Saxon Women and the Church: Sharing a Common Fate* (Woodbridge, 1992), p. 289. See also Introduction, p. 14.
[78] *Felix's Life of Saint Guthlac*, ed. and trans. B. Colgrave (Cambridge, 1985), pp. 120–1, 124.
[79] Griffiths, 'Siblings and the Sexes', pp. 41–4.
[80] Ibid., p. 45.
[81] C. Maillot, 'Bernard de Clairvaux et la fratrie recomposée', *Médiévales* 54 (2008), 13–34; see also McLaughlin, 'Survivors and Surrogates', p. 47.
[82] Maillot, 'Bernard de Clairvaux', pp. 27–31; Cîteaux was founded in 1098; the first female house associated with the order was founded in the time of the second abbot, Stephen Harding, receiving donation of lands between 1120 and 1125. See B. L. Venarde, *Women's Monasticism and Medieval Society: Nunneries in France and England: 890–1215* (Ithaca NY, 1997), pp. 73–4 and C. H. Berman, *The Cistercian Evolution: The Invention of a Religious Order in Twelfth-Century France* (Philadelphia, 2000).

proximity. Contemporary churchmen feared that the presence of women – even sisters – could elicit carnal thoughts. Jean Gerson (1368–1429), the eldest of twelve siblings, wrote both letters and treatises to help his six sisters in their spiritual lives; yet he records that he was troubled by sexual thoughts when he saw them.[83] The biblical story of Amnon and Thamar, half-brother and sister, and children of King David, was often adduced as evidence that sisters might incite lustful thoughts in their brothers.[84] The Knight of La Tour-Landry, who compiled his book of instruction for his daughters around 1371–2, cites the rape of Thamar to warn against intimacy with members of the opposite sex. The Knight makes an exception for husbands, fathers and sons, but he urges that any woman 'that clenly wylle kepe honoure and worship ought not to abyde alone with a man alone'.[85]

As primogeniture began to take hold, the Church offered opportunities for advancement to younger sons. Not all brothers approved of this career path, even for their juniors. Caesarius of Heisterbach (c. 1180–1240) relates the trials of a man who was a canon of Bonn cathedral. His knightly brothers sent a young man to him with a message purporting to be from his mother to lure him outside the foundation, then kidnapped him. Nevertheless, he managed to escape and returned to the order, this time for good.[86] That aristocratic brothers should object to one of their number choosing the religious life seems curious, given that the aspirant would thus remove himself from kin-group competition for property. An ecclesiastical career seems to have been viewed as less manly and less noble than the knightly vocation, and the brother's choice in this exemplum may, as we shall see in chapter four, have challenged norms of sibling solidarity. Although brothers flourish when they choose different paths in life from their siblings, extreme de-identification can be regarded as an affront, provoking the very discord that the deviating brother had hoped to avoid.[87]

---

[83] McGuire, 'Late Medieval Care and Control of Women' (p. 33, n. 98) and McGuire, 'Jean Gerson and the End of Spiritual Friendship'. See also Ledwige, 'Relations de famille'. Cf. *Index exemplorum*, ed. Tubach, no. 4424, p. 337 in which a woman begs her brother, a monk, to come to see her after many years of separation. He visits, accompanied by two fellow-monks, but tells her they can never meet again, because she is a woman.

[84] Amnon's rape of his half-sister was avenged by her brother Absalom, bringing discord to the kingdom of Israel (2 Samuel 8). See Griffiths, 'Siblings and the Sexes', pp. 50–1.

[85] William Caxton, *The Book of the Knight of the Tower*, ed. M. Y. Offord, EETS ss 2 (Oxford, 1971), p. 87.

[86] Caesarius of Heisterbach, *The Dialogue on Miracles*, i.13, ed. H. von E. Scott and C. C. S. Bland, 2 vols (London, 1929), I: 20–1. Cf. Geoffroi le Grand Dent's murder of his brother in the tale of Mélusine, discussed in chapter four.

[87] Bank and Kahn, *The Sibling Bond*, pp. 104–11.

Royal Siblings

Aristocratic sibling groups might also share similar destinies. Eleanor of Provence (1223–91) and her three sisters all became queens through marriage; the two elder sisters married Henry III of England and Louis IX of France, and the two younger sisters married the kings' younger brothers.[88] That all four sisters became queens was remarkable enough for Dante to comment on it in *Il Paradiso*: 'Quattro figlie ebbe, e ciascuna reina, / Ramondo Beringhiere' ('Four daughters, and each one of them a queen / Had Raymond Berenger').[89] The brother-in-law relationship between Louis and Henry was crucial to thirteenth-century Anglo-French diplomacy. Matthew Paris records the king's observation that it was right to make peace with Henry by ceding him land, acknowledging the extended affinal group: 'Nonne duas sorores desponsavimus, et fratres nostri reliquas? Omnes quotquot ex illis ortum sunt producturae vel producendae, vel producturi vel producendi, tanquam fratres erunt et sorores' ('Have we not married two sisters, and our brothers the other two? All that shall be born of them, both sons and daughters, shall be like brothers and sisters').[90] Sibling and affinal bonds, and the links between cousins, are associated with harmonious diplomatic relationships and the resolution of long-standing Anglo-French conflict. Louis and Henry were fortunate that their younger brothers were able to claim other kingdoms outside their own domains; these distant territorial interests contributed to peace and stability at home. Richard had indeed risen in rebellion against his brother several times in the early years of his reign, but marriage to the queen's sister allied him closely to the queen's party and he did not rebel again.[91]

Within earlier royal dynasties, or indeed elsewhere in Europe in the thirteenth century, the prosperity and peacefulness of the kingdom depended on the survival of one (and preferably only one) mature heir per generation. '[D]eux ou plusieurs fils, mais un seul trône, un héritage, un honneur, et c'est le conflit' ('two or more sons, but only one throne, one inheritance, one honour, and it's conflict').[92] The Carolingian dynasty's success stemmed in part from the demise of men who might otherwise, as in the often fratricidal earlier Merovingian conflicts, have contested the succession.[93] Hákon IV, king of Norway for much

---

[88] Howell, *Eleanor of Provence*, p. 137.
[89] Dante, *Paradiso* VI: lines 133–4, cited from http://www.danteonline.it/italiano/opere.asp?idope=1&idlang=OR.
[90] Howell, *Eleanor of Provence*, p. 137; Matthew Paris, *Chronica Majora*, ed. H. R. Luard, 7 vols (London, 1872–3), V: 481.
[91] N. Vincent, 'Richard, First Earl of Cornwall and King of Germany (1209–1272)', *DNB*, 2004; online edn, Jan 2008, http://ezproxy.ouls.ox.ac.uk:2117/view/article/23501, accessed 19 July 2012.
[92] L. Leleu, 'Frères et sœurs ennemis dans la Germanie du Xe siècle', *Médiévales* 54 (2008), 35–52 (p. 35).
[93] Russell, *Medieval Demography*, p. 114. See also Duby, *The Knight, the Lady*, p. 247

of the first half of the thirteenth century, stipulated that only the legitimate heirs born to him and his queen could inherit the crown.[94] Emphasizing the importance of Christian marriage over casual concubinage, Hákon's move won Church approval, even as it excluded his own eldest son from the succession.[95] By ending the custom by which any descendant of previous Norwegian kings might be regarded as a plausible royal candidate, Hákon successfully terminated the civil wars which had racked the kingdom for over a century.

The early Frankish and twelfth- and early-thirteenth-century Norwegian royal dynasties were by no means exceptional; fraternal royal rivalry was rife across Europe. In 1198 Pope Innocent III wrote to Duke Andrew of Hungary to reproach him for making war on his brother, King Imre, instead of fulfilling a crusading vow made on his deathbed by his father Béla III.[96] Innocent threatened anathema and invoked fraternal obligation, praying optimistically that 'the affection of mutual charity' might unite the warring brothers 'as it united the paternal blood and the maternal womb'.[97] Strongly stigmatized by the Church, fratricide was regarded as second only to parricide in sinfulness, though the prize of the throne might be worth the stigma. The recurrent political conflicts between royal or noble brothers recorded in historical material find a clear reflection in pseudo-history and in foundation myths, as we shall see in chapter four.

Siblings' Marriages

If the father were dead, brothers arranged their sisters' marriages, exercising a 'fratriarchal' authority.[98] Sibling involvement in marriage arrangements tended to be 'determined . . . by the particular timing of the marriage and the demographic composition of the family at that time [rather] than by any clearly articulated set of marital rules'.[99] From the twelfth century onwards in north

---

on the lords of Amboise's successful strategy for limiting the number of heirs per generation.

[94] See J. Jochens, 'The Politics of Reproduction: Medieval Norwegian Kingship', *American Historical Review* 92 (1987), 327–49, here pp. 347–8; Sturla Þórðarson, *Hákonar saga Hákonarsonar*, in *Det Arnamagnæanske håndskrift 81A fol.: Skálholtsbók yngsta*, ed. A. Kjaer and L. Holm-Olsen (Oslo, 1926–86), p. 492; C. Larrington, 'Queens and Bodies: The Norwegian Translated *Lais* and Hákon IV's Kinswomen', *Journal of English and Germanic Philology* 108 (2009), 506–27 (pp. 512–13).

[95] See Duby, *The Knight, the Lady*, pp. 41–2, on Charlemagne's restrictive marriage policy for his children.

[96] C. Rousseau, 'Kinship Ties, Behavioural Norms and Family Counselling', in *Women, Marriage, and Family*, ed. Rousseau and Rosenthal, pp. 325–47.

[97] Ibid., p. 336.

[98] See Introduction, p. 6, and Pateman, *The Disorder of Women*, pp. 33–53, for fraternal oppression as an aspect of patriarchy.

[99] C. Johnson, 'Marriage Agreements from Twelfth-Century Southern France', in *To Have and to Hold*, ed. Reynolds and Witte jr, pp. 215–59 (p. 244).

and west France, but rather later in southern Europe where Roman law had prevailed, the provision of a dowry terminated a sister's inheritance claims.[100] Elsewhere, in parts of northern Europe, women could return their dowry to the paternal estate on their father's death in the hope of gaining a larger share than that received at marriage; if the family's property had expanded since the daughters' marriages they could thus profit from it.

Royal and aristocratic sisters often contracted marriages which took them to live far away from their birth kindred, limiting their future interactions with their siblings. By contrast, in lower social classes, sisters and brothers might live in close proximity to one another and maintain friendly relations after marriage.[101] Some miracle stories mention siblings visiting each other's houses and offering help and advice with children. Two daughters of the lord of Tolentino in the central Italian Marche, their brother Manfred and his wife Ymilia were all present one evening around 1305, when Manfred's and Ymilia's baby, who was nursing at her mother's breast, suddenly became lifeless. After an impassioned appeal to the local saint, the baby revived.[102] Didier Lett concludes from the same Tolentino sources that the strength of ties between siblings after marriage in this part of Italy depended heavily on the customs of virilocality and patrilocality.[103] Brothers established the marital home near their father, or even within their father's house, while sisters lived elsewhere with their husbands. Thus brothers are recorded as acting together and visiting one another, and sisters-in-law are often present at the events which give rise to the Tolentino miracle testimonies. However, the married sisters did not tend to move very far; they could often be found at the childbeds of their sisters and sisters-in-law. The strength of sibling relations is crucially affected by geographical proximity; wives continued to hold and to exercise 'des droits au sein de leur groupe natal, et des obligations vis à vis leurs membres' ('rights within the bosom of their birth group and obligations towards its members') when they could easily visit or communicate with their families.[104] Boccaccio's *Decameron* illustrates how, in fourteenth-century Italian urban communities, married siblings often intervened in one another's lives – as we shall see in chapter seven.

The ideology of romantic love and the doctrine of consent changed medieval thinking about marriage from the eleventh century onwards. Earlier, married women might be envisaged as occupying the problematic position of 'exchanged

---

[100] Fossier, 'The Feudal Era', pp. 407–29 (p. 418); Duby, *The Knight, the Lady*, pp. 96, 103.
[101] D. Lett, 'Liens adelphiques et endogamie géographique dans les Marches de la première moitié du XIVe siècle', *Médiévales* 54 (2008), 53–68. In England, in contrast, in the thirteenth and fourteenth centuries, girls in the Lincolnshire villages of Weston and Moulton moved about fifteen miles away when marrying, a day's journey. See Smith, 'Hypothèses', pp. 127–9 and Goldberg, *Women, Work*, p. 212.
[102] Finucane, *Rescue of the Innocents*, pp. 91–2.
[103] Lett, 'Liens adelphiques'.
[104] M. Godelier, *Métamorphoses de la Parenté* (Paris, 2004), p. 164.

women', in Gayle Rubin's terminology.[105] Heroic legend and poetry frequently explored the implications of the sister privileging her affective ties with her brothers over her bond with her husband. Conversely, and especially after the birth of children, the sister might develop new loyalties – often unwelcome from her birth-family's point of view – allying herself with the kin-group into which she married.[106] In Thietmar of Merseburg's *Chronicle*, for example, the monk-author recounts how her sibling loyalty apparently had a stronger affective hold on his mother than maternal love.[107] Thietmar narrates how in 994 three of his maternal uncles were captured by Viking pirates.[108] Negotiations were undertaken to exchange these high-ranking noblemen for other hostages so that the uncles could arrange for ransom-payment. Thietmar was sent by his mother as hostage for his uncle Sigifridus. Thietmar set out for the Viking ship, but his uncle had already managed to escape, and thus he was spared the exchange.[109]

While marriage created new alliances through the exchange of women, wives continued as social actors, both within the new marital family and within their birth families.[110] The new-made alliance might hold, conferring benefits on all involved, or it might founder. Martin Aurell notes the inherent fragility of agreements contracted between feuding groups through marriage in the medieval period:

> L'ennui est qu'au Moyen Âge tout accord est par définition instable ... le lien matrimonial est soluble dans le sang de la défaite militaire et dans l'encre du traité trahissant une alliance précédente.
>
> ('The problem is that in the Middle Ages every accord is by definition unstable ... the marriage bond is dissolvable in the blood of military defeat and in the ink of a treaty which betrays a previous alliance.')[111]

The Embrones and Peveres were among the most important patrician families of Genoa where, in 1226, Giovanna Embrone's husband Nicolà was murdered by her brothers. Giovanna's Pevere brothers had previously forced her to make a

---

[105] See Introduction, pp. 11–12, on exchanged women. On the ideological changes in medieval marriage, and in particular the doctrine of consent, see *Viator* 4 (1973), special issue on marriage, and H. A. Kelly, *Love and Marriage in the Age of Chaucer* (Ithaca NY, 1975).

[106] Such affinal tensions are explored in chapter seven.

[107] Compare Klagsbrun, *Mixed Feelings*, p. 113.

[108] Thietmar von Merseburg, *Chronicon* IV.33–5, in *Die Chronik des Bischofs Thietmar von Merseburg und ihre Korveier Überarbeitung. Thietmari Merseburgensis Episcopi Chronicon*, ed. R. Holtzmann, MGH Scriptores 6, Scriptores rerum Germanicarum, Nova Series 9 (Berlin, 1935); *Ottonian Germany: The Chronicon of Thietmar of Merseburg*, trans. D. Warner (Manchester and New York, 2001), p. 168.

[109] See Leleu, 'Frères et sœurs ennemis', pp. 37–8.

[110] See Introduction, p. 12.

[111] M. Aurell, 'Rompre la concorde familiale: typologie, imaginaire, questionnements', in *La parenté*, ed. Aurell, pp. 9–59 (p. 33).

will excluding her daughter in favour of her three siblings. After Nicolà's death, Giovanna retreated to a convent. Her brothers soon persuaded her to demand release from her vows; Giovanna claimed that she had been out of her mind with grief when she made them.[112] Although the Embrones and the Peveres exchanged a public kiss of peace the following year this did not end the feud for an Embrone murdered a Pevere in 1232.[113] Such stories could be multiplied indefinitely from medieval sources: hostility, even murder, between affines is a recurrent sibling theme. Geographical distance reduced the probability of conflict between brother and brother-in-law, just as the development of different identities diminished the opportunity for strife between brothers.

Where the sister's marriage took her far from her kindred, the likelihood that she would feel profound sorrow at leaving behind her siblings, perhaps never to see them again, was acknowledged. In 1203 Pope Innocent III took up the case of the estrangement between Philip Augustus of France and his queen, Ingeborg of Denmark, reminding the king how Ingeborg had left her loving siblings to come to his kingdom, 'Reliquerat siquidem fratres et sorores, ut tibi matrimonialiter adhaereret, essetisque duo in carne una' ('she has thus left her brothers and sisters in order to cleave to you in marriage, and you are two in one flesh'), Innocent notes.[114] This invocation of sibling love is doubtless a rhetorical trope, adapting Genesis 2. 24, which urges a man to leave father and mother and cleave to his wife. Nevertheless the pope's observation serves to draw the recalcitrant king's attention to Ingeborg's kindred. The marriage had been arranged by Ingeborg's brother, Knut VI of Denmark; vehemently refusing on his sister's behalf to accept Philip Augustus's argument that the marriage could be annulled on the grounds of consanguinity, he had appealed to Innocent's predecessor Celestine III to rule in the dispute.[115]

Brothers thus continued to take an interest in their sisters after marriage, under some inheritance systems they stood to inherit from their sister and the relationship with her sons might be particularly close (see below, p. 38). Bede relates how the seventh-century King Penda of Mercia attacked Cenwalh of Wessex when the latter put away his wife, Penda's sister, and married another. Penda's anger was both political and personal; the rejection of the affinal bond signalled a rupture in the two kingdoms' diplomatic relations.[116] Cenwalh took

---

[112] S. Epstein, 'The Medieval Family: A Place of Refuge and Sorrow', in *Portraits of Medieval and Renaissance Living: Essays in Memory of David Herlihy*, ed. S. K. Cohn and S. Epstein (Ann Arbor MI, 1996), pp. 149–71 (p. 153). See also D. O. Hughes, 'Domestic Ideals and Social Behavior: Evidence from Medieval Genoa', in *Medieval Families*, ed. Neel, pp. 124–56 (p. 143).

[113] Epstein, 'The Medieval Family', p. 153; see also S. Epstein, *Wills and Wealth in Medieval Genoa: 1150–1250* (Cambridge MA, 1984), pp. 91–6.

[114] PL 215: col. 198.

[115] See Duby, *The Knight, the Lady*, pp. 205–6, G. Conklin, 'Ingeborg of Denmark, Queen of France, 1193–1223', in *Queens and Queenship in Medieval Europe*, ed. A. J. Duggan (Woodbridge, 1997), pp. 39–52, and now D. L. d'Avray, *Dissolving Royal Marriages: A Documentary History, 860–1600* (Cambridge, 2014), ch. 6.

[116] *Bede's Ecclesiastical History of the English People* III.3, ed. and trans. B. Colgrave and

refuge with King Anna of East Anglia. Here he accepted the Christian faith and successfully reconquered his kingdom, but Bede does not explain how his marital issues were resolved. Lower down the social scale, in late-medieval Paris, widows looked for their brothers' aid in legal matters.[117] Sisters might also offer support: Jeanne Lablonde accompanied her widowed sister Lucette to testify to the abuse of Lucette's daughter at the hands of her husband.[118] In cases where the widow sought to get control of her dower, or if she wished to remarry, she might have to bring suit against her own siblings to gain access to the financial resources she required.[119]

Brothers were often responsible for making the social and financial arrangements for their sisters' remarriages, privileging the family's interests over the sister's desires. In fifteenth-century Florence, husbands, who were frequently twenty or more years older than their wives, tended to leave young widows. Their children would be reared by their paternal kin, while the widow was usually required to return to her birth family, so that her father or brothers could marry her off again.[120] 'All Florentine families pursued the same combination of contradictory desires, pressuring their widowed daughters-in-law to leave their dowries in their husbands' (and children's) estates and encouraging their widowed daughters to reclaim their dowries and contract new marriages', notes John Najemy.[121]

Older sisters might sometimes take a hand in their brothers' marital arrangements, though this is less easily documented. In one case, heard in the York Consistory Court in 1365, Alice Roucliff's mother had previously entered into an agreement with John Marrays that her underage daughter would marry him, but that there should be no intercourse until she was old enough. John lived in the household of his sister Annabile Marrays. Annabile gave evidence that Alice had told her that she and John had attempted to consummate the marriage, and that Alice now wanted the wedding to be solemnized. John and the bride's mother had earlier concluded an agreement under which John agreed to pay a sum of money if he did not wait until the agreed time for consummation: Annabile wanted to safeguard her brother's position with regard to his liability to pay Alice's mother. She was also Alice's confidante and had some influence in advancing the solemnization of the marriage.[122]

R. A. B. Mynors (Oxford, 1969), pp. 232–5.

[117] C. Jeanne, 'Seules ou accompagnées? Les veuves parisiennes et leurs fratries à la fin du moyen âge', *Médiévales* 54 (2008), 69–81.

[118] Ibid., pp. 75–6.

[119] Ibid., p. 77.

[120] C. Klapisch-Zuber, *Women, Family and Ritual in Renaissance Italy* (Chicago, 1987), pp. 28–46 and pp. 120–30.

[121] J. Najemy, *A History of Florence, 1200–1575* (Oxford, 2006), p. 235.

[122] F. Pedersen, 'Marriage Contracts and the Church Courts in Fourteenth-Century England', in *To Have and to Hold*, ed. Reynolds and Witte jr, pp. 303–9; P. J. P. Goldberg, *Women in England: c. 1275–1525: Documentary Sources* (Manchester and New York, 1995), pp. 58–80.

Nephews and Nieces

Both nobles and ecclesiastics took an interest in their siblings' offspring. The aristocratic practice of hypergamy equipped a sister's children with a maternal uncle who would not compete with them for their paternal inheritance, and who might be wealthier and more powerful than their own father.[123] Thus, as Beitscher notes, one solution to the sibling competition exacerbated by primogeniture was for younger sons to undertake their knightly training with the maternal uncle (*avunculus*). This removed them from the orbit of their father and older brother, who retained control of the family estates, and reduced the opportunity for conflict.[124] Martin Aurell observes that maternal uncles and nephews – Mordred and Tristan, for example – only fall out in legend. Normally maternal uncles and sisters' sons were expected to acknowledge their reciprocal bonds: Thietmar of Merseburg's accession to his mother's demand that he offer himself as hostage in the place of his maternal uncle was discussed above. After the Benedictine Reforms, the imposition of clerical celibacy prevented high-ranking ecclesiastics from producing offspring – or at least none that could be acknowledged. The sister's son was consequently trained and promoted as his ecclesiastic uncle's natural successor.[125] Thus Gerald of Wales (*c.* 1146–1223) might reasonably have expected to succeed to the see of St David's after his maternal uncle, David fitz Gerald, had the king and archbishop of Canterbury not intervened to veto him.[126]

The relationship between father's brother and brother's son was more problematic. A deceased elder brother's children had at least some claim on his inheritance: when a kingdom was at stake, the outlook for brother's sons might be grim. Richard III made sure that his brother's children did not survive their incarceration in the Tower. King John of England was certainly implicated in the death of Arthur of Brittany, who had some claim to the throne through his father Geoffrey, third son of Henry III. John also imprisoned Arthur's sister, Eleanor of Brittany, until her death in 1241.[127] Not all paternal uncles conform to the 'wicked uncle' stereotype. Gilles Lecuppre notes how Charles de Valois (1270–1325) offered his strong support and loyalty to the last three Capetian monarchs, all his paternal nephews.[128] In many cases, as Lecuppre argues, the pressure for continuity works in favour of the dead king's brother, rather than his untried heir: 'Le frère incarne l'identité, l'enfant l'altérité, voire l'extranéité' ('The brother embodies identity; the child alterity, even extraneousness').[129] A young

---

[123] Aurell, 'Rompre la concorde', p. 21.
[124] Beitscher, '"As the twig is bent"'.
[125] Cf. the origin of the term *nepotism*; see Réal, *Vie des saints*, pp. 493–500.
[126] Aurell, 'Rompre la concorde', p. 22.
[127] Ibid., pp. 19–22; J. C. Holt, 'King John and Arthur of Brittany', *Nottingham Medieval Studies* 44 (2000), 82–103.
[128] G. Lecuppre, 'L'oncle usurpateur à la fin du Moyen Âge', in *La parenté déchirée*, ed. Aurell, pp. 147–56 (p. 147).
[129] Ibid., p. 153.

nephew has little chance of success against his *patruus*; if he rises against the usurper, his rebellion offers a pretext for putting the heir to death, even though popular and retrospective sentiment may often be on the younger man's side.[130]

Death and Mourning

'Death only ends a life: it does *not* end a relationship', propose Bank and Kahn.[131] Siblings remember their dead. Public memorializing of the dead in Viking-age (and later, medieval) Scandinavia very often fell to the sibling, who paid for the erection of large stones, often decorated and inscribed in the runic alphabet with information about the dead family member. Birgit Sawyer has argued that the erection of runestones was driven largely by issues of inheritance; they functioned both as a public announcement of death and as an enumeration of those who stood to inherit from the dead person.[132] Analysis of the runic corpus shows that the overwhelming majority of sibling dedications (nearly 400) are commissioned by brother(s) commemorating their brother(s) or their father.[133] Twelve inscriptions are sponsored by a mixed sibling group who commemorate brothers, while fourteen inscriptions show sisters remembering their brothers. Sisters are often included in memorializations in which the whole family is named; in the Hassmyra inscription from Sweden a certain Holmgautr notes that his dead wife Óðindísa was a good sister to Sigmundr.[134] The carving of each word incurs costs in time, money and materials: the expansion of these inscriptions beyond the bare minimum record necessary for legal purposes points to the existence of warm emotional bonds between siblings and affines in Viking-age and medieval Scandinavia.

By the end of the medieval period, private personal writings, such as the *Hausbücher* discussed earlier, and the Italian *ricordanze*, become valuable sources for sibling affective bonds. While such family record-books have the primary function of noting births, marriages and deaths, they sometimes incorporate surprisingly emotional writing about the events they chronicle. The Florentine Giovanni di Pagolo Morelli (1371–1444) wrote a formal eulogy for his sister, known as Méa, who had recently died in childbirth. After the death of Giovanni's father and grandfather Méa looked after her brother for about four years.

---

[130] See Holt, 'King John', pp. 95–9 for the role of Peter of Wakefield and various chroniclers in raising questions about John's accession and Arthur's death.
[131] Bank and Kahn, *The Sibling Bond*, p. 271.
[132] B. Sawyer, *The Viking-Age Rune-Stones: Custom and Commemoration in Early Medieval Scandinavia* (Oxford, 2000), pp. 107–10; see now J. Jesch, 'Runic Inscriptions and the Vocabulary of Land, Lordship and Social Power in the Late Viking age', in *Settlement and Lordship in Viking and Early Medieval Scandinavia*, ed. S. M. Sindbaek and B. Poulsen (Turnhout, 2011), pp. 31–44.
[133] Warm thanks to Judith Jesch for help in analysing the runic database: http://www.runforum.nordiska.uu.se/samnord/.
[134] Västmanland inscription 24.

She was of normal height, with very beautiful hair, shining and blonde, with a very beautiful figure, so genteel that she was a delight. And among her beauties, she had hands like ivory, so well-made that they seemed painted by the hand of Giotto. . . . In everything she did she was most virtuous: refined and pleasing in her speech, unaffected and restrained in delivery, and eloquent. She was a self-confident, frank woman with a virile soul, abundant in all virtues. She could read and write as well as any man.[135]

Giovanni's praise for his sister contains the conventional elements of a formal portrait, as well as details which seem strikingly closely observed – the hands like those in a Giotto painting, for example. The portrait is full and lifelike, and Giovanni's regard for his sister is clear. Outside these late personal memoirs, siblings have limited opportunity to record how they lamented their brothers and sisters. Resignation to the death of siblings is explored in saints' lives, particularly those composed in the early part of the period. These depict the devout brother or sister experiencing emotions of loss – mourning, anger and guilt – must be painfully reconciled with a faith-filled understanding that the dead person has been gathered to the Lord and is now in heaven.[136] In contrast, the vengeance imperative fuelled blood-feud; the obligation to avenge a murdered brother seems to have been hard to eradicate, even when Christian ethics and laws which regulated compensation for killing were well established.[137]

Half- and Step-Siblings

Medieval families could be complex. The death of one or other parent and the remarriage of the surviving partner created half-siblings from the new union, or brought within the household step-siblings with no genetic connection to the former family unit. Step-siblings might be regarded as part of a larger household or *familia* for whom the head of household took responsibility, as Jenny Kermode shows for late-medieval English towns, while other medieval sources scrupulously distinguish them from the original family.[138] Expressions such as '"the children of his father's wife" or the "husband of his father's sister" indicat[e] that they are not really seen as siblings', Ruth Mazo Karras notes of a fourteenth-century Prussian source.[139] Illegitimate or step-siblings could be absorbed into the labour force in farming or peasant families; here they could earn a living, whether or

---

[135] Giovanni di Pagolo Morelli, *Ricordi*, in *Mercanti scrittori*, ed. V. Branca (Milan, 1986), p. 153. Translation from *Women in Italy, 1350–1650: Ideals and Realities: A Sourcebook*, ed. M. Rogers and P. Tinagli (Manchester, 2005), p. 107.
[136] See chapter three, below, pp. 90–2.
[137] See chapter two, pp. 64–9.
[138] J. Kermode, 'Sentiment and Survival: Family and Friends in Late Medieval English Towns', *Journal of Family History* 24 (1999), 5–18.
[139] R. M. Karras, 'Invisible Women', *Medieval Feminist Forum* 39 (2005), 15–21, discussing here scribal usage in the Book of Aldermen (Schöppenbuch) from Bartenstein in what is now Poland in 1458.

not they expected to inherit from the deceased biological parent. They were thus less likely to enter into legal conflicts with step- or half-siblings. In aristocratic families fathers often made separate provision for stepchildren or illegitimate offspring. As the Anglo-Saxon examples discussed below indicate, stepbrothers in the paternal line also compete fiercely with their step-siblings: step-fraternal solidarity is easily abandoned as a social norm when a throne is at stake.

Anticipated inheritances could be jeopardized by expansion within the family, especially if step-siblings become converted to half-siblings with the birth of children to a second or subsequent marriage. The anxiety that a new set of children with a second wife could supplant the offspring of the first wife is frequently explored in imaginative literature, shaping the widespread perception of the stepmother as wicked.[140] Before primogeniture and the gradual abandonment of concubinage took hold, royal succession was considerably complicated by the existence of different sets of half-siblings who shared a father. Kings in Anglo-Saxon England, for example, were chosen from a group of male kindred related by blood to the last king, and the eldest son was not necessarily selected by the council to rule. Pauline Stafford has documented the rivalry between first and subsequent sets of brothers in the royal house of Wessex in the later Anglo-Saxon period.[141] Two sons and two stepsons of Emma of Normandy acceded to the English throne during the eleventh century.[142] The cohort's fluctuating fortunes were determined by shifting factional influences, not least the support of their mother, who was certainly instrumental in the rapprochement between Harthacnut and his successor and half-brother, Edward the Confessor. Harthacnut's treatment of Edward 'was perhaps moved by brotherly love, as the encomiast alleges, but one might also discern the influence of Emma, keen to maintain her own position by ensuring that one kingly son should be followed by another', as M. K. Lawson suggests.[143]

Such evidence as can be found for step-children suggests that their prospects, in terms of inheritance and marriage arrangements, are determined by their surviving parent and step-parent rather than by their step-siblings who have no jurisdiction over them. Blood ties, even if only via one parent, are significant; the next chapter explores how the obligation to avenge a slain brother was imagined as falling on half-brothers as well as full-brothers.

---

[140] See P. Watson, *Ancient Stepmothers: Myth, Misogyny and Reality* (Leiden, 1995).

[141] P. Stafford, 'The King's Wife in Wessex, 800–1066', in *New Readings on Women in Old English Literature*, ed. H. Damico and A. Hennessy Olsen (Indianapolis, 1990), pp. 56–78. See also P. Stafford, 'Sons and Mothers: Family Politics in the Early Middle Ages', in *Medieval Women*, ed. D. Baker (Oxford, 1978), pp. 79–100.

[142] M. K. Lawson, 'Harthacnut (c. 1018–1042)', *DNB*, 2004, http://ezproxy.ouls.ox.ac.uk:2117/view/article/12252, accessed 19 July 2012; E. Tyler, 'Talking about History in Eleventh-Century England: The *Encomium Emmae* and the Court of Harthacnut', *Early Medieval Europe* 13 (2005), 359–83, for discussion of Emma's role in the production of the *Encomium* and its management of her relationships with her sons. See also P. Stafford, *Queen Emma and Queen Edith: Queenship and Women's Power in Eleventh-Century England* (Oxford, 1997).

[143] Lawson, 'Harthacnut'.

Quasi-sibling Relationships

Beside half- and step-sibling relationships, a range of other quasi-sibling relationships were possible, leaving aside the fraternal/sororal models of the monastery or convent. The most prominent of these is the foster-bond. This might take several forms: emergency fostering of an orphan with relatives, as in the cases of Peter Damian and Giovanni di Pagolo Morelli discussed above or patronal fostering in which high-ranking families fostered the children from less highly ranked kinships, typical in England and much of continental Europe from the ninth century onwards.[144] Another type of fostering – so-called cliental allegiance fosterage – entailed high-ranking families sending their children to live with families of lower status.[145] Prevalent in Ireland, parts of Celtic Britain and in Scandinavia, especially Iceland, this practice confirmed relative social status, but it also created powerful affective links and expectations of political and military support between chieftains and lesser-ranking families from outside the clan.[146] Fostering created life-long bonds between foster-siblings. Although in the Icelandic family sagas with their focus on feuding, foster-brothers can end up killing one another in adulthood, in other kinds of saga they are depicted as setting out into the world together, sharing the profits from trading and raiding. Fostering could be conflated with knightly training by the maternal uncle in continental European contexts.[147] Since foster-brothers did not directly compete with one another for inheritance or authority within a clan group, the bonds between them might be especially enduring. Writing of twelfth-century Irish conditions, but also reflecting on Welsh custom, Gerald of Wales laments how, if men nowadays have any bonds of love or fidelity 'it is only for their foster-sons and foster-brothers'.[148] Foster and kin relationships entail different political and emotional ties: 'loyal allegiances of fosterage, linked with endemic assassinations within ruling dynasties, are copiously attested in medieval Irish annals', notes Peter Parkes.[149]

Fosterlings of different genders may have fallen in love with one another, resulting in successful marriages. Chivalric practice in twelfth-century and later

---

[144] P. Parkes, 'Celtic Fosterage: Adoptive Kinship and Clientage in Northwest Europe', *Comparative Studies in Society and History* 48 (2006), 359–95 (pp. 359–60).

[145] Ibid., pp. 359–60.

[146] A. Hansen, 'Fosterage and Dependency in Medieval Iceland and its Significance in *Gísla saga*', in *Youth and Age in the Medieval North*, ed. S. Lewis-Simpson (Leiden, 2008), pp. 73–86; Parkes, 'Celtic Fosterage', p. 362.

[147] D. Kullmann, *Verwandtschaft in epischer Dichtung. Untersuchungen zu den französischen chansons de geste und Romanen des 12. Jahrhunderts* (Tübingen, 1992), pp. 88–92.

[148] Gerald of Wales, *Topographia Hibernica* III.7, in *Giraldus Cambrensis Opera*, ed. J. S Brewer *et al.* 8 vols, V, ed. J. F. Dimock (London, 1867), vol. 5, pp. 167–8. Cited from Parkes, 'Celtic Fosterage', p. 365; see also L. B. Smith, 'Fosterage, Adoption and God-Parenthood: Ritual and Fictive Kinship in Medieval Wales', *Welsh History Review* 16 (1992), 1–35.

[149] Parkes, 'Celtic Fosterage', p. 367.

France often meant that a child destined to marry the child of a neighbouring noble family might be fostered with its future in-laws; growing up aware of their marital destiny the future spouses would come to know each other well. Although this seems a humane custom, particularly in the case of child betrothals, there is some psychological evidence that children reared together tend not to regard one another in a sexual light.[150]

When a woman acted as wet-nurse for another's child, quasi-sibling bonds, so-called 'milk kinship', could result.[151] The theologian and encyclopaedist Alexander Neckham was born on 8 September 1157, the same night as the future king of England, Richard I 'Lionheart'. Neckham tells us that his mother Hodierna was Richard's wetnurse, and he enjoyed his milk-brother's patronage later in life.[152] Gerald of Wales includes milk-siblings (*collactaneos*) among his categories of non-related individuals whom the Irish preferred to their own blood-kin: fostered from earliest infancy, Irish foster-siblings and milk-siblings are easily conflated.[153] Unlike foster-sibs or the milk-brother or sister, godchildren do not appear to regard themselves as bound in a quasi-sibling relationship, despite being subject to the kinds of marriage prohibitions in force for blood relationships. Adoption, in a form comparable with the modern practice, was not generally practised in northern Europe. It seems to have been feasible under certain circumstances; Guibert de Nogent's mother probably adopted the infant she took into the household to ameliorate her husband's suffering in Purgatory (see p. 20 above).[154] Adoption or quasi-adoption was most likely to occur where there were no surviving legitimate heirs, and therefore adoptive children did not impinge on or create new sibling bonds.

The final form of quasi-sibling bond evidenced in medieval sources is sworn-brotherhood. In late Anglo-Saxon England, during the course of a multi-generational blood-feud, Ealdred becomes the sworn-brother of Carl, son of Thurbrand, whom Ealdred had previously murdered. The two men plan to

---

[150] The so-called Westermarck hypothesis; see A. P. Wolf, *Sexual Attraction and Childhood Association: A Chinese Brief for Edward Westermarck* (Stanford, 1995); D. Lieberman, J. Tooby and L. Cosmides, 'Does Morality have a Biological Basis? An Empirical Test of the Factors Governing Moral Sentiments Relating to Incest', *Proceedings of the Royal Society: Biological Sciences* 270 (2003), 819–26. Compare also the case of John Somerford and Joan Brereton, who after living together as children for ten years, refused to ratify the marriage on reaching the age of puberty: Orme, *Medieval Children*, p. 336.

[151] P. Parkes, 'Fosterage, Kinship, and Legend: When Milk was Thicker than Blood', *Comparative Studies in Society and History* 46 (2004), 587–615.

[152] J. Goering, 'Neckam, Alexander (1157–1217)', *DNB*, 2004, http://ezproxy.ouls.ox.ac.uk:2117/view/article/19839, accessed 22 July 2012.

[153] Gerald of Wales, *Topographia Hibernica*, pp. 167–8. In Arthurian texts, King Arthur's unquestioning devotion to his often difficult foster-brother Kay, the sharp-tongued seneschal, derives from Kay's mother having nursed and raised the infant king. See further examples under *collactaneus* in the *Dictionary of Medieval Latin from British Sources* (Oxford, 1975–2013).

[154] M. M. Sheehan, *Marriage, Family, and Law in Medieval Europe: Collected Studies*, ed. J. K. Farge (Cardiff, 1996), p. 258 and n. 33

journey to Rome together, but are delayed; Ealdred stays with Carl, and is treacherously murdered by him as they are out walking together. Ealdred's grandson, Earl Waltheof of Northumbria, thirty-five years after the killing of Ealdred in 1038, has Carl's sons and grandsons murdered at a feast.[155] This is one of the earliest references to sworn-brotherhood; it is hard to tell whether Carl simply changes his mind about the relationship, or whether he entered it in order to catch Ealdred off-guard in order to prosecute his vengeance.

Later in the period, adult men of chivalric rank would establish ritual friendship, a pact often sealed by taking the Eucharist together after swearing to mutual love and the obligation to avenge the brother.[156] In Henry V's army in 1421, two squires, Nicholas Molyneux and John Winter, swore a compact intended to augment *lamour et fraternite* ('love and brotherhood') which already existed between them, becoming *freres darmes* ('brothers in arms') in the church of St Martin at Harfleur.[157] Molyneux and Winter agreed to arrange ransom for one another if one were captured, to stand hostage for the other, and to pool their gains of war for later investment back in London. Most famous – indeed infamous – among such friendships was that of Edward II and Piers Gaveston; contemporary chroniclers observed how the prince decided at first sight to bind himself to Gaveston in a *fraternitatis fedus* ('convenant of brotherhood'), a bond of love which he regarded as unbreakable.[158] Kenneth McFarlane argues that in the fifteenth century sworn-brotherhood as practised between men-at-arms was strictly a business arrangement; Alan Bray concludes that the relationship was rooted in strong affective, if not necessarily erotic, feelings.[159] Literary sworn-brotherhoods are consistently imagined as primarily affective relationships, as chapter eight shows; those who actively solicit such relationships without a pre-existing dimension of love and loyalty are exactly those who should be eschewed.

Conclusion

Medieval sibling experience across the lifespan is strongly inflected by gender and by social class: norms for sibling interaction and behaviour varied significantly for brother and sister, for noble and for peasant. Nevertheless, the cultural expectation that siblings will love and support one another is evidenced across the continent and throughout the period, at the same time as many historical

---

[155] See 'De Obsessione Dunelmi', in Symeonis Monachi, *Opera Omnia*, ed. T. Arnold, Rolls Series 75, 2 vols (London, 1882–5), I: 215–20, and C. J. Morris, *Marriage and Murder in Eleventh-Century Northumbria: A Study of* De Obsessione Dunelmi (York, 1992). Thanks to Tom Lambert for this reference.

[156] See A. Bray, *The Friend* (Chicago, 2003), ch. 1 *in extenso*.

[157] Ibid., pp. 16–17; K. McFarlane, 'A Business Partnership in War and Administration, 1421–1445', *English Historical Review* 78 (1963), 290–310 (p. 309).

[158] Bray, *The Friend*, pp. 27–9.

[159] McFarlane, 'A Business Partnership', pp. 292–3, n. 7.

sources acknowledge the possibility of sibling conflict. Mortality, especially infant and child mortality, could alter birth order, promoting a younger child to the position of preferred heir. Inheritance patterns and dowry customs determine which sibs inherit, which marry, which migrate, which enter the church, and which other families become linked to the original family through marriage alliances. In adulthood, sisters would usually marry; continuing links with their siblings would be determined by the distance between the wife's new home and her parents' or siblings' houses. When brothers married, the relationship between their family and the affinal group could be harmonious and profitable to all involved. But it might also, especially when a marriage was arranged to settle a conflict between two groups, become troubled and violence recur.

The consequences of primogeniture encouraged brothers often to choose different paths in life, in the hope of minimizing sibling conflict. In the late-medieval period, when demographic collapse in the wake of the Black Death had freed up resources, brothers often banded together in new enterprises: bringing new land under the plough or investing their capital in the emerging merchant companies. Sisters usually retained strong links with their blood-kindred and expected to maintain their rights within the family, even after marriage. Brothers tended to take an interest in their sisters' children, though brothers' offspring were regarded as competition in the transmission of power or inheritance. Ideas of fraternity shaped peer relations; beyond the immediate family people (mostly, but not always, men) might form fictive sibling relations with their coevals through institutions such as fostering and sworn-brotherhood. What remains largely occluded in the analysis of historical or quasi-historical material about medieval siblings are the affective elements: 'these private unspoken aspects of a sibling relationship which are so difficult to detect'.[160]

Chapter two investigates the most culturally powerful of all bonds in the medieval imagination: love and loyalty between brothers. In saga, heroic legend, epic, ballad and romance, brothers sacrifice everything for one another, going to the ends of the earth to avenge a murdered half-brother, renouncing kingdoms or sacrificing life itself. Rivalry is sublimated into fraternal love, but separation maintains brotherly affections: the paradigm identified in this chapter of marked differentiation, of achieving complementarity, and choosing 'different roads' is also recognized as a successful fraternal strategy in literary texts.

---

[160] Bank and Kahn, *The Sibling Bond*, p. 21.

2

'Berr er hverr á bakinu nema sér bróður eigi':[1] Fraternal Love and Loyalty

Introduction

Holed up on a steep-sided island off Iceland's north coast, the outlaw Grettir and his younger brother Illugi face Grettir's enemies, who have climbed up the island's precipitous cliffs. Already mortally ill, Grettir can scarcely defend himself. When Illugi throws a shield over his brother and fights until he is overcome, Grettir tersely observes, 'Berr er hverr á bakinu nema sér bróður eigi' ('Bare is the back unless one has a brother'). Once Grettir is dead, Illugi refuses to save his own life by swearing to renounce vengeance on his brother's slayer. Defying the cowardly Þorbjǫrn hook, Grettir's chief opponent, he chooses to follow his brother in death rather than live with the shame of forswearing vengeance for him.

Grettis saga is probably one of the latest of the *Íslendingasögur* (sagas of Icelanders) to be composed.[2] Probably late fourteenth century in date, it relates events from the early eleventh century filtered through a later-medieval consciousness of Grettir's historical situation. Grettir's ancestors were relative late-comers to Iceland, and Grettir himself is incapable of settling to the life of a farmer as his older brother Atli does. He pursues a no-longer-viable career as a Viking: a life of raiding and fighting anachronistic within his northern Icelandic farming community and which ends in his outlawry. Like many other brothers, Grettir and Atli preserve their warm fraternal relationship through clear differentiation: one fights, one farms, and Grettir displays no interest in inheriting land from his father.[3] Illugi's fraternality is differently imagined. The boy is profoundly attached to the brother he scarcely knows; as a much

---

[1] 'Bare is the back unless one has a brother', *Grettis saga*, in *Grettis saga Ásmundarsonar, Bandamanna saga, Odds þáttr Ófeigssonar*, ed. Guðni Jónsson, ÍF 7 (Reykjavík, 1936), p. 260.

[2] *Íslendingasögur* recount in prose the histories of Icelandic families between the settlement (roughly 870) and around 930. Broadly realistic, though not without supernatural elements, they were composed between the early thirteenth century and the late fourteenth century.

[3] See, on individual differences, Cicirelli, *Sibling Relationships*, pp. 46–52 and Bank and Kahn, *The Sibling Bond*, pp. 62–4.

younger sibling he idealizes, even hero-worships, his habitually absent brother.[4] Although Grettir has strikingly fractious relationships with his father and with the young men of his age-cohort in the district, he remains emotionally close to both his brothers, avenging the death of Atli, and sharing a small hut for several years with Illugi without evident strain.[5]

Grettir's remark about the exposed existence of a man with no brother is proverbial; it occurs in sibling and non-sibling contexts elsewhere in Germanic literature.[6] In Saxo Grammaticus's account (c. 1200) of the slack young Danish king Frothi III, it is deployed when Ericus the Eloquent and his faithful half-brother Roller enter the king's hall. Frothi's hall-servants delight in laying greased animal hides on the hall-floor, jerking them from under the feet of the unwary to make them trip and look ridiculous. As Ericus struggles to keep his balance, Roller catches him from behind. Ericus praises him by quoting the proverb, which gains extra traction from the physical situation: 'nudum habere tergum fraternitatis inopem' ('a brotherless man has a bare back').[7] Ericus and his half-brother had resolved their sibling rivalry at an earlier stage of their lives. Ericus's sorceress-stepmother had tried to give her own son Roller an advantage over his half-brother by preparing a portion of magically enhanced food for him; the wise Ericus, recognizing her intention, devoured the food himself. Realizing that her plan had gone astray, Roller's mother begged Ericus always to help Roller, to which Ericus answered 'ad astandum fratri *natura* pertrahi' ('[I] was *naturally* drawn to stand by [my] brother') (my italics).[8] Roller is Ericus's only brother; older than his half-brother, Ericus wields the strong social advantage of seniority, but he also is clever enough to notice and to frustrate his stepmother's attempt to even up the distribution of *sapientia* between the two brothers.

These two Scandinavian stories of brotherly loyalty do not simply epitomize the best kinds of fraternal relations, they foreground the positive aspects of brotherhood which recur in sibling narratives across medieval Europe: love, solidarity and uncomplaining acceptance of the different roles allotted to them by birth order. Contemporary psychological theory argues that sibling attachment – 'high access', a shared childhood, according to Stephen Bank and Michael

---

[4] On idealization, see Bank and Kahn, *The Sibling Bond*, pp. 92–3.
[5] See C. Larrington, 'Awkward Adolescents: Male Maturation in Norse Literature', in *Youth and Age in the Medieval North*, ed. S. Lewis-Simpson (Leiden, 2008), pp. 145–60.
[6] http://www.usask.ca/english/icelanders/proverbs_BNS.html. Compare Kári's metaphorical use of the proverb in *Njáls saga*, ed. Einar Ólafur Sveinsson, ÍF 12 (Reykjavik, 1954), ch. 152, p. 436, in praise of an ally, despised as cowardly by his own wife, who nevertheless has bravely fought alongside him. Similarly the Old English wisdom poem *Maxims I* contrasts the friendless man who risks being eaten by wolves on his travels with the brothers who will be successful if they act together even in as dangerous an adventure as fighting against a boar or a bear, in *Poems of Wisdom and Learning in Old English*, ed. T. A. Shippey (Cambridge and Totowa NJ, 1976), pp. 72–3.
[7] Saxo, *GD* V.3.8 (all citations from online version); Saxo, *HD*, p. 128.
[8] Saxo, *GD* V. 2.9; translation adapted from Saxo, *HD*, p. 125.

Kahn – is an important predictor of warm sibling relations in adulthood.⁹ Yet, as noted in chapter one, medieval siblings often did not grow up together. The emotional bonds forged by joint childhood experiences were necessarily replaced or reinforced by a powerful social imperative enjoining absolute fraternal love and loyalty, and theorized as genetically encoded, transmitted in the brothers' shared blood. Varying marriage patterns across Europe dictated whether half-brotherhood was more likely to result from a patriarch whose serial marriages produced children by different wives, or whether a young widow might bear children to a succession of husbands. Medieval sibling narrative tends to foreground shared paternality when half-brothers have strong affective bonds; problematic half-brotherhood, as in the case of Hildibrandr, discussed below, is more closely associated with sharing a mother. Contemporary medical emphasis (ultimately deriving from Aristotle) on the predominant influence of semen rather than uterine material in determining a child's physical and mental qualities underlies the distinction.¹⁰ Patrilocality also suggests that children who share a father will grow up with knowledge of one another's existence; by contrast, virilocality often entails a mother leaving her first set of children behind on remarriage. Thus she may produce further offspring who are unaware of their maternal half-sibs' existence. The author of *Grettis saga* depicts Grettir as inspiring loyalty and love in all his brothers, including his older Norwegian half-brother Þorsteinn. Even if they are raised separately and even if they are only half-brothers, brothers *should* love one another unconditionally. The norm of fraternal love comes second only to the requirement for filial obedience to the father in medieval European minds.

Alert to the wiles of stepmothers and sorceresses, Ericus realized which portion of the snake-liquor-infused dinner would benefit him, while Roller observed his mother's cooking, but failed to anticipate her intentions. He lacked the initiative to insist on his share of the unpleasantly dark-coloured porridge which conferred wisdom, eloquence and the understanding of the language of birds and beasts. Through a combination of disposition and opportunity, a combination which, as Cicirelli notes, is crucial to differentiating siblings, from the moment he fails to seize the porridge Roller is destined to be the less successful younger brother, the follower, not the leader.¹¹ To reassure both step-mother and brother from his position of comparative advantage, Ericus continues to insist that brotherly loyalty is innate in him. Roller's career as trusted lieutenant prospers through maintaining solidarity with his clever sibling. Ericus's fortune is made by his shrewdness and eloquence; he wins the hand of the king's sister, while less-fortunate Roller is given Frothi's cast-off queen, the Hunnish Hanunda, divorced for adultery. Despite his heroic size and fighting ability, Roller always tags along behind his sharp-witted half-brother; but by

⁹ Bank and Kahn, *The Sibling Bond*, pp. 9–15.
¹⁰ T. Laqueur, *Making Sex: Body and Gender from the Greeks to Freud* (Cambridge MA, 1992), pp. 55–62.
¹¹ Saxo, *HD* V. 2.6–9; Saxo, *HD*, pp. 123–5; Cicirelli, *Sibling Relationships*, pp. 46–52.

accepting his limitations and by displaying exemplary loyalty he benefits socially from Ericus's rise in royal favour. Roller relies on Ericus's patronage rather than parlaying his fraternal connection for his personal advantage; the brothers together model an ideal half-brother relationship which mirrors contemporary understanding of the centrality of kin-networks in early-medieval courts.

Brotherly Solidarity

In his *Travels*, composed in the mid-fourteenth century, the fictive voyager 'Sir John Mandeville' relates how, nearing death, Jenghiz, the great khan of Cathay, gathered his twelve sons. Taking an arrow from each of them, he bound them together and invited each son in turn to break the bundle. All failed, whereupon the Khan instructed the youngest son to untie the bundle and to snap each one individually. Asking his sons why the bundle could not be broken and why the youngest was successful, the khan points the moral: 'treuly thus wil it faren be you. For als longe as yee ben bounden togedere in iii. places, that is to seyne in loue, in trouthe, and in gode accord, no man schalle ben of powere to greue you'.[12] But if brotherly love and trust break down, he warns, they will all be destroyed. Jenghiz dies; his eldest son takes over his kingdom, 'and his othere bretheren wenten to wynnen hem many contrees and kyngdomes vnto the lond of Pruysse and of Rossye ... but thei weren alle obeyssant to hire elder brother'.[13]

Solidarity, respect and mutual support between brothers is central to the social construction of fraternality throughout the medieval period. Yet brothers acting together in sustained concert are less frequent in medieval literature than might be expected. This absence is one of the cultural entailments of primogeniture: the oldest brother cannot go adventuring with his siblings for he must stay at home to oversee the farm or the estate, or indeed the kingdom of Cathay. Younger brothers, in contrast, must strike out for themselves. The key to harmonious fraternal relations is thus the pursuit of separate destinies, though brothers will usually provide mutual aid when it is requested. The eldest brother maintains his symbolic authority over the younger brothers, even if exercised at a distance. This narrative pattern – brothers heading in different directions – reflects the psychological process of 'borderwork': the struggle between siblings for adequate differentiation.[14] Same-sex siblings in particular strive to overcome their identification as interchangeable by parents and outsiders, repeatedly behaving in ways which serve to establish: 'I am me; I am not you'.[15] Fraternal differentiation is thus crucial for the narrative hero.

---

[12] *Mandeville's Travels*, ed. M. Seymour (Oxford, 1967), p. 165.
[13] Ibid., p. 165.
[14] Rosenthal, *Patriarchy and Families of Privilege*, p. 111; Apter, *Sister Knot*, p. 110. See also Introduction, p. 6.
[15] Apter, *Sister Knot*, p. 110.

Groups of undifferentiated, even unidentified, brothers are found in folk-tale or else play minor roles in higher-status genres: romance heroes often fight against indistinguishable groups or *fratries* of brothers whose only function is to establish the protagonist's heroic or chivalric credentials.[16] So, in Sir Thomas Malory's 'Tale of Sir Gareth', Gareth kills the Black Knight, and overcomes his brothers, the Green Knight, the Red Knight and finally Sir Persaunt of Inde; through his victories Gareth inculcates proper chivalric mores in the surviving brothers and recruits them to successful membership of the Round Table.[17] Sir Persaunt of Inde is the only closely characterized member of this fraternity, otherwise only differentiated by the colour of their armour. More usually, brothers are clearly distinguished from one another. 'Siblings make each other different', note Sutton-Smith and Rosenberg: some degree of counter-identification between brothers is crucial for positive sibling relations.[18] Extreme differentiation, complete de-identification from the values and beliefs of other siblings often exacerbates conflict, for, as discussed in later chapters, brothers should be different, but not *too* different in their life-choices.

Medieval romance often engages with the impact of primogeniture (whether strict or modified) on norms of brotherly solidarity. In the early-thirteenth-century *Parzival*, Wolfram von Eschenbach notices and laments the sudden change in fortune of the hero's father Gahmuret when his own father Gandin, king of Anjou, dies. Wolfram is explicitly critical of primogeniture as an institution; prevalent in north and west France (and ascribed by him to Galoes's kingdom of Anjou), it was being introduced to his native Thuringia around the time that he was composing the poem:[19]

> (daz ist ein wârheit sunder wân)
> daz der altest bruoder solde hân
> sîns vater ganzen erbeteil.
> Daz was der jungern unheil,
> daz in der tôt die pflihte brach
> als in ir vater leben verjach.
> Dâ vor was ez gemeine:
> sus hâtz der alter eine.[20]

('(this is undeniably true) – that the eldest brother should have his father's

---

[16] C. Vial, 'Entre création et destruction: les liens adelphiques dans les récits arthuriens de langue anglaise', in *Frères et sœurs*, ed. Cassagnes-Brouquet and Yvernault, pp. 151–69. I borrow the useful *fratrie* from French to designate cohorts of brothers; the English 'fratry' has a rather different sense.
[17] 'Tale of Sir Gareth of Orkney' in Sir Thomas Malory, *Le Morte Darthur*, ed. P. J. C. Field, Arthurian Studies 80, 2 vols (Cambridge, 2013), I: 223–88.
[18] Sutton-Smith and Rosenberg, *The Sibling*, p. 2.
[19] *Parzival*, trans. C. Edwards, Arthurian Studies 56 (Cambridge, 2004), pp. xv–xvi. I am grateful to Cyril Edwards for discussion of the relevance of inheritance issues in the civil war of 1198–1208 after the death of Emperor Heinrich IV.
[20] Wolfram von Eschenbach, *Parzival*, ed. K. Lachmann, 6th edn (Berlin and New York, 1998), I.5.3–10.

entire inheritance. This was a curse upon the younger ones – that death caused a breach of such duties as their father's life had vouchsafed them. Before all had been shared – now the elder possesses it alone.')[21]

Gahmuret is consequently deprived of 'sus bürge unde lant' ('his castles and land') (5.24) when his elder brother Galoes succeeds to the throne. When the nobility come to renew their fealty to the new king they beg Galoes to exhibit 'bruoderlîche triwe' ('brotherly loyalty') (6.15) and to grant Gahmuret a *hantgemælde* ('a lord's estate') (6.19).[22] Such a grant would, in effect, endow the younger brother with an estate which would bring with it both lordship and a title. This would be a radical innovation under a strict primogeniture system, for it could entail the foundation of a dynastic 'Seitenlinie' ('side-branch'), creating rival claims in future generations.[23] Replying to the nobles, Galoes asserts that he wishes to do right by his brother, noting sympathetically, 'er hât wênc, und ich genuoc' ('He has little, I have ample'), and he makes a strategic counter-offer.[24] Better than a *hantgemælde*, Galoes claims, Gahmuret shall have riches and he may share the title of 'Angevin' with his brother. Gahmuret can remain in Galoes's household and be his *ingesinde*.[25] Thus Galoes nimbly skirts the question of lordship and closes down the possibility of a separate title. Although his promise of wealth and a shared dynastic name appears generous, the status of the *ingesinde* is a kind of vassalage which does not require homage.[26] The nobles respond well to Galoes's counter-offer, but Gahmuret politely refuses his brother's proposal – for him this is an unacceptable option.[27]

> Hêrre unde bruoder mîn,
> wolt ich ingesinde sîn
> iwer[28] oder decheines man,
> sô het ich mîn gemach getân

---

[21] *Parzival*, trans. Edwards, p. 2.
[22] *Parzival* I.6.19; trans. Edwards, p. 3. The implications of *hantgemælde* are contested; see R. Schmidt-Wiegand, '"hantgemælde", Parzival 6, 19: Rechtswort und Rechtssinn bei Wolfram von Eschenbach", in *Studien zu Wolfram von Eschenbach: Festschrift für Werner Schröder zum 75. Geburtstag*, ed. K. Gärtner and J. Heinzler (Tübingen, 1989), pp. 333–42 and H. Noltze, *Gahmurets Orientfahrt: Kommentar zum ersten Buch von Wolframs "Parzival"*, Würzburger Beiträge zur deutschen Philologie (Würzburg, 1995), pp. 41–3.
[23] Noltze, *Gahmurets Orientfahrt*, p. 43.
[24] *Parzival* I.7.6; *Parzival*, trans. Edwards, p. 3.
[25] Here I follow the interpretation of Noltze, *Gahmurets Orientfahrt*, pp. 39–45. For the more commonly held view that Galoes is warmly generous in his offer to Gahmuret, see, for example, F. Gentry, 'Gahmuret and Herzeloyde: Gone but not Forgotten', in *A Companion to Wolfram's* Parzival, ed. W. Hasty (Columbia SC, 1999), pp. 3–11.
[26] 'Vasallität ohne Lehen', Noltze, *Gahmurets Orientfahrt*, p. 47.
[27] 'keine annehmbare Option', ibid., p. 49.
[28] As Noltze notes, brothers would normally use the familiar form to one another; Gahmuret's address of Galoes first as *Hêrre* and then with the formal pronoun *iwer* signals a degree of alienation.

('My lord and brother, if I wished to belong to your or any man's retinue, then I would have it made').[29]

Gahmuret would rather set out to make his fortune and reputation overseas than be an *ingesinde*, dependent on his brother's generosity. Conflict between the brothers is averted; both negotiate the inheritance crisis with tact, paying careful attention to one another's face. Gahmuret's willingness to remove himself from Anjou and to take service with another lord who is not related to him by blood not only solves the immediate difficulty, it preserves, albeit at arm's length, the warm relationship between the two brothers. Gahmuret does not reject his family's core chivalric values, but rather lays claim to an enhanced version of them. He is indeed highly successful in his career as knight-errant, winning the love of two queens and siring two sons. Although Gahmuret dies young in the service of the Baruch Baldug, nevertheless Galoes is killed before his younger brother, felled in a joust.[30] Gahmuret mourns him fiercely; although he does not return to rule the kingdom in person he lays claim to Anjou and transmits his sovereignty over the territory to his posthumous son and grandson.[31]

Romance usually leaves the tensions generated by differential inheritance customs unexplored; its target aristocratic and bourgeois audiences are left to infer that limited prospects spur the romance hero to embark on making his own fortune. The young man's departure from home is effective in reducing fraternal rivalry over parental resources and encourages the expansion of the kindred's wealth-base by a strategic marriage alliance. Leaving the *fratrie* is crucial to identity formation in romance, enabling the young man to develop and display his own personality traits, to escape the dominance of the elder brother and to emerge as a mature man, ready to found his own family. High male mortality rates among the militarized European aristocracy resulted in the frequent failure of the male line, and afforded opportunity for late-medieval social ambition through strategic marriage to heiresses. Brothers then invoke the mutual aid norm to help one another in expanding the larger kin-group's sphere of influence. In the late-fourteenth-century French romance of *Mélusine*, four of the heroine's many sons leave home in pairs to seek their fortunes, after an explicit and clear-sighted discussion about their individual prospects with their mother.[32] Urian and Guyon note there are already eight brothers, and the *fratrie* might eventually total many more.[33] Going off on chivalric adventure

---

[29] *Parzival* I.7.19–2; translation adapted from *Parzival*, trans. Edwards, p. 3.
[30] *Parzival* II.30.13–18 (death of Galoes).
[31] *Parzival* II.32–3 (Gahmuret's mourning); II.39 (Gahmuret assumes the throne); II.303 (Herzeloyde styled Queen of Anjou); XVI.303 (Kardeiz inherits Anjou).
[32] Prose version: Jean d'Arras, *Mélusine. Roman du XIVe siècle*, ed. L. Stouff (Geneva, 1974); English translation, *Melusine; or, the Noble History of Lusignan*, trans. D. Maddox and S. Sturm-Maddox (University Park PA, 2012). Poetic version: Coudrette, *Le Roman de Mélusine ou Histoire de Lusignan*, ed. E. Roach (Paris, 1982), trans. into modern French as *Le Roman de Mélusine*, trans. L. Harf-Lancner (Paris, 1993).
[33] Jean d'Arras, *Mélusine*, p. 83; *Melusine*, trans. Maddox and Sturm-Maddox, p. 73. The discussion scene is absent from Coudrette (p. 157).

is a practical and face-saving response to the situation; as in Gahmuret's case a rhetorical appeal to honour and reputation occludes the brothers' effective self-disinheritance. Their willingness to cede their share of the patrimony gains them Mélusine's support: she finances their voyage and delivers wise counsel about the chivalric life. The elder of each pair wins a bride and a kingdom for himself, then assists his younger brother in achieving the same success. The strategy works well for Urian and Guyon de Lusignan who gain the princesses and thrones of Cyprus and Armenia respectively: as the king of Cyprus's brother is king of Armenia, the brothers marry cousins. Antoine and Renaud achieve similar success in Luxembourg and Bohemia.[34] With the third pair of brothers, the pattern fails, however. Geoffroy la Grand Dent and Fromont should perhaps have followed their seniors' example, but the choleric Geoffroy undertakes his giant-killing exploits alone while pious Fromont elects to become a monk – the disastrous outcome of this deidentificatory move is discussed in chapter four. Although Mélusine is of supernatural origin, her husband Raimondin was only a minor nobleman, dependent on his uncle's favour, before his fairy wife took him in hand.[35] By suppressing fraternal rivalry and working cooperatively, Raimondin's sons become important royal players in a Europe which is only partly imaginary.[36] At the climax of the romance six sons of Lusignan unite to defend Alsace from its enemies. Fraternal loyalty extends to providing military support to Renaud's wife's uncle: although the affinal connection is relatively distant, the king of Alsace had been instrumental in arranging Renaud's marriage to his niece and his inheritance of the kingdom of Bohemia.[37]

In romance, the only son longs to have a brother and is usually delighted when he finds a long-lost sibling in adulthood. Arthurian tradition features a number of brothers who have been long separated or who have never known of each other's existence. Despite his closeness to his cousins Bors and Lionel with whom he was raised by the Lady of the Lake, Sir Lancelot is overjoyed to learn that Hector de Mares, a noble and accomplished knight whom he knows only by sight, is in fact his illegitimate half-brother: 'De ceste chose fu Lanceloz moult liez et moult joianz plus que qui li donnast la millor cité que li rois avoit' ('Lancelot was happier and more joyful at this news than if he had been given the king's best city'), relates the narrator.[38] When Lancelot and

[34] On the romance as the history of a lineage, see E. Baumgartner, 'Fiction and History: the Cypriot Episode in Jean d'Arras's *Mélusine*', in *Mélusine of Lusignan*, ed. Maddox and Sturm-Maddox, pp. 185–200, especially pp. 194–6.

[35] See S. Knight, *Arthurian Literature* (Basingstoke, 1983), p. 76, on the search for heiresses; also C. Larrington, 'The Fairy Mistress: A Medieval Literary Fantasy', in *Writing and Fantasy*, ed. C. Sullivan and B. White (Harlow, 1999), 32–47.

[36] As Maddox and Sturm-Maddox note, Jean d'Arras's *Mélusine* 'is a rich embodiment of paradoxes of all sorts', not least in its generic instablity 'in combining fiction and history in a single work', *Melusine*, p. 1.

[37] Jean d'Arras, *Mélusine*, p. 282; *Melusine*, trans. Maddox and Sturm-Maddox, pp. 208–12.

[38] *Lancelot: roman en prose du XIIIe siècle*, ed. A. Micha, 8 vols (Geneva, 1978–82), IV: ch. 78, quotation p. 228; *L-G*, III: 369, episode from pp. 167–9.

Hector finally meet, Lancelot runs to his brother with a cry of 'Frere, ne me conoissiez vos pas?' ('Brother, don't you recognize me?'); their mutual rejoicing baffles those others present who do not know of their kinship.[39] On the same day Banin identifies himself to Lancelot as his father's godson, and is also warmly welcomed as a new member of the kin-cohort. Both Hector and Banin are careful to acknowledge Lancelot as their lord, 'mes sires et mes freres', for although Lancelot seems to be younger than Hector, he is the legitimate son and thus has seniority.[40] The existing social hierarchy is not disrupted nor will contention over inheritance arise. Consequently Lancelot's joy at learning that a distinguished member of the Round Table is his half-brother is both deeply felt and untroubled. Hector strategically notes that his recognition by the lineage bolsters their collective chivalric strength: 'que nostre lignages en sera plus doutez touz les jorz que nos vivrons mes' ('because of this our line will be more greatly feared for long as we live').[41] The loyalty of Lancelot's lineage to their lord, rather than to Arthur, entails their departure into French exile with him; consequently Arthur is deprived of their military support in his decisive battles against Mordred. In the *Mort Artu*, Hector dies shortly before Lancelot at the hermitage where the surviving members of the lineage have transformed themselves into a spiritual fraternity. In Malory's *Morte Darthur* Ector arrives at the hermitage just after his half-brother's death and he delivers a moving eulogy over his body.[42] That Ector should fail to locate his kin-group's new 'felyscype' until Lancelot is dead emphasizes Malory's clear perception that bonds of blood tend to be inimical to the ideals which Arthur had sought to promulgate through his Order.

By contrast, the *Morte Darthur*'s history of Sir Gareth traces an individual sibling's attempt to shed or avoid an unwelcome fraternal identification. When Gareth arrives incognito at Arthur's court and elects to work in the kitchens for a year before being knighted, he has a double motivation. He intends to dissociate himself from his own brothers already at Arthur's court: Gawain, Agravain and Gaheris, and to acquire Lancelot as his mentor. Gareth's attempts to distinguish himself from his brothers are successful up to a point; he prevails upon Lancelot to knight him and he establishes a chivalric reputation independent of the expectations of prowess generated by his lineage. At the end of his 'Tale' two of his brothers marry into Gareth's wife's kin-group, ostensibly forming a new affinal grouping. As the behaviour of Gawain and his brothers declines into the worst kind of vicious and unchivalric feuding later in the text, Gareth effectively disowns them, and ostentatiously allies himself with a different chivalric faction within the court. Yet he cannot opt out of the relationship; even if he does not wish to be Gawain's brother, Gawain will not renounce his

---

[39] *Lancelot*, ed. Micha, V: ch. 91, pp. 111; *L-G*, III: 336.
[40] *Lancelot*, ed. Micha V: ch. 91, p. 111; *L-G*, III: 336.
[41] *Lancelot*, ed. Micha, V: ch. 91, p. 112; *L-G*, III: 336.
[42] Malory, *Le Morte Darthur*, ed. Field, I: 339.

Fraternal Love and Loyalty

bond with Gareth.[43] Gawain's kin-oriented instinct, epitomized by his refusal to downgrade or abandon the fraternal vengeance imperative, will be a major cause of the destruction of the Round Table.[44]

Two *Íslendingasögur* offer striking examples of brothers who go on adventures together, *Njáls saga*, discussed below, and *Egils saga*'s Þórólfr and Egill. This saga, composed in the early thirteenth century, quite possibly by the author and chieftain Snorri Sturluson, relates the histories of two sets of brothers: Þórólfr and Grímr, and in the next generation, Egill and the second Þórólfr.[45] Exemplifying their temperamental differences, Grímr prefers to stay at home on the family farm while, until he is brought down by slanderers, Þórólfr pursues a political career in the service of King Haraldr Fairhair of Norway. The first pair of brothers lead distinctly separate lives and form closer bonds with foster-brothers or with friends than with each other. Egill and Þórólfr's fraternal relations are more complicated than those of the previous generation. The teenage Egill's behaviour is tiresomely attention-seeking in a mode typical of younger siblings, and he effectively bullies his more sensible elder brother into taking him to Norway.[46] Þórólfr's forebearance with Egill's lack of self-control and his patient negotiation with King Eiríkr on his brother's behalf exhibit the responsible behaviour typical of firstborns; consequently he risks the king's esteem and forfeits the queen's favour.[47] When Egill's attack on the queen's brother makes it impossible for Þórólfr to return to his wife in Norway for the winter, the journey to England which they undertake instead leads indirectly to Þórólfr's death. The brothers fight in the service of King Æthelstan at the Battle of Vinheiðr (Brunanburh in English sources). Egill's forebodings about the king's decision to deploy the brothers separately on the day of the main battle turn out to be entirely justified. Like his uncle and namesake, Þórólfr is too trusting in the rightness of the decisions of kings, while Egill knows that brothers prosper best together. Without Egill by his side, Þórólfr's back is indeed fatally bare and he dies a hero's death. Egill mourns his brother profoundly. He buries him, composes moving elegiac verses for him, and he exacts handsome compensation for his loss from the king.[48]

The postponed revelation that Egill is in love with his sister-in-law explains much of his difficult behaviour while in Norway. Illness – whether strategic or psychosomatic – prevents him from attending his brother's wedding and he 'acts out' once he has recovered, behaving boorishly in the presence of the royal couple and killing their favourite retainer.[49] After Þórólfr's death, Egill

---

[43] G. Allen, 'Sibling Solidarity', p. 179; see further C. Larrington, 'Sibling Relations in Malory's *Morte Darthur*', *Arthurian Literature* 28 (2011), 57–74, in particular pp. 63–8.
[44] See below, pp. 66–7.
[45] *Egils saga Skalla-Grímssonar*, ed. Sigurður Nordal, ÍF 2 (Reykjavík, 1933); *Egils saga*, trans. C. Fell (London, 1993).
[46] See on later-born siblings, Klagsbrun, *Mixed Feelings*, pp. 64–79.
[47] See on firstborns, ibid., pp. 48–52.
[48] *Egils saga*, ed. Sigurður Nordal, pp. 139–48.
[49] Ibid., pp. 105–14; Torfi Tulinius has proposed a psychoanalytic reading of Egill as

may, as Torfi Tulinius argues, feel guiltily ambivalent about his situation; he has been bereaved, he has exacted revenge on Þórólfr's killer, and now his way is clear to woo his brother's wife (and former foster-sister).[50] Whether or not Torfi's psychoanalytic approach convinces, the author of *Egils saga* undertakes a thoughtful exploration of sibling psychology, probing the complex connections between inherited character traits, birth-order effects, and social context and habitual behavioural patterns in his doubled pairs of brothers.

In *Njáls saga* the sons of Njáll form a cohort which assimilates half-brothers, foster-brothers and brothers-in-law to various degrees. Despite their marriages they largely live together at the paternal farm and they constitute a highly significant faction in south Iceland's local politics in the late tenth and early eleventh centuries. Njáll has three sons with his wife Bergþóra: the contentious and violent Skarpheðinn, Helgi and Grímr, as well as an illegitimate (*laungetinn*) son, Hǫskuldr. This fraternal group is augmented by the addition of two brothers-in-law who marry Njáll's daughters, a foster-brother Þórhallr, the brother of Helgi's wife, and, a rather later actor in the saga, Njáll's foster-son Hǫskuldr Þráinsson. His father had been killed by his *de facto* foster-brothers; his history is discussed in chapter eight.

Helgi and Grímr demonstrate little individualism, whether within or beyond the fraternal group, until they suddenly decide to leave their father and elder brother, to set sail on a trading voyage.[51] In the Pentland Firth they are attacked by a number of Scottish ships; only the arrival of the Hebridean Kári Sǫlmundarson, who enters the battle on their side, saves them from disaster. Kári is in the service of the Earl of Orkney, and the two brothers join him in raiding around the British Isles. The following year the comrades set sail for Norway, where the brothers' loyalty to Þráinn Sigfússon, an Icelander whom they know from home, antagonizes Norway's ruler, Hákon jarl. Once again Kári negotiates a successful outcome. On their return to Iceland, Kári marries the men's sister and becomes a key member of the fraternal alliance. The repercussions of these events will take a generation to play out, but finally Þráinn's refusal to compensate the brothers for the losses they suffered in Norway on his account will lead to his death at the hands of the Njálssons, the death of Þráinn's own son many years later, and the burning of Njáll and his sons in their home.

Helgi and Grímr's bid to establish their independence from their father and elder brother thus brings mixed success. When they ask his permission to go abroad, Njáll prophesies, 'þó munuð þit fá sœmð í sumu ok mannvirðing, en eigi ørvænt, at af leiði vandræði, er þit komið út' ('though you will gain honour and reputation in some respects, difficulties may be expected to come from

---

motivated by unconscious sibling hostility and sexual jealousy in his relationship with Þórólfr. See *Skáldið í skriftinni: Snorri Sturluson og Egils saga* (Reykjavík, 2004), especially pp. 75–80.

[50] Torfi Tulinius, *Skáldið í skriftinni*, p. 178. For romantic attraction between foster-siblings, see chapter eight, pp. 227–32.

[51] *Njáls saga*, ed. Einar Ólafur Sveinsson, pp. 201–25.

your journey if you do go abroad').⁵² Njáll is right; the brothers might easily have perished in the fight in the Pentland Firth had not a new big brother in the form of Kári come to their rescue. The brothers return from their formative adventure abroad having acquired a new (and more level-headed) older brother than Skarpheðinn, and with enhanced reputations, but they also now nurture a grudge against Þráinn which will ultimately cost many lives, including their own. Breaking away from the sibling group in order to reshape their identities as traders and raiders is only partially successful, and they remain subordinate to their dominant elder brother, and to their brother-in-law Kári. His enduring and highly valued membership of the fraternal cohort is sealed by his marriage to their sister, an affinal tie which seems to obviate direct competition with Skarpheðinn, the leader of the *fratrie*.

The sons of Njáll, with their affines and foster-sibs, form an exceptionally tight-knit group whose activities demonstrate the sibling capacity to gang up together against anyone who threatens their face or their interests.⁵³ The collective exhibits a strong group-ego, one which pursues unhealthily self-centred ends: the band of brothers mutates into a gang whose behaviour and goals are regarded as anti-social by many in the community. Skarpheðinn is clearly the gang-leader; his domineering is typical of an arrogant eldest brother. Often insolent to his father and rarely consulting his juniors, Skarpheðinn systematically sabotages any hope of alliance with the most powerful men in Iceland in order to settle the case for the killing of Hǫskuldr Hvítanessgóði (see chapter eight).⁵⁴ His younger brothers fail either to challenge his decision or to act on their own account. When all three brothers are killed in the consequent burning, their brother-in-law Kári must avenge them. Sibling solidarity brings fatal consequences here as the charismatic eldest brother's anti-social orientation drags his other siblings towards an avoidable catastrophe. Helgi and Grímr's alliance with a different and better kind of brother in choosing Kári does not save them from the toxic dynamic of the sibling group, but it does at least assure vengeance for their deaths and opens up the possibility of finally settling the feud. Operating primarily in the interest of the larger kin-group, often reinforcing the eldest brother's authority over his younger siblings, the fraternal solidarity norm does not necessarily benefit the individual. Considered in a larger context, this solidarity can become highly anti-social in its effects.

Medieval moral literature demonstrates the power of normative expectations of fraternal solidarity, even within devout Christian discourse. The *Index exemplorum* summarizes a significant number of stories which address loyalty between brothers.⁵⁵ Fraternal themes include narratives about forgiveness between brothers: the king of England forgives his brother for trying to usurp the throne, while a knight is advised by an abbot that if he forgives his brother's

---

⁵² Ibid., p. 181.
⁵³ Mitchell, *Siblings*, p. 103.
⁵⁴ *Njáls saga*, ed. Einar Ólafur Sveinsson, pp. 297–306.
⁵⁵ *Index exemplorum*, ed. Tubach.

sin against him, God will forgive him.⁵⁶ In the popular, widely circulated story-collection the *Gesta Romanorum*, a brother cheats his own brother of his inheritance – a frequent cause of fraternal strife which will recur in chapter four – and he is sentenced to be executed; the defrauded brother intercedes with the emperor for him and saves his life.⁵⁷ The devil often tries to stir up strife between brothers in exempla; in one tale he is defeated by the meekness with which a younger brother allows his older brother to beat him.⁵⁸ Although passivity and violence are not conducive to warm fraternal relationships, the younger's submission reinforces the ideologically powerful notion of hierarchy within fraternal groups, the eldest brother assuming parental authority over the sibling group once he has inherited. In another tale, brothers prove unable to argue with one another even when they try to do so, while another monastic pair succeed in keeping the fraternal peace when one willingly cedes the cell's only sleeping mat to the other.⁵⁹

Brothers who jointly inherit a kingdom together more often than not become ferocious enemies.⁶⁰ Geoffrey of Monmouth's *Historia regum Britanniae* contains a striking number of episodes in which brothers double-cross each other for the sake of power, but the chronicle and pseudo-history genres also offer examples of brothers whose unity proves the truth of Jenghiz Khan's fable of the arrows. In the *Historia*, Belinus and Brennius agree to divide Britain between them: Belinus the elder taking the lion's share, 'Troiana consuetudo' ('according to Trojan custom'), while Brennius makes do with Northumbria.⁶¹ When the brothers fall out, Belinus seizes the whole kingdom, and Brennius retreats to Gaul from where eventually he launches an invasion. In an echo of the story of Coriolanus, their mother appeals to Brennius to forgive his brother, and, in an astute, if partial, summation of recent events, she notes that Brennius's exile among the Allobrogi has been beneficial: he has won a princess as wife and become heir to a mighty dukedom. Brennius and Belinus are reconciled – exhibiting Mitchell's principle of sudden 'reversal of hatred into love', typical of sibling relations – unite forces and, with the aid of Brennius's in-laws, they ravage Gaul and Italy, finally conquering Rome.⁶² After this joint triumph they wisely choose separate paths once more: Belinus returns to rule Britain peacefully for many years, giving his name to the London district of Billingsgate, while Brennius, still a problematic younger sibling, remains in Italy, 'populum inaudita tyrannide afficiens' ('afflicting its people with unheard-of tyranny').⁶³

---

⁵⁶ Ibid., p. 65: no. 791; no. 793.
⁵⁷ *Gesta Romanorum: or Entertaining Moral Stories*, trans. C. Swann (London, 1824), pp. 146–7.
⁵⁸ *Index exemplorum*, ed. Tubach, p. 66, no. 798.
⁵⁹ Ibid., p. 66, no. 806; no. 807.
⁶⁰ See chapter four.
⁶¹ Geoffrey of Monmouth, *History of the Kings of Britain*, ed. Wright, trans. Reeve, pp. 48–59.
⁶² Mitchell, *Siblings*, p. 41.
⁶³ Geoffrey of Monmouth, *History of the Kings of Britain*, ed. Wright, trans. Reeve, pp. 58–9.

A later legendary British king, Morvidus, sires five sons, whose interactions exemplify the problems of brothers sharing rule. The eldest fulfils the expectations of the primogeniture system and makes an excellent king, but when he dies his brother Arthgallo succeeds him. In Geoffrey's view, Arthgallo is lamentably democratic, promoting the low-born at the expense of the nobility until he is finally deposed and replaced with his brother Elidurus. After five years, Elidurus, out hunting, encounters his unhappy brother who has returned from exile. Unable to muster support to regain the throne, he is wandering in the forest searching for his former friends. His plight leads Elidurus to take pity on him: 'cucurrit . . . et amplexatus est illum, infinita oscula ingeminans' ('He ran to embrace him, showering him with kisses').[64] Elidurus compels the nobility to submit to Arthgallo once again, and returns the crown to him. Having learned the error of his ways, Arthgallo now promotes aristocratic interests and reigns successfully for the next ten years. When he dies, Elidurus, nicknamed the *pius* ('dutiful'), regains the throne, only for his two younger brothers to depose and imprison him. When both of them are dead, the luckless Elidurus wins the throne a third time.[65] Geoffrey's quasi-history illustrates very clearly the politico-historical truths that medieval kingdoms prosper when there is only one adult male heir, and that the survival of more than one son to manhood is highly conducive to civil war.[66] Elidurus's fraternal solidarity is exemplary; his strong sense that age hierarchies ought to be maintained encourages him to take a chance on Arthgallo's reform. Yet his personal style of kingship fails to command the support either of his brothers or the nobility until all other options are exhausted.

Beyond these traditional paradigms of behaviour for brothers in power – furiously rivalrous or exceptionally loyal, in the manner of Elidurus, as chronicled by Bede or Gregory of Tours, and elaborated by Geoffrey in the *Historia* – later historical or quasi-historical writing offers a more nuanced picture of fraternal politics. William Miller notes that neither the *Íslendingasögur*, relating events taking place between c. 870 to 1030, nor the *samtíðasögur* ('contemporary sagas'), dealing with the late twelfth and thirteenth centuries, mention a single instance of fratricide.[67] In both fictionalized and historicized saga-genres, brothers may pass through fraught and ambivalent phases in their relationships, but they always manage to reach some accommodation. *Íslendinga saga*, among other things a biography of the thirteenth-century writer and politician Snorri Sturluson, was largely composed by Sturla Þórðarson, Snorri's nephew. The work illustrates how, even though Snorri was fostered from the age of five in the south of Iceland, away from his significantly older brothers, Sighvatr, eight years his senior, and Þórðr, thirteen years older, their

---

[64] Ibid., pp. 62–3.
[65] Ibid., pp. 62–5.
[66] See chapter one, p. 32–3.
[67] W. I. Miller, *Bloodtaking and Peacemaking: Feud, Law and Society in Saga Iceland* (Chicago, 1997), p. 160.

fraternal tie did not weaken. Sighvatr and Þórðr are depicted as very close to one another, but when they fall out over the inheritance from their mother, Snorri astutely argues that 'bræðr aldri skulu á skilja um fé' ('brothers should never quarrel over money').[68] He strategically distracts Þórðr by noting that all three brothers have inherited a chieftaincy from their father which Sighvatr has retained in his control. Sighvatr's transfer of the chieftaincy to his son and their nephew, Sturla Sighvatsson, creates a new bone of contention between the brothers: Snorri persuades Þórðr to join forces with him against their middle brother. Unlike his two younger brothers, Þórðr finally dies in his bed aged 72, but until that day, although the three brothers continue to ally themselves in ever-changing configurations of two against one, they never deploy violence directly against one another.

The real conflicts between the brothers – in particular between the interests of Sighvatr and Snorri – are fought out in the next generation. Sighvatr's son Sturla is reported as having blinded and castrated his cousin, Snorri's son Órækja. The truth of this charge is in doubt, for in his later appearances in the saga Órækja appears to be unscathed.[69] Although the Sturlusons are assiduous in avoiding open battle, the next generation contains too many ambitious sons and sons-in-law for each to have his own sphere of influence and conflict becomes inevitable.[70] Sighvatr's lineage is almost eliminated when he and all except one of his sons die at the battle of Ǫrlygsstaðir in 1238. After the battle, in a trope familiar from heroic literature, one of Sighvatr's sons, Kolbeinn, asks to be executed before his brother, Þórðr.[71] Kolbeinn cannot bear to witness his brother's death, conscious as he is that the revenge imperative extends not only to this brother, but to the rest of the kinship, all but exterminated by Sighvatr's enemies. His wish is granted to him.[72] In the war-torn thirteenth-century Icelandic polity, fraternal norms of solidarity are maintained when all other social bonds come under strain. While Geoffrey's pseudo-history is patterned by alternating fraternal rivalry and solidarity, reflecting his pragmatic understanding of dynastic politics, Sturla's account of events which occurred within living memory testifies to the vital importance of the fraternal bond.

Twins

Twins might be imagined as representing a particular challenge to the task of differentiation so crucial to successful fraternal identity formation. Yet

[68] *Sturlunga saga*, ed. Jón Jóhannesson, Magnús Finnbogason and Kristján Eldjarn, 3 vols (Reykjavík, 1946), I: 303.
[69] Ibid., I: 395.
[70] See Torfi Tulinius, *Skáldið í skriftinni*, pp. 181–204 for discussion of the Sturlung fraternal relations and the possibility that *Egils saga* closely reflects these.
[71] *Sturlunga saga*, ed. Jón Jóhannesson *et al.*, I: 437.
[72] For vengeance for Sighvatr and his sons, see the whetting of Steinvǫr in the next chapter, pp. 93–4.

they are surprisingly rare in medieval European romance. Nor, when they do occur, do medieval twins particularly *resemble* one another; absolute physical interchangeability is characteristic of sworn-brothers, not twins.[73] *À propos* of the modern cinematic convention of good twin / bad twin, Juliet Mitchell argues that humans are fundamentally unsettled by the concept of twinship: in striving to 'overcome the dilemma of being too nearly the same as another [so] we need to make crude differences', she suggests.[74] Such radical oppositions are absent in medieval twin narratives, for, even in the face of infant hardship, the well-born twin will always finally manifest the innate qualities deriving from his noble blood.

Twinship (or even more rarely, and always allied to supernatural elements, triplethood) invites authors to consider the effects of nature versus nurture on sibling cohorts.[75] The late romance *Valentine and Orson* (first translated into English in the early sixteenth century, but based on a lost fourteenth-century French original) relates the highly divergent fate of twin brothers, separated when their mother gives birth to them in the forest. It explores the effects of different childhood experiences on boys who share an identical genetic inheritance. Valentine is nobly brought up and becomes an outstanding knight while his brother Orson (*ours*-son or Bear's son) is reared by bears and becomes a Wild Man. The brothers' sharply differing early lives produce highly polarized physical and intellectual differences: Orson is both stronger and hairier than his brother and he lacks human language. Despite an upbringing which, like that of Perceval, excludes knowledge of chivalry, Orson is instinctively attracted to his brother's knightly accoutrements. Valentine succeeds in overcoming him in battle and brings him out of the forest into the civilized world. Here Orson learns gradually to jettison his animal traits and become skilled in both the practice and discourse of chivalry.[76] The two young men do not realize that they are brothers until much later in the romance when their parentage is revealed. Their reaction to the discovery is even more emotional than that of Lancelot, discussed above: 'Than Valentyne that was rauysshed for Ioye came to Orson and in wepynge moche tenderly kyssed his mouthe And Orson on the other syde enbrased hym and c[o]lled hym in castyinge oute grete syghes anguysshous.'[77] Although it is not clear which twin was born first, Orson serves and obeys Valentine as if he were the elder brother, for Valentine is his senior in chivalric terms.

The topos of twinship thus opens up, but does not closely interrogate, the important question: how fair is primogeniture? In the Anglo-Norman romance

---

[73] See chapter eight.
[74] Mitchell, *Siblings*, p. 213.
[75] See the discussion of the *Roman de Silence*, in chapter five and of *Lai le Freine* in chapter three.
[76] *Valentine and Orson*, trans. H. Watson, ed. A. Dickson, EETS os 204 (Oxford, 1937); see also D. Yamamoto, *The Boundaries of the Human in Medieval English Literature* (Oxford, 2000), pp. 187–96.
[77] *Valentine and Orson*, p. 141.

Boeve de Hamtoun and its Middle English and Old Norse translations, Bevis's wife Josiane sends her male companions away when she is about to give birth to twin boys in the forest.[78] By the time Bevis returns, the lady has been abducted, leaving her babies behind. Bevis thus has no idea which of the boys is the elder, but nevertheless he makes a determination in the matter, asking a forester whom he meets shortly afterwards to foster one child, to baptize him Guy after Bevis's father, and (in the Middle English version only) to make sure he is given chivalric training.[79] The second child is given to a fisherman with the instruction to name him Miles, but without the chivalric stipulation.[80] Both children are eventually restored to their parents and grow up to become worthy knights. As a result of Bevis's arbitrary decision, Guy is chosen (in both the Anglo-Norman and Old Norse versions) to inherit two-thirds of his maternal grandfather's kingdom and is given the title of king, while Miles, merely a duke, inherits the remaining third. Significantly, the Middle English Auchinleck manuscript version trades this careful inheritance distinction for a winner-takes-all outcome: Guy is awarded the whole kingdom while Miles gets nothing.[81] In all versions, Miles eventually marries the daughter of the king of England on the understanding that he will inherit from his father-in-law.[82] The English romance employs the inheritance solution which would prove so successful for the brothers in the later *Roman de Mélusine*: like other noble younger sons under strict primogeniture, the junior twin of romance acquires a new estate or kingdom through his heroic feats and an advantageous marriage.

The arbitrary treatment of the twins in *Bevis* suggests that the underlying reason for the paucity of twin stories in medieval romance is precisely the unassailable cultural importance of the first-born. Twin narratives ought perhaps to problematize the very different social outcomes for males born only minutes apart, yet in romance they do not. The issue is tactfully avoided in *Bevis*, and in *Valentine and Orson*; in both texts reasonably equitable outcomes are eventually assured for the apparently younger twin. Josiane's asking the men to withdraw when she gives birth is usual medieval practice, but her isolation highlights the difficulty of determining which twin is the elder.[83] The labouring mother cannot

---

[78] For the Anglo-Norman and Old Norse texts, see *Bevers saga*, ed. C. Sanders (Reykjavík, 2001); for the Middle English romance, see *Bevis of Hamptoun*, in *Four Romances of England* ed. R. B. Herzman, G. Drake and E. Salisbury (Kalamazoo, 1999). For the birth of the twins see *Bevers saga*, ed. Sanders, pp. 240–7; *Bevis of Hamptoun*, ed. Herzman *et al*. lines 3619–46.

[79] *Bevers saga*, ed. Sanders, p. 255; *Bevis of Hamptoun*, ed. Herzman *et al.*, lines 3710–44

[80] Surprisingly, Miles is named after his mother's former husband, whom she murdered on her wedding night, but perhaps the etymology of the name (Latin: *miles* 'soldier') guarantees future martial prowess.

[81] *Bevers saga*, ed. Sanders, pp. 302–3; *Bevis of Hamptoun*, ed. Herzman *et al.*, lines 4011–13.

[82] *Bevers saga*, ed. Sanders, pp. 356–9; *Bevis of Hamptoun*, ed. Herzman *et al.*, lines 4555–75.

[83] As the taboo against Présine's husband witnessing her in childbirth confirms (see chapter three, p. 82)

necessarily testify to relative seniority; only a midwife, if one were present, could confirm which twin is born first. At the end of *Parzival* Wolfram, whose reservations about primogeniture were noted earlier, reassures his audience that the twin sons of Condwiramurs and Parzival will each be provided with separate inheritances, obviating the need for the fraternal negotiations undertaken in their grandfather's generation. Kardeiz will rule over his parents' secular kingdoms (including Anjou), while Loherangrin will succeed to his father's Grail kingdom.[84] Neither of Parzival's sons will be obliged to pursue the knight-errant career of Gahmuret, a path which gained him fame, but also arguably a premature death in military service in the Middle East.[85]

The Icelandic *fornaldarsaga* ('legendary saga') *Hrólfs saga kraka* recounts the history of the ancestors of King Hrólfr of Denmark as a prologue to Hrólfr's own history; the saga, as we shall see, is strikingly interested in lateral relationships. Hrólfr's great champion, Bǫðvarr Bjarki, is the youngest of three triplet brothers born to Bera, a peasant's daughter, and the royally born Bjǫrn of Norway: their names signify 'bear' and 'she-bear'.[86] Bewitched by a wicked stepmother, the boys' father regularly takes bear-form. After Bjǫrn dies, hunted down by his own father's warriors, pregnant Bera is forced to eat some of his bear-flesh by the step-mother. As a result of this breach of taboo, the three sons are born part-animal: differentiation by birth order is reinforced by the apportioning of distinguishing characteristics.[87] The eldest, Elg-Fróði, is human from the waist up and an elk from the waist down. Þórir hundsfótr has dog-paws instead of feet, while Bǫðvarr looks human, but has a bear-nature. The three brothers go their separate ways on adulthood. Elg-Fróði becomes a highway robber; when Þórir hundsfótr leaves home, Fróði offers him a halfshare in the booty from his robberies. Another fate lies in store for Þórir: following Fróði's advice, he is chosen as king of Gautland. After avenging his father, Bǫðvarr visits Fróði and Þórir and then takes service with King Hrólfr of Denmark. Here he has a splendid career as the best of the king's champions, until Hrólfr's half-sister Skuld and her husband attack him in strength.[88] During the battle Bǫðvarr is nowhere to be seen, but a mighty bear is observed fighting by Hrólfr's side: Bǫðvarr in the animal form inherited from his father. By employing magic, Skuld's army overcomes the king and his champions, but their victory is short-lived. Elg-Fróði and Þórir come to avenge their brother and put Skuld to death.

In this story the brothers are born within minutes of each other, and, in a pattern typical of folk-tale, the youngest achieves the most fame, compensating for his

---

[84] *Parzival* XVI.303, 823; *Parzival*, trans. Edwards, pp. 257, 263.
[85] See above, p. 52.
[86] *Hrólfs saga kraka* in *FSN*, I: 44–69; death of Bǫðvarr, I: 105; *The Saga of Hrolf Kraki*, trans. J. Byock (London, 1998), pp. 37–55; death, p. 78.
[87] *Fornaldarsögur* (legendary sagas) deal with heroic or romance material, set in Scandinavia before the settlement of Iceland. Composed from the early thirteenth century onwards, some of them incorporate European romance and *Märchen* motifs as well as heroic legend.
[88] See further chapter five.

lack of advantage under normal primogeniture rules.[89] Each brother chooses a different path in life, and Fróði, whose name means 'wise', assumes a prophetic role in directing his brothers to better fortune than he achieves, unable, because of his elk-deformity, to be accepted by normal human society. Triplethood, as distinct from twinship, is clearly envisaged as supernatural in causation and outcome. Despite the family's relative poverty, each son inherits differentially; that Bǫðvarr the youngest does best out of the division and gains his father's sword underlines a folkloric inversion of normal inheritance expectations. Despite their physical differences, the brothers successfully work through the usual areas for fraternal conflict. Although he grumbles when he gets a smaller share of his father's treasure and a less impressive weapon than the sword which Bǫðvarr inherits, Fróði generously offers to share his life of outlawry with his brothers, and declares how much he loves Bǫðvarr when he swears to avenge him. Bǫðvarr demonstrates his own loyalty to Þórir by refusing the opportunity to have sex with his brother's wife. These two brothers are apparently indistinguishable (apart from their feet), but Bǫðvarr immediately reveals his identity to the lady when he secretly substitutes for her husband. He and his sister-in-law thereafter spend their nights in conversation. The youngest and most normal-looking brother, as often the case his mother's favourite, is the one entrusted with the history of his father's death and thus he seizes the chance to take single-handed vengeance on his step-grandmother. Paternal vengeance inaugurates his heroic career; Bǫðvarr becomes the right-hand man of one of the greatest kings of the north, the subject of a well-known heroic lay (the *Bjarkamál*) and he is swiftly avenged by his own brothers when he falls in defence of his sovereign. The fraternal love and solidarity of the Bear's Sons offers a thematic counterpoint to the hostility of Skuld and Hrólfr's brother-in-law. The saga explores over a number of generations, as we shall see in later chapters, the negotiation of shared rule between brothers and the dissatisfaction and enmity of those excluded from the division of power: sisters, their husbands, and sister-sons.[90]

Avenging the Brother

Even when brothers go their separate ways in medieval narrative, the obligation to avenge the brother's death is never dissipated by that separation. Thus when he hears of Grettir's and Illugi's deaths, their half-brother Þorsteinn drómundr leaves Norway to pursue their slayer Þorbjǫrn hook as far as Constantinople. When Hook (as he is called in the saga's coda) boasts of his killing of Grettir, displaying the hero's short-sword Grettisnaut which he had used to behead him, Þorsteinn persuades him to hand over the sword to be admired, and immediately kills him with it.[91] Þorsteinn drómundr had earlier prophesied

---

[89] Jackson, 'Ambivalence and the Last-Born'.
[90] See chs. 4 and 5, pp. 115 and 148.
[91] *Grettis saga*, ed. Guðni Jónsson, pp. 271–4.

to Grettir that his arm, though puny in comparison with Grettir's brawny limbs, would avenge his death; for him the distinction between brother and half-brother has no significance.[92] The saga's final lines relate that the vengeance taken for Grettir was noteworthy in Icelandic tradition because the avenger went to such lengths to track down Hook.[93] Þorsteinn's subsequent picaresque adventures in Constantinople draw heavily on the Tristan legend; his quixotic prophecy to his half-brother and its fulfilment evidently attracted distinctive romance elements into the saga structure. His long-distance vengeance should probably be regarded as a nostalgic fourteenth-century reflection on a much earlier social norm.

In *Njáls saga*, Njáll's illegitimate son Hǫskuldr is killed by a certain Lýtingr in revenge for the death of Þráinn Sigfússon, whose falling-out with the Njálssons was discussed above. Hǫskuldr's mother Hróðný reacts to the news of her son's death with remarkable self-control and calculation, bringing his body to Njáll's farm and displaying it to Njáll and his sons. Everyone present understands the implications of the scene she so carefully stages, but Hróðný drives the point home:

'Þér fel ek á hendi, Skarpheðinn, at hefna bróður þíns, ok þó at hann sé eigi skilgetinn, þá ætla ek þó, at þér muni vel fara ok þú munir þó mest eptir ganga.'

('I place it in your hands, Skarpheðinn, to avenge your brother, and even though he is not legitimate, I expect that you will behave well, and you will still pursue this most.')[94]

Njáll's legal wife Bergþóra concurs with Hróðný that Skarpheðinn is obliged to avenge his half-brother; neither Njáll nor Skarpheðinn object to Hróðný's choice of the eldest half-brother as chief avenger, even though she has, as Miller notes, a brother of her own who could equally take revenge on her behalf.[95] Skarpheðinn, Helgi and Grímr succeed in killing Lýtingr's brothers, but a peace-deal is concluded before the culprit himself can be slain.[96] What signifies about Hǫskuldr Njálsson is not his illegitimacy, nor, particularly, the existence of strong affective bonds between him and his brothers, but rather his blood-membership of the fraternal group. The collective honour of the Njálssons is severely damaged by the blow struck against an unsuspecting and relatively easy target (Hǫskuldr was not involved in the feud with Þráinn). Their fraternal group identity remains threatened until they achieve revenge

---

[92] Ibid., pp. 137–8.
[93] Ibid., p. 290: 'at hans var hefnt út í Miklagarði, sem einskis annars íslenzks manns' ('that he was avenged out in Constantinople, unlike any other Icelandic man').
[94] *Njáls saga*, ed. Einar Ólafur Sveinsson, p. 252.
[95] W. I. Miller, 'Choosing the Avenger: Some Aspects of the Bloodfeud in Medieval Iceland and England', *Law and History Review* 1.2 (1983), 159–204 (p. 191).
[96] That Hǫskuldr Þráinsson Hvítanessgóði successfully intercedes with Njáll on Lýtingr's behalf contributes both to Hǫskuldr's eventual murder by them and to the eventual burning of father and sons. See further Miller, 'Choosing the Avenger'.

on the two unmourned 'óeirðarmenn' ('violent men'), the brothers who were willing parties to the killing, even if the prime instigator, Lýtingr himself, escapes punishment.

How can a man survive the death of his brother? Only by taking vengeance for him: if vengeance is impossible, the trauma is intensified. Malory regards the final disintegration of the Round Table as caused, at least in part, by the conflict between the 'felyscype' of Arthur's court and the older values of blood-loyalty exemplified in the Orkney lineage.[97] When Gareth and Gaheris are accidentally killed by Lancelot while rescuing Guenevere from the fire to which she has been condemned for adultery, Gawain's emotional reaction to his brothers' death is the most dramatic of any male character in the whole of Malory's narrative:

> he felle downe and sowned, and longe he lay there as he had ben dede. And whan he arose oute of hys swoughe he cryed oute sorowfully and seyde 'Alas!' And forthwith he ran unto the kynge, criynge and wepyng.[98]

To distract Gawain from his grief, Arthur suggests that they plan 'a remedy for to revenge theire dethys', one of the few instances in the final part of the narrative where Arthur takes an active role in the political situation. He succeeds in transforming Gawain's sorrow for his brothers into an unassuageable anger, a move that binds his remaining nephew closely to him for Gawain cannot achieve his vengeance without Arthur's resources. Yet Arthur's tactic backfires: however much Lancelot explains, apologizes or offers to do penance, Gawain will not forgive him for Gareth's death, while Arthur has ill-advisedly ceded the possibility of negotiating between the two factions. Gawain recognizes and accepts that his brother 'loved hym [Lancelot] bettir than me and all hys brethirn and the kynge bothe'.[99] What Gawain cannot bear and cannot forgive is the terrible mischance that caused Lancelot unwittingly to kill Gareth: that the preferred friend, the better-than-brother, as Gawain sees it, should have betrayed the man who loved him so.[100]

In the *Mort Artu* (and earlier in the Vulgate cycle), Guerrhet, Gaheriet and Lancelot are on warm enough terms, but Lancelot neither knighted nor mentored Gauvain's brother(s), and the text handles their deaths very differently. Agravain, Guerrhet and Gaheriet meet their deaths during Guenièvre's rescue. The

---

[97] As Elizabeth Archibald has noted, Malory does not employ the concept of fictive fraternity for the Round Table knights, reserving the term 'brother' for full or half-brothers. See E. Archibald, 'Malory's Ideal of Fellowship', *Review of English Studies* 43 (1992), 311–28, p. 315, n. 15.

[98] Malory, *Le Morte Darthur*, ed. Field, I: 888.

[99] Ibid., I: 887.

[100] The English *Stanzaic Morte*, a primary source for Malory, does not show Lancelot killing either Gaheriet or Gaheries (as they are called in this text). Indeed he strongly denies responsibility for their deaths to Gawain, whose vengefulness seems the more reprehensible. *Stanzaic Morte Arthur*, cited from *King Arthur's Death: The Middle English Stanzaic Morte Arthur and Alliterative Morte Arthure*, ed. L. D. Benson, rev. E. E. Foster (Kalamazoo, 1994).

unmourned Agravain is deliberately targeted by Lancelot since his accusations made the adultery public. Guerrhet (a comparatively minor character) is killed by Bors, while Hector knocks off Gaheriet's helmet so that Lancelot fails to recognize him and he is killed in the general mêlée.[101] Gauvain's emotional reaction to their deaths is intensified by Arthur's decision deliberately to display the bodies to him. Lancelot does not apologize to Gauvain in the *Mort*; he neither explains the mischance of Gaheriet's death nor refutes the accusation that Gauvain's brothers were killed through treachery, and Gauvain's vengefulness consequently seems more justified. Only as he is dying does Gauvain make his peace with Lancelot; he requests that the inscription on the tomb he will share with Gaheriet be amended to explain that the deaths were caused 'par l'outrage de monseigneur Gauvain' ('by the uncontrolled behaviour of lord Gauvain'), rather than by Lancelot as the epitaph had previously declared.[102] Gauvain thus seizes the last word in the narrative of his own and his brothers' death, finally recognizing his culpability in the Round Table's destruction.

In the *Morte Darthur*, by contrast, Gawain's anguish is poignantly complicated by his realization that Gareth loved Lancelot more than he loved his own brothers. Malory's innovations in Gareth's history – if they are his – develop his interest in the tensions between brotherhood through blood and the fictive fraternity of knightly companionship. Throughout the *Morte Darthur*, but especially in its final movement, the obligations entailed by blood ties are depicted as problematic while freely chosen bonds of love and service, binding knights such as Urré and Lavayne to Lancelot, outlast even the Round Table's destruction.[103] Malory's wholesale incorporation of material from the Post-Vulgate *Suite de Merlin*, a text which revolves around feuds between groups of brothers, foregrounds the sibling-gang effect as characteristic of the Orkney cohort. As with the Njálssons, fraternal solidarity primarily benefits the senior brother whose leadership is experienced as anti-social both by subordinate brothers and by the larger social community.[104]

Christian moralists identified blood-vengeance for kin-group members as an extremely powerful secular ideal which would take many centuries to eradicate. Exemplary literature engages critically with the obligation for fraternal vengeance; while one exemplum notes as a general principle that when a brother is killed the family will rise in revenge, other exempla recommend forgiving even a brother's murderer as the most difficult test of Christian forgiveness.[105] So strongly does the renunciation of vengeance pull against deeply rooted social norms that it attracts exceptional moral reward. In *Sólarljóð*, an Icelandic Christian poem probably dating from the thirteenth century, the poet invokes traditional wisdom, warning that enemies should never be trusted, however

---

[101] *La Mort le Roi Artu: roman du XIII*ᵉ *siècle*, ed. J. Frappier (Geneva, 1964), pp. 127–33.
[102] Ibid., p. 224.
[103] See further, Larrington, 'Sibling Relations', pp. 71–2.
[104] Mitchell, *Siblings*, p. 103.
[105] *Index exemplorum*, ed. Tubach, p. 65, no. 790; p. 268, no. 3438.

plausible they appear. Yet this observation is complicated by an exemplum in which a certain Sǫrli agrees to settle for his brother's death with Vígólfr, the chief slayer. The murderers drink with Sǫrli in reconciliation, but the next day they kill and dismember him, throwing his body down a well. Sǫrli's soul, the poet declares, will go straight to heaven, while the murderers will spend a long time in hellish torment.[106] Inherited common sense about not trusting one's enemies merges with the most challenging Christian demand for eschewing vengeance in favour of forgiveness, Even though Sǫrli acts foolishly in social terms by riding through a lonely valley with known killers, in salvational terms his forgiveness of his murderers merits immediate heavenly reward. The Icelandic law-code and Christian moral teaching offered viable ideological alternatives to feud and vengeance, but these old lineage-based values proved hard to shift both within the Icelandic polity and in the imaginative world of Icelandic writers.

Until it was finally displaced by civil law, the obligation of blood-vengeance was central to medieval societies. Its long survival may be explained by the premise that honour inheres in kindred-collectives; to injure or kill one member of a lineage is to damage the standing of all of its members. The revenge imperative also has a clear psychological function. A particular anguish is imagined for those who cannot achieve vengeance for brothers, a despair which, as in Illugi's case, makes one's own death seem preferable. The emotional consequences of the failure to avenge a brother fuse with culturally suppressed mourning for childhood sibling bereavement. 'With no other sibling available to continue the identity process, the survivor is truly bereft, and has for a partner in the dialectical dance for self-definition only the dead sibling's ghost', Bank and Kahn note.[107] As observed in chapter one, contemporary medieval documents scarcely refer to the grief of sibling childhood bereavement, though almost every adult must have experienced it. This grief, and the guilt which it engenders, 'guilt... for this unholy wish that everyone has', finds its reflection in the powerful emotions unleashed in medieval narratives when an adult brother dies.[108] The unconscious murderous impulses produced in childhood by the brother's birth resurface with the brother's loss; they provoke violent and often apparently irrational reactions, finding expression in revenge narratives which seek somehow to erase the sibling's death.[109] Private, individual grief is recuperated through narratives which – although they cannot undo sibling

---

[106] *Sólarljóð*, ed. C. Larrington and P. Robinson, in *Poetry on Christian Subjects*, 2 vols, Skaldic Poetry of the Scandinavian Middle Ages 7, gen. ed. M. Clunies Ross (Turnhout, 2007), I: vv.19–24. See also C. Larrington, 'New Thoughts on Old Wisdom: Norse Gnomic Poetry, the Narrative Turn and Situational Ethics' (forthcoming).

[107] Bank and Kahn, *The Sibling Bond*, p. 272.

[108] Mitchell, *Mad Men and Medusas*, p. 245.

[109] Mitchell, *Siblings*, pp. 169–71 takes issue with the earlier psychoanalytic view that sibling loss in adulthood does not result in 'disordered mourning' behaviour. The murder of a sister is differently understood; it is a rarer occurrence in medieval writing, and the reactions which it elicits are not scripted as precisely; see pp. 97–101 below.

loss – at least bring a kind of closure through retributive violence and the restoration of family honour.

Accidental Fratricide

For medieval authors, the emotion produced by the adult brother's death outweighs all other kinds of grief.[110] Narratives which deal directly with the death of the beloved or the unrecognized brother at his own brother's hands allow the exploration of the murderous fantasies generated by sibling rivalry as crystallized in the brother's killing. Stories in which brothers accidentally come into conflict with their own lost brothers constitute a popular medieval story-arc. The brother is acknowledged only as he dies at his brother's hand; love, guilt and shame combine in a dense cluster of sibling emotion. The accidental fratricide topos where the slayer is compelled by honour and custom offers a sibling parallel to the universal Sohrab-and-Rustum tale, in which father and son fight incognito and the father kills his son. These narratives are multivalent in their exploration of unacknowledged sibling rivalry, loss and survivor-guilt. They also permit imaginative rehearsal and resolution of the fear of fratricide. The vicissitudes of chance in warrior societies, where separated brothers give individual allegiance to different lords or where deliberate rage-filled killing is integral to battle-success, throw up opportunities for incognito fratricide. Courting one's own death, imagining that death as a consequence of fraternal conflict is, as Mitchell suggests, an act of 'disturbed mourning'; the accidental fratricide narratives thus engage with the trauma of sibling loss at a cultural level.[111]

The fates of two such knightly brothers are related early in Malory's *Morte Darthur*. Balin and Balan are devoted to one another, achieve mighty feats when fighting shoulder to shoulder, and yet they end by killing one another in single combat. Balin's adventures begin with a sword brought to court by a damsel which only the best of knights can draw from its scabbard. Balin succeeds where others fail, but when he refuses to return the sword, the damsel prophesies that 'ye shall sle with that swerde the beste frende that ye have and the man that ye moste love in the worlde, and that swerde shall be youre destruccion'.[112] Merlin reveals that the damsel's brother had killed her lover in knightly combat, and that the sword was created for her to take revenge on him, a blind but highly suggestive motif. Balin is reunited with his brother Balan:

---

[110] See chapter three for discussion of sisterly recuperation of the dead brother in the fantasies explored in fairy- and folk-tales. Cf. Bank and Kahn, *The Sibling Bond*, pp. 271–95.

[111] Mitchell, *Siblings*, p. 169.

[112] Malory, *Le Morte Darthur*, ed. Field, I: 50. See also J. Mann, '"Taking the Adventure": Malory and the *Suite du Merlin*', in *Aspects of Malory*, ed. T. Takamiya and D. Brewer, Arthurian Studies 1 (Cambridge, 1981), pp. 71–91 and Larrington, 'Sibling Relations', pp. 60–3.

'Whan they were mette they put of hyr helmys and kyssed togydirs and wepte for joy and pité' – and together they capture Arthur's enemy King Royns of North Wales.[113] This victory restores Balin to Arthur's favour; the presence of his sibling-peer, mirroring and completing him, allows Balin at last to function successfully as a unitary self.[114] When he separates once more from his brother, Balin's fortune declines catastrophically. When he comes to a castle where custom demands that a newcomer must fight against the resident champion, he is persuaded at the last minute to exchange his shield for one which does not identify him. Thus he engages unwittingly with his brother, retained at the castle after defeating the previous champion, and they slay one another. The brothers are buried together, for 'We came bothe oute of one wombe . . . and so shalle we lye bothe in one pytte'.[115] The fate of the two brothers, both in their French and English versions, originates in the clash between the damsel's brother and her lover.[116] Even though that particular plot-line is developed no further, the contrasting themes of ill-fated heterosexual desire and exemplary sibling loyalty are strikingly explored within the tale. Frustrated desire and sibling hatred, generated in the sword-bearing damsel through her brother's killing of her lover, are projected on to Balin and Balan, significantly, the only fratricides in the *Morte Darthur*. Knightly convention, both the starkly inhumane custom of compelling a knight to remain in one place and to kill his challengers until he is killed in his turn, and the tradition of not revealing one's name until the joust's end, underlie the tragedy of the two brothers; the damsel's curse interacts with the Arthurian world's arbitrary conventions to bring about the tragic outcome.

That fear of fratricide haunts Malory's text: a similar incognito battle between Gawain and Gareth is only averted by the interference of Lyonet, their sister-in-law. Bors and Lionel (as discussed further in chapter four) narrowly escape killing one another during the Grail Quest. The potentially tragic consequences of failing to recognize the brother shape audience expectations in other, earlier romances. In *Parzival*, Wolfram makes knowing play with the narrative possibility of accidental fratricide when he concludes his hero's secular career with a fight against his unrecognized Moorish half-brother. Particoloured Feirefiz, son of Gahmuret and the queen of Morocco, was born before Gahmuret married Herzeloyde and fathered Parzival. Wolfram signals Feirefiz's existence early in his narrative; the elder brother, as is typical for this plot-motif, knows of his younger half-sibling's existence, while the younger remains in ignorance about his elder sib. Parzival's lineage, his complicated web of maternal and paternal relations, is disclosed to him serially by various uncles and by his cousin Cundrie. Thus, although he learns that he has a half-brother when Cundrie contrasts the two siblings after Parzival's failure at the Grail Castle, he does not realize who Feirefiz is until they have fought

---

[113] Malory, *Le Morte Darthur*, ed. Field, I: 55.
[114] Mitchell, *Mad Men and Medusas*, p. 106.
[115] Malory, *Le Morte Darthur*, ed. Field, I: 73.
[116] Larrington, 'Sibling Relations', pp. 61–2.

one another to a standstill. As with the battle between Bors and Lionel, God intervenes to prevent catastrophe. Parzival's sword breaks in his hand and Feirefiz courteously forbears to continue the battle.[117] Although the audience must be apprehensive that the topos of unwitting fratricide is in play, by the time the fight begins the narrative has already begun to move towards its happy resolution and the suspense is not prolonged. Notwithstanding Feirefiz's non-Christian status, the warmth between the two brothers is just as powerful as the love between Lancelot and Hector de Maris. In contrast to the sons of Ban, Parzival and Feirefiz are both legitimately born, but there is no rivalry. Parzival is quick to acknowledge his elder brother's seniority, refusing to address him with the familiar pronoun *du*, despite Feirefiz's friendly request that he should do so. When Cundrie tells Parzival that he can choose a single companion to accompany him on his return to the Grail Castle to fulfil his destiny by asking the Grail Question, he unhesitatingly chooses his new sibling.[118] Only once Parzival is himself a king – and the Grail king at that – does he feel that he and the newly baptized Feirefiz share a social rank which permits the use of familiar forms: 'ich mac nu wol duzen dich / unser rîchtuom nâch gelîchet sich' ('I can now address you familiarly, since our possessions are just about equal').[119]

Two Scandinavian versions of the accidental fratricide topos demonstrate changing attitudes to brother-killing. The story is a development from the older tradition of Hildebrand and Hadubrand, part of which is preserved in the Old High German *Hildebrandslied*. Hildebrand and his son are ranged on opposing sides in battle; although Hildebrand identifies himself to Hadubrand, the latter refuses to believe that his father has returned from service with Theodoric of the Goths and battle is joined. The lay is incomplete, but Irish, Persian and Russian analogues, in addition to references elsewhere in Germanic tradition, indicate that the father kills his son.[120] The two fratricidal versions of Hildebrand's tragedy are preserved in Saxo's *Gesta Danorum* and in the later Icelandic *Ásmundar saga kappabana*.[121] Two half-brothers grow up separately: the older is aware of the younger's existence, while the younger does not know he has a half-brother. Finally, through a combination of female goading and the operation of fate, the brothers are forced to fight in single combat and the older dies, though not before he utters a death-song. This reveals the dying man's fraternal relationship with the victor, and, in the case of Saxo's Hildiger,

---

[117] *Parzival* XV.342, 14; *Parzival*, trans. Edwards, p. 236.
[118] Refusing to use 'du': *Parzival* XV.349, lines 21–2; *Parzival*, trans. Edwards, pp. 238–9; Feirefiz as sole companion, *Parzival* XV.383–4; *Parzival*, trans. Edwards, p. 250. Noltze, *Gahmurets Orientfahrt*, p. 49, comments on pronoun usage and its variations in *Parzival*.
[119] *Parzival* XVI.314, lines 1920; *Parzival*, trans. Edwards, p. 260.
[120] See A. T. Hatto, 'On the Excellence of the "Hildebrandslied": A Comparative Study in Dynamics', *Modern Language Review* 68 (1973), 820–38. Saxo does not relate the son-killing, although he connects Hildiger with the Germanic Hildebrand-tradition. In *Ásmundar saga kappabana*, Hildibrandr kills his son in a berserk rage on his way to fight against his half-brother.
[121] Saxo, *GD*, 7.9.5; Saxo, *HD*, p. 221. *Ásmundar saga kappabana*, in *FSN*, I: 383–408.

expands on the ethical implications of the elder brother's knowledge.

Rather than dwelling on the fratricidal theme, the Icelandic saga foregrounds the operation of a curse laid on the two brothers' swords by the smiths who forged them. More than one of the saga's minor characters observes that the two antagonists are similar in appearance and bear similar swords, sustaining audience anticipation of mutual fratricide, but, as in Saxo, the younger half-brother survives.[122] Saxo's account takes the ethical dimension of Hildiger's dilemma very seriously; though he has never previously met his half-brother Haldanus, and though he is himself a violent and tyrannical man, he shrinks from knowing fratricide. Hildibrandr in *Ásmundar saga* has no such introspective moments; his awareness of the curse instils a fatalism in him. While Hildiger fears lest he kill his brother, Hildibrandr knows that his brother Ásmundr will kill him. Although *Ásmundar saga kappabani* was written down a good century or so after Saxo composed his *Historia*, Saxo drew on earlier Icelandic sources for his version, in particular some earlier version of the *Death-Song*. Despite the *Death-Song*'s implication that both brothers die at one another's hand, like Balin and Balan, generic pressures cause both Saxo and the saga-author to bypass the topos's traditional outcome. In Saxo's history, Haldanus must survive in order to father the famous Danish king Harald Battle-Tooth once the pollution of kin-killing has been ritually lifted from him. The saga's bridal-quest framework demands that Ásmundr should win his princess, despite the considerable moral qualms he feels when he learns the price he has paid for her vengeance on Hildibrandr, her father's slayer.[123]

These two related versions of unwitting brother-killing test the general rule that fratricide is the worst crime imaginable. When brother kills full brother in romance, as in 'The Tale of Balin and Balan', the killer cannot survive the experience; if he does not die from the wounds inflicted by his brother, he takes his own life.[124] Though still appalled by the fratricidal act, half-brothers in pseudo-history and romance may survive their slaying of a half-sibling as long as they act in ignorance, however wilful. This absolves them of the fratricidal intention, and allows them to survive, and even to prosper, once their blood-guilt has been dealt with. Saxo externalizes Haldanus's guilt; the consequence of his crime against his kindred is a failure to increase that kindred through siring a son until the pollution is ritually expiated. Ásmundr's unease at killing within the kindred is internalized; he tries to suppress the knowledge of his fratricide, and angrily projects his guilt onto princess Æsa. She maintains that destiny, in the form of the accursed sword, brought about the fratricide, dispelling Ásmundr's anxiety and guilt and enabling a happy ending.

[122] The prose text implies that both brothers will die; Hildibrandr's poem regrets that one brother was born to kill the other.
[123] M. Ciklamini, 'The Combat between Two Half-Brothers: A Literary Study of the Motif in *Ásmundar saga kappabana* and *Saxonis Gesta Danorum*', *Neophilologus* 50.2 (1966), 269–79; concluded, 50.3 (1966), 370–9.
[124] In ballad, as we shall see in chapter four, the fratricide must go into exile, severing his ties to his lineage.

The treatment of fratricide is highly genre-specific. Foundational legends, chronicle and pseudo-history, as discussed in chapter four, permit, even reward, fratricide in the pursuit of territorial gain or political power. In legends, such as that of Romulus and Remus, kin-killing is subsumed into sacrifice.[125] The legendary history of Britain, and Frankish history as narrated by Gregory of Tours, recognizes fratricide as an inevitable outcome when there are multiple heirs; chronicle takes a pragmatic view of power politics and family loyalty. Divine punishment is seldom unleashed on the surviving brother in these genres, for his success in carrying forward the dynasty proves him to be the victor, the hero appointed by fate. With its close focus on family dynamics, romance recognizes that the possibility of fratricide generates powerful narrative tension, either to be dispelled in a last-minute recognition scene, or tragically fulfilled in a death which is difficult, though not impossible, to expiate.

Conclusion

The fraternal relationship is the most profoundly experienced bond in medieval literature. Although highly inflected by birth order, brotherhood is a lifelong relationship imagined by medieval authors as a model of exemplary, unswerving love and loyalty. Fraternal closeness is a powerful cultural construction, regarded as operative even between half-brothers, and between siblings who, when brought up separately, scarcely know one another. Medieval authors also recognize that the solidarity of fraternal cohorts and the tyranny of birth-order could inhibit the full development of individual identity. Brothers flourish best when they choose separate paths in life, differentiating themselves through the careers they select. This strategy enables them to achieve complementarity, to distribute skills and personality traits between them. If individual differentiation is taken too far, resulting in the rejection of crucial shared cohort values, rivalry may be exacerbated and fraternal conflict precipitated, rather than avoided, as chapter four will show. Complementarity, rather than complete polarization, is what profits the brotherly collective.

Primogeniture, and birth order more generally, shapes the destinies of brothers in medieval narratives. Older brothers assume quasi-paternal responsibility and leadership within the sibling group. Younger brothers must make their fortunes away from the family, seeking new possibilities which remove them from direct competition with their other siblings. Primogeniture is a cultural given in romance: older brothers regard sole inheritance as their right while younger brothers must make the best of their lot. Dissent from the status quo is unusual; as we shall see in chapter four, fratricide driven by primogeniture tends to occur only in ballad and in pseudo-history. When brothers remain closely enmeshed with one another, the fraternal group can easily become

---

[125] W. Burkert, *Homo Necans: The Anthropology of Ancient Greek Sacrificial Ritual and Myth*, trans. P. Bing (Berkeley CA, 1983), and see chapter four.

a gang, directing the aggression of sibling rivalry outwards onto non-group members and converting brotherly solidarity into an anti-social threat. The gang-mentality chiefly benefits the gang-leader: junior members of the cohort find themselves sacrificing their individual aspirations to group identity and its collective aim. Even when separated, brothers are consistently imagined as cognizant of their obligation to avenge one another, whatever the social cost. Thus the brother demonstrates his love and loyalty without having to negotiate his differences with a living sibling; equally he manages to resolve some of the complex emotions evoked by sibling bereavement through a violence experienced as cathartic.[126] On a psychological level, the vengeance imperative in literary texts speaks to the widespread experience of child or adult sibling loss, offering a fantasy expiation for the guilt experienced by the survivor. Nevertheless, texts which critically examine vengeance as a social phenomenon often problematize it through sibling-framed questions. How far does that obligation extend? Can it be eschewed in favour of forgiveness? And, are sisters – as debated in the next chapter – to be included within that imperative?

Individual difference between brothers is by no means fully accounted for by birth order, since younger sons often possess qualities of initiative and daring which their elder brothers either lack or cannot responsibly exercise. Medieval writers are interested in exploring the relative effects of nature and nurture on sibling groups. How far are family traits heritable (and thus associated with predestination), and how far do young men make their own fortunes? Twin studies in medieval narrative are somewhat limited in extent; the uneasy questions they provoke about the fairness of primogeniture are fudged in the interest of maintaining the social status quo. Although loyalty and affection is expected between half-, step- and full-brothers, differing inheritance expectations solidify social relations in genres such as romance and saga. Outside chronicle and pseudo-history, brothers go to extraordinary lengths to avoid breaching the taboo against fratricide; in romance the accidental brother-killer must perish or else he finds himself accursed.

Brothers are thus 'good to think with' when deep social change is at stake. Sibling dynamics are dramatized in the literary explorations which chart the slow move away from blood-vengeance to legal redress, or which anticipate the reasons for the modification of strict primogeniture among the twelfth-century French aristocracy. To think about brothers is also to think laterally about family, about loyalty as a social norm extended beyond the fraternal cohort to friends, business partners, affines and brothers-in-arms, and about the ways in which medieval models of fraternity anticipate the extension of fraternity as an increasingly inclusive ideal in later European history.[127] Fraternity, as Juliet Flower MacCannell argues, overthrows patriarchal order, to replace the Father, not with the 'privileged son and heir, but only one among brothers'. Yet the establishment of this order depends more than ever upon the 'suppression of

---

[126] Cicirelli, *Sibling Relationships*, pp. 185–98.
[127] See for example, MacCannell, *Regime of the Brother*.

the "sister"', a suppression which perpetuates the asymmetry which medieval authors perceived in cross-sibling relations.[128]

Relations between sisters, and between cross-sex siblings, are imagined differently from fraternal bonds. Individual differentiation is accomplished chiefly through gender for cross-sex siblings, while the fates of sisters are less markedly determined by birth order. Sisters function interchangeably both within and outside the family, and their task in individualizing themselves is rendered more difficult by the impossibility of embarking on heroic adventure as their brothers do. Sisters are often separated from one another in adulthood by marriage, while brothers leave to go adventuring before their sisters are of an age to forge strong affective bonds with them. However, as the next chapter will show, although these bonds between sisters and sisters, or sisters and brothers, are not regarded as being as fundamental to medieval social and religious ideology as are fraternal bonds, love, loyalty and sacrifice also significantly shape women's and cross-sex sibling relationships.

---

[128] Ibid., p. 12 and p. 3.

3

'Io v'ho cara quanto sorella si dee avere':[1] Sisters, and their Brothers

Introduction

The previous chapter showed how brothers are imagined as working to reconcile the drive for differentiation from their male siblings with the strong social norm of kinship solidarity. However, opportunities for sisters to demonstrate love and loyalty are much rarer in medieval narratives. Girls often marry young; if they are of high social status they frequently live far from their natal family in their husband's household. Enduring what Claude Lévi-Strauss calls 'the hard fate of exiles', their interactions with their siblings tend to become restricted.[2] Meetings with other sisters who have also married away or who are in the convent are limited; this consideration accounts for the relative paucity of medieval stories about pairs of sisters when one or both are married.[3] In lower-status families by contrast the historical sources examined in chapter one show that married sisters very frequently spent time together, helping one another with childbirth and child-raising and socializing in family groups (see p. 34). In fourteenth-century urban literature, such as the *Decameron*, when a sister marries into another mercantile family she simply moves to another street in the city and her siblings remain closely involved in her life.[4]

For medieval authors, women only become interesting to write about when they become old enough to marry. Although sisters are often imagined to be rivalrous, particularly in matters of love as we shall see in chapter five, a number of medieval stories in different genres show that sisters can also be loyal and self-sacrificing. 'Intense loyalty and sustained caregiving are not based on simple strategic or temporarily convenient alliances', note Bank and Kahn: 'Loyalty involves feeling and identification with the other person; it also requires tangible action.'[5] This chapter focuses on sisterly loyalty, whether expressed for another sister or for a brother, through the kind of 'tangible action' that complicates the

---

[1] 'I hold you as dear as one should hold a sister'. Giovanni Boccaccio, *Decameron* II.3; my translation (with thanks to Gervase Rosser).
[2] Lévi-Strauss, *Elementary Structures of Kinship*, p. 306.
[3] See Queen Eleanor of Provence and her sisters in chapter one (p. 32), for example.
[4] See chapter seven for instances of sibling interaction after marriage in the *Decameron*.
[5] Bank and Kahn, *The Sibling Bond*, p. 113.

plots of medieval narrative as often as it resolves them. The chapter also examines brothers' positive regard for their sisters and the limits to that regard. Juliet Mitchell argues that unresolved sibling relationship issues can result in social groups who 'do not relate to each other on the basis of a mutual recognition of the other's consciousness'.[6] The patriarchal prioritization of men's interests produces such failures of recognition, for sisterly subjectivity, sisters' agency, is not reckoned with on the same basis as the interests of brothers, and thus brothers can be unpleasantly surprised by their sisters' apparent uncooperativeness.[7]

Sibling borderwork allows siblings to control their psychological anxiety about identity. The fear of interchangeability, of the erasure of individuality, is overcome by insisting on the differentness of siblings and refusing to allow one brother to substitute for another. Medieval brothers do not have to work to establish their difference from their sisters, for their preferential gender status (almost always) makes the task otiose. Sisters, though, have good reason to be anxious, for they simply *are* more interchangeable than brothers in the prevailing social systems (even if this is a condition which can sometimes operate to women's advantage). Positive brother–sister interactions are shaped by different, often highly asymmetric, kinds of loyalty; sisters love and help their brothers as individuals, while brothers tend to take a more instrumental view of their sisters, valuing them as much for the alliances they can bring through their marriages as for the childhood intimacy they may have shared. Leonore Davidoff suggests that in nineteenth-century Western families, 'girls' personal loyalty towards, and involvement with their brothers' concerns may have been stressed, while the boys in the family took for granted both their right and their duty to turn to external pursuits'.[8] This pattern of sisterly involvement with their brothers' fates and brothers' relative indifference to their sisters' futures, except in terms of alliance-making or achieving Christian salvation, is also evident in medieval literature.

This chapter examines first the positive relationships of sisters with one another in medieval literature and then investigates the affectionate bonds between cross-sex siblings. I begin by considering narratives in which a sister successfully differentiates herself from another sister: she achieves romantic happiness by insisting on sisterhood and thus re-establishing her sisterly membership of her high-status lineage.

Substituting for the Sister: Sisterly Loyalty

In Marie de France's late-twelfth-century poem *Fresne*, a foundling gives up her noble lover when he is urged to marry someone of his own status.[9] Evidence of

---

[6] Mitchell, *Siblings*, p. 132.
[7] See chapter five for exploration of this theme.
[8] L. Davidoff, 'The Sibling Relationship and Sibling Incest in Historical Context', in *Sibling Relationships*, ed. P. Coles (London, 2006), pp. 17–47 (p. 21).
[9] Marie de France, 'Fresne' in *Lais*, ed. and trans. A. Micha (Paris, 1994); pp. 98–125;

lineage and a dowry are crucial to marriage negotiations, and Fresne possesses neither. When Fresne selflessly thinks to decorate the bridal bed with one of her few possessions from her infancy, an embroidered cloth, the bride's mother identifies it as the token that she left with one of her twin daughters when she abandoned her as a baby.[10] Fresne is united with her sister Codre, the legitimate bride, who gladly makes way for her newly recovered sister to marry the duke whom she loves – and who loves her. The recognition token is a traditional motif in stories about abandoned children, yet where twins are concerned it might be expected that Codre's mother and the sisters themselves would notice a resemblance between the two women. However, as previously noted, physical identicality is either absent or not remarked upon in medieval twin stories.[11] The interchangeability of Fresne and Codre is strongly figured by their twinship; the only distinction between them is that one sister has a publicly acknowledged lineage and a handsome dowry while the other does not.[12]

In *Fresne*, Codre loses little by her sacrifice; she marries another nobleman and had no emotional investment in wedding the man who becomes her brother-in-law. Moreover, as Elizabeth Archibald notes, the relationship between Codre and her new husband would have been incestuous in eccelesiastical law, thanks to her sister's previous sexual history.[13] Solidarity and love between sisters is most clearly displayed when questions of love and marriage are at stake: these two sisters did not need to share a childhood in order to feel loyalty and affection for one another. Same-sex siblings 'have common ground and can identify with one another more easily'; sisters in particular have a capacity for imaginative identification with one another that reinforces empathy.[14] A brother would be very much less likely to cede the woman he had intended to marry to his own brother; when two brothers desire the same woman intense rivalry rather

The Lais of Marie de France, trans. G. Burgess and K. Busby (Harmondsworth, 1999), pp. 61–7. See also the Middle English version, 'Lai le Freine' in *The Middle English Breton Lay*, ed. A. Laskaya and E. Salisbury (Kalamazoo, 1995), and E. Archibald, 'Lai le Freine: The Female Foundling and the Problem of Romance Genre', in *The Spirit of Medieval English Popular Romance*, ed. A. Putter and J. Gilbert (Harlow, 2000), pp. 39–55.

[10] The twins' mother had previously criticized another woman for bearing twins, claiming that this was evidence of intercourse with two different men. Whether this belief was genuinely held in the medieval period is unclear; certainly Fresne and her sister are not the result of adultery. See E. Kooper, 'Multiple Births and Multiple Disaster: Twins in Medieval Literature', in *Conjunctures: Medieval Studies in Honor of Douglas Kelly*, ed. K. Busby and N. J. Lacy (Amsterdam, 1994), pp. 253–69.

[11] Compare Bǫðvarr bjarki and his brothers, and Valentine and Orson in chapter one.

[12] For a thoughtful discussion of twinning themes and the retrospective legitimization of Fresne, see M. T. Bruckner, '*Le Fresne*'s Model for Twinning in the *Lais* of Marie de France', *Modern Language Notes* 121 (2006), 946–60.

[13] E. Archibald, *Incest and the Medieval Imagination* (Oxford, 2001), p. 226; see, however, Duby, *The Knight, the Lady*, p. 70, on the frequency of relationships which were technically incestuous in twelfth-century France.

[14] Bank and Kahn, *The Sibling Bond*, p. 125; Klagsbrun, *Mixed Feelings*, p. 98.

than renunciation is the more likely result.[15] Masculine self-sacrifice of this kind is enabled, however, when sibling rivalry is absent; a sworn-brother *will* freely yield up the woman he loves to his companion if his friend's happiness depends on it.[16]

Sibling plots feature strongly in ballads. These strip away the incidental conventions of characterization found in other genres to focus on powerful emotions and extremes of behaviour.[17] The Scots ballad classified as Child 62, 'Fair Annie', shares *Fresne*'s themes of sister-substitution and the centrality of lineage and dowry.[18] Annie has borne Lord Thomas seven sons, yet he decides to marry a high-born lady, apparently for her dowry. When the new bride asks the weeping Annie about her family, their relationship is revealed. The bride declares:

> 'If the Earl of Wemyss was your father,
> I wot sae was he mine;
> And it shall not be for lack o gowd
> That ye your love sall tyne'.   *(lose)*   (62A.v.30)

Annie's sister owns seven ships; she promises to give three to Annie as dowry and four to her eldest son. Annie can now marry Lord Thomas, and the bride rejoices that she can 'gae maiden hame'. In 62C the gift of ships is explicitly said to be the lost sister's dowry; in 62J, somewhat duplicitously, the lord claims that he had visited the sisters' family home in search of Annie's dowry rather than with the intention of gaining a new wife, though he certainly returns with one. At the beginning of the ballad, however, he brags that he will fetch a wife who is 'a brighter and a fairer dame / Than ever ye hae been'. When he abducted the twelve-year-old Annie, he complains, he acquired no 'gowd and gear'. The new bride clearly remembers her lost sister for she notices their resemblance. Annie's sister's loving generosity, like Codre's, is made easier by the absence of erotic interest in her future brother-in-law. Even so, the loyalty she exhibits to Annie entails some emotional cost: in version 62B, though she gladly cedes her place to her sister, she is also rueful. When she returns to her father's house, she will be mocked for leaving home a wife but coming home a maiden, she sighs, and her loss of status momentarily troubles the happy ending.

Medieval romance imagines young women as possessing an agency and mobility which they could not easily have exercised in real life, and in this genre girls give effective moral and practical aid to their sisters. In Malory's 'Tale of Sir Gareth', Lyonet goes to Arthur's court in search of a champion to rescue

---

[15] See chapter four.
[16] See chapter eight.
[17] Although the ballads adduced in this book are recorded in the eighteenth or nineteenth centuries, they usually have medieval settings, and often have analogues in other medieval genres. They cannot be regarded as 'medieval' in quite the same sense as romance or saga, for example, but their direct and dramatic treatment of sibling emotion makes them an important source for premodern sibling imaginings.
[18] *English and Scottish Popular Ballads*, ed. F. J. Child, 5 vols (New York, 1884), II: 63–83.

her sister Lyonors from the implacable Red Knight of the Red Launds, who is besieging her castle.[19] Though Lyonet treats with contempt the apparent kitchen-boy Gareth, who takes on the quest, by the time they arrive at Lyonors's castle he has proved his mettle and they have reached a mutual understanding. After Gareth's victory, Lyonet prevents him and her sister from consummating their love by conjuring up a phantom knight through her hitherto unguessed magical ability. Gareth is attacked so severely that the anticipated sexual encounter is thwarted on two separate occasions. A modern reader might impute jealousy to Lyonet, who, in other reflexes of this plot-type, ultimately weds the victim of her insults once he has proved himself, but it is doubtful that Malory's conception of Lyonet's psychology is so complex.[20] Rather, Lyonet acts as moral guardian to her sister, impelled by sisterly regard to safeguard Lyonors against yielding up her virginity before the marriage has been formalized. When Gareth and her sister remonstrate with her about her policing of Lyonors's premarital chastity, she insists that 'all that I have done ... shall be for your worshyp and us all'.[21] Malory's fifteenth-century gentry readership would have noted the importance of Lyonet's actions in making sure that, despite the intimacy between the two betrothed young people, the marriage is properly contracted in the presence of Gareth's mother and uncle, King Arthur, before sexual union takes place.[22]

Thus a crisis related to a young woman's marriage once again offers an opportunity to explore sisterly loyalty. The Red Knight's siege of Lyonors's castle is intended primarily as a challenge to the Round Table, yet he also regards Lyonors as his lady, warning Gareth who is gazing at her, 'leve thy beholdyng ... she is my lady, and for hir I have done many stronge batayles'.[23] Lyonet takes an active interest in arranging her sister's marriage by bringing a better suitor (the incognito son of the king of Orkney) to the castle as Lyonors's champion. The more surprising then that after the defeat of the Red Knight it is revealed that the two sisters have a brother, Sir Gringamour, who has made no effort to defend his beleaguered sister, and who takes a strikingly lax view of the need for Lyonors to maintain her chastity.[24] Gringamour is evidently anxious to secure the Orkney prince as a brother-in-law, and he urges Lyonet neither to offend nor to drive away their sister's suitor.[25] Lyonet is a highly proactive sister, expressing sisterly loyalty through 'tangible action', indeed interfering with her sister's sexual pleasures in a way that might well elicit annoyance in

---

[19] Malory, *Le Morte Darthur*, ed. Field, I: 223–88.
[20] Cf. La Cote Male Tayle and the Damoiselle Maledysaunt, ibid., I: 360–75.
[21] Ibid., I: 262.
[22] See K. Cherewatuk, *Marriage, Adultery and Inheritance in Malory's* Morte Darthur, Arthurian Studies 67 (Cambridge, 2006), pp. 1–23.
[23] Malory, *Morte Darthur*, ed. Field, I: 250.
[24] For a structural explanation of Gringamour's failure to aid his sister, see below, p. 98. Gringamour cannot marry his sister, and must therefore wait for an appropriate challenger to the besieging knight to lift the siege and win the lady.
[25] See C. Larrington, 'Sibling Relations in Malory's *Morte Darthur*', *Arthurian Literature* 28 (2011), 57–74.

the amorous lady. As Terri Apter notes, conflicting emotions of protectiveness and resentment are strongly reciprocal elements in sister-relationships, and Lyonors does not thank Lyonet for her intervention.[26] Indeed, she defiantly tells her brother that since she and Gareth are betrothed, 'I shame nat to be with hym nor to do hym all the pleasure that I can', and Gringamour concurs with her point of view.[27] Nevertheless, Lyonet's wisdom about the responsibilities of lateral relations is vindicated. Not only does her concern for her sister's honour contrast with their negligent brother's casualness, but she intervenes later in the Tale to prevent her new brothers-in-law from accidentally killing one another.[28] Lyonet's profound engagement with sibling and affinal loyalties is rewarded when she marries Gareth's brother Gaheris at the end of the Tale, achieving an equal match with her sister. Fraternal doubling resolves the issue of sisterly rivalry and permits Malory to suppress the Damesell Malydysaunt plot-arc (in which the critical damsel weds the knight she persecutes) since there are more than enough princes of Orkney to go round.

Sisterly Solidarity

Modern siblings, Ann Goetting observes, tend to form coalitions against their parents when they perceive injustice or oppression.[29] Medieval sisters too are sometimes imagined as offering resistance to their parents' authority; their rebellions are the more disturbing because their rejection of the prevailing family dynamic has the power to disrupt social – in particular, patriarchal – structures. The romance of Mélusine begins with an episode illustrating just such a disastrous outcome to sisterly solidarity. In the prose version of Jean d'Arras's *Histoire de Mélusine* and in its fifteenth-century English translation, Mélusine's history is prefaced by a prologue about her parents.[30] This relates how King Hélinas broke a taboo placed on him by Présine, Mélusine's mother: he should never see her in childbed.[31] Hélinas broke this promise when Présine gave birth

---

[26] Apter, *Sister Knot*, pp. 137–75.
[27] Malory, *Morte Darthur*, ed. Field, I: 262.
[28] See above, p. 70.
[29] Goetting, 'Developmental Tasks', pp. 705–6, and Bank and Kahn, *The Sibling Bond*, pp. 322–4.
[30] Jean d'Arras, *Mélusine*, ed. Stouff, pp. 5–15, and *Melusine, part I: Text, Notes and Commentary*, ed. A. K. Donald, EETS es 68 (Oxford, 1895; repr. 2010), pp. 11–12. Cf. also *Le roman de Mélusine*, ed. Roach; trans. L. Harf-Lancner.
[31] Hélinas trespassed against strongly entrenched gender norms, for childbirth was, without exception, a business only for women, cf. Bellisent's and Josiane's birthing in the forest discussed in chapter two. See also G. M. Gibson, 'Scene and Obscene: Seeing and Performing Late Medieval Childbirth', *Journal of Medieval and Early Modern Studies* 29 (1999), 7–24 (p. 9); P. McCracken, *The Curse of Eve, the Wound of the Hero: Blood, Gender, and Medieval Literature* (Philadelphia, 2003), pp. 77–91; and L. Haas, 'Women and Childbearing in Medieval Florence', in *Medieval Family Roles: A Book of Essays*, ed. C. Jorgensen Itnyre (New York and London, 1996), pp. 87–99.

to triplets: Mélusine and her sisters. If twinship, as Gabrielle Spiegel argues, flags up 'formless and unassimilatable duplications and sinister replications', triplethood sets up even greater expectations of contrast and similarity.[32] Key sibling issues of solidarity, identity and differentiation are intensified by the sisters' triplet status, and as in the case of Bǫðvarr bjarki and his brothers, the multiple births signal the supernatural element in their bloodline.[33]

As the eldest, Mélusine encourages her sisters to punish their father's trangression and they imprison him within a mountain, where he perishes. Aptly, Hélinas's enclosure echoes the circumstances of his trespass; for his curiosity about how – and what – his wife liberates from her womb he is confined to a womb-like space from which he can never be freed. Furious Présine fractures the sisters' solidarity; she punishes them with forcible separation and differentiation, ending the 'sinister replication' which made parricide possible. Through the individual taboos placed upon them, Présine's daughters are destined to replay their mother's challenge to masculine respect for female privacy and self-determination. Mélusine's husband Raimondin performs little better than Hélinas in observing his wife's injunction against trying to discover what she does on Saturdays when, penetrating her privacy with his sword-point, he spies on her in her serpent form. Mélior is fated to conduct a non-competitive test of male stamina while refusing to constitute its prize. The only man who succeeds in the vigil of the Sparrowhawk ruins his lineage's fortunes by insisting on erotic satisfaction as his reward.[34] Palestine, the last sister, is removed from these contested and gendered spaces; enclosed within Mount Canigou in Roussillon she awaits the man from her lineage who can win the treasure she guards. Success in this quest will bring the ultimate chivalric and Christian prize: domination over the Holy Land, the territory that bears her name.[35]

The sisters' unified response to their father's trespass against the tabooed witnessing of childbirth, that central domain of femininity, cannot be allowed to go unpunished, and it is their mother who reinforces the patriarchal order. Among brothers, solidarity is a recognized norm; even when, as often happens

---

[32] G. M. Spiegel, 'Maternity and Monstrosity: Reproductive Biology in the *Roman de Mélusine*', in *Mélusine of Lusignan*, ed. Maddox and Sturm-Maddox, pp. 100–24 (p. 105). Cf. R. Girard, *Violence and the Sacred*, trans. P. Gregory (Baltimore and London, 1977), p. 56.

[33] See above, chapter two, p. 63.

[34] A descendant of Mélusine's son Guy of Armenia succeeds in the test, only to insist on claiming Mélior as his prize. She notes that since he is a descendant of her sister's son, she is (in effect) his aunt; the liaison would be incestuous as well as contravening the terms of the curse. Jean d'Arras, *Mélusine*, pp. 796–809; Coudrette, *Mélusine*, ed. Roach, pp. 302–14; trans. Harf-Lancner, pp. 133–9. See Spiegel, 'Maternity and Monstrosity', pp. 115–17. On the contemporary fortunes of the king of Armenia, Léon of Lusignan, see Baumgartner, 'Fiction and History' (pp. 186–7).

[35] This feat is not even attempted in Jean d'Arras's version; in Coudrette, Geoffroy resolves to win his grandfather's treasure, but dies before he can set out, *Mélusine*, ed. Roach, pp. 325–7.

in Malory, a group of brothers acts in an unchivalric fashion, sallying in numbers out of a castle, until defeated by a Round Table champion, their fraternal loyalty is positively valued.[36] The strong political connection between sibling dynamics and the development and maintenance of social structures was, as we have seen, well understood in medieval Europe, for loyal fraternal cooperation offers a crucial model for guilds, chivalric and monastic orders and other kinds of fictive brotherly associations. Solidarity between brother and sister, as in the case of Orestes and Electra, for example, is imagined as facilitating the overthrow of tyranny and the establishment of a new political order, while fraternal rivalry can be envisaged as destroying not only family bonds, but the entire political process.[37] But when sisters rise up together against father or husband existing hierarchies are shattered, and disaster results for the women and for the polities which they inhabit. Sisterly unity in these tales enables a resistance that is highly disruptive to the maintenance of the male lineages from which political authority derives.

Three related texts recount the British origin myth: the Anglo-Norman poem *Des Granz Geanz*, its Latin derivatives and the Prologue to the Middle English *Brut* chronicle, an episode in which a group of sisters rebel against their marriages.[38] In the Middle English version, the sisters, led by the eldest, Albina, are offended at being made to marry below their status and they refuse to fulfil their wifely duties. Recalled to their father's home to be rebuked for their behaviour, the sisters take decisive collective action: they murder their undesirable husbands and are consequently exiled. Like many nobly born medieval women, they strongly object to being married below their status: 'I am come of a more hyere kynges blod þan my housbond is', Albina insists.[39] Her complaint signals the limits to hypergamy, discussed in chapter one as an aspirational marriage strategy which could bring the benefit of a powerful maternal uncle for a sister's sons.[40] For every lesser noble aspiring to improve his social status through marrying up, there may well have been an Albina, unwilling to jeopardize her standing by marrying too far down. In this tale, patriarchal authority errs

---

[36] See Vial, 'Entre création et destruction', and C. Serp, 'Fratrie, fraternité et fratricide dans le cycle Lancelot-Graal', in *Frères et sœurs*, ed. Cassagnes-Brouquet and Yvernault, pp. 201–9.

[37] R. D. Hinshelwood and G. Winship, 'Orestes and Democracy', in *Sibling Relations*, ed. Coles, pp. 75–96.

[38] The Middle English prologue is based on, but differs significantly from, the Anglo-Norman poem *Des Granz Geanz*, which forms the prologue to some manuscripts of the Anglo-Norman Prose *Brut*, and which also has a Latin derivative, *De Origine Gigantum*. See L. Johnson, 'Return to Albion', *Arthurian Literature* 13 (1995), 19–40 for bibliography. The story is calqued on the tale of Hypermnestra and the other Danaides (Ovid, *Heroides*, XIV), in which fifty sisters are ordered to marry fifty brothers, their cousins. All but one, Hypermnestra, murder their husbands. See T. Drukker, 'Thirty-Three Murderous Sisters: A Pre-Trojan Foundation Myth in the Middle English Prose *Brut*', *Review of English Studies* 54 (2003), 449–63.

[39] Drukker, 'Thirty-Three Murderous Sisters', p. 457.

[40] See chapter one, p. 38.

when it counters the individual acts of wifely disobedience by summoning the women back to the home which they identify with their proudly maintained social aspirations; the recall enables collective action – rarely available to noble women separated through the virilocal consequences of marriage – and, like Mélusine and her sisters, they seize the opportunity to act out their subversion.

The exiled sisters land on what will ultimately become the island of Britain and name it *Albion* after their ringleader. Husbandless, their copulation with the devil gives rise to a race of giants who still populate the island when the Trojan-descended hero Brutus arrives to settle it. Albina and her sisters are not intentional revolutionaries, deliberately seeking to overthrow patriarchal order. In contrast to the epic achievement of Brutus's later domination of the island, their foundation of the new polity is both unintended and unruly. Albina's earlier land-taking populates Albion with brutes and savages whom Brutus must annihilate. Her story tropes the chaotic royal politics of eleventh-century England, subdued by William of Normandy's invasion: post-Conquest anxieties about the new Norman dynasty's legitimacy generate a myth contrasting the disorderly rule of women with the discipline and order of men. Consequently Albina's rebellion reappears in a number of pseudo-historical texts composed in Norman England.

In the earlier Anglo-Norman and Latin versions the sisters' murderous plans are frustrated when the youngest betrays their intentions to her husband, and the disobedient women are set adrift. These thirty-three sisters, all but one loyal to one another, cannot be tolerated in their native land, for their solidarity is more threatening to order than the actions of the triplets in the tale of Mélusine. Nor, unlike Brutus, can they be properly regarded as the mothers of the new nation they accidentally found, for their giant offspring are wild and uncivilized, dwelling in caves, not cities, and they are hostile to humans. That Albion/Albanie is the kingdom ruled by Mélusine's luckless father Hélinas before his imprisonment by his triplet daughters suggestively links these two narratives of husband-killing and near-parricide.[41] Brutus is required to exterminate the old order, the giants who figure nature rather than culture; through his giganticide and his renaming Albion as Britain, he shapes the country's future history, assimilating it to patriliny and civilization. Yet Brutus's multiple erasures of the dangerous effects of sisterly unity cannot, in the longer term, achieve a lasting and peaceable fraternal polity. Only highly exceptional brothers will, as Geoffrey of Monmouth and his successors show, share the rule of Britain without resorting to the treachery and murder embedded in the island's occluded prehistoric past.[42]

---

[41] S. G. Nichol, 'Melusine between Myth and History: Profile of a Female Demon', in *Mélusine of Lusignan*, ed. Maddox and Sturm-Maddox, pp. 137–64 (p. 161).

[42] See chapter two for brothers who manage to negotiate shared rule in Geoffrey's British history and chapter four for those who do not.

Taking Care of the Brother

Sisters and brothers in medieval narrative are always so highly differentiated by their gender that the establishment of individuality in relation to a cross-sex sib is not generally a site of struggle. Only in rare circumstances does a brother or sister cross, in rhetorical or social terms, the border between gender and personhood. In the probably thirteenth-century Icelandic *Gísla saga*, a Norwegian father, Þorbjǫrn, successfully goads his son Gísli into attacking his sister Þordís's wooer when the family's honour has been compromised by the suitor's failure to make a formal marriage offer. In his incitement Þorbjǫrn claims that he must have bred daughters, not sons, since Þordís's brothers seem so complacent about her reputation. The accusation is highly effective; only the death of the offender can now rid Gísli of the taint of being, rhetorically, his own sister, and he speedily recuperates his gender status by killing the reluctant suitor.[43] Conversely, in a group of later (probably fourteenth-century) Norse romances, the princess with no siblings turns herself into a fictive male, a *meykonungr* or maiden-king, in order to remedy her lack of brothers.[44] Having achieved a kind of masculinity, signalled by male attire and a change of name, the *meykonungr* successfully rules her kingdom, leads its army into battle and takes offence if she is not addressed by her masculine name. When she is conquered – as she always is – by her future husband, she is forced to relinquish her new name and clothing along with much of the authority she has over her patrimony, and she must marry. That both these examples are drawn from Iceland highlights the extreme importance of strictly policing the border between gender roles both in medieval Icelandic society and in the saga-age society it imagined for itself.[45]

Juliet Mitchell identifies the sister as displaying three different aspects to her brother. She 'both cares for and destroys: the lateral would-be murderer, the nurse and the lawgiver'.[46] In this section I explore the sister's role as 'nurse and lawgiver', as nurturer and as an embodiment of particular types of family ethics. The caregiver appears chiefly in traditional and popular literature, while the lawgiver, as we shall see, unsettles the chivalric ethic by pressing the claims

---

[43] *Gísla saga*, in *Vestfirðinga sögur*, ed. Björn K. Þórólfsson and Guðni Jónsson, ÍF 6 (Reykjavík, 1953), pp. 24–5. In the E-version of the saga, Gísli acts very promptly to prevent the suitor Bárðr's further infringement of the family honour; in the Y-version, he tries hard to get his siblings' friend Kolbeinn to desist from the compromising visits. When Gísli finally kills Kolbeinn, Þorbjǫrn explicitly withdraws the accusation that he has fathered daughters, not sons.

[44] M. Kalinke, *Bridal-Quest Romance in Medieval Iceland*, Islandica 46 (Ithaca NY, 1990), and now Jóhanna K. Friðriksdóttir, *Women in Old Norse Literature: Bodies, Words and Power* (New York and London, 2013), pp. 107–33.

[45] See P. M. Sørensen, *The Unmanly Man: Concepts of Sexual Defamation in Early Northern Society*, trans. J. Turville-Petre (Odense, 1983).

[46] Mitchell, *Siblings*, p. 57. The destroyer, the would-be murderer, will appear in chapters five and seven which explore the consequences when the brother–sister relationship is compromised through triangulation with another man, usually the sister's lover.

of kinship-oriented revenge against the overarching imperatives of the fictive and homosocial brotherhood of knights, invoking an older ethical system in order to critique new social norms.

Sisters, especially older sisters, are consistently imagined as nurturing and caring for their brothers; they reflect and model expectations of sisterly caregiving in non-aristocratic or motherless families.[47] Popular genres, such as fairy- and folk-tale, preserve stories in which the brother–sister relationship is affectionate and loyal, and in which the sister is effective at warding off danger from her brother and herself, or releasing him from enchantment.[48] If in the *Märchen* the sister rescues her brothers through patience, loyalty and dedicated application to difficult tasks, brothers are markedly less likely to come to their sisters' aid, unless they appear at the last minute in order to finish off the villain who threatens their sibling's life.[49] The capacity of sisters to release their brothers from enchantment and restore them to human adulthood, like the tales of vengeance discussed in the previous chapter, speaks to psychological reactions to sibling loss. Modern psychology has uncovered the effects of sibling loss on surviving children at the time of bereavement and in later adulthood: guilt, grief, anger, feelings of exclusion from parental mourning and anxieties about identity – must I now replace, indeed become, my dead sibling? – are typical reactions.[50] These brother–sister *Märchen* propose that the lost sibling(s) *can* be recovered if the survivor-sister only loves them enough, if she is prepared to suffer terrible torments to restore them to life in human form. The tales reverse sibling death through a fantasy of resurrection: death shares a structural equivalence with magical transformation. Just as the enchantment of the brother can be revoked, so death can be negated through the power of a sister's love. Grief and guilt are erased and all live happily in a restored sibling cohort.

Folk- and fairy-tales thus place siblings in extreme situations where uncomplicated love and loyalty saves the sibling or half-sibling pair from a

---

[47] Bank and Kahn, *The Sibling Bond*, pp. 125–38.
[48] See I. Vielhauer, *Bruder und Schwester: Untersuchungen und Betrachtungen zu einem Urmotiv zwischenmenschlicher Beziehung* (Bonn, 1979), pp. 11–14, and J. and W. Grimm, *Kinder- und Hausmärchen: Jubiläums-Ausgabe*, 3 vols, ed. H. Rölleke (Stuttgart, 1982), I: 100–8 for Tale 15, 'Hänsel und Gretel'; *The Complete Fairy Tales of the Brothers Grimm*, 3rd edn, trans. J. Zipes (New York, Toronto, London, 1992), pp. 53–8. Cf. also, Tale 9, 'Die zwolf Brüder (The Twelve Brothers), *Kinder- und Hausmärchen*, I: 71–7; *Complete Fairy Tales*, pp. 32–6; Tale 25, 'Die Sieben Raben', *Kinder- und Hausmärchen*, I: 154–6 (The Seven Ravens) *Complete Fairy Tales*, pp. 91–3 and M. Tatar, *The Hard Facts of the Grimms' Fairy Tales* (Princeton, 1987), pp. 146–8.
[49] Cf. Tale 46, 'Fitchers Vogel' (Fitcher's Bird) (ATU Type 311, very similar to Type 312, Bluebeard), in Grimm, *Kinder- und Hausmärchen*, I: 235–9; trans. *Complete Fairy Tales*, pp. 155–8.
[50] See for example D. E. Balk, 'Adolescents' Grief Reactions and Self-Concept Perceptions Following Sibling Death', *Journal of Youth and Adolescence* 12 (1983), 137–61, and now *Children's Encounters with Death, Bereavement, and Coping*, ed. C. A. Corr and D. E. Balk (New York, 2010). Cf. Bank and Kahn, *The Sibling Bond*, pp. 271–95.

horrible fate.[51] In other genres, sisters are less likely to have to disenchant their bewitched brothers, and their freedom of action is often restricted by their social status. Yet, even when the sister's agency is limited, some narratives recognize how a sister's perceptiveness and advice may help an unhappy brother when the rest of the family ignores his feelings. In 'Lord Thomas and Fair Annet' (Child Ballad 73), only Lord Thomas's sister advises him to marry his beautiful but poor lover in preference to the well-dowered 'nut-brown bride', 'Lest ye sould sigh and say, Alace / What is this we brought hame?' (73A10).[52] But Thomas succumbs to his family's desire for 'gowd and gear' and weds the 'nut-brown bride'. At the wedding, seeing her rival's loveliness, the 'nut-brown bride' stabs Fair Annie through the heart. Lord Thomas kills the bride and then himself. Thomas's sister's advice to marry for love could have averted the family tragedy: the ballad recognizes the sister's perspective as differing from that of the other kindred. The sister empathizes with her brother's conflicting emotions, for she understands the difference between love and the attraction of the dowry. Moreover, she herself has no stake in the fortune which her sister-in-law will bring, since she will leave the family when she marries in her turn. Her liminal position, already perhaps in transition to her marital family, allows a disinterested perception of her brother's situation, and she alone gives full weight to the importance of erotic love for his future happiness.

The thirteenth-century Icelandic *Laxdæla saga* incorporates a notably romance-like interest in emotion, not just in the homosocial bonds between men, but also in the complex feelings involved in both heterosexual and sibling relationships.[53] Unlike most *Íslendingasögur* it seems to have been influenced by the French Arthurian romances and the *lais* of Marie de France, which were translated into Norwegian at the court of King Hákon IV in the early thirteenth century: both the translations and the repertoire of emotions they contained were transmitted to Iceland shortly afterwards.[54] In this saga, another understanding sister is the only person who can talk to her brother about his broken heart. When Kjartan returns home from a long stay in Norway, he finds that his foster-brother Bolli has married Guðrún, the woman whom Kjartan loves. Kjartan's sister Þuríðr approaches him at the spring-games, speaking to him sympathetically and directly.[55] She relays the common gossip that he is pining for Guðrún, begs him not to fall out with his once dearly loved foster-brother Bolli, and suggests that he might also marry, urging him to consider his friend's sister Hrefna. 'Kjartan tók vel undir þetta ok kvað hana vel mála leita' ('Kjartan responded well to

---

[51] See Davidoff, 'The Sibling Relationship', p. 37.
[52] *Ballads*, ed. Child, II: 179–99.
[53] S. Kramarz-Bein, '"Modernität" der *Laxdæla saga*', in *Studien zum Altgermanischen: Festschrift für Heinrich Beck*, ed. H. Uecker (Berlin, 1994), pp. 421–42.
[54] See *The Arthur of the North*, ed. M. Kalinke (Cardiff, 2011); Sif Rikhardsdóttir, *Medieval Translations and Cultural Discourse: The Movement of Texts in England, France and Scandinavia* (Cambridge, 2012), pp. 26–9.
[55] *Laxdæla saga*, ed. Einar Ólafur Sveinsson, pp. 137–8.

this, and said she was talking sense'), the saga reports.[56] Vindicating Þuríðr's counsel, the marriage is a loving one on both sides; after Kjartan's death Hrefna dies of sorrow.[57] Þuríðr's tactful intervention respects Kjartan's grief, a state of mind which the rest of the family has tried to ignore, but she also suggests a way to help her younger brother move forward and find happiness elsewhere. 'On the whole, ... brothers benefit from their sisters' care', observes Klagsbrun of the older sister – younger brother relationship. The older sister can take the place of the mother in nurturing the young man; here Þuríðr helps him out of the emotional impasse in which he has become trapped.[58]

Cross-sex siblings learn from one another about how to get on with members of the opposite sex; a good relationship with a sister or brother lays a strong foundation for a successful marriage. Þuríðr's approval of Hrefna underlines the importance of cross-sex influence when a brother or sister chooses a sexual partner. By marrying women like their sisters or men like their brothers, siblings unconsciously seek partners who allow them to continue their established sibling roles.[59] We bring 'the sibling self ... to a marriage', notes Coles; Kjartan's warm and trusting relationship with his sister is replicated in his marriage to his sister's friend.[60]

Emotional warmth is imagined as normative between brothers and sisters, even when siblings were not reared together. This norm is deployed to clever effect in a tale narrated in the *Decameron* (II.5).[61] Visiting Naples, young Andreuccio incautiously accepts an invitation to a young woman's home. Here, primed by an older woman who recognizes the young man and knows his family, the girl embraces him with many tears and claims that she is his lost half-sister, concocting a story that her mother had been seduced by his father during a stay in Palermo. Andreuccio is thus persuaded to stay overnight at his new sibling's house; subsequently she robs him and casts him out into the street. Notable in this story is how passionately the 'sister' greets her supposed half-brother and Andreuccio's joyful readiness to trust in a newly discovered sibling. His exclamation, 'Io v'ho cara quanto sorella si dee avere' ('I hold you as dear as one should hold a sister'), reflects the norm of cross-sex sib affection, even if its comparative phrasing ironically reminds the audience that this woman is no sister at all.[62] Andreuccio might have been less easily gulled had the woman claimed a sudden sexual passion for him, but her claim to siblinghood disarms him precisely through the expectation that trust and emotional warmth should characterize the brother–sister relationship, even on first meeting.[63]

[56] Ibid., p. 137.
[57] See chapter eight for the foster-brothers' final conflict.
[58] Klagsbrun, *Mixed Feelings*, p. 123.
[59] E. Morley, 'The Influence of Sibling Relationships on Couple Choice and Development', in *Sibling Relationships*, ed. Coles, pp. 197–224.
[60] Coles, *Sibling Relationships*, p. 82.
[61] *Decameron* II.5; *Decameron*, trans. Waldman, pp. 87–99.
[62] Ibid.; my translation (with thanks to Gervase Rosser).
[63] The supposed sister's gender and illegitimacy would reassure Andreuccio that she

Merchants were highly mobile in fourteenth-century Italy; evidently their travel between cities could facilitate the establishment of unofficial second families. When in the early twelfth century Peter Abélard noted in his *Ethics* that it is difficult to recognize one's sister, he may have been thinking of geographically scattered and unknown half-siblings of the type that Andreuccio's self-styled sister purports to be.[64]

Family separation is a staple of medieval romance; when a long-lost brother and sister meet, they too experience an instant attraction to one another. In Wolfram von Eschenbach's early-thirteenth-century epic *Willehalm*, courtly delicacy prevents lady Gyburg from pressing her husband's reticent new recruit on his family origins, but Rennewart, it transpires, is indeed her brother. When Rennewart falls out with the cooks in Willehalm's household who mistreat him by singeing off his whiskers, Willehalm sends his wife to try to calm him.[65] Gyburg immediately senses something about the young man: 'Ir ougn im nie gewancten: / eteswaz se an im erblicte, / dâ von ir herze erschricte' ('all the time she did not take her eyes off him for she discerned something in him which startled her deep in her heart').[66] She asks him about his family and Rennewart replies by remarking that Gyburg reminds him very much of his sister. He begs her to question him no further, but the foundations have been laid for a recognition scene later in the poem: 'der vrouwen tet ir herze kuont / daz si niht erfuor wan lange sidr' ('the lady's heart was telling her something which she did not find out until a long time later').[67] In fact *Willehalm* is unfinished, and so the emotional climax of the brother's and sister's confirmation of their relationship is never attained. Comparison with Wolfram's French source, *Rainouart*, suggests that he intended the poem to end with the sibling reunion, and, very likely, Rennewart's baptism and marriage to Willehalm's niece, Alyze. The siblings' memories of childhood and their physical similarity, remarked on by the poet, bring Gyburg's elder-sister caretaking instincts to the fore. She understands instinctively how to manage Rennewart's rage and distress at the loss of the signifier of his manhood: his singed-off whiskers. In a symbolically significant move, she laps Rennewart in her cloak, manifesting her unconscious impulse to protect her younger brother. Gyburg's suspicions that she has found her brother evoke intense, if still secret, joy; Rennewart's less intense response is to place instant trust in the lady who reminds him of his long-lost sister. Sibling emotion is not quite reciprocal here; the asymmetry is produced by Wolfram's greater interest in Gyburg's interior processes. Gyburg's tact, finesse and sympathy, befitting a Christian countess, contrast with Rennewart's hard-to-

---

could have no claim on his patrimony; cf. Lancelot and Ector in chapter two, p. 54
[64] Peter Abelard, *Ethics*, ed. and trans. D. Luscombe (Oxford, 1971), pp. 26–7. See chapter six, pp. 157–62.
[65] The significance of Rennewart's beard will be discussed in chapter seven.
[66] Cited from: http://www.hs-augsburg.de/~harsch/germanica/Chronologie/13Jh/Wolfram/wol_wio6.html. (290: 16–18). Translation from: *Willehalm*, trans. M. M. Gibbs and S. M. Johnson (Harmondsworth, 1984), pp. 148–9.
[67] *Willehalm*, 291, 2–3; trans. Gibbs and Johnson, p. 148.

control emotionality, wildness and hypermasculinity, qualities which Gyburg's husband can harness in his battle against the brother-and-sister's pagan kindred. Failing the civilizing effects of baptism and marriage, Rennewart remains a dangerously unmanageable adolescent, tractable only within the sibling dyad.

Mourning the Brother; Avenging the Brother

Luce Irigaray remarks on the imbalance between the social and emotional implications of the loss of the brother and the loss of the sister for the surviving sibling: 'Le frère est déjà investi d'une valeur pour la sœur, dont celle-ci ne peut le gratifier en retour, sinon en lui rendant un culte dans la mort' ('the brother is already invested with a value for the sister, a value that she cannot offer him in return, except by devoting herself to his cult after death').[68] Hagiographic literature in the early-medieval period sometimes depicts close sibling interaction, a warmth facilitated by the existence of double houses and less strict rules of enclosure. These saints' lives give free rein to the feelings of pious sisters when their brothers die. Two moving accounts of sisters mourning their adult brothers illustrate the emotional tension between the faith-filled knowledge that the brother is already in heaven and the profound grief of the sisters left behind. Sibling identification remains a powerful determinant of an individual's understanding of him- or herself, whether the sibling is dead or alive: death cannot erase the sibling bond.

The late-seventh-century Frankish saint Anstrude gives full voice to her grief when, apparently acting on behalf of her convent, her brother Baldwin goes to negotiate in a legal case with some clan enemies and is murdered.[69] Anstrude is torn between acceptance of God's will and her own sorrow; first weeping, then struggling to justify her tears, she calms herself sufficiently to embark on a formal elegy.[70] Using rhetorical tropes which contrast past and present, Anstrude seeks to persuade herself and her audience that – even though he has abandoned his sister in this life – Baldwin has triumphantly achieved the martyr's palm. Anstrude's lament and eulogy for her brother is the most extensive mourning speech we have uttered by a sister for a brother in medieval literature and it amply demonstrates the depth of feeling which the hagiographer imagines as existing between the siblings:

Iam iam redis ad me, frater karissime, heri vivus, hodie occisus; heri dimisi

---

[68] Irigaray, 'L'éternelle ironie' (p. 270); translation adapted from 'The Eternal Irony', trans. G. Gill (p. 217).

[69] *Vita Anstrudis abb. Laudunensis*, MGH, SS rer. Merov. 6, ed. B. Krusch and W. Levison (Hannover, 1913), pp. 66–78; *Sainted Women of the Dark Ages*, trans. J. A. McNamara and J. Halborg with E. G. Whatley (Durham NC, 1992), 'Life of Anstrude', pp. 289–303. See also Lett, *Frères et Sœurs: Histoire d'un lien*, pp. 175–6; Réal, *Vie de saints, vie de famille*, pp. 486–7.

[70] *Vita Anstrudis*, c. 5, p. 69.

te incolumem, hodie recipio te ad sepeliendum. Frater, frater animo meo amantissime!

('Now, now you come back to me, dearest brother. Yesterday you were alive, today slaughtered. Yesterday, I sent you out unhurt; today I receive you back for burial. Brother, brother, best loved of my soul!')[71]

Anstrude blames herself for persuading her brother to attend the court case at which he was killed; an important constituent of her reaction is guilt: 'Heu me... frater innocens, ut quid te misi consiliis crudelissimorum hominum!' ('Alas for me, innocent brother, that I sent you off at the advice of those cruellest men!').[72] Her lament oscillates between profound grief and hard-won submission to God's judgement: 'precor vos, licet sim turbata privatione fratris, ut animae eius memores sitis in orationibus vestris, ut crudeliter interempti anima possideat paradisi gaudia' ('I pray you, despite my own pain at the loss of my brother, that you will remember his soul in your prayers so the soul of one cruelly slaughtered may possess the joys of paradise').[73]

Felix's Latin *vita* of the Anglo-Saxon saint Guthlac, dating from 730–40, describes the dramatic collapse of Pega, Guthlac's sister, when she hears that her brother is dead:

velut in praecipitium delapsa, se solo premens, inmensi macroris molestia medullitus emarcuit, lingua siluit, labrum obmutit, omnique vivali vigore velut exanimis evanuit.

('she fell down in a headlong fall, and as she lay upon the ground she withered away to the very marrow by the mighty affliction of her grief; her tongue was silent, her lips were mute and she lost all life and strength, just as if she were dead.')[74]

Pega's body performs the grief to which she may not give voice, lest she seem to question the ways of God. She had not seen her brother for many years: Guthlac's deathbed message to her reveals that he had avoided her in life so that they might meet again in heaven. Whether his love for Pega, the most devout of his siblings, represented a particular threat to his eremitic resolve is unclear.[75] Unfortunately, *Guðlac B*, the Old English poetic account of the saint's death, breaks off in the middle of the messenger's announcement of his lord's death to the 'wuldres wynmæg' ('delightful maiden of glory').[76] The messenger's own lament, deploying many tropes of masculine grief at personal loss, occupies

---

[71] Ibid., c. 9, p. 70; *Sainted Women*, p. 295.
[72] *Vita Anstrudis*, c. 6, p. 69; *Sainted Women*, p. 294.
[73] *Vita Anstrudis*, c. 8, p. 70; adapted from *Sainted Women*, p. 295.
[74] *Felix's Life of Saint Guthlac*, ed. and trans. B. Colgrave (Cambridge, 1985), pp. 158–61.
[75] J. T. Schulenburg, *Forgetful of their Sex: Female Sanctity and Society, ca. 500–1100* (Chicago and London, 1998), pp. 300–1.
[76] *The Guthlac Poems of the Exeter Book*, ed. J. Roberts (Oxford, 1979), pp. 123–4. Quotation: line 1345.

a good thirty lines; it seems likely that the Old English poet would similarly have elaborated Pega's response and would have provided valuable insight into normative Anglo-Saxon expression of sibling mourning.

Faith enables both sisters to recover from their loss. Though Baldwin's murderers slander Anstrude to Ebroin, the mayor of Theuderic's palace, and he plans to send her into exile, her steadfastness in confronting Ebroin's soldiers, and a miraculous intervention, convince Ebroin to become her supporter and friend. Pega takes over Guthlac's dwelling after her brother's death; she maintains his shrine, uses his relics to perform healing miracles and determines who is worthy to approach the saint's tomb. She thus regains a kind of intimacy with her brother through his relics, ensuring his continuing presence in her life as well as in her prayers.[77] Pega's vigorous promotion of her saintly brother's reputation becomes the guiding principle of her life; while this testifies to the strength of the emotional tie, there is also a payoff in terms of enhanced influence for the sister in maintaining and directing her brother's nascent cult. Later in the medieval period, spiritual sisters are less able to leave their convents to adminster their brothers' legacy, and styles of sibling intimacy change into, for example, the female mystic / fraternal amanuensis dyad.[78]

Mourning for the adult cross-sex sibling's death, as Irigaray intimates, generates different behavioural responses in either sex.[79] A brother's killing calls for vengeance; if no surviving brother is available a sister may take on the task of eliciting revenge. The female 'whetter', urging vengeance for a family member's death, is a trope found in the *Íslendingasögur*.[80] The whetting woman stands between two men or groups of men: the dead and those whom she identifies as potential avengers. Her speech act (the *hvǫt*) is inflected by her private emotion, by social convention (she must be closely related to the victim), and by strategic considerations: her auditors must recognize her right to act. She must thus maximize the effectiveness of her speech; this often involves theatrical staging and highly rhetorical language. The female whetter brings the private emotional world into the public domain; she ignores or circumvents ideologically sanctioned legal process, harnessing older social conventions to redress her loss and her family's honour. A number of *Íslendingasögur* are interested in exploring this tension between official ideology, older deep-rooted vengeance imperatives and the private, feminized domain of emotion, and in tracing its consequences.[81]

Sisters thus find themselves involved in procuring vengeance for their brothers. In the relatively late *Harðar saga*, a narrative which interestingly

---

[77] *Felix's Life*, ed. Colgrave, p. 169; Schulenburg, *Forgetful of their Sex*, pp. 301–2.
[78] See Griffiths, 'Siblings and the Sexes' (pp. 39–45) and chapter one, p. 30.
[79] How brothers respond to their sisters' deaths is discussed below.
[80] See J. Jochens, *Old Norse Images of Women* (Philadelphia, 1996), pp. 162–203, and offering a counter-argument, Jóhanna K. Friðriksdóttir, *Women in Old Norse Literature*, pp. 10, 24–45.
[81] Among these are *Njáls saga*, *Laxdœla saga*, *Gísla saga* and *Heiðarvíga saga* and the saga discussed below.

foregrounds sibling themes, a sister's vengeance for her brother forms the saga's climax.[82] Alienated from their father, their mother dead, Þorbjǫrg and Hǫrðr are unusually close for cross-sex siblings in medieval Iceland. Þorbjǫrg prophesies to her brother when he is twelve years old that he will die violently and she will obtain vengeance for him. Hǫrðr later becomes leader of a notorious band of outlaws. At odds with his brother-in-law Indriði, Þorbjǫrg's husband, he tries and fails to burn both Indriði and his sister in their house. Nevertheless, Þorbjǫrg rides to a meeting where an attack on the outlaws is planned and publicly declares that she will bring about the death of the man who kills her brother. Indriði is a member of the attacking party when Hǫrðr is killed, but shrinks from the fatal blow. Þorbjǫrg later draws a knife on him when they are in bed together; although she is easily disarmed, her violent and symbolic action is a prelude to talking terms.[83] Only when Indriði kills the unfortunate man who struck Hǫrðr his death-blow is Þorbjǫrg appeased. Reconciled with her husband, she gains public kudos for her determination to avenge her brother. The death of the immediate slayer is not sufficient for her, however. Together with Hǫrðr's widow, Þorbjǫrg continues to plot vengeance on more of the killers; only the death of Hǫrðr's older son in a further revenge attack terminates the women's campaign.

Þorbjǫrg cannot save her brother, but she achieves sufficient vengeance for his death to save her face and to make her speech acts – her prophecy to Hǫrðr, her public threat and her whetting of her husband – effective; indeed the *hvǫt* usually succeeds in its immediate aims in the sagas of Icelanders. In the *samtíðasaga* (contemporary saga) *Þórðar saga kakala*, another sister tries to elicit her husband's support for her brother in taking vengeance for the deaths of their father and brothers. Steinvǫr, Sighvatr Sturluson's daughter and Þórðr kakali's sister, tests out the extent of her personal influence and rhetorical power in her brother's cause.[84] When Þórðr comes to her home to solicit help for vengeance for their father and brothers on his enemies Gizurr and Kolbeinn ungi, Steinvǫr asserts that her husband Hálfdan will certainly render assistance, or else their marital *samþykki* (accord) will be at an end. Steinvǫr offers a direct challenge to Hálfdan's masculinity – if he is slow to respond, she will take up weapons and lead men herself, while handing over to her husband the keys to the dairy. The use of gender-specific topoi in Steinvǫr's challenge signals the proximity of her speech to the *hvǫt*, and to the suggestions of effeminacy that

---

[82] *Harðar saga ok Holmverja*, ed. Þorhallur Vilmundarson and Bjarni Vilhjálmsson, ÍF 13 (Reykjavík, 1991) explores the relationships of two cross-sib pairs in two generations of the same family; Torfi's over-involvement with his sister Signý, Hǫrðr's mother, and her objection to her marriage to a much older man sow the seeds of Hǫrðr's tragic destiny.

[83] Compare Þórdís in *Gísla saga*, discussed in chapter seven, who attacks and seriously wounds her brother's slayer; it is not clear whether she intended to kill him.

[84] Þórðr is the only son of Sturla to survive the Battle of Ǫrlygsstaðir, mentioned in the previous chapter (p. 60). *Þórðar saga kakala*, in *Sturlunga saga*, ed. Jón Jóhannesson *et al.*, II: p. 6.

are conventional in *níð* or legal insult.⁸⁵ Although she is driven by still-prevailing cultural beliefs about sibling solidarity, Steinvǫr's rhetoric is criticized as *málóð* (vehement) by the narrator and as *ákafa* (forcefulness) by her husband. From Hálfdan's perspective, Þórðr's chances of success look unpromising at this early stage of his campaign and he answers his wife directly rather than addressing his brother-in-law. He is elderly, he argues, unused to participation in politics, and unwilling to commit himself until he sees how much further support can be mustered. Steinvǫr's whetting, surprisingly, fails. Although the saga author deploys a trope effective in the *Íslendingasögur* genre, it is identified by the other actors in the scene, and by the author himself, as excessive. Steinvǫr's sisterly desire for vengeance for her family has no purchase on her prudent husband.

The saga-author's deliberate employment of the *hvǫt* reflects his understanding of generic distinctiveness; Steinvǫr's auditors within the saga recognize her aims, but reject her strategy. In the social conditions of the thirteenth century, the female-uttered *hvǫt* has lost whatever rhetorical effectiveness it might once have had. Although Steinvǫr claims the moral and emotional right to assist her brother in vengeance, whether Halfdan will render assistance to Þórðr is determined by political pragmatism. Subsequently Steinvǫr actively solicits support from one of Iceland's two bishops for her brother, but she fades from the narrative once Þórðr's campaign is properly under way.

In the Arthurian Post-Vulgate cycle, specifically in the *Queste del Saint Graal*, two courtly sisters seek vengeance for their brothers's deaths, with no greater success than Steinvǫr.⁸⁶ A comparable tension between family solidarity, the vengeance imperative, and official (here chivalric) ideology is explored through the sisters of two significant Arthurian knights, Perceval and Yvain of Cenel (one of the many doubles of Arthur's nephew Yvain). Both women go to great lengths to prosecute vengeance on their common enemy, Gauvain. After Gauvain and his brothers have killed all Perceval's brothers, the sons of Pellinor, in vengeance for Pellinor's slaying of their father Lot of Orkney, Perceval's (unnamed) sister sets up an elaborate *aventure-piège* (adventure-trap) at a tower on an island.⁸⁷ The first knight to arrive seeking adventure is sworn to remain and to kill all comers without mercy until such time as he himself is overcome and replaced by the victor. When the custom forces him to fight against Gauvain's brother Gaheriet, Perceval persuasively argues that the earlier oath of fictive brotherhood sworn by the two knights on joining the Round Table invalidates the oath to fight to the death given by Gaheriet to Perceval's sister. The two knights amicably leave the island together.⁸⁸ Later Gauvain faces Lancelot's half-brother, Hector, the

---

[85] See Jóhanna K. Friðriksdóttir, *Women in Old Norse Literature*, pp. 18–19.

[86] *La version Post-Vulgate de la* Queste del Saint Graal *et de la* Mort Artu: *Troisième partie du Roman du Graal*, ed. F. Bogdanow, 4 vols (Paris, 1991–2000); *L-G*, IV and V.

[87] F. Wolfzettel, 'Le *Roman d'Erec* en prose du XIIIe siècle: un anti-*Erec et Enide*?', in *The Legacy of Chrétien de Troyes*, ed. N. J. Lacy, D. Kelly and K. Busby, 2 vols (Amsterdam, 1988), II: 215–28 (p. 224).

[88] *La Folie Lancelot: A Hitherto Unidentifed Portion of the Suite de Merlin Contained in MSS B. N. fr. 112 and 12599*, ed. F. Bogdanow, Beihefte zur Zeitschrift für romanische

current champion, and he too persuades him to prioritize the Round Table oath over the custom of the castle. The vengeance of Perceval's sister is frustrated, though Gauvain leaves the island with her curses ringing in his ears.[89]

The next time Perceval's sister appears in the text she has reverted to the quasi-saintly role she plays in the Vulgate *Queste*; having abandoned her family-oriented vengefulness she willingly sacrifices her life to heal the Leprous Lady.[90] Her ethical re-alignment marks a move away from the opposition between private revenge and public punishment exacted by Arthur on knights who contravene the Round Table's code. At first Perceval's sister seizes agency in prosecuting her vengeance; her multiple sibling losses provoke her into a kind of hysteria. In the hope of destroying Gauvain's lineage, and through the custom of killing all comers, the sister tries to annihilate her fraternal loss, but this scheme is futile in the face of the Round Table's homosocial oaths.[91] Fictive brotherhood proves stronger than the sister's rage, and she finds consolation at last in Christian acceptance of suffering and self-sacrifice. This textual trajectory brings Perceval's sister to an understanding of a still higher law: the Christian ethic which the Grail Quest seeks to promote as a challenge to the corrupt and problematic chivalry practised by Arthur's most-highly regarded knights in this Cycle.

Later in the Post-Vulgate *Queste*, Yvain of Cenel meets a dishonourable death – being burned alive – when Lamorat's kindred avenge his death on the young knight, simply because of his Round Table membership. This vengeance should by rights have been visited on Gauvain, Lamorat's murderer, but he prudently retreats when he reads the threat to Round Table knights posted at the gate of the castle where Yvain is slain.[92] When Yvain's sister learns how ignobly her brother died, she too swears vengeance on Gauvain: 'Je n'avray ja mais joye devant que j'en soye vengee et que je l'aie fait morir de male mort' ('I'll never be happy until I'm avenged and make him die a hard death').[93] The girl enlists the help of Sir Patrides, whom Gauvain promptly kills, and then of King Bademagu. Once again the Round Table's powerful ideology of brotherhood outweighs the imperative for private revenge: Bademagu will not disregard his oath by killing Gauvain.[94] Later, Yvain's sister denounces Gauvain to his uncle at Camelot and Arthur responds forcefully, threatening Gauvain with expulsion from the Round Table. Yet, despite the mounting death-toll of good knights at Gauvain's hands in the course of the Post-Vulgate Grail Quest, Arthur cannot or will not act against his nephew.[95]

Sibling solidarity encourages Yvain's sister to regard herself as an agent of

---

Philologie 109 (Tübingen, 1965), p. 99; *L-G*, V: 39.
[89] *La Folie*, ed. Bogdanow, pp. 123–31; *L-G*, V: 38–101.
[90] *Version Post-Vulgate*, ed. Bogdanow, III: 65–75; *L-G*, V: 333–9.
[91] On hysteria as an effect of sibling trauma, see Mitchell, *Mad Men and Medusas*.
[92] *Version Post-Vulgate*, ed. Bogdanow, II: 172–96; *L-G*, V: 347–52.
[93] Ibid., I: 178, *L-G*, V: 349.
[94] Ibid., II: 175–96; *L-G*, V: 349–52 (p. 194), *L-G*, V: 352.
[95] Ibid., II: 462; *L-G*, V: 312.

vengeance for her brother's death. The text, in contrast, positions her as a hysteric as defined by Juliet Mitchell: a woman who has over-invested in a now-disrupted sibling relationship.[96] She is confined to a marginalized position that allows Arthur to ignore her; her reappearances with a succession of avengers and her reiterated verbal denunciations of Gauvain demonstrate the sister's strongly textual function: insistently to call attention to the damaged ideal of chivalry embodied by the king's nephew in the Post-Vulgate *Queste*'s bleak version of the Arthurian world.[97] Much later in the narrative, Yvain's sister publicly shames Gauvain as he is denied entry to the Grail Castle.[98] Calling out from within the Castle, where she appears to be resident, she crows that Perceval will succeed in the Quest where Gauvain has failed. Like Perceval's sister, this sister too has had to abandon her quest for revenge, recognizing that Arthur and his compromised Round Table will not enforce ethical standards on the king's nephew, and that the court's lost values cannot be recuperated by the Quest. The trajectories of both sisters emphasize, in Judith Butler's phrase, 'how kinship secures the conditions of intelligibility by which life becomes livable, by which life also becomes condemned and foreclosed'.[99] These sisters only have textual existence because of their brothers' chivalric activities, but their search for recognition of their right to revenge – or to justice – is negated by the unreformable nature of the Arthurian court. Only by abandoning the imperative for revenge for their brothers can the two sisters find peace. Perceval's sister sacrifices herself for an unworthy object in the Leprous Lady, but in so doing, she transforms herself into a type of Christ. Yvain's sister learns to leave vengeance to God, since earthly institutions fail her. Becoming part of a sacred sisterhood within Corbenic, she renounces her place in the disintegrating chivalric world. Mourning becomes a private affair; though sisterly grief is respected, the ethic of vengeance which these sisters represent cannot reform the chivalric system as an institution. Although bonds of fictive brotherhood are privileged over blood-ties when sisters demand justice, Round Table membership does not save knights from death at the hands of their fellow knights. Arthur's failure to regulate his family's obsession with honour compromises the ethics of the Round Table in this Cycle, and, as suggested in the previous chapter, is instrumental in the downfall of Camelot. This critique of the chivalric ethos, symbolized by the sister's single-minded, but finally futile, quest for justice for her brother, is typical of the larger concerns of the Post-Vulgate Cycle. Composed by clerics who themselves stood outside the institution they wrote about, the Cycle probes the gulf between Christian morality, the law of the family and the corrupt court over which Arthur presides; the authors harness the fantasy that the brother must be avenged, even

---

[96] Mitchell, *Mad Men and Medusas*, p. 221.
[97] The role of 'brother's keeper', typical of the older sister as caretaker and substitute mother, can indeed, as Bank and Kahn observe, be a thankless one: *The Sibling Bond*, pp. 125–34.
[98] *Post-Vulgate Queste*, ed. Bogdanow, III: 257; *L-G*, V: 368.
[99] J. Butler, *Antigone's Claim: Kinship between Life and Death* (New York, 2000), p. 23.

by a sister if no male agent is available, to explore the failure of both family-oriented ethics and courtly notions of honour. In sagas the sister's demand for vengeance will only succeed if larger social interests are served by its execution; in the romances, her private, emotion-driven desire for revenge is depicted as excessive, hysterical, impossible. A brother's vengeance for his brother within the same saga and romance genres is, by contrast, expected, comprehensible and very often successful. Responses to the redefinition of vengeance effected by social change – the extension of civil law and the centralizing authority of the king – are imaginatively explored in both genres, and the sibling inflection of the issue teases out its ethical dimensions in unpredictable ways.

Policing the Sister

One consequence of the power asymmetry between brothers and sisters is that brothers are expected to take responsibility for their sisters' conduct. Thus they are depicted compelling their sisters to conform to social norms, or defending their honour – usually defined in sexual terms. Ballads again present extreme cases. In 'Proud Lady Margaret' (Child Ballad 47), a woman subjects her suitors to a riddle competition and executes all who cannot answer.[100] Finally a man appears who is as wise in riddling as she, and he answers her questions successfully. Margaret is willing to give herself to the victor, but he reveals himself to be her brother, returned from the grave to tell her to abandon her pride in her cleverness and her social status. Brother Willie's intervention leaves Margaret weeping, perhaps in penitence. The brother's obligation to oversee his sister's behaviour and make clear to her the consequence of her sinfulness, even beyond death, links this ballad with a common exemplum theme.[101] Instead of praying the sister out of purgatory, this brother returns from there in person in order to save his sister's soul. Moreover, Brother Willie's spectral impersonation of a suitor evokes the threat of brother–sister incest, a strong ballad preoccupation.[102] Margaret's apparent unwillingness to accept a normal exogamic marriage calls up its dangerous opposite: a transgressive union which threatens to breach the crucial boundaries between brother and sister, and between the living and dead. Willie's corrective influence recalls Margaret to proper acceptance of social norms as well as to spiritual reform.

In romance, brothers are sometimes impelled to fight for their sister's honour against besieging knights or predatory giants, a role in which they frequently fail. In Chrétien de Troyes's *Le Chevalier au Lion*, Gauvain's nephews are pitted against a giant who threatens to outrage their sister and they cannot defeat their

---

[100] *Ballads*, ed. Child, I: 425–31.
[101] Typical might be *Index exemplorum*, ed. Tubach, p. 337, no. 4425. An abbot sees his dead sister tormented by dragons because of her neglect of her mother. After masses are said for her, she reappears to tell him that she is now saved.
[102] See chapter six.

enemy. Only a superlative outsider knight, in this case Yvain (and his lion), can remove the threat. Yvain's married status precludes him from receiving Gauvain's niece as his prize, but in other romances the sister's peril provides an opportunity for her rescue by a hero from outside the family, and permits her to find a superior husband. The frequency of this romance motif explains Gringamour's failure to defend Lyonors in the 'Tale of Sir Gareth', discussed above (p. 80). A sister's unwanted suitor is better repelled by a desirable future husband than by the brother whom the sister cannot wed; what appear to be fraternal deficiency in fact operates to reinforce the exogamic marriage norm.

In the fourteenth-century English poem *The Jeaste of Syr Gawain*, based on an episode in one of the *Continuations of Perceval*, Gawain is attacked first by the father, then by each of the brothers of the girl he has seduced.[103] The maiden freely yielded herself to Gawain, that inveterate ladies' man, and her brothers are serially shamed and defeated. Although Gawain overcomes each opponent in turn, his fight with the final brother, Brandles, ends inconclusively because darkness is falling. Furious Brandles beats his sister black and blue and the poem concludes bleakly for the girl: she wanders away into the forest, never to see her family again. In the early-thirteenth-century *Continuation*, the seduction of Bran de Lis's sister took place some years before the confrontation between Gauvain and her brother. Here the battle concludes when the lady intervenes, presenting her fine son Ginglain (elsewhere the *Bel Inconnu* or 'Fair Unknown') to his father and maternal uncle, and the men are reconciled.[104] The *Jeaste* lacks such a reconciliation-coda and thus figures a trial of strength between Gawain and the successive challengers, one which regulates the men's relative knightly status.[105] The unfortunate sister, like many other Arthurian damsels, functions largely as the pretext for the fight. As he incites each brother to attack Gawain, her outraged father observes that a substantial wrong has been done: property rights in their daughter and sister have been irretrievably damaged and a lack of respect shown to them.[106] In the earlier text, the sister's dishonour is effaced by her son's heroic nature and the seducer's willing recognition of the splendid young man he has fathered; the family is appeased by its public connection to the prestigious Gauvain. In the later poem, originating in a more popular oral context, the sister's disgrace cannot be undone. Whether or not she gives birth to Gawain's bastard, her family has definitively expelled her.

So-called 'honour'-killings usually result either in the death of the suitor or the death of the brother in medieval literature. The sister escapes with her life, since to kill a woman is regarded as even more shameful than enduring

---

[103] 'The Jeaste of Sir Gawain', in *Sir Gawain: Eleven Romances and Tales*, ed. Thomas Hahn (Kalamazoo, 1995).

[104] See M. Aurell, 'Rompre la concorde familiale: typologie, imaginaire, questionnements', in *La parenté*, ed. Aurell, pp. 9–59 (p. 39).

[105] Hahn, *Introduction*. http://www.lib.rochester.edu/camelot/teams/jeastint.htm

[106] Compare Weisner, 'Comparing Sibling Relationships across Cultures'; see also Cicirelli, 'Sibling Relationships in Cross-Cultural Perspective'.

her dishonour.[107] Women are seldom murdered in medieval romance or saga (they tend to die spontaneously of grief when tragedy strikes), and thus their male kin are rarely required to avenge them. In 'Young Benjie' (Child Ballad 86), Benjie murders his lover Marjory after a lover's quarrel; Marjory's three brothers find the corpse and watch over it, hoping for Marjory to revive and reveal the culprit.[108] When Marjory's ghost identifies Benjie, the brothers are ready to take revenge:

> Sall we Young Benjie head, sister?
> Sall we Young Benjie hang?
> Or sall we pike out his twa gray een,
> And punish him ere he gang?[109]

Their sister's ghost is content with having the killer blinded; she requires her brothers to maintain Benjie about the house so that every seven years he can be taken to the stream where he drowned his lover and prompted to rehearse his repentance for the murder. Fraternal protectiveness of the sister extends not only to avenging her on her killer, but also to taking account of her post-mortem wishes about the nature and extent of that vengeance.

A significant exception to the rule that brothers rarely avenge sisters is the case of Svanhildr, whose history is related in a number of Old Norse and Latin sources.[110] Svanhildr is to marry Jǫrmunrekkr, king of the Goths, but she becomes compromised by a relationship with his son Randvér and Jǫrmunrekkr executes both wife and son. Hence Svanhildr's mother Guðrún Gjúkadóttir dispatches her remaining sons, borne to her third husband Ionákr, to avenge their half-sister.[111] The brothers Hamðir and Sǫrli regard their mission as futile, observing that their mother will now lose all three of her children: 'þú erfi at ǫll oss drykkir / at Svanhildi ok sono þína' ('you may drink the funeral-ale for us all, for Svanhildr and for your sons').[112] Well aware of the strength of numbers arrayed against them, the brothers frame their arguments against attacking their brother-in-law by recalling past vengeance murders in the family; underlying their reluctance is an implicit assumption that sisters do not need to be avenged as brothers so unequivocally do. Guðrún's insistence on revenge for the daughter whom she bore to her first and best-loved husband, Sigurðr, in preference to the survival

---

[107] Saints' lives are an obvious exception, though here female martyrdom is largely a feature of narratives set in a pre-medieval period.
[108] *Ballads*, ed. Child, II: 281–3.
[109] Ibid., 86A, v. 19.
[110] In the *Poetic Edda*, in the prose introduction to the poem *Guðrúnarhvǫt*, the poem itself and in *Hamðismál*; see *The Poetic Edda: Volume I, Heroic Poems*, ed. U. Dronke (Oxford, 1969). It is reprised in brisk summary in Snorri Sturluson, *Edda: Skáldskaparmál: Introduction, Text and Notes*, ed. A. Faulkes (London, 1998), and at somewhat more length in *Vǫlsunga saga: The Saga of the Vǫlsungs*, ed. and trans. R. G. Finch (London, 1965), as well as in Saxo, *GD* VIII.
[111] Guðrún's earlier history is discussed in chapter seven.
[112] *Guðrúnarhvǫt*, v. 8, in *Poetic Edda*, ed. Dronke, p. 148.

of her sons, enrages the young men.[113]

As the furious brothers ride off to fulfil Guðrún's will, they meet their half-brother Erpr, whose riddling offer of aid further provokes them, and they strike him down. Erpr deploys the important conceptual metaphor of the members of a kindred as limbs of the body: siblings come in pairs like hands and feet. His offer to help 'sem fótr ǫðrum' ('as one foot does the other') is violently rejected by his uncomprehending half-brothers who retort: 'Hvat megi fótr fœti veita / né holdgróin hǫnd annarri?' ('How can a foot help a foot / or a hand grown from flesh help a hand?')[114] The brothers achieve partial success in maiming Jǫrmunrekkr because they are invulnerable to weapons and they cut off their brother-in-law's hands and feet. But their delay in striking off the head enables Jǫrmunrekkr to exhort his men to stone his assailants. As they die, Hamðir and Sǫrli realize that, had he lived, Erpr the third brother would have beheaded the victim in a timely way. Failing to grasp the real implications of Erpr's invocation of the limb metaphor, Hamðir and Sǫrli negate the strength of the (half)-fraternal bond by their murder and they die only because they rejected his aid. The obligations of the bond with their half-sister are, in contrast, an issue which the poem offers up for discussion.[115] Half-brothers, as seen in chapter two, must be avenged in heroic literature; Svanhildr's gender rather than her half-sibling status inflects the brothers' view of their sibling bond. In contrast to the sisters of the Post-Vulgate *Queste* who insist in vain on vengeance for their murdered brothers, Hamðir and Sǫrli make a pragmatic objection to sacrificing their lives to the vengeance imperative for their older half-sister; they thus confirm the asymmetry in cross-sex sibling emotional priorities noted by Irigaray.[116]

Sibling Old Age

Brother–sister relations are often plunged into crisis through conflict with the sister's husband or sexual partner.[117] Yet, when marriages are over and the search for new sexual partners abandoned, the mature brother and sister can achieve an uncomplicated, deeply loving stage in their relationship.[118] Sibling

---

[113] See Jochens, *Old Norse Images of Women*, p. 147; David Clark, 'Undermining and En-gendering Vengeance: Distancing and Anti-Feminism in the Poetic Edda', *Scandinavian Studies* 77 (2005), 173–200 (p. 179), and C. Larrington, '"I have long desired to cure you of old age": Sibling Drama in the Later Heroic Poems of the Edda', in *Revisiting the Poetic Edda: Essays on Old Norse Heroic Legend*, ed. P. Acker and C. Larrington (New York and London, 2013), 140–56.

[114] *Hamðismál* v. 13.3–4 in *Edda*, ed. Dronke. See also chapter four, pp. 113–15.

[115] See C. Larrington, 'Stjúpmœðrasögur and Sigurðr's Daughters', *in Á austrvega. Saga and East Scandinavia. Preprint Papers of The 14th International Saga Conference*, Uppsala, 9–15 August 2009, ed. A. Ney, H. Williams and F. Charpentier Ljungqvist, 2 vols (Gävle, 2009), II: 568–75; and Larrington, '"I have long desired', pp. 151–3.

[116] See n. 68 above.

[117] See chapter seven.

[118] See C. Larrington, *King Arthur's Enchantresses: Morgan and her Sisters in Arthurian*

rivalry dissipates with age; elderly, widowed siblings sometimes set up home together, finding a renewed closeness in reminiscing about their shared past and acting as one another's memory-keeper.[119] One constant in the story of King Arthur, from the mid-twelfth century onwards, is the appearance of his sister Morgan le Fay after his final battle. In the earliest source (in which she is not yet his sister, Geoffrey of Monmouth's *Vita Merlini, c.* 1150), Arthur is brought to Morgen in her island home and she is optimistic that she can heal him of his mortal wounds. However, he remains with her in the Fortunate Isles and does not return to Britain. In some French *chansons de geste*, such as *La Bataille Loquifer*, and the late *Le Bâtard de Bouillon* (c. 1350), Arthur and Morgan, by now sister and brother, are depicted as living together in Avalon, where they preside over chivalric adventures undertaken by visiting knights. Their sibling relations are renewed in a kind of second childhood from which age, disease, sexuality and death are excluded. Morgan's former erotic desires are sublimated into wisdom and the nurturing of visiting heroes, while Arthur puts aside politics and dynastic concerns for patronage and philosophizing.

These Mediterranean reflexes of the idealized sibling bond, in which sexual desire and worldly ambition are transformed into a quietly loving relationship, are foreshadowed in the story of Merlin and his sister in the *Vita Merlini*.[120] After Ganieda is widowed, she joins her brother, who has recovered from his earlier madness, in his forest retreat. Here she too gains the gift of prophecy.[121] Brother and sister dwell together far away from courts and temporal power in their simple, harmonious, woodland home, yet they still channel a riddling understanding of the world they have renounced through their prophetic insight. When spouses are dead and children far away, brothers and sisters, like Merlin and Ganieda, willingly spend time together, reinterpreting their shared past experiences to provide crucial emotional support for one another.[122]

Conclusion

'Loyalty is a major theme or dimension of sibling relationships', as Bank and Kahn observe.[123] Medieval authors understood this characterization as central:

Tradition (London, 2006), pp. 45–50.
[119] See Goetting, 'Developmental Tasks', p. 710 and Allen, 'Sibling Solidarity', p. 180. Cf. Cicirelli, 'Feelings of Attachment'.
[120] See Geoffrey of Monmouth, *Vita Merlini / Life of Merlin*, ed. and trans. Basil Clarke (Cardiff, 1973), and A. O. H. Jarman, 'The Merlin Legend and the Tradition of Welsh Prophecy', in *The Arthur of the Welsh*, ed. R. Bromwich, A. O. H. Jarman and B. F. Roberts (Cardiff, 1991), pp. 117–45 (pp. 132–6).
[121] *Vita Merlini*, ed. Clarke, pp. 130–1, line 1468.
[122] See Cicirelli, 'Feelings of Attachment', and Cicirelli, *Sibling Relationships*, pp. 115–22.
[123] See Bank and Kahn, 'Intense Sibling Loyalties', p. 251.

the siblings discussed in this chapter express their love and loyalty through self-sacrifice and nurturing. Caring *for* the sibling is largely a female role; although brothers care *about* their sisters, this care is not normally displayed in tenderness. Yet brothers do not normally employ direct violence against their sisters, and they often value their advice. Narratives about sisters interacting lovingly with one another are notably sparser than brother–sister stories, but the plentiful tales of sisterly rivalry discussed in chapter five are counterbalanced by this chapter's exploration of sisterly solidarity and renunciation. Nor is the obligation of vengeance for a dead sibling restricted to those narratives of fraternal revenge discussed in chapter two. A sister's loss of a brother or a brother's loss of a sister is keenly felt and it can unleash a violence which, though usually conforming to prevailing social norms, can perpetuate feud within and between families. Nevertheless, the obligation to avenge a sister's death is less pressing than the imperative for vengeance for a brother.

The analysis of sisters and cross-sex sibling pairs in this chapter confirms the intuition that sisters are, on some level, regarded as interchangeable with one another, at least until they are married. Sisters are less individualized than brothers in their roles, both within the family, and often when viewed from the perspective of outsiders such as possible sexual or marriage partners. The differentiation process so crucial to ordering fraternal relations does not occur between sisters, for each girl anticipates a similar destiny for herself: to be exchanged in marriage. Complementarity is thus less easily envisaged and not noticeably achieved: it is marriage, not distinctive identity development, which effects separation between sisters and reduces the potential for conflict. In romance and epic the family vengeance ethic is powerfully interrogated: can and should a sister succeed in avenging a brother, unique and irreplaceable as he is? In saints' lives, by contrast, the sister can recuperate the lost brother through memorialization and, in Pega's case, by overseeing his emerging cult. That a sister's killing should be equated with a brother's, as Guðrún argues of Svanhildr's murder, shocks and enrages Svanhildr's half-brothers. When their mother employs the rhetoric normally used to urge revenge for a male killing, she successfully provokes her sons to action, but ordinarily a sister's life does not matter so much.

The birth of the sibling teaches the child that seriality is in the order of things, observes Mitchell.[124] The child's 'unique grandiose self' is put at risk by the arrival of the sibling, but as it learns to negotiate that trauma, it makes the transition 'between murder versus being annihilated on the one hand, and, on the other hand, tolerance of self and other, self-esteem and respect for the other'.[125] Same-sex and cross-sex siblings come to make that transition, to love, respect and to nurture the other, though the power asymmetries between genders in medieval societies result in different styles in expression of sibling love and loyalty. Bank and Kahn confirm that these positive emotions 'can coexist with

---

[124] See Mitchell, *Siblings*, pp. 43–4 on 'the law of the mother'.
[125] Ibid., p. 215.

rivalry, conflict, and competition'; when the sibling trauma is not managed, 'murder [and] being annihilated' emerge as a real threat in adults siblings' interactions with one another.[126] The next chapter will trace how, beginning with the first murder which is also the first fratricide, different kinds of fraternal conflict are at the centre of some of the most compelling medieval narratives.

---

[126] Bank and Kahn, 'Intense Sibling Loyalties', p. 251

4

'Næs þæt andæges nið':[1] Fraternal Hatreds

Introduction

For medieval Christians, human history began with a fraternal killing.[2] After Cain 'slog his broðor swæsne' ('struck his dear brother'), and the earth swallowed Abel's blood, 'bealoblonden niþ' ('hostility mixed with evil'), as the Old English *Exeter Maxims* note, became widespread amongst mankind.[3] Fratricide and the impulses which underlie it can never be eliminated, for fear of replacement by the brother, that one who is the same as you, that one who can take your place, is deeply embedded in the psyche. 'Because each sibling evokes the danger of the other's annihilation, siblings are going to want to kill each other. This murderousness is forbidden, and must be transmuted to aggressive play and healthy rivalry', suggests Juliet Mitchell.[4] Where sibling trauma – the fear of substitution or of failing to differentiate – is successfully processed, love, respect, self-esteem and strong loyalties result. On a social level, as well as in the individual psyche, repeated cultural work is required to uncover and resolve the dark urge to destroy the sibling. The brother comes to be perceived as a 'monstrous double' in Girard's terms: one whose existence menaces his brother, but also one who threatens larger social structures, whose desires distort and threaten the cultural order.[5] Mythology perpetually returns to the fratricidal theme; foundation tales recognize how the sacrifice of the brother inaugurates the beginning of a new kind of order. As chapter two's discussion of accidental fratricide showed, brother-killing is a recurrent locus of horror that signifies powerfully in medieval narrative. Brothers slay one another over inheritances, kingdoms and women. Often, however, the trigger for the killing is a comparatively trivial matter, but one which nevertheless strikes to the heart of fraternal fears of displacement and loss of identity. 'Pathologies of the borderline' – apparently minor infringements of previously negotiated distinctions – provoke a sibling fury that astonishes by its violence.[6]

---

[1] 'That was no one-day feud', *Maxims I c*, line 59b, in *Poems of Wisdom and Learning in Old English*, ed. T. A. Shippey (Cambridge, 1976), p. 72.
[2] Genesis 4. 1–16.
[3] *Maxims I c*, line 62a, ed. Shippey, p. 74.
[4] Mitchell, *Siblings*, p. 10.
[5] R. Girard, *Violence and the Sacred*, trans. P. Gregory (London, 2005), pp. 152–78.
[6] Mitchell, *Siblings*, p. 31.

Cain and Abel, and their Reflexes

The story of Cain and Abel, the ur-feud for Old English poets, resonates through the medieval imagination. Cain's quarrel with Abel challenges the premise that brothers prosper in adult life when they choose separate paths: when they establish differentiation and agree to minimize the arena for competition and direct comparison. For these brothers *are* strongly differentiated: Cain, the elder, is an arable farmer, 'a tiller of the ground', and Abel is 'a keeper of sheep'. But when the time of offering came, God 'had respect unto Abel', but 'unto Cain and to his offering he had not respect'.[7] Why not? Only God knows, and so, as Ricardo Quinones observes, 'The *arbitrariness of preference* thus compounds the tragedy of differentiation and brings home the fact of division in a way that is particular to the Cain–Abel theme'.[8]

God the Father promised authority ('thou shalt rule over him') to the older sibling, but then favoured Abel's 'firstlings of his flock' over Cain's 'fruit of the ground'. Cain's response to the provocation is coldly premeditated: 'it came to pass that Cain rose up against Abel his brother, and slew him'.[9] Competition between siblings for parental favour may have an evolutionary origin, 'looking beyond actual family provision to possible survival conditions, when competition will be a life-or-death matter'; getting more food, more wealth, more love than one's sibling seems crucial to survival.[10] Such primitive competitive instincts must be controlled and repressed by the eldest brother if he is indeed to wield authority over the rest of the cohort; here Cain signally fails.

Late-medieval English mystery plays expand on the biblical outline of the brothers' interaction, fleshing out Cain's murderous rage and Abel's provoking humility. The cycle dramatists model Abel in line with traditional biblical exegesis as a type of Christ, and present Cain, who often compounds his sin with blasphemy and cursing, as a contemporary warning against anger and pride. The playwrights also sought explanations for God's arbitrariness. The sacrifice which differentiates the brothers is thus often equated with tithing by the plays' clerical authors: since Cain fails to tithe properly, his sacrifice is unacceptable.[11] In the fifteenth-century Chester play of Cain and Abel, he grumpily declares that although he has plenty of corn, he will choose stalks from which the grain has fallen or which have been part-eaten by animals: 'God, thou gettest noe other of mee, / be thou never so gryme'.[12] Abel, in contrast, offers 'the best

---

[7] Genesis 4. 4–5.
[8] R. Quinones, *The Changes of Cain* (Princeton, 1991), p. 9; Quinones's italics.
[9] Genesis 4. 8.
[10] Citation from Apter, *Sister Knot*, p. 139. See further *Sister Knot*, pp. 137–44 for a broadly evolutionary interpretation of sibling rivalry, following D. Mock, *More than Kin and Less than Kind* (Cambridge MA, 2004); cf. F. J. Sulloway, *Born to Rebel* (London, 1998).
[11] See for example G. G. Coulton, *The Medieval Village* (Cambridge, 1925, repr. 1989), pp. 279–306.
[12] *The Chester Mystery Cycle*, ed. R. M. Lumiansky and D. Mills, 2 vols, EETS ss 3.

beaste ... of all my flocke with harte free'.[13] God's promise that Abel will obey his elder is fulfilled; he walks meekly aside with his brother when asked to do so and is promptly killed. When God challenges Cain about the murder he is defiant: 'I cannot tell / of my brother. Wottys thou not well / that I of him had noe keepinge?' Cursed by God and sentenced to exile, Cain swiftly repents of his sin and, in an added scene, he takes a touching farewell of his parents.[14]

The Chester cycle offers a relatively orthodox treatment. The Towneley cycle playwright, in contrast, presents a Cain who is already a type of rage from the moment he appears on stage. Shouting and blustering, at his ploughboy, his oxen and his placatory brother, Cain responds to Abel's gentle greeting with obscenities, 'Com kis myne ars, me list not ban / ... Thou should haue bide til thou were cald'.[15] Abel's reminder that it is time to tithe is met with wisecracks – Cain owes God nothing, he never borrowed so much as a farthing from him – and Abel has to nag and chivvy him into making the sacrifice. Cain's initial tactic after the murder is to hide from God in a hole; when asked where his brother is, he blurts out the truth: 'I trow at hell ... or somwhere fallen on slepyng'.[16] His fury is not assuaged by the murder and he meets God's curse with defiance. Forcing his boy falsely to proclaim a pardon for him, Cain wanders off stage, visibly enacting the sin of despair by refusing to show remorse or to ask forgiveness.

These two mystery plays take strikingly different approaches to Cain's and Abel's fraternality. Revelling in dramatic characterization, showing Cain's irascible personality and Abel's piously irritating obedience to divinely ordained rules, the Towneley playwright understands how brothers can simply get on one another's nerves until one of them snaps. Foregrounding Christian teaching, the Chester cycle makes Abel a clear type of Christ and shows his brother's immediate repentance, foreshadowing the remorse of Judas. Nevertheless, Cain's sin cannot be forgiven for God's curse is upon him to the seventh generation. The Chester play depicts Cain as already guilty because of his grudging attitude to tithing – an attitude no doubt shared by many in the play's audience – and God's troubling favouritism is thus explained away. The sibling relationship, centre-stage in Towneley, is subordinated here to the quasi-paternal relationship with a God recast as a just, rather than an alarmingly capricious, father.

For Old English poets, Cain's monstrous legacy, as 'an accursed outcast and criminal, one for whom no recuperation is possible', was imaginatively productive; his history provided an aetiology for the intractable problem of feud.[17] In *Beowulf*, Cain's lineage in the shape of Grendel and his mother continue to feud against the other descendants of Adam, killing Hrothgar's thanes and consuming their bodies. Brother-slaying is, however, displaced in the poem

(Oxford, 1974, 1986), I: lines 535–6.
[13] Ibid., I: lines 557–8.
[14] Ibid., I: lines 618–20; 631–2.
[15] 'Cain and Abel' in *The Towneley Plays*, ed. M. Stevens and A. C. Cawley, 2 vols, EETS ss 13–14 (Oxford, 1994), I: lines 57–61.
[16] Ibid., I: lines 345–8.
[17] Quinones, *Changes of Cain*, p. 40.

away from the domain of the monstrous and is projected back into the human world; *Beowulf* is, as Tom Hill has recently suggested, thematically engaged with fratricide.[18] Beowulf silences Unferð when he concludes his account of his marine exploits with the sharp accusation that Unferð has performed no such feats. On the contrary:

> ðu þinum broðrum   to banan wurde,
> heafodmægum;   þæs þu in helle scealt
> werhðo dreogan

('you became the killer of your brothers, your close kinsmen; for this you will suffer damnation in hell').[19]

The circumstances of Unferð's crime against his brothers are unknown to us, although an Anglo-Saxon audience might have been familiar with his history.[20] His name occurs nowhere else in Germanic legend, and although some scholars have speculated that the brother-slaying must have been accidental, or a sin of omission, or explicable in terms of tribal politics, Beowulf's deployment of this terrible accusation goes unchallenged.[21] That an apparent fratricide should occupy an honourable place in Hrothgar's retinue, rather than wandering, like Cain, in exile, calls into question the ethics of the Danish court; as Ben Reinhard argues, the references to Unferð in Heorot intimate an 'atmosphere rife with suggestions of feud and fratricide'.[22]

Anglo-Saxon individuals and their kings repeatedly sought to regulate blood-feud and to develop legal processes for peace-making, whether in the eighth century when *Beowulf* may have been composed, or the eleventh century when it was written down.[23] Tribal feuding might range brothers on different sides: sworn loyalty to one's lord overrode blood-ties. Epitomized in the Hildebrand-tradition (examined in chapter two), this dilemma may perhaps explain Unferð's apparent culpability. Fratricide sharply problematizes the reciprocal structures of feud, occurring as it does within the micro-community of the family. Beowulf's

---

[18] T. D. Hill, 'Hæðcyn, Herebeald, and Archery's Laws: *Beowulf* and the *Leges Henrici Primi*', *Medium Ævum* 81.2 (2012), 210–21.

[19] *Klaeber's Beowulf and the Fight at Finnesburh*, ed. R. D. Fulk, R. Bjork and J. D. Niles (Toronto, 2008), lines 587–9. 'helle' ought perhaps to be emended to 'healle', see A. Orchard, *A Critical Companion to* Beowulf (Cambridge, 2003), pp. 252–3, and references there.

[20] C. Y. Rich, in 'Unferth and Cain's Envy', *South Central Bulletin* 33 (1973), 211–13, perceptively argues that Unferth's attack on Beowulf is motivated by Cain's besetting sin in the Old English *Genesis*, envy (*invidia*; *æfsta*).

[21] Summarized by S. Gwara, *Heroic Identity in the World of Beowulf* (Leiden and Boston, 2008), pp. 127–9, and see now B. Reinhard, 'Grendel and the Penitentials', *English Studies* 94.4 (2013), 371–85, particularly pp. 381–3.

[22] Reinhard, 'Grendel', p. 383.

[23] See P. Hyams, 'Feud and the State in Late Anglo-Saxon England', *Journal of British Studies* 40 (2001), 1–43, especially pp. 5–6, and R. Fletcher, *Bloodfeud: Murder and Revenge in Anglo-Saxon England* (Oxford, 2004).

own uncle had killed his brother during an archery contest, a killing consistently interpreted by the poem and by critics as accidental. Nevertheless, in a number of medieval narratives where royal succession is at stake, as in the tale of Tydeus discussed below, mishaps with bows and arrows eliminate rivals in such a way that intention cannot be proved. These 'accidental' deaths cannot be expiated. Hreðel cannot execute vengeance on his surviving son, nor is the killer condemned to exile; he is not disqualified from succeeding to the throne after his broken-hearted father's death. That these two brothers are named Herebeald (the victim) and Hæðcyn (the slayer) and that the weapon is a stray missile suggestively connects the episode to the death of the god Baldr (cf. *–beald*) in Norse myth, slain by his blind brother Hǫðr (cf. *Hæð-*) through the machinations of the ambiguous figure of Loki.[24]

The Baldr-legend is recounted in detail in Snorri Sturluson's early-thirteenth-century *Prose Edda*, and alluded to in the eddic poem *Vǫluspá* (dating from around 1000).[25] In Snorri's account, when Loki discovers that the mistletoe was omitted from the catalogue of material objects that had sworn never to harm Baldr, he fashions a dart from the tender young plant. Placing it in Hǫðr's hands, he encourages the blind god to participate in the game which the other gods are playing. The missiles that they hurl at Baldr bounce harmlessly off him – but the mistletoe-dart strikes Baldr dead, his loss one of the portents of *ragna rǫk*, the doom of all the gods.[26] Hǫðr does not intend the death of his brother: as in the case of Beowulf's uncles, the killing occurs in the context of a game and he is as much Loki's victim as Baldr is.[27] 'The killing is devastating because it was done by a brother, and it could not be undone', remarks John Lindow in his wide-ranging study of the Baldr myth and vengeance.[28] The accident in the *Beowulf* episode does not initiate a cycle of vengeance. In the mythic context, Óðinn, Baldr's bereaved father, who can beget new sons more easily than the aged Hreðel, arranges for the death of Hǫðr, the *handbani* (technical slayer), as a poor recompense for the death of Baldr.[29] Loki, the *ráðbani* (plotter of the killing), cannot be killed, for he and Óðinn are sworn blood-brothers, and Loki's fate is written differently. Baldr's avenger also – paradoxically – becomes a fratricide

---

[24] See *Klaeber's Beowulf*, ed. Fulk *et al.*, pp. xlvii–viii, for discussion of this connection; also S. Jurasinski, *Ancient Privileges: Beowulf, Law and the Making of Germanic Antiquity* (Morganstown WV, 2006), pp. 113–48 for the legal understanding of accidental fratricide.

[25] Snorri Sturluson, *Edda: Prologue and Gylfaginning*, ed. Faulke, pp. 45–8; *Edda*, trans. Faulkes, pp. 48–51.

[26] See Introduction, p. 15.

[27] Hǫðr's blindness is not mentioned elsewhere in northern myth or legend; Heather O'Donoghue has plausibly connected the motif with the death of Cain, shot by the blind Lamech: 'What has Baldr to do with Lamech? The Lethal Shot of a Blind Man in Old Norse Myth and Jewish Exegetical Traditions', *Medium Ævum* 72 (2003), 82–107.

[28] J. Lindow, *Murder and Vengeance among the Gods: Baldr in Scandinavian Mythology* (Helsinki, 1997), p. 181.

[29] *Beowulf*, lines 2462–71.

through his vengeance, but, as a half- rather than full brother to Hǫðr, Váli can expiate his kin-slaying. Like Haldanus and Ásmundr in the Hildebrand tradition, the half-brother is not irremediably polluted by killing a half-brother.[30]

Ynglinga saga is a quasi-historical saga which begins the great compendium of Scandinavian kings' lives, *Heimskringla*, probably composed in the 1230s by Snorri Sturluson. Here a mysterious mutual fratricide appears at an early stage in the legendary history of the Swedish kings. Two Swedish royal brothers, Alrekr and Eiríkr, were enthusiastic tamers and riders of horses. One day the brothers ride away from their retinue to a plain where they intend to race their horses. Later they are both found dead there: their heads are smashed in, 'en ekki vápn hǫfðu þeir nema bitlana af hestunum' ('and they had no weapons with them except the bits of the horses').[31] Unlike the recurrent murderous brothers in Geoffrey of Monmouth, discussed below, there is no suggestion that the brothers are in competition for the kingdom; the mutual fratricide is apparently occasioned by the purest sibling rivalry, presumably a quarrel over who had the better horse. One of a series of bizarre deaths ascribed by Snorri to members of the Yngling dynasty, this killing has no resonances of foundational sacrifice. As an emblematic example of sibling hatred, it is succeeded in Snorri's narrative by another, more clearly motivated, brother-murder, discussed below.

Lindow analyses the northern myths and legends of fratricide (including the Hildebrand-tradition discussed in chapter two) as addressing the problems generated by kinslaying and vengeance within families; such violence was particularly salient in thirteenth-century Iceland, where these stories were preserved. 'As the usual rules of feuding broke down during the course of the thirteenth century and open warfare took its place, as fratricide became an increasingly real possibility, narratives about the unraveling world of the æsir must have seemed apt', Lindow posits.[32] The fratricide theme is indeed foregrounded across genres in the thirteenth-century Icelandic literary context: in Snorri's mythography, eddic poetry, and the legendary saga of Hildibrandr and Ásmundr. Explored at a distance in narratives of the legendary past or projected forward into the past-yet-future timescale of *ragna rǫk*, these brother-slayings distantly figure contemporary Icelandic anxieties about unceasing violence within and beyond the kindred. Moreover, as noted in chapter two, neither the sagas of Icelanders nor contemporary sagas feature any fratricides at all.[33] This omission suggests that more realist genres shied away from considering such psychically disturbing killings, whether occurring in the historical past or in the civil war which raged in contemporary Iceland.

---

[30] See chapter two.
[31] Snorri Sturluson, *Heimskringla*, ed. B. Aðalbjarnarson, 3 vols, ÍF 26–8 (Reykjavík, 1941–51), I: 39–40. Snorri's source for these deaths was a probably ninth-century poem, *Ynglingatal*, composed by Þjóðólfr of Hvín, vv. 10–11.
[32] Lindow, *Murder and Vengeance*, p. 178.
[33] Miller, *Bloodtaking and Peacemaking*, p. 160.

European ballad tradition preserves a fratricidal tale in which one brother kills another; possible motivations for the slaying are explored across the different versions. 'The Twa Brothers' (Child Ballad 49) relates how two school-age brothers playfully wrestle with one another, and one fatally wounds the other with a knife that was in his pocket.[34] In versions A and C the killing seems to be accidental. The dying John provides his distraught brother with a story to tell the rest of the family: he should claim that John has gone off to England to seek his fortune. John's true love must, however, hear the truth: that he lies in the churchyard. In other versions Willie deliberately stabs his brother during the wrestling; in version B he regrets his impulsive action immediately. In version H John asks whether it is for his gold, his money or his land that his brother has killed him and Willie replies that it is for the 'land sa broad / That I have killed thee', a motive shared with a number of other fratricides. Sibling murder must not pay off: Willie cannot profit from his brother's death. If fratricide does not result in mutual slaying, the surviving brother is expelled from the community. So Willie takes Cain's path into the wilderness, whence he shall never return before 'the sun and moon dances on the green, / And that will never be'.[35]

The different versions of 'The Twa Brothers' tease out a range of motivations for fratricide. Some propose that the killing is sheer accident (but, like the archery mishaps discussed above, can such fateful events be truly accidental)? Willie's immediate regret in version B speaks to the ambivalent and labile emotions of 'Siblings . . . [who] love where they hate'.[36] That the brothers are still young enough to be at school is significant; Willie sublimates his primitive infant murderousness into sibling rough play until his underlying hostility suddenly resurfaces and he strikes his brother down. Version H rationalizes the attack within a familiar framework: Willie is the younger brother who covets the elder's inheritance. This proliferation of motives for the killing confirms the underlying psychological complexities which the ballad allusively explores.

Recorded in the Finnish *Kalevala*, the story of Untamo and Kalervo demonstrates just how speedily petty fraternal squabbles, a quite literal patrolling of the sibling borderline, can escalate into murder.[37] The two brothers Untamo and Kalervo own neighbouring farms.[38] Untamo trespasses on Kalervo's property and Kalervo retaliates. One lays fishing-traps in the other's water, the other takes the fish he has caught, provoking a fist-fight. Kalervo sows oats behind Untamo's house, and so, inevitably, 'A bold ewe from Untamo's farm ate the oats Kalervo had sown / Kalervo's fierce dog ripped up the ewe from Untamo's farm'.[39] From minor

---

[34] *Ballads*, ed. Child, II: 438–45.
[35] Ibid., I: 435–44. Version D (p. 444).
[36] Mitchell, *Siblings*, p. 103.
[37] The traditional poems on which the *Kalevala* was based, like many other European oral traditions, were not recorded until the nineteenth century (though arguably the medieval period continues well into that century in parts of northern Europe).
[38] http://runeberg.org/kalevala/31.html; *The Kalevala*, trans. F. P. Magoun jr (Cambridge MA, 1969), Poem 31, pp. 223–4.
[39] *Kalevala*, trans. Magoun, p. 223.

incidents of brotherly unneighbourliness, the feud intensifies: finally Untamo gathers his forces and kills all of Kalervo's family except for a single woman. Pregnant by Kalervo, she is taken home as a slave.[40] The collective oral poets of the *Kalevala*-tradition understand how, within close-knit agricultural communities where farm-land is scarce and must be hacked out of the surrounding forests, minor infringements of land and other rights become unforgiveable offences in the brothers' minds. Childish tit-for-tat retaliation escalates into deliberate annihilation of almost all the other brother represents; significantly, Kalervo's unborn son will carry the feud into the next generation.

Untamo's excessive reaction to minor infringements on his property recalls the analysis of Cain's and Grendel's besetting sin as envy.[41] Sibling envy does not operate at a logical level, by reckoning up the actual value of the eaten crops or the stolen fish, but rather it reflects and replays the catastrophic emotions of sibling displacement.[42] Feelings of emptiness and issues of possession, of never having enough and of wanting what the other has only because he has it, stem from unresolved childhood sibling trauma.[43] And so, converted in these stories into hysterical excess, envy of the brother's horse or his well-received sacrifice, or resentment at his sheer existence figured by his unregulated grazing of sheep, all end in murder. Thus the tragedy of Cain plays out across medieval narratives, staging fraternal murderousness as generated by the most trivial of causes. Not all fratricides are triggered by such minor infringements of the sibling borderline; a number of tales, notably preserved in classical history or in chronicle, depict how medieval brothers also fight for the largest possible stakes: the crown and the kingdom.

Foundational and Royal Fratricide

> Very early [the Cain theme] entered into alliance with the foundation sacrifice, and very late it joined league with the concept of the double. These two associations suggest that at its heart Cain-Abel reveals an encounter with the lost brother, the sacrificed other, who must be gone but who can never be gone.[44]

Quinones's intuition that the Cain complex also shapes fratricidal episodes in

---

[40] It is prophesied that her son Kullervo will avenge his father on his uncle, carrying the feud on into a new generation: how Kullervo fulfils the prophecy, and his miserable fate, is related in chapter six.

[41] See note 20 above.

[42] See C. J. Moser, R. Jones, *et al.*, 'The Impact of the Sibling in Clinical Practice: Transference and Countertransference Dynamics', *Psychotherapy: Theory, Research, Practice, Training* 42 (2005), 267–78, especially pp. 272–4.

[43] Mitchell, *Mad Men and Medusas*, pp. 203–45. See also Mitchell, *Siblings*, p. 41.

[44] Quinones, *Changes of Cain*, p. 3; the brother as (monstrous) double will be discussed below.

which a polity is inaugurated or revolutionized helps to account for the recurrent brother-killings of dynastic histories. These narratives often frame fratricide as figuring civil war, and, as we shall see, cannibalism is also part of this nexus. On a pragmatic rather than strictly symbolic level, intra-familial conflict is regarded as an inevitable concomitant to the struggle for power. In medieval versions of Statius's epic poem, the *Thebaid*, exemplified here from John Lydgate's *Siege of Thebes* (1421), Ethyocles, the elder son of Oedipus, assumes the throne after his father's death, agreeing to relinquish it to his brother Polymyte (as he is called in this text) after a year.[45] The lords of Thebes, whose plan this is, hope to circumvent the inevitable problems caused by a plurality of brothers and a single inheritance by instigating this apparently equitable strategy.[46] They anticipate that brotherly love will persuade the brothers to agree to the plan of alternation: 'Of on hert / as brother vnto brother // euerich of hem / to regnen after other, // ʒeer be ʒeer'.[47]

The optimistic lords reckon without the intransigence of the first-born and the mistrust of the younger brother. Despite the mutual oaths sworn before all the gods, Polymyte suspects his brother will try to assassinate him and he leaves Thebes, taking refuge with Adrastus, king of Argos. Here he is joined by Tydeus of Caledonia, who had killed his brother while out hunting: '[he] casuelly / lete his Arow Slippe, / he slough his broder / callëd Menalippe'.[48] For his part in this convenient accident, Tydeus has been exiled.[49] Lydgate's source, the Prose *Roman de Thèbes*, reiterates the phrase *par grand mescheance* at this point, insisting that Fortune had caused the death of Tydeus's brother. Lydgate too, translating his source with the telling word *casuelly*, 'relies on the suppression of ethical causation', as Will Sweet observes.[50] Lydgate's narration nevertheless retains a significant ambiguity with regard to intention.[51] In the

---

[45] See D. Battles, *The Medieval Tradition of Thebes: History and Narrative in the Old French Roman de Thèbes, Boccaccio, Chaucer, and Lydgate* (London and New York, 2004), and W. Sweet, 'Lydgate and Scottish Lydgateans' (unpublished D.Phil. thesis, University of Oxford, 2009), pp. 49–82. Lydgate's primary source is the popular prose *Roman de Thèbes*. This is edited in *Prose, Verse, and Truth-Telling in the Thirteenth Century: An Essay on Form and Function in Selected Texts, Accompanied by an Edition of the* Prose Thèbes *as Found in the* Histoire ancienne jusqu'à César, ed. M. Lynde-Recchia (Lexington KY, 2000), itself based on Orosius's *Historiae adversus Paganos*.

[46] See chapter one, pp. 32–3.

[47] John Lydgate, *The Siege of Thebes*, ed. R. R. Edwards (Kalamazoo, 2001). Part II, lines 1115–16.

[48] Ibid., Part II, lines 1277–8. The forest, as the deaths of any number of medieval heroes demonstrate, is the site *par excellence* of murder (compare the fate of Sîfrît in chapter seven), accidental killing (Raimondin's uncle, see below), and murder framed to look like a hunting accident (Boves in *Daurel et Beton*, discussed in chapter eight). The name Menalippus first occurs in the Prose *Roman*, p. 148.

[49] That the death occurred in the context of a hunting accident derives from Boccaccio's *De Genealogia Deorum*. See *Lydgate's Siege of Thebes*, 2 vols, ed. A. Erdman and E. Ekwall, EETS es 108, 125 (Oxford, 1930), II: 6–8 on sources and II: 108–9 on this episode.

[50] The *Roman* adds that in some accounts the victim is said to be Tydeus's uncle.

[51] Sweet, 'Lydgate and Scottish Lydgateans', p. 81. See Statius, *Thebaid: Books 1–7*, ed. D. R. Shackleton Bailey (Cambridge MA and London, 2003), I: 402–3.

Thebaid, impelled by the *horror* of his act, Tydeus flees his own kingdom; in Lydgate (though not the Prose *Roman*) he is exiled as punishment.[52]

The two refugees marry Adrastus's two daughters and thus become brothers-in-law. Unlike the sons of Mélusine (chapter two) who were able to parlay new kingdoms for themselves through advantageous marriages, neither Polymyte nor Tydeus have any prospect of inheriting Argos: if Polymyte wants a kingdom he must regain the throne of Thebes. Tydeus visits Ethyocles to discover his intentions; he learns that the king has no intention of ceding the throne to his brother and flatly denies any agreement between them.[53] Consequently Adrastus, Tydeus and Polymyte (and their allies) make war as the Seven against Thebes. When Polymyte and Ethyocles finally meet in battle, 'lik two Tygres in her ragë wood', Polymyte runs his brother through.[54] Suddenly overcome by remorse, he dismounts and tries to aid him by pulling out the spear, but Ethyocles seizes the opportunity to strike Polymyte to the heart with a dagger and both brothers die on the field. Ethyocles' refusal to share the throne destroys the hopes of the Theban council for peace and for an equal sharing of monarchy – an institution whose etymology encodes the very paradox the Thebans had hoped to negotiate. Ethyocles receives honourable burial, but Creon, the 'olde Tyraunt', Jocasta's brother, is elected king and refuses to allow the bodies of Polymyte and the dead Greeks to be decently buried.[55] The narrative ends with Theseus's expedition against Thebes which utterly destroys the ill-fated city, as narrated in Boccaccio's *Teseida* and Chaucer's 'Knight's Tale'.

Elsewhere on the battlefield, the accidental fratricide Tydeus dies at the hands of a Theban whom tradition consistently names as Melanippus.[56] Tydeus's dead brother, named Menalippe both in the Prose *Roman de Thèbes* and in Lydgate's text, is thus invoked; the collocation of fratricidal themes is neatly emphasized by the chiming names. Just as Polymyte and Ethyocles die by each other's hand on the battle-field, so some version of Tydeus's own slain brother materializes among the Theban warriors to strike him down. The dying Tydeus calls on one of his companions to bring him Melanippus's head and he gnaws on it as he finally expires. The symbolic equivalence of civil war, fratricide and cannibalism are made horribly manifest by this bizarre form of vengeance. Consequently Dante summons up Tydeus when he introduces the tragic figure of Ugolino in the *Inferno*, acknowledging the link primarily through an extended metaphor

---

[52] See *Thebaid*, lines 402–3 and the earlier vernacular versions: Benoît de Ste Maure, *Roman de Thèbes*, 2 vols, ed. L. Constans (Paris, 1890), p. 35, lines 669–72, and the Prose *Roman de Thèbes*, p. 148.
[53] *Siege of Thebes*, ed. Edwards, Part II, line 2249; see Sweet, 'Lydgate and Scottish Lydgateans', p. 82.
[54] *Siege of Thebes*, ed. Edwards, Part III, line 4274.
[55] Ibid., Part III, line 4385. Sophocles' *Antigone* was of course unknown to medieval readers.
[56] The Prose *Roman* very likely derives the brother's name from that of Tydeus's future slayer, *Roman de Thèbes*, ed. Constans, p. 328.

comparing the two men as cannibals.⁵⁷ Ugolino's place of torment, fittingly, is Caina, the domain of Cain and other fratricides.⁵⁸ The Alberto degli Alberti brothers, one a Guelph, the other a Ghibelline, who killed one another in a quarrel over their inheritance sometime after 1282 are the first figures remarked by Dante in Caina, while Pisa, where Ugolino met his terrible fate, is identified by Dante as *novella Tebe* 'a new Thebes', cementing his connection of the Theban fratricidal topos and contemporary Tuscany.⁵⁹

These multiple brother-killings – committed by Cain, Polyneices and Eteocles, and the Alberti brothers – symbolize for Dante the fratricidal nature of civil strife. Achieving democracy, even in the limited form understood in medieval city-states, in early parliaments, or within guilds or monastic organizations, can, it has been argued, be understood as dependent on the resolution of symbolic sibling conflict. Aside from the recurrent rivalries produced by strict primogeniture in ruling families, a mature community politics demands that the individual relinquish his egoistical interests, for the social self must be understood as, pre-eminently, the sibling self, the one which must learn how to interact with its peers. '[T]he harsh ethic of fairness among "sibling" equals' encourages the subject or citizen to generalize the family experience into 'the democratic demand for equality and fair redistribution', argue Robert D. Hinshelwood and Gary Winship.⁶⁰ When viable social organization has yet to be established or when it has broken down, the dislocation is frequently symbolized by warring brothers, those who cannot or will not subscribe to the 'harsh ethic of fairness'.⁶¹ The dangers of internal division within royal or noble lineages are strongly highlighted by these narratives, but they also resonate with the aspirations of other classes to establish democratic, or at least fraternalistic, social institutions. The fratricide topos can be understood as marking an early, politically primitive or regressive stage within a state that is figured as a family. Only once some version of peaceable fraternality has evolved can a lasting and mature politics come into being.

Such royal rivalries as the Roman and Theban fratricides are widespread in medieval literature, both borrowed from, but also emerging independently of,

---

57 Dante, *L'Inferno*, Canto XXXIII, ed. and trans. J. D. Sinclair (New York, 1939), repr. 1981.
58 The voice of Cain himself is heard in *Purgatorio* 14, on the Terrace of Envy, crying: 'Anciderammi qualunque m'apprende' ('Everyone that finds me shall slay me'). These are Cain's words uttered after killing Abel but before God marks him as inviolable (Dante, *Purgatorio*, Canto XIV, line 133). Caina is where the reader would also expect to find another fratricide, Gianciotto Malatesta, who murdered his brother Paolo because of the latter's affair with Gianciotto's wife, Francesca (da Rimini). Indeed, when Dante and Virgil encounter the two lovers in the circle of the lustful, Francesca prophesies that 'Caina attende chi vita ci spense' ('Caina waits for the one who quenched our life'). Dante, *Inferno*, Canto V, lines 106–8.
59 R. Quinones, *Foundation Sacrifice in Dante's Commedia* (University Park PA, 1994), pp. 26–7; Dante, *Inferno*, Canto XXXIII: line 89.
60 Hinshelwood and Winship, 'Orestes and democracy', pp. 86–7.
61 Hinshelwood and Winship, 'Orestes and democracy', p. 87.

classical tradition. Brothers will either learn to negotiate equitable shares of the kingdom or else they will destroy one another. In the Old Norse *fornaldarsaga* (legendary saga) *Hrólfs saga kraka*, the line of the Danish kings, the Skjǫldungs, begins with two brothers, Halfdan and Fróði who initially divide Denmark between them.[62] Driven by envy, Fróði attacks Halfdan and burns him in his hall. Halfdan's two sons survive, protected by their foster-father and sheltered by their older sister Signý until they can finally avenge themselves on their uncle. These two brothers then hold the kingdom jointly until Hróarr wisely marries the daughter of the king of England and takes power there, leaving Helgi in sole charge of Denmark. Relations between the brothers are cordial; Hróarr declares publicly that he is happy with his power-base in Northumbria, and he does not begrudge his younger brother the Danish throne, provided he can have a coveted family heirloom, a splendid ring. Helgi willingly consents to this. The second generation thus successfully negotiates power-sharing, comparable with those sons of Mélusine, and of Bevis of Hamton, discussed in chapter two. Through the acquisition of new territory for one to govern and the arrangement of acceptable compensation, the brothers settle their inheritance equitably.

Or so Hróarr and Helgi believe. Their sister, in contrast, perceives herself as slighted, feeling that her brothers have not acknowledged the help she and her husband gave them in regaining the throne and avenging their father. Signý provokes her son Hrókr to demand for himself either a third of Denmark or the ring which Hróarr possesses; he derives his claim through the principles of partibility and transmission of rights through the female line. The contest over the ring ultimately leads to the death of Hróarr and the maiming of his cousin. Failure to extend the sibling settlement to Signý and the exclusion of her lineage from the fraternal negotiations thus generates further conflict. Signý could not win herself a new kingdom through marriage, but she might have been appeased by the distribution of chattels, symbolized by the ring. The saga offers for consideration the question of how far sisters and their sons might have a claim on territory and treasure, and the difficulties which arise when there are insufficient resources to satisfy all parties. The saga's sympathies clearly lie with the two brothers; Signý's ambition for her 'grimmr ok harðla ágjarn' ('fierce and very covetous') son is punished when he is maimed by his two uncles. Hróarr cuts off Hrókr's feet when his sister's son throws the contested ring in the sea, while Helgi breaks his arms and legs in vengeance for Hróarr's death, leaving him shamefully incapable. Hrókr's dismemberment reflects the important conceptual metaphor of members of the family as members of a body.[63] The kindred's internal bonds are destroyed by Hrókr's greed and his murder of his mother's brother: the punishments visited on him by his two

---

[62] *Hrólfs saga kraka* in *FSN*, I; translation, *The Saga of Hrolf Kraki*, trans. J. Byock (London, 1998).
[63] As discussed in the previous chapter, p. 100.

uncles avoid the crime of kinslaying while making visible on his body the damage done to the lineage and its interests.[64]

Early in Geoffrey of Monmouth's *Historia regum Britanniae*, Mempricius murders his brother Malin during talks about sharing the kingdom: he then rules despotically, killing both his family members and the nobility. Abandoning his wife for the pleasures of sodomy, Mempricius meets his end when, during a hunting expedition, he is surrounded by a pack of ravening wolves and 'miserrime deuoratus est' ('is miserably devoured'); his horrible end figures his own wolfishness in murdering his kinsmen.[65] Ferreux and Porrex, two brothers who hold the kingdom after the death of Leir and his daughters also quarrel. Porrex expels Ferreux who, like many another British king, returns from exile with foreign aid and kills his brother, only to be slain in turn by their grief-stricken mother.[66] The readership of Geoffrey and his translators, spreading far beyond Geoffrey's original Angevin patrons, could draw their own conclusions about the models of sibling behaviour most conducive to a harmonious polity at all social levels.

Indeed, examples of brothers who fight one another for political power could be multiplied from both historical and pseudo-historical medieval sources. Geoffrey's *Historia* shows a repeating pattern of royal fratricide: one which alternates with pairs of loyal and loving brothers who peacefully negotiate power-sharing, and with sole heirs or heiresses to the throne. Gregory of Tours's sixth-century account of early Frankish kings depicts equally fractious fraternal relations, exacerbated by the custom of concubinage which multiplied royal sons, and by the Merovingian kings' apparent disregard for the sanctity of oaths. As depicted in these historical or pseudohistorical accounts, royal sibling conflict is concretely connected with contemporary conditions for kingship: where a number of kingly candidates could plausibly claim the kingdom through blood, the incentive to fight for the throne was extremely strong. As noted in chapter one, the Church was eventually instrumental in regularizing royal inheritance in line with generalized primogeniture customs, and it tried to mediate between warring royal brothers, eventually decreasing, if not completely preventing, such sibling strife.[67]

---

[64] Warring brothers are the founders of Denmark in Saxo Grammaticus's account of Danish legendary history: Lothar is captured by his brother Humbli and forced to abdicate, Saxo, *GD*, I; Saxo, *HD*, pp. 14–15.

[65] Geoffrey of Monmouth, *History of the Kings of Britain*, ed. Wright, trans. Reeve, pp. 34–5.

[66] This drama of family tensions which forms the plot of *Gorboduc* (1561), arguably the first theatrical tragedy to be written in English. Geoffrey of Monmouth, *History of the Kings of Britain*, ed. Wright, trans. Reeve, pp. 44–7; Thomas Norton and Thomas Sackville, *Gorboduc* in *Minor Elizabethan Drama, Vol I, Pre-Shakespearean Tragedies* (Letchworth, repr. 1959).

[67] See above, chapter one, p. 33.

The Brother in the Monastery

In his life of St Patroclus, Gregory of Tours shows how learning might give an older brother airs. Once he has begun to go to school, Patroclus's brother Antonius comes to despise little Patroclus, who is working as a shepherd, looking after the family's flocks. At dinner he contemptuously orders, 'Sit further away from me, you peasant. You herd sheep, while I study letters; the care of such a task ennobles me, while you are made common by your work'.[68] Patroclus immediately abandons the sheep and enrols at school, where he soon surpasses his brother in learning. As early as the sixth century, then, non-noble classes are depicted as perceiving the advantage of education and clerical careers for their sons. Frankish saints' lives, among other early texts, often relate how religious siblings supported their brothers and sisters in fulfilling their own vocations. Monastic careers were regarded as honourable for noble men and women in early Anglo-Saxon England, for example; since virginity was not a prerequisite for taking monastic vows, it was entirely possible to retire to the religious life after having produced offspring to continue the lineage.[69] Moreover, as Sarah Foot observes, 'many commentators have concluded that life within an Anglo-Saxon minster was, for all classes of society, little removed from life within any noble household'.[70]

In later accounts, sibling support for another sibling's vocation can be more obviously lacking. Perhaps surprisingly, since a brother in the cloister entails one rival fewer for the paternal inheritance, a number of exempla – and one well-developed narrative – recount the strong hostility of knightly brothers to their sibling's decision to enter a monastery. Caesarius of Heisterbach relates two tales of religious whose vocation is challenged by their kin. In one exemplum, as discussed in chapter one, a man is enticed out of his foundation by his brothers, and kidnapped; he escapes and returns to the order with renewed enthusiasm for the ecclesiastical life. Less happily, Caesarius follows this tale with another in which knightly brothers entice their monastic brother out of his foundation. He elects to stay outside, but dies insane.[71] These stories point to an eleventh- and twelfth-century belief among the aristocracy that a clerical calling was somehow unmasculine and unworthy; this apparent contempt for the ecclesiastical life would only be dissipated by the rise of clerical bureaucracies within royal courts

---

[68] Gregory of Tours: *Life of the Fathers*, trans. E. James, 2nd edn (Liverpool, 1991), p. 66; Réal, *Vies de saints*, p. 479.

[69] See F. W. Stenton, *Anglo-Saxon England* (Oxford, 1970), pp. 160–1, for Bede's anxieties about this practice as expressed in a letter to Bishop Ecgbert of York in 734.

[70] S. Foot, *Monastic Life in Anglo-Saxon England, c. 600–900* (Cambridge, 2006), p. 248; see also D. Schneider, 'Anglo-Saxon Women in the Religious Life: A Study of the Status and Position of Women in an Early Mediaeval Society' (unpublished Ph.D dissertation, University of Cambridge, 1985), p. 73.

[71] Caesarius of Heisterbach, *Dialogue on Miracles*, i.xii–xiv, ed. Scott and Bland, I: 20–1.

in the later twelfth and thirteenth centuries.[72] When whole groups of brothers and sisters, such as Bernard of Clairvaux and his siblings, elected to enter the monastic life, a noble kindred might be left short of heirs. Bernard's youngest brother, according to various exempla collections, decided to take the tonsure only after much agonizing; as the last brother still in the world, he was anxious about allowing the family lands to pass out of the fraternal group's control.[73]

In socio-historical terms the stories discussed above, often composed and transmitted by the very monks who were striving to retain their noble recruits, point to a reluctance, even in the late twelfth century when Caesarius was collecting his material, for noble families to regard the cloister as a solution to the problem of younger sons. Although the exempla do not spell out the circumstances in which siblings seek to recover their monastic brothers for secular life, the sudden availability of a marriageable heiress, or the death of one or more brothers destined to inherit parts of the patrimony, suggest themselves. Child oblates might themselves turn against the vocation to which they had been vowed at a very young age, and seek their brothers' assistance in escaping from their foundations. Admission to the monastery was often accompanied by substantial donations of land, donations which other members of the kin-group might later seek to reclaim. Usurpation of previously agreed settlements would be greatly facilitated if the brother withdrew from the foundation which had control of the gift.[74]

The move into the monastery also unsettles the prevailing model of fraternity as determined by blood. Although Bernard successfully converted his lateral kin-group into a monastic brotherhood, a brother's choice of spiritual brethren over his own genetic brothers disturbs the sibling group's idea of itself. Hence perhaps, in the Mélusine tradition, the furious reaction of Geoffroy la Grand Dent to the news that his brother Fromont intends to join the monastery of Maillezais.[75] Geoffroy's elder brothers (as noted in chapter two) prospered by setting out into the world in pairs, winning themselves wives and kingdoms, but Geoffroy seems to be happy to fight alone, without the support of the brother closest to him in age. When he learns that Fromont has entered Maillezais, Geoffroy's rage is excessive. He foams at the mouth like a wild boar, recalling the animal implicated in his father's accidental killing of his uncle, and indeed the beast which furnishes his own distinguishing mark: the tusk that protrudes

---

[72] See C. S. Jaeger, *The Origins of Courtliness – Civilizing Trends and the Formation of Courtly Ideals – 939–1210* (Philadelphia, 1985), pp. 19–30.

[73] *Index exemplorum*, ed. Tubach, p. 50, no. 603.

[74] Cf. Beitscher, '"As the twig is bent"', pp. 188–90. Thanks to Tom Lambert for useful discussion on this point.

[75] Jean d'Arras, *Mélusine*, ed. Stouff, pp. 250–2 and J. H. M. Taylor, 'Mélusine's Progeny: Patterns and Perplexities', in *Melusine of Lusignan*, ed. Maddox and Sturm-Maddox, pp. 165–84. On the historical background to this episode, see *Melusine; or, the Noble History of Lusignan*, trans. D. Maddox and S. Sturm-Maddox (University Park PA, 2012), pp. 7–8.

through his cheek.[76] Geoffroy, Coudrette tells us, would rather see his brother hanged – a distinctly low-status fate – than become a monk and he reproaches his parents for not having endowed Fromont with estates and castles and for failing to arrange a marriage for him.[77] Geoffroy sets fire to Maillezais, burning down most of the monastery and killing a hundred monks, among them his brother. When all are dead, the madness lifts from Geoffroy and he immediately comprehends the magnitude of his sin. Cursing himself as a worse sinner than Judas – in terms not dissimilar to those employed by Cain in the Chester play – he departs, weeping bitter tears of remorse. He sets sail for Northumberland, leaving his parents to deal with the aftermath of his crime and Fromont's death, a trauma that will destroy both their marriage and Mélusine's hopes of salvation.

The noble patrons of Jean d'Arras and Coudrette's work may have regarded the preference for entry into a humble priory over the pursuit of high ecclesiastical office as an unworthy choice: Raimondin's initial reaction was to try to persuade his son to join a more fashionable and aristocratic foundation. Geoffroy's fury, explained only in terms of his choleric and boar-like nature, remains relatively unmotivated, but his excessive rage against Fromont invites the consideration that more-deeply rooted sibling issues are in play. For fraternal rage is essentially narcissistic: Geoffroy is provoked by his brother's choice to be different from him. His sibling fury stems less from the primary act of differentiation, but rather from his interpretation of Fromont's choice as a deliberate deviation from the chivalric value system prevailing among the other siblings.[78] Geoffroy's older brothers chose paths which called for a minimal level of differentiation between each sibling pair and the rest of the fraternity: in winning different kingdoms and marrying their heiresses, they successfully achieved complementarity.[79] Fromont, the brother with whom Geoffroy most closely identified, dared to be different, to refuse the similarities which the sons of Mélusine shared by virtue of their birth and to select a strategy of complete de-identification, of becoming exactly what his brothers, in particular Geoffroy, the loner and giant-killer, were not.[80] By leaving the world in which his other brothers had been so successful, Fromont rejects, in Geoffroy's eyes, the man that he has become: Fromont damages his brother's sense of himself at a level which provokes an excessive and infantilized rage. Bank and Kahn recognize this phenomenon as 'polarized rejection', the development of an identity which is perceived as antagonistic to the other sibling's own self-image.[81] Like Cain before him, Geoffroy cannot accept

---

[76] See L. Harf-Lancner, *Les fées au Moyen Âge* (Paris, 1984), pp. 177–8.
[77] Coudrette, *Le roman de Mélusine*, ed. Roach, p. 225, line 3508; trans. Harf-Lancner, p. 95; cf. Jean d'Arras, *Mélusine*, p. 250; *Melusine*, trans. Maddox and Sturm-Maddox, p. 178.
[78] Bank and Kahn, *The Sibling Bond*, pp. 104–11. See Introduction, p. 8 for discussion of complementarity as implying healthy evolution of individual identity.
[79] Bank and Kahn, *The Sibling Bond*, pp. 62–4.
[80] On differentiation, counter-identification and deidentification, see Moser, Jones *et al.*, 'The Impact of the Sibling', p. 271, and Charles, 'Sibling Mysteries'.
[81] Bank and Kahn, *The Sibling Bond*, pp. 104–11. Intriguingly, the therapeutic instance they

that his brother should choose *not* to be his second self. In an access of primitive rage, he destroys both his brother and those who have chosen the same destiny; the effect on his parents is utterly tragic. Unlike Cain and the other fratricides considered above, Geoffroy's remorse leads him to penance and to the rebuilding of Maillezais; although he cannot restore his shattered family, he finds common cause with his remaining brothers in defending the kingdom of Alsace.[82]

Sexual Jealousy

Even if brothers manage to negotiate the struggle for political supremacy and settle inheritance issues amicably, they may still come into conflict when they are rivals for the same woman. 'One wants what the other person wants and mimes that person's desires', as Juliet Mitchell notes: a brother covets a woman not necessarily for her own charms, but simply because his brother desires her also.[83] When siblings enter into sexual competition, where intensified desire comes into play, mimetic desire converts the beloved brother into a Girardian 'monstrous double'. Unlike rivalry for the kingdom, where there is only one prize, and its value is uncontested, rivalry over a woman is complicated by the existence of other equally fitting love-objects. Why must the brother choose precisely *this* woman? '[T]*he subject desires the object because the rival desires it*. In desiring an object the rival alerts the subject to the desirability of the object', Girard proposes.[84] Thus the subject–rival dyad is both reconstituted and triangulated; their shared desire unites the two brothers as doubles, but each brother comes to perceive the other as monstrous, as an Other who must not only be overcome, but finally be destroyed.[85]

As seen in earlier chapters, ballads often depict the most unmediated forms of sibling emotion. 'Lord Ingram and Chiel Wyet' (Child Ballad 66) tells of two brothers who 'laid baith their hearts on one lady', Lady Maisry.[86] Lord Ingram honourably asks her family for her hand, while Chiel Wyet seduces her. Though Maisry states her preference for marrying the chiel, her father arranges the marriage with Lord Ingram. 'I wonder what ails my one brother / he'll not let my love be', the chiel comments when he hears too late of the wedding, signalling the younger brother's intuition that the elder has asked for Maisry's hand purely to spite him. In the bridal bed, Lord Ingram discovers that his wife is already pregnant. When she reminds him that she had told earlier him of her affair with

cite here is of a younger brother who chooses to become a priest in order to de-identify himself with his bullying older brother. F. Schachter *et al.*, 'Sibling Deidentification', *Developmental Psychology* 12 (1976), 418–27, argue that 'deidentification is a mechanism for resolving sibling rivalry, a Cain Complex' (p. 427).

[82] See chapter two, p. 53.
[83] Mitchell, *Mad Men*, p. 25.
[84] See Girard, *Violence and the Sacred*, pp. 154–5; his italics.
[85] Ibid., p. 170.
[86] *Ballads*, ed. Child, II: 126–36.

his brother, Lord Ingram nobly offers to take responsibility for the baby, but she refuses to name him as father. Chiel Wyet bursts into the chamber and murders his brother, who stabs him in return. Both brothers fall dead, while the bride runs mad and swears she will live from now on as a beggar-woman. Now at last, she admits, Lord Ingram has gained her respect for his magnanimous reaction to her pregnancy. In the B version of the ballad, Lord Ingram chastely lays a sword between him and his bride, intending to renounce her to his brother in the morning, but the fight between the brothers forestalls this happy outcome. Chiel Wyet sometimes kills himself after slaying his brother; in version B, Maisry also kills herself after giving birth to the chiel's son, leaving the household weeping 'for the bonnie babe / That lay blabbering in her bleed'.[87]

As older brother, Lord Ingram has inherited the title and is the desirable match; the younger chiel has fewer prospects, but clearly knows how to charm. While Lord Ingram shows an older brother's maturity and understanding in his reaction to Maisry's plight, the chiel manifests the simmering rage of the younger brother whose social position and erotic object are claimed, as of right, by the older. The type of resentment epitomized by Cain, the older brother's anger at being displaced by the new arrival, is refracted differently in a younger brother. For him, the elder brother has always been there, always in the way, and, under primogeniture, he takes the lion's share of family resources. The younger sibling's acceptance of the social status quo thus founders on his brother-double's desire for the woman he loves; it precipitates him into blind murderousness. Too late does the dying Ingram gesture to his brother with the cup with which he had intended 'to hae drunken her o'er to thee'; in annihilating his brother, the chiel destroys himself.

As Gertrude remarks in John Updike's novel of 2000, *Gertrude and Claudius*, 'the brother of one's husband is a figure of interest, providing another version of him – him recast, as it were, by another throw of the dice'; this observation might stand as an epigraph to many of the fraternal murders discussed below.[88] Fraternal murder lies at the heart of Amleth's story, as recounted in Saxo's *Historia Danorum*. Rørik succeeds to the throne of Denmark and appoints the brothers Orvendil and Fengi as governors of Jutland. When Orvendil has distinguished himself by overcoming a notable pirate in single combat, he wins Rørik's daughter Gerthruda as his wife.[89] Infuriated by his brother's successes, Fengi murders him in order to obtain Gerthruda, adding, as Saxo observes, incest to his other crimes. Amleth, son of Orvendil and Gerthruda, is assisted in his quest for vengeance on his uncle by his foster-brother and sister, characters whose love and friendship contrasts with Fengi's lack of sibling loyalty.[90] Saxo's spare narrative gives little insight into Fengi's feelings, and still less into Gerthruda's, but it suggests that the fratricide is doubly motivated: both by sexual passion

---

[87] Ibid., Version A, II: 438.
[88] John Updike, *Gertrude and Claudius* (London, 2000), p. 48
[89] Saxo, *GD* III. 6; Saxo, *HD* III. 83.
[90] Amleth's foster-relationships are discussed in chapter eight.

and by fraternal envy at Orvendil's preferment. More vivid psychological characterization distinguishes the fratricidal Swedish King Alrekr's two sons: outgoing, popular Yngvi and silent, imperious and quarrelsome Álfr.[91] It is not clear who is the elder, but Yngvi is named first in *Heimskringla*. Yngvi habitually travels abroad raiding, while Álfr rules over Sweden. On one occasion Yngvi comes home to Uppsala and sits up late feasting while his brother goes early to bed. Álfr's wife Bera, also of a sociable disposition, stays up to chat to her brother-in-law. When her husband orders her to bed, telling her that he does not want to be kept awake by her conversation with his brother, Bera retorts that the woman who was married to Yngvi rather than Álfr might count herself lucky. This remark infuriates Álfr, particularly when his wife repeats it on other occasions. When he finds his brother once more in conversation with Bera and sitting, significantly, in the king's high seat, Álfr finally attacks him. Yngvi retaliates: both fall dead and are buried together. Here the fraternal rivalry seems to be rooted both in fundamental personality differences and in varying life experiences, although it is clearly exacerbated by sexual jealousy. The brothers had at first chosen 'different roads', and kept out of one another's way; strategies of counter-identification and separation successfully managed sibling conflict. But Yngvi's return sparks Álfr's antagonism. His fund of stories from his raiding days are alluring to Bera, who seems to be bored with her stay-at-home husband; like Gertrude she regards Yngvi as representing 'another throw of the dice', not a 'monstrous double', but rather a more attractive version of the man she married. Álfr is profoundly threatened by the brother who looks set to displace him in his wife's affections and perhaps in his rule, but, by destroying his sibling, he also destroys himself.

Another Norse legend shows the hero successfully resisting the provocation to identify his brother and rival as his 'monstrous double' and to deal with him accordingly. At the conclusion of the eddic poem *Helgakviða Hjǫrvarðzsonar*, Helgi faces a fatal duel against a certain Álfr.[92] Just before the battle Helgi discovers that his own brother Heðinn has formally sworn – and now bitterly regrets – an oath to take Helgi's valkyrie bride Sváva as his own. Though this does not ultimately matter to Helgi, since he is doomed to die in the duel with Álfr, Heðinn's vow, which he himself can barely account for, is strikingly emblematic of the fraternal ambivalence which the eddic heroic poems frequently explore.[93] Heðinn's apparent lapse into nursery envy, wanting what his brother has and acting to get it, miming rather than truly experiencing desire for Sváva, is motivated by the appearance of a disturbing figure, a trollwoman riding a wolf whose sexual overtures Heðinn rejects. This female and her wolf-mount are identified by Helgi as his *fylgjur*, his 'fetches', supernatural figures whose appearance

---

[91] See above, p. 109 for Alrekr; Álfr and Yngvi, Snorri Sturluson, *Heimskringla*, I: 41–2.
[92] In *Edda*, ed. Neckel and Kuhn; *Edda*, trans. Larrington, pp. 125–7.
[93] See C. Larrington, 'Sibling Drama: Laterality in the Heroic Poems of the Edda', in *Myth, Legends, and Heroes: Studies in Old Norse and Old English Literature in Honour of John McKinnell*, ed. D. Anlezark (Toronto, 2011), pp. 169–87.

signals dynastic change. When Heðinn fails to respond to the troll-woman as an erotic object, his sexual desire is deflected away from her towards his brother's beloved and perhaps acts out an unconscious jealousy and resentment of his successful sibling. On a dynastic level, however, the troll-woman-fetch foresees that Helgi is doomed and arranges for the continuation of the lineage via a union between Heðinn and Sváva. While Helgi is surprisingly forgiving of his brother when he confesses what he has done, Sváva's response to the exchange of brothers is harder to read, 'Mælt hafða ec þat . . . myndiga ec lostig at liðinn fylki / iofur ókunnan armi veria' ('I declared this . . . I would not willingly, if my lord were gone, hold a prince of no reputation in my arms').[94] The poem neither relates whether Sváva is mollified by Heðinn's vow to avenge Helgi, nor if his mission is successful. Brothers are not interchangeable as sexual partners in the way that sisters often are, especially when, as is frequently the case in eddic heroic tradition, the beloved hero was freely chosen by the woman. The difference between the heroic Helgi and Heðinn, who only figures in the story when he blurts out his desire for his brother's love, is too marked for Sváva to accept him as a subsititute with equanimity.[95] Yet fraternal love rises above both mimetic desire and the irruption of the monstrous – the troll-woman and her wolf-steed – into the brothers' relationship; Helgi cedes his beloved to Heðinn. The death of one of the doubles solves the problem, even if from a Girardian perspective, it is the wronged, unmonstrous brother who dies.

Mimetic sexual desire equals rivalry for power in its capacity to disrupt the fraternal relationship. It is more difficult for the brother to cede the desired woman to his rival than for the sister to give way to her bridegroom's beloved, as in the stories of Freine and Fair Annie analysed in chapter two; sexual pride is more tightly bound up in a brother's taking possession of a woman than in a sister's unconsummated marriage to a man she does not love. Lord Ingram (if only in version B and too late) and Helgi are able to find the magnanimity to yield the woman they love to their brother. Although their renunciations are qualified by Ingram's realization that his bride is pregnant by his brother and Helgi's foreboding that he is doomed, nevertheless both brothers privilege the fraternal bond over their possession of the beloved, and, at least in Helgi's case, the threat of fratricide is averted. Other brothers cannot resist mimetic desire; its effect on previously loving siblings is to convert one into a murderous and monstrous figure who can only be appeased by his brother's death.

Managing Fraternal Rage

Helgi's encounter with Heðinn dissipates their conflict, largely because the hero is already doomed. While heroic legend and pseudo-history frequently recur to the theme of fraternal hostility, romance rarely attends centrally to

---

[94] *Helgakviða Hjǫrvarðzsonar*, v. 42.
[95] See Larrington, 'Sibling Drama', pp. 173–4.

fraternal concerns, except in the Arthurian cycle or the separated-twins story of Valentine and Orson.[96] When the romance hero sets out into the world, he typically leaves his family behind, or else he is engaged in a quest to find his lost family; if he needs a loyal friend he either takes his foster-brother or he acquires a sworn-brother.[97] A striking exception to romance's lack of interest in fraternal relations is the late-fourteenth-century English outlaw romance, the *Tale of Gamelyn*.[98] *Gamelyn* amply demonstrates both dimensions of the fraternal bond: the persistent treachery of the hero's elder brother Sir John and the staunch loyalty of his middle brother, Sir Ote. At the beginning of the romance, their father bequeaths to Gamelyn, the youngest, a portion which is three times that of the two older brothers' inheritance. The folk- and fairy-tale motif of the youngest sibling as the parental favourite threatens to be so disruptive to the social status quo that the father's advisors strongly counsel against this disposition. In vain, however: Sir John's attempts to recover his lost patrimony from Gamelyn furnish the romance's plot.

Gamelyn is overly trusting. Relying on the strength of verbal commitments, time and again he falls for his elder brother's false promises and he is driven into outlawry through his brother's machinations.[99] Unlike Sir John, Sir Ote shows exemplary solidarity; he even goes bail for his brother's appearance in court. This loyalty is strongly tested when Gamelyn arrives only at the very last minute to save Ote from being hanged by John. As he rushes into court Gamelyn swears that it is his eldest brother who shall hang, and, unexpectedly in a family romance, he keeps his vow. Neither reconciliation nor family reunion is possible when the fraternal relationship has broken down so catastrophically. The father's erratic division of inheritance – the root of the conflict – is erased, for the king decrees that Ote take the land in parage after John's death and that Gamelyn should hold it from him. For all his violence and individualism, Gamelyn is reintegrated into his family once it is purged of its '"shrewed," that is diabolic, bad leader: primogeniture is recuperated and all in the family is again well', Knight and Ohlgren comment.[100] The eccentric inheritance disposition provokes the sibling crisis: the romance's narrative impetus come from the breach of the primogeniture norm, and it offers contrasting models of fraternal rage and solidarity as reactions to that crisis. The relationship between Ote and Gamelyn is properly reconstituted through the king's external authority while John's execution eliminates a family member who would neither recognize nor uphold its sibling norms.

[96] See chapter two above, p. 61.
[97] See chapter eight.
[98] *The Tale of Gamelyn*, in *Robin Hood and Other Outlaw Tales*, ed. S. Knight and T. H. Ohlgren (Kalamazoo, 1997).
[99] C. Donnelly, 'Aristocratic Veneer and the Substance of Verbal Bonds in "The Weddynge of Sir Gawen and Dame Ragnell" and "Gamelyn"', *Studies in Philology* 94 (1997), 321–43. See also R. Kaeuper, 'A Historian's Reading of *The Tale of Gamelyn*', *Medium Ævum* 52 (1983), 51–62 for a comparison of the *Tale* with contemporary court records.
[100] *Tale of Gamelyn*, Introduction.

Genres popular with aristocratic and gentry audiences, such as Arthurian romance, regard fratricide with unmitigated horror; the accidental mutual killing of Balin and Balan is memorialized by Merlin in his inscription on their joint tomb, and the happy ending of Malory's 'Tale of Sir Gareth' is saved by Lyonet's timely halting of the battle between Gareth and his brother before it becomes fatal.[101] During Malory's version of the Grail Quest, a further fratricide is averted only by divine intervention.[102] When Lionel is seized, bound and beaten by unknown knights, rather than rescue his anguished brother, Bors elects to defend a gentlewoman who is about to be raped. Later Bors is shown his brother's corpse, though this is in fact a diabolical delusion, sent to bring him to despair and to turn him aside from the Quest. Shortly afterwards, Bors joyfully discovers Lionel alive and well. But Lionel is furious with Bors for abandoning him and he accuses his brother of unexampled treachery: 'For never arste ne ded no brothir to another so grete an untrouthe'.[103] Although Bors kneels down to beg forgiveness and mercy for his fraternal dereliction, calling him 'Fayre swete brothir', implacable Lionel issues a formal challenge. He rides Bors down and is about to smite off his head, when first a hermit and then Sir Colgrevaunce, a fellow Round Table knight, intervene to try to prevent the fratricide. Lionel kills both men. Bors warns him that a fight between brothers can only end in death and eternal damnation for both of them, 'for if hit befelle, fayre brothir, if that I sle you other ye me, we both shall dye for that synne'.[104] Bors is finally provoked to draw his sword in self-defence, but a heavenly voice forbids him to strike. A fiery cloud appears between the brothers and they both fall unconscious. When they revive, Bors begs Lionel as his 'fayre swete brothir' once again to forgive him, and this time Lionel accepts his apology, though he does not return the epithet of 'brother'. 'The narcissistic love of the-other-as-the-self explodes in murderousness once it is realized that there cannot be another self', Mitchell notes.[105] Lionel cannot accept that Bors could discount the primary affective tie in his world, his relationship with his brother, by valuing more highly the imperative to help a woman, crucially – in terms of Grail Quest ethics – in order to preserve her virginity. Bors is not, or is no longer, Lionel's second self; that realization provokes the sibling confrontation, the 'explosion into murderousness'. That Lionel seeks to kill his brother, knowing his identity, and that Bors's provocation to self-defence risked fratricide on his own account, magnifies the sinfulness of Lionel's murderous intention. No human, whether priest or fellow-knight, can assuage Lionel's sense of aggrievedness and betrayal; only God's direct intervention can frighten him into a grudging forgiveness.

Medieval Norse society regarded the custom of *mannajafnaðr* (comparing

---

[101] See chapter two, pp. 69–70.
[102] Malory's account of the episode closely follows his French source in the *Queste. La Queste de Saint Graal*, ed. A. Pauphilet (Paris, 1975), pp. 175–80; 187–93; Malory, *Le Morte Darthur*, ed. Field, I: 736–8; 743–7.
[103] Ibid., I: 743.
[104] Ibid., I: 746.
[105] Mitchell, *Siblings*, p. 35.

men) as an entertaining pastime, a higher form of gossip which served to establish the relative standings of men within a community. Unsurprisingly, as reported in the sagas, such comparisons frequently ended in conflict.[106] *Heimskringla* gives an extensive account of one such instance. In the saga of the sons of King Magnús, King Eysteinn initiates a *mannajafnaðr* with his brother Sigurðr in order to enliven a dull feast. The comparison begins by measuring their relative physical skills (*íþróttir*). Sigurðr notes that in their youth he could always beat Eysteinn at wrestling, though he was a year older; Eysteinn ripostes that he was more agile. Sigurðr could always duck Eysteinn when they swam together, but Eysteinn could swim just as far and was far better at ice-skating, 'en þú kunnir þat eigi heldr en naut' ('but you were no better at that than a cow'), he adds provocatively.[107] Sigurðr is bigger and stronger; Eysteinn is better-looking and knows more about the law. From this point onwards, the brothers skirt dangerously close to insult: Eysteinn does not always keep his promises, while Sigurðr refuses help to everyone who asks for it. Sigurðr sailed around the Mediterranean and visited Jerusalem (the first Norwegian king to do so) while Eysteinn 'sazt heima meðan sem dóttir fǫður þíns' ('sat at home meanwhile like your father's daughter').[108] Eysteinn's financial support for his brother's expedition, he retorts, was the equivalent to paying a dowry for his brother – the implications of effeminacy in the gambits of both brothers verge on the unforgiveable. Sensing this danger perhaps, they switch topics: Sigurðr has achieved great feats abroad, but Eysteinn has improved conditions in Norway, building harbours and raising beacons. The last word goes to Eysteinn. To Sigurðr's remark that he swam across the Jordan and tied a knot in a thicket, and his challenge to his brother to untie it, Eysteinn merely shrugs. He is not about to go to the Holy Land; when Sigurðr returned from his travels all he had left was a single ship to contribute to his brother's fleet, unlike, it is implied, earlier Norwegian kings whose Mediterranean raiding brought both fame and material gain.[109] Wisely, both brothers stop the game at this point. Although they are furious with one another, they nevertheless succeed in keeping the peace between them for the remainder of their lives. Eysteinn died in 1123. Although Sigurðr began to show signs of insanity, his erratic behaviour was tolerated by the Norwegian nobility and he continued to rule until his death in 1130.

Eysteinn seems to have initiated the contest because Sigurðr had taken as his mistress a young woman to whom Eysteinn seems to have had an attachment – though she was too low-born for marriage to be in question. As in the case of Yngvi and Álfr, related towards the very beginning of *Heimskringla*, the

---

[106] See for example the consequences of the comparable game of naming what one puts one's trust in, in *Víga-Glúms saga*, ch. 14, ed. G. Turville-Petre (Oxford, 1940), pp. 23–5; *Víga-Glums saga*, trans. J. McKinnell (Edinburgh, 1987), pp. 83–7.
[107] Snorri Sturluson, *Heimskringla* III: 259–62, here pp. 259–60.
[108] Ibid., III: 261. Compare Gísli's provocation when his father claims that, judging by Gísli's forebearance when his sister is dishonoured, he must have fathered daughters not sons, as discussed in chapter three, p. 85.
[109] Haraldr harðráði, for example, whose history is related earlier in *Heimskringla*.

charismatic brother who can enthral women with tales of foreign travel uses his wider experience as cultural capital in order to become intimate with his brother's beloved.[110] Yet the dialogue between the brothers also highlights real questions about the changing nature of kingship in the twelfth-century north. In Scandinavian prehistory, Yngvi's raiding enhanced his prestige while Álfr appeared quite uncharismatic in his role as stay-at-home king. By 1100, kingship is differently understood. Eysteinn's knockout gambit is his assertion that he has enormously benefited his country by building churches, founding monasteries, helping sea-farers and administering the laws, while his brother has opted for travel and celebrity, for a heroic reputation when he comes home. Yet Sigurðr has also squandered the resources his brother had given him and has nothing material to show for his adventures. Twelfth-century kingdoms need adminstrator-kings, not itinerant raider-heroes, Snorri's text suggests. The escalation from childish boasts to real antipathy – and the gendered language of traditional insult – nevertheless suggests that the strategically complementary styles of kingship that these two brothers have chosen had prevented serious political conflict, perhaps even war, between the sons of Magnús. The *Heimskringla* account was composed about a hundred years after the death of the two kings and its author was well aware that almost a century of civil war would follow Sigurðr's death.

This chapter about fraternal hatred ends then with Snorri's imagined scene of successful conflict management between two royal brothers. In contrast with the pseudo-historical brothers Alrekr and Eiríkr, who killed one another with their horse-bits in the earliest saga in the compendium, and with Yngvi and Álfr, rivals for a woman who enjoyed Yngvi's conversation, these two historical Norwegian kings are depicted as having learned to contain, if not to relish, their sibling differences. Their rivalry has not dissipated; like many adult siblings each one rakes over childhood events to bolster and maintain what Bank and Kahn identify as a 'frozen image' of one another.[111] Their initial rehearsal of their complementary skill-sets reinforces the idea that both natural talent and deliberate decision-making have influenced their individual development. Nevertheless, Eysteinn and Sigurðr seem to have succeeded in sublimating their antipathy into a grownup version of 'aggressive play and healthy rivalry'.[112] They attend, each in their different way, to Norway's needs, building public works and increasing its international standing, and each has achieved a mature style of leadership in his chosen domain, reinforcing their successful strategy of counter-identification.[113]

---

[110] See above, p. 122.
[111] Bank and Kahn, *Sibling Bond*, pp. 73–4.
[112] Mitchell, *Siblings*, p. 10.
[113] Cf. Hinshelwood and Winship, 'Orestes and Democracy'.

Conclusion

Struggles for political power, differences over inheritance, and sexual jealousy occasion fraternal conflict in medieval narratives. Astonishingly trivial causes – a dead sheep or a superior horse – provoke an infantile rage whose outcome is very frequently death, whether by an archery accident, through a pocket knife which slips when wrestling in play, or by a deliberately wielded sword. Psychoanalytic and psychological theories illuminate the complexities involved in successful resolution of sibling hatred: the elder brother must learn to live with the sibling who he fears will displace him, and to accept that his younger brother is not his second self. His task, like that of his younger brother, is to establish a separate, a complementary identity. The medieval younger brother must learn to accept that the older brother is indeed the winner-who-takes-all and that he cannot usurp his place or his social position. Brothers obsessively patrol the borderline between them, checking for, and reacting with excessive emotion to, any perceived encroachment. Choosing a different path in life can postpone sibling conflict, often indefinitely, if the brothers remain apart. When counter-identification is construed as deliberate deidentification, however, as when brothers' choice of a monastic vocation is abhorred by their knightly siblings, and spiritual fraternity is made to substitute for blood-kinship, the brother's behaviour is regarded as an intolerable affront and sibling murderousness is exacerbated.

Medieval imaginations recognized that brothers could harbour irrational hatred of one another, hatred which the medieval psychology of sin largely construed as envy, identified with the root cause of Cain's murder of his brother. As Quinones observes, 'the divisions of the brothers within the Cain-Abel rubric show a great capacity to assume the nature of rival principles and thus enter into great dualistic schemes'.[114] These contrasting binaries – older/younger, stay-at-home/adventurer, knight/monk, husband/seducer – are mostly addressed through violence in the medieval narratives considered in this chapter. Yet, since the brother *is* also the second self, such violence annihilates the self who commits the killing and the fratricide rarely benefits from his crime for long. Sisterly hatred stems from the same psychological fears of displacement displayed by brothers, intensified by their marked substitutability in patriarchal (or fratriarchal) 'exchanges of women'. Disputes over inheritance and sexual rivalry generate competition between sisters, just as they do between brothers. Although sisters rarely kill one another, their quarrels, as the next chapter shows, are as bitter, as petty, and as deeply rooted as any fraternal conflict.

---

[114] Quinones, *Changes of Cain*, p. 9.

5

'Te souviegne de ce que je suis ta seur':[1] Sisters and Hostility

Introduction

Quarrels between sisters in medieval narratives are not so different from those between brothers; they range in scale from petty rivalries to conflicts which affect the destinies of outsiders beyond the family group, even – in a couple of texts – determining rule in Arthur's Britain. As suggested in chapter three, the relative interchangeability of sisters, and the fact that similar adult lives, centring on marriage and motherhood, lie ahead of girls means that they are less often depicted as antagonizing one another through such common fraternal strategies as counter-identification or rejection. As among brothers, the surface motivations for sisterly disputes are most frequently sexual rivalry or inheritance claims, but girls can fall out with one another over less substantial matters: sibling competitiveness can manifest itself at an early age. In his late-twelfth-century collection of exemplary stories, Caesarius of Heisterbach relates a delightful story of two little girls being educated in a monastery of his order in Frisia. The two sisters are highly competitive in the classroom, but one falls ill. Fearing that she was lagging behind in her studies while her sister was making great progress, the poorly child asked to see the prioress and offered to ask her mother for six denarii which she would give to the prioress if she would suspend her sister's studies until the patient was well enough to study again. The prioress, Caesarius reports, laughed at this, but was impressed by the little scholar's enthusiasm.[2] Just so, the rivalries between older pairs of sisters often seem petty and spiteful at the level of attack and response, but such quarrels function as proxies for female anxieties about extremely serious issues.

Quarrelling over Gawain

Gawain's knightly demeanour, and that of his companions, becomes a bone of contention between sisters in three related Arthurian texts. The ostensible

---

[1] 'Remember that I am your sister'; *Erec: Roman arthurien en prose*, ed. C. Pickford (Geneva and Paris, 2nd edn, 1968), p. 163; L-G, IV: 300.
[2] Caesarius of Heisterbach, *Dialogue on Miracles*, iv.25, ed. Scott and Bland, I: 222. Cf. also *Index exemplorum*, ed. Tubach, p. 337, no. 4423 for a similar story.

proposition is whether a man's worth can be judged by his appearance: a group of ladies, including two sisters, gaze from afar at unknown knights and leap to conclusions about their courage and social status.[3] The fullest and most dramatic version of the sisters' quarrel occurs in Heinrich von den Türlin's early-thirteenth-century romance *Diu Crône*.[4] Here the quarrel between the two sisters appears to build on a pre-existing mutual dislike. Flursensephin, the elder sister, observes Gawein and his companion arriving in a town where a tournament is to take place. She remarks that he and his companion Quoikos look like merchants dishonourably pretending to be knights in order to stave off potential robbers. Little Quebeleplus, her younger sister, contradicts her, arguing not only that the two men carry themselves like knights, but, she adds provocatively, either will be capable of defeating Flursensephin's own chosen knight, Fiers of Arramis, in the tournament. Flursensephin flies into a violent rage, rebuking Quebeleplus for daring to have an opinion at all. Quebeleplus persists that it is wrong for ladies to malign unknown men; she will adopt the stranger as her knight and urge him to defeat Flursensephin's sweetheart. Flursensephin responds with:

> einen ôrslac . . .der was alsô grôz
> daz ir von bluote hin gôz
> beidiu nase unde munt,
> dâ von sie wol drîstunt
> nider viel ûf daz pflaster.

('such a blow on the face that she fell three times to the ground and blood poured from her nose and mouth.')[5]

Quebeleplus makes her way to the house where Gawein is staying and recruits him as her champion. She asks him to avenge her against her sister by defeating Fiers, but requests that, unlike the other knights in the tournament, he should not contend for her sister's hand. Quebeleplus's father Leigamur, who has surrounded the house with his knights on the spiteful advice given by his elder daughter and who now attacks Gawein's party, is defeated by Quoikos. Apologizing to Gawein, he chuckles when he hears why his younger daughter is present. Quebeleplus leaves Gawein her sleeve as token.

At the tournament Fiers and Leigamur are taken prisoner, to Flursensephin's astonishment and chagrin. The two captives are given to Quebeleplus to do with as she wishes, while Flursensephin is awarded to Gawein. He declines her hand, asking that she be betrothed to Quoikos. Thus, for her disobliging comments about the appearance of Gawein and Quoikos and her aggression towards her younger sister, Flursensephin is punished both by losing her

[3] Cf. the equivalent scenes in the *Conte del Graal* and *Parzival*, discussed below.
[4] Heinrich von dem Türlin, *Diu Crône*, ed. G. Felder (Berlin and Boston, 2012), lines 17678–18679; *The Crown*, trans. J. W. Thomas (Lincoln NE and London, 1989), pp. 199–210.
[5] *Diu Crône*, ed. Felder, lines 17844–9; *The Crown*, trans. Thomas, p. 201.

sweetheart and being made to marry one of the men she was disparaging. Although Quoikos has acquitted himself well in the tournament, he is not of Gawein's rank. Quebeleplus, too young herself to marry, has successfully sabotaged her sister's romantic hopes.

In the *Conte del Graal*, where the Sisters' Quarrel episode originates, the emphases are somewhat different.[6] The elder sister is less violent to her younger sister, La Pucelle aux Petites Manches (the Maiden with the Small Sleeves) and Gauvain contents himself with presenting the girls' father and the elder's beloved to the younger sister as her prisoners before riding off in search of further adventure. Although the moral implications of the story – the judging eyes of women, the offence caused by disparaging knights and demoting them to the class of merchants – remain the same, Heinrich's version considerably intensifies the sisterly rivalry. The elder sister is more comprehensively punished both for her cruelty to her sibling and for her critical remarks about Gawein. Wolfram von Eschenbach, by contrast, develops Chrétien's quarrel between the sisters over the merits of Gawan in a very different direction.[7] In *Parzival* the elder sister Obîe's nastiness towards her sister and her insulting treatment of Gawan is entirely psychologized. Obîe has driven away her royal lover (and foster-brother) Meljanz by an over-emphatic insistence that he should offer her knightly service if he is to woo her, and her misery at the rift she has caused with him makes her behave savagely and erratically towards her family and to strangers. The outcome of the battle in *Parzival* is narratively more satisfying than in the *Conte del Graal*, for Gawan effects two reconciliations: one between Meljanz and Obîe's father, the king's former guardian, and between the king and his beloved. The scenes between Gawan and the younger sister Obîlot who retains him as her knight are altogether charming; Obîlot's little friend Clauditte observes that the girls possess only dolls with which they could reward Gawan's service, but she offers to let Obîlot have any of her dolls to present to him if they are prettier than Obîlot's own.[8] Clauditte's generosity counterpoints the unpleasant behaviour of Obîe both towards her little sister and to Gawan; a freely chosen friend is more understanding and loyal than the conflicted sibling.[9]

In these three versions of the Sisters' Quarrel, the elder sister's anxiety about her marital prospects is palpable; the episode foregrounds how the relative powerlessness of the noble girl to determine her own fate causes her to misuse such power as she has over her younger sister. Wolfram observes that the people of Bearosche think it is high time that their duke's daughter Obîe should

---

[6] Chrétien de Troyes, *Le Conte del Graal*, ed. C. Méla in *Chrétien de Troyes: Romans*, ed. M. Zink (Paris, 1994), lines 4884–5583 ; Chrétien de Troyes, *Perceval: The Story of the Grail*, in *Arthurian Romances*, trans. D. D. R. Owen (London, 1993), pp. 440–9.

[7] Wolfram von Eschenbach, *Parzival*, ed. Lachmann 6th ed., Bk VII; *Parzival*, trans. Edwards, Bk VII.

[8] *Parzival*, ed. Lachmann, VII.372: 15–21; *Parzival*, trans. Edwards, pp. 108–27.

[9] See Apter, *Sister Knot*, pp. 186–202, for how female friendships seek both to avoid and to reproduce the sister-relationship.

become someone's *amie*, but Obîe's alienation of her royal suitor means the cancellation, or at least postponement, of her marriage arrangements.[10] The younger sister, still a child, has no such stake in the tournament. She speaks from a clear-eyed apprehension of the truth about knightly appearance and has the freedom to exercise a little girl's charm over Gawan and his companion. The episode recognizes typical sisterly dynamics: the capacity of the younger sister to torment the elder by bringing her insecurities into the open, and the elder's desire to demonstrate her authority through disciplining, even bullying, her younger sister. Victor Cicirelli foregrounds the role of older siblings as 'socializing agents', teaching younger siblings what is appropriate to their age and gender. 'Younger siblings learn values, knowledge, and skills that help them to develop cognitively, emotionally and socially, as well as values and knowledge about the larger society (such as respect for elders) that prepares them for future living'.[11] But Cicirelli also observes that rigid sibling hierarchy can allow the older sibling to tyrannize the younger; Flursenphin's brutal attack on her sister contrasts with the merely verbal sparring of Obîe and Obîlot, and her excessive behaviour perhaps merits the punishment which Quebeleplus's retaliation brings down on her.

Thus older sisters assert a right to correct and teach their younger sisters, while younger sisters make use of their intuitive understanding of their sisters' inner lives to tease and provoke: Obîlot does not improve her older sister's frame of mind by mentioning her sister's aggrieved lover Meljanz in the same breath as Gawan. As Bank and Kahn note, 'Siblings know well the arsenal of weapons each possesses; they are usually able consciously to calculate, calibrate, plan and control their aggressive actions and hostile statements'.[12] These different versions of the sisters' quarrel over Gawan highlight in varying degrees the enduring tensions in sisterly relationships, and offer naturalistic depictions of elder-sister bossiness and younger-sister torment. They also recognize that the marriageable girl's impending change of status is a site of tension for her siblings. While brothers concern themselves with the advantages of the new alliance forged through the marriage, sisters become sensitized to their own future marital prospects. Even a much younger sister, who does not yet participate directly in the competition for a husband, sees the arrival of her sister's possible suitors as an opportunity to test out her own attractiveness and social skills. Thus the three younger sisters play-act the role of courtly love-object with Gawan/Gawein; Obilôt's and Claudite's childish notion that their dolls might be a suitable gift for Gawan contrasts with Obilôt's panicky realization that her knight must have her sleeve as a token for the tournament, and that she

---

[10] *Parzival*, ed. Lachmann, VII.345 ; *Parzival*, trans. Edwards, p. 110.
[11] Cicirelli, *Sibling Relationships*, pp. 75–9 (p. 78); see also Cicirelli, 'Sibling Relationships in Cross-Cultural Perspective', p. 9.
[12] Bank and Kahn, *The Sibling Bond*, p. 199; see further on sisters' empathetic understanding of one another as facilitating hostile moves, Apter, *Sister Knot*, pp. 78–84.

has nothing suitable to offer. Obilôt capitalizes on the problems that Obîe's rejection of Meljanz have caused her parents to cement her own standing as a parental favourite; she charms her father into providing her with a lavish new set of clothes at the same time as she practises her feminine persuasiveness on the responsive Gawan.

Sisters and Inheritance

The introduction of primogeniture solves some problems of sibling rivalry – each brother knows in advance where he stands in terms of inheritance, and the younger brothers can plan their careers accordingly – but it brings others in its wake. When inheritance practice is in the process of change, literary texts lay bare the emotional implications of newly emerging legal provisions as they impact on family relationships. Where there are no male heirs, competition between sisters over their patrimony can be as intense as the brotherly rivalries explored in the previous chapter. A seminal sibling conflict which influences depictions of sisterly hostility across a number of later texts is the legal case instituted by a younger against her older sister in Chrétien's *Yvain: Le Chevalier au Lion*. The different versions of this quarrel, in French, German, English and Norse, shed light on norms for the division of inheritance between sisters under the specific legal systems of the land where the translation is made, while the episodes also differently characterize the intransigence of the elder and the attitude of the younger sister. In *Yvain* the dispute between the two daughters of the lord of Noire Espine begins when the elder sister announces that she will take the entire patrimony for herself and disinherit her younger sister.[13] The younger sister intends to take her case to Arthur's court; the elder sister forestalls her by arriving there first and enlisting Gauvain as her champion in judicial combat. When the younger sister can find no champion of her own, she sets out in search of Yvain, the 'Chevalier au Lion'. Yvain is located and the pair return to court just in time for the combat. The king tries to persuade the elder sister to compromise; addressing the younger, he explains that he has asked the elder to yield 'votre droiture' ('your rightful portion').[14] Nevertheless, because the latter has already demanded judicial combat, the king seems powerless to enforce what he regards as a more equitable settlement, and the battle proceeds. The two disguised knights fight to a draw, and everyone, including the queen, begs the elder sister to cede a third or a quarter of her land to the younger.[15] Finally the king tricks her by asking where she might be – that damsel who 'par

[13] Chrétien de Troyes, *Le Chevalier au Lion*, ed. D. Hult, in *Chrétien de Troyes: Romans*, ed. Zink; see also G. Armstrong, 'Questions of Inheritance: Le Chevalier au Lion and La Queste del Saint Graal', in *Rereading Allegory: Essays in Memory of Daniel Poirion*, Yale French Studies 95 (1999), 171–92 and D. Maddox, *The Arthurian Romances of Chrétien de Troyes: Once and Future Fictions* (Cambridge, 1991), pp. 69–76.
[14] *Le Chevalier au Lion*, ed. Hult, line 4783.
[15] Ibid., lines 6173–4.

force et par male merci' ('by force and with evil intention') has disinherited her sister.[16] Inadvertently admitting to her malicious desire to see her sister reduced to beggary, the elder speaks up. Although the sympathies of the narrator and the court are very much aligned with the younger sister, as Donald Maddox observes, the settlement the king imposes remains imprecise: the younger will hold an unspecified amount of land in fief from the elder.[17] Under primogeniture the usual practice would be for the elder to designate between a quarter and a third – the very amount the court had suggested – for other siblings to hold, but there is no guarantee in *this* settlement that the grudging elder sister will be so generous.[18] Arthur could have specified the giving of land in *parage*, a system coming back into vogue in Chrétien's day. This would have left the younger sister holding the land from the king as suzerain, instead of remaining subject still to the vagaries of the elder sister, but the king does not demand this.[19] For Maddox, this indicates hasty judgement on Arthur's part, and a wish to be done with the matter, rather than ensuring that the ends of justice are served.[20]

Other adaptors of the Rival Sisters episode are uneasy about the uncertain legal disposition in the French text. In Hartmann von Aue's version, the younger sister is so appalled by the blood shed in the combat that she is ready to renounce her claim entirely; the king is so 'harte erbolgen' ('seriously angry') with the elder sister that he refuses to accept her offer.[21] Finally, pointing out that her champion Gawein is claiming to have lost the battle (as of course is Iwein), the king puts enough pressure on the intransigent elder girl for her to agree to share the inheritance.[22] Oaths are sworn and, the narrator assures us, the younger gets her rightful portion: 'sî ir teil ze rehte enpfie'.[23] The Norse translator of the poem disposes of the matter fairly speedily after the fight is concluded. In *Ívens saga* the king briskly declares that he will arbitrate: 'en meyjarnar skyldu skipta til helmings allt þat er þær erfðu eptir föður sinn' ('and the maidens were to divide equally everything they had inherited from their father').[24]

The fourteenth-century English translation *Ywain and Gawain* regards the legal issues pertaining to the two sisters as being more important than their

---

[16] Ibid., line 6381.
[17] Maddox, *Arthurian Romances*, pp. 77–8.
[18] P. Jonin, 'Aspects de la vie sociale au XIIe siècle dans *Yvain*', *L'information littéraire* 16 (1964), 47–54.
[19] Duby, *The Knight, the Lady*, p. 276, notes that at the time the romance was being composed, *parage*, which had fallen out of fashion with the twelfth century's enthusiasm for simple primogeniture, was being gradually restored.
[20] Maddox, *Arthurian Romances*, pp. 77–8.
[21] Hartmann von Aue, *German Romance III: Iwein, or The Knight with the Lion*, ed. and trans. C. Edwards, Arthurian Archives (Cambridge, 2007). The younger sister's offer of renunciation, lines 7380–94 (line 7410).
[22] 'ich teil ir liute unde lant' ('I will share with her the people and land'), *Iwein*, line 7785.
[23] *Iwein*, line 7791.
[24] *Ívens saga*, ed. and trans. M. Kalinke, in *Norse Romance II: The Knights of the Round Table*, ed. M. Kalinke (Cambridge, 1999), pp. 94–5.

personal relationship. The translator rarely departs far from his French exemplar, but he makes a point of declaring that Arthur's decision constitutes a legal precedent for the partibility of land, 'þis land was first, I understand / þat ever was parted in Ingland'.[25] Here the younger sister is awarded half of the patrimony, but she holds it from the elder in 'tenure in parage', for in England by this period parage was very common. Thus the estate is not divided, and the elder sister continues to hold the whole inheritance from Arthur. The poet of the English *Ywain and Gawain* may have had specialist legal knowledge, allowing him to adjudge the most equitable settlement and assign its origin to Arthur, who is more favourably viewed by the English poet than he is by Chrétien.[26] Arthur has a sound, contemporary, legal understanding; where the male line failed, inheritances were customarily shared between female heirs in England from the late twelfth century onwards.[27]

In the French *Roman de Silence* by Heldris de Cornouailles, the romance's plot, in which an only daughter has to cross-dress as a man and become a social male in order to inherit, is driven by the problem of inheritance by twin sisters.[28] Before Silence was born, two earls had married twin sisters and, when their father died, each earl contended that his wife was the elder and should inherit. One noble is willing to compromise and to share equally; the other refuses. The resulting judicial combat leaves both knights dead, and thus the king of England enacts a law forbidding women to inherit. As Sharon Kinoshita notes, the king's 'ruling belatedly compensates for the monarchy's inability to control the violence unleashed by triangulated male desires – two indistinguishable counts vying for one piece of land – by stripping *women* of their customary rights of inheritance.'[29] When displaced onto the women's husbands, the inheritance-driven quarrel results in mutual destruction rather than the eventual compromise and settlement which the two unmarried sisters are able to achieve with Arthur's guidance in the *Ywain*-episode. This prelude to the history of Silence also confronts directly the challenge that twinship presents to primogeniture, contrasting with the evasions of the male twin-romances discussed in chapter two.

The inheritance quarrel between sisters also becomes productive in another mode, that of allegory as deployed within the romance genre. In an adventure

---

[25] *Ywain and Gawain*, ed. A. B. Freedman and N. T. Harrington, EETS os 254 (Oxford, 1964), lines 3767–8.

[26] K. Busby, 'Chrétien de Troyes English'd', *Neophilologus* 71 (1987), 596–613, here p. 606; *Ywain and Gawain*, ed. Freedman and Harrington, pp. xxvi and 130–1.

[27] S. L. Waugh, *The Lordship of England: Royal Wardships and Marriages in English Society and Politics, 1217–1327* (Princeton, 1988), p. 16; see also S. Kinoshita, 'Heldris de Cornuälle's *Roman de Silence* and the Feudal Politics of Lineage', *PMLA* 110 (1995), 397–409 (pp. 399–400).

[28] Heldris de Cornouailles, *Silence: A Thirteenth-Century French Romance*, ed. and trans. S. Roche-Mahdi (East Lansing MI, 1992), in particular lines 281–4. Compare the discussion of male twins and inheritance in chapter two, pp. 62–3.

[29] On the legal background to the romance see Kinoshita, 'Heldris de Cornuälle's *Silence*', p. 400.

in the Grail Quest, similarly recounted in the *Queste* and in Malory, the rival sisters are converted into allegorical principles.[30] In this episode Bo(o)rs is asked to fight for a younger sister against an older one. King Amanz (Malory's Anyawse) had loved the older sister and had given her all his lands, but her rule was so evil that he revoked the gift and gave it to the younger. Now Amanz/ Anyawse is dead, the older sister is seeking to seize back the inheritance. The older sister symbolizes the Old Law; the younger the New Law. Bo(o)rs is, of course, decisively victorious over the champion of the Old Law and the elder sister is left with nothing. In the *Queste*, the elder continues to make trouble for the younger; envy, that besetting sibling sin, is not dispelled in defeat: 'l'autre dame pot la guerroia puis toz les jorz de sa vie, come cele qui toz jorz avoit envie sor li' ('the other lady harried her always . . . as one who nursed an undying envy all her life').[31] Malory awards Bors a total victory: 'the old lady fledde with all hir knyghtes' and all those who hold fiefs of her agree to do homage to the younger.[32]

The late-twelfth or early-thirteenth-century French romance *La Mule sans Frein*, which may also have been composed by Chrétien, is framed by the theme of sisterly rivalry, this time given a more comic inflection.[33] A girl on a bridleless mule comes to Camelot seeking a knight who can recover for her the missing accoutrement. Keu offers himself as her champion, but turns back at the sight of a dangerous sword-bridge, much like that in Chrétien's *Le Chevalier à la Charete*. Gauvain successfully takes on the adventure and wins the bridle which is in the possession of the mule-rider's sister. '[J]e sui sa suer et ele est moie' ('I am her sister and she is mine'), the lady admits.[34] Gauvain politely declines the lady's offer of herself and hastens back to Camelot where the bridle is returned to the girl, and she goes on her way once again.[35] The contest between the sisters must owe something to Chrétien's inheritance quarrel, but the story is so sparely told that the significance of the dispute is obscured.[36]

---

[30] *La Quête du Saint Graal*, ed. F. Bogdanow (Paris, 2006), pp. 428–40; *The Quest of the Holy Grail*, trans. P. Matarasso (Harmondsworth, 1969), pp. 184–7; Malory, *Le Morte Darthur*, ed. Field, I: 734–5, and see further Armstrong, 'Questions of Inheritance'.

[31] *La Quête*, ed. Bogdanow, p. 440; *Quest*, trans. Matarasso, p. 187.

[32] Armstrong, 'Questions of Inheritance', pp. 189–91 notes that the theme of inheritance rights is also taken up by the fiend in female form who tempts Perceval, but here the younger sister is eliminated: Malory, *Le Morte Darthur*, ed. Field, I: p. 710.

[33] *La Mule sans Frein*, in *Two Old French Gauvain Romances*, ed. R. C. Johnston and D. D. R. Owen (Edinburgh and London, 1972); see also D. D. R. Owen, 'Paien de Maisières — A Joke that Went Wrong', *Forum for Modern Language Studies* 2 (1966), 192–6; cf. also D. D. R. Owen, 'Two More Romances by Chrétien de Troyes?', *Romania* 92 (1971), 246–60.

[34] *Mule*, ed. Johnston and Owen, line 970.

[35] See I. Arseneau, who reads the romance as essentially parodic, 'Gauvain et les métamorphoses de la merveille: déchéance d'un héros et déclin du surnaturel', in *Une étrange constance. Les motifs merveilleux dans la littérature d'expression française du Moyen Âge à nos jours*, ed. F. Gingras, Collections de la République des Lettres. Symposiums (Québec, 2006), pp. 91–106.

[36] See Owen, as in n. 33 above.

Sisters and Hostility

In *Diu Crône* the lost bridle and the theme of sisterly rivalry are re-combined; both erotic interests and issues of inheritance and of sovereignty are at stake in the episode.[37] Gawein comes to the castle of Queen Amurfina, and falls in love with her.[38] Passing a Perilous Bed test, he spends the night with her. Amurfina seems aware of Gawein's reputation as a seducer, for she makes doubly sure of her new lover by sharing a love-potion with him. This causes him to lose his memory for some time: since Amurfina's literary origins are in the fairy-mistress trope, Heinrich teases his audience with the notion that Gawein may find that he has been trapped in the castle for three hundred years.[39] However, a plaque commemorating his earlier feats against Amurfina's father restores Gawein's memory, and after pledging to marry his lady, he sets out once more.

When Gawein arrives at Amurfina's castle, Heinrich remarks that she and her sister Sgoidamur have inherited a magic bridle from their father; this is apparently a bridle of sovereignty. The sisters were intended to share it, but Amurfina has appropriated the bridle and driven Sgoidamur away from her inheritance. Sgoidamur has set out to Karidol (Camelot) to request assistance in retrieving the bridle. Amurfina had originally sent for Gawein in order to secure him as her champion, but does not, once she has fallen in love with him, mention the bridle to him. Thus when Sgoidamur appears at Karidol to request a champion at Pentecost, the traditional occasion for adventure, and after Kei has failed the challenge, Gawein willingly undertakes the quest, unaware that he is acting against his fiancée's interests.[40] He sets off on Sgoidamur's mule and, crossing the Sword-Bridge, comes to a revolving castle, where he becomes involved in a beheading game with the castle's lord, a certain Gansguoter. He is revealed as the uncle of the two sisters, and, moreover, is living with Arthur's mother who had disappeared some years previously. After a series of adventures devised by Gansguoter Gawein is awarded the bridle. Only now does Gansguoter outline the complex family relations behind the adventure, telling Gawein that Amurfina is waiting to greet him elsewhere in the castle.

When Gawein and Amurfina arrive together at Arthur's court, Sgoidamur is overjoyed to have the bridle restored to her mule, but alarmed to see her sister in Gawein's company. Ginover (Guenevere) makes peace between the two sisters and an accommodation is reached. Sgoidamur receives the bridle and acknowledges that she is now subject to Gawein; he bestows her upon Gasozein de Dragoz (probably of otherworld origin, he appears to be Ginover's former lover; see p. 150 below). When Sgoidamur consents, a double wedding is celebrated. Gawein thus tactfully solves the problem of Gasozein's passion for

---

[37] See L. Jillings, 'The Rival Sisters Dispute in *Diu Crône* and its French Antecedents', in *An Arthurian Tapestry: Essays in Memory of Lewis Thorpe*, ed. K. Varty (Glasgow, 1981), pp. 248–59; Jillings argues that the bridle motif and the inheritance plot had already been combined in an antecedent to the German romance.

[38] *Diu Crône*, ed. Felder, lines 7667–9128; *The Crown*, trans. Thomas, pp. 86–101;

[39] N. Thomas, *Diu Crône and the Medieval Arthurian Cycle*, Arthurian Studies 50 (Cambridge, 2002), p. 101.

[40] *Diu Crône*, ed. Felder, lines 12611–13934; *The Crown*, trans. Thomas, pp. 141–55.

Ginover which had earlier caused him to abduct and attempt to rape her, secures this problematic knight as a brother-in-law and neutralizes the dissatisfaction of his sister-in-law.[41] Sgoidamur and Gasozein are to take over Amurfina's castle, so removing him from court and returning him to the world of fairy. The previously autonomous Amurfina relocates to Karidol, putting her firmly under the authority of Ginover and her husband. Most importantly for Gawein's continuing adventures, he has gained Gansguoter as an ally; the lord and his territory have affinities with the Grail. Gawein's later success in the text's Grail-adventure will owe everything to Gansguoter's support.[42]

The Rival Sister story thus functions differently across the various romances in which it appears. In Chrétien and his translators the main focus is on the equitableness of different kinds of inheritance practice; at a time when primogeniture was already customary, it may seem odd that the elder sister's contention that she should be sole inheritrix should be questioned. But, as chapter one sets out, strict primogeniture had already come under pressure by the end of the twelfth century: younger sons were beginning to hold lands in fief from their older brothers, the solution to the quarrel which Arthur eventually proposes in Chrétien's text. Moreover, the younger sister needs some provision for a dowry when she weds. Although as her champion Yvain ought to win her hand along with her law-suit, as a married man he cannot secure her future in this way. Nor, given his amorous track-record, will Gauvain compensate the older sister's loss by offering himself as husband. The younger sister's plight and the elder's selfish behaviour thus points up the inherent difficulties in the inheritrix's situation. Her father dead, and by definition having no brothers, she may imagine that the privileges of primogeniture grant her the freedom to do as she wishes with her inheritance, but social pressure operates to ensure that she makes adequate provision for her younger sister – as indeed a brother would.

The significance of the magic bridle in *La Mule sans Frein* is unclear; its recovery leads to no visible benefit for the younger sister, and the elder's loss is nugatory. Heinrich, by contrast, makes multivalent use of the motif to accomplish suitable marriages for the two sisters, to solve the problem of Ginover's putative lover, to secure the moral stature of Gawein as a faithful married man rather than an amorous seducer, to bring Gawein's fairy-mistress wife safely into the courtly world and to remove the problematic figure of Gasozein from the ambit of Ginover and Arthur. Sisterly rivalry is extinguished through the orderly and appropriate re-distribution of status, property and husbands. When later in the text Amurfina and the rest of the court are persuaded (falsely) that Gawein has been killed, Sgoidamur offers her sister warm sympathy and understanding.[43]

---

[41] See S. Samples, 'An Unlikely Hero: The Rapist-Knight Gasozein in *Diu Crône*', *Arthuriana* 22.4 (2012), 101–19.

[42] Thomas, *Diu Crône*, p. 5; p.97.

[43] *Diu Crône*, ed. Felder, lines 17173–311; *The Crown*, trans. Thomas, pp. 194–5; see also C. Larrington, 'Mourning Gawein: Performing Grief in *Diu Crône*', in *Arthurian Emotion: Voice, Mind, Body*, ed. F. Brandsma, C. Larrington and C. Saunders (Cambridge, forthcoming).

Normal sisterly intimacy and love has resumed now that each has a husband and a castle or kingdom of her own.

Fair shares for all is a central sibling concern.[44] Francine Klagsbrun, who observes that sibling rivalries break out anew in quite petty ways on the death of the parents and the division of parental possessions, argues that 'for siblings money is also something more than money. It has symbolic meaning... money is emblematic of the sibling's worth in the eyes of parents. It validates each one's history in the family'.[45] Just so with castles and bridles: unlike the rigid entailments of strict male primogeniture, the choices of the inheritrix are, in legal terms, less constrained. The elder sister seems to be expected to share her inheritance with her sister in some way: the repetition of the sister-inheritance motif across the romance genre indicates a normative understanding of estate division between sisters, and the difficulty in enforcing it. '[A] major task of middle-aged siblings is... the achievement of the division of parental property ... without rancor and bitterness', observes Cicirelli, whose reference to middle-aged siblings reflects current demographic patterns.[46] Medieval siblings were likely to inherit from their parents rather earlier in the life-span, when dowry and marriage prospects for sisters might still be in flux.[47]

Clearly the symbolic bridle cannot be divided equally between sisters, and its existence triggers rivalrous manoeuvres to gain possession of it. In *Diu Crône* the contention is settled when both sisters are married and thus provided for, and solidarity and affection resumes between them, while *La Mule* leaves unclear whether the restoration of the bridle to the sister who comes to Camelot marks the end of the battle between the sisters. The bridle signifies control – whether self-control or the husband's control of his wife – and it thus functions as an ambiguous but suggestive symbol of sisters' emergence into adulthood and the reconfiguring of childhood rivalries into adult competition.

Erotic Competition and Sexual Jealousy

Sgoidamur may have hoped to win Gawein as her husband through his acceptance of the Bridle Quest. That he returns from it with her sister as his betrothed could have been galling, but Heinrich intends the joy of a double wedding as conclusion to this episode and has no interest in developing a characterization of these sisters as erotic rivals. Whether well-born or not, in medieval narratives a woman is rarely able freely to choose herself a husband. Rather she must wait for a suitor to present himself and hope that she passes muster in his eyes. The same theme of powerlessness which underpins the 'Rival Sister' story, and the normally sublimated understanding that sisters

---

[44] Apter, *Sister Knot*, pp. 137–44.
[45] Klagsbrun, *Mixed Feelings*, pp. 271–2.
[46] Cicirelli, 'Sibling Relationships in Adulthood', p. 460.
[47] See chapter one, pp. 18–19.

are competitors, comes into clearer focus once a suitor is in view. Yet openly acknowledged rivalry would breach conventions of female decorum; age-hierarchy often dictates that the eldest should marry first, and if her seniority is not observed, trouble can ensue. The Knight of the Tour-Landry, writing for his two daughters, warns them of the poor impression girls can make when suitors come on their first visit. In his anecdote a knight comes to ask for the hand of a young woman. But, knowing that her suitor was to visit, the vain girl chose to wear only 'a streyght cote furred' in order to show off her figure. As the weather was very cold, the girl looked pale and unhealthy, while her younger sister, who had not anticipated inspection as a marriage prospect, was warmly dressed and had a 'rede and fresshe' colour. The knight promptly chose the younger sister as his bride. After the marriage, he notes with surprise that his sister-in-law, now sensibly dressed, looks ruddier and fairer than his wife. The wife smugly explains her sister's mistake in arraying 'her self in the most praty maner that she couthe for to shewe her body praty and small and well shapen', and she counts herself lucky that she won her husband's love that day through her sister's error of judgement.[48] The Knight does not comment further on the story, but the fact that the husband is now alert to his sister-in-law's attractiveness suggests future complications in the two sisters' relationship. Husbands' desire for their wives' sisters as a recurrent literary trope is explored in chapter seven.

Writing expressly for two sisters, the Knight calls up further apposite tales of contrasting pairs of sisters whose marital fates depend on their conformity to moral and social standards. A second tale in the *Book* relates how the emperor of Constantinople had two daughters. The younger was pious and God-fearing, while her elder sister mocked her nightly prayers for the dead and complained that they prevented her sleeping. Two knights fall in love with the sisters and an amorous rendezvous is arranged. But when the pious sister's lover steals within her bed-curtains he sees a thousand men in their winding-sheets surrounding the bed and flees in terror: his lady's virtue is preserved. The lover of the scornful elder sister meets no such supernatural obstacle, with the result that she falls pregnant by him. The emperor has her drowned and her lover flayed alive, while the younger sister, her virginity narrowly preserved by her piety, is rewarded with marriage to the king of Greece.[49] In a succeeding exemplum, another pious elder sister makes a good marriage while her spoiled younger half-sister behaves in a disorderly fashion in her own household. Finally her furious husband accidentally puts out one of her eyes when striking a servant with whom she is carousing. Mutilated, she loses the love of her husband and all, comments the Knight severely, through her own fault.[50] These sisters do not explicitly compete with one another for husbands, but the pious and demure girl, the Knight suggests, will make a good match because the wise suitor will

---

[48] Caxton, *The Book of the Knight of the Tower*, ed. Offord, pp. 158–60.
[49] Ibid., pp. 15–16.
[50] Ibid., pp. 17–19.

recognize her excellent character qualities, while her flighty sister will remain unmarried, or bring about her own ruin, or try her husband's patience beyond endurance.

As the allegorized application of the inheritance quarrel in the *Queste*-narrative indicates, pairs of sisters who embody opposed moral qualities and their contrasting fates are frequently employed in exemplary tales. Relying on the connection between the feminine grammatical gender of many abstract nouns in Latin and their personification in female form, the *Gesta Romanorum* makes frequent use of the good sister / bad sister trope.[51] So, for example, in the tale of the 'Dowries Given by the Emperor to his Two Daughters', one daughter (symbolizing the world) is beautiful, and whoever gains her as a husband gets no dowry, while the other daughter has as dowry the kingdom of heaven. Nevertheless, when the elder daughter is married 'with grete worshippe and gladnesse', the younger weeps on account of her ugliness, until her father comforts her with his explanation of the differing dowries. Shortly afterwards a 'gentile knyght' comes wooing the ugly daughter and wins her, and the empire besides.

The sisters discussed above are compared by their suitors, husbands and fathers, and one is denigrated relative to the other. Except in the first exemplum, where the successful younger sister crows over her, presumably still unwed, elder, these sisters do not openly compete for husbands. The sisterly relationship comes under very evident strain, however, when there is only one desirable suitor and more than one marriageable woman, particularly if the suitor is of high social rank. The ballad 'The Twa Sisters' (Child Ballad 10) dramatizes the extreme sexual jealousy of one sister for another, especially when principles of birth order hierarchy are transgressed: Sweet William loves the younger sister more than the elder. When the opportunity presents itself, the elder pushes her younger sister into the river.[52] In version 10C the younger sister pleads for her sister to pull her out, offering half of her land – only for the sister to retort that she will inherit all the land once her sister is dead – compounding the inheritance and erotic motivations for sisterly hostility. The younger sister offers to renounce William, but her sister reckons that she will gain him anyway. The older sister's jealousy is manifest: 'Your cherry cheeks and your yellow hair / Garrd [made] me gang [go] maiden evermair'; this, and her sense of entitlement, prove fatal for the younger. The crime is discovered when the drowned sister's body floats into a mill-pool and the miller, or a passing harper, makes a harp from it, shaping the breast-bone into the instrument's frame and stringing it with the dead girl's hair. When played before the king and queen, the harp speaks of its own accord, identifying the sister as the murderer. In some versions the

---

[51] *Early English Versions of the Gesta Romanorum*, ed. S. J. H. Herrtage (London, 1879), pp. 48–50 (King Lear and his daughters); pp. 132–5 (Allegory of Four Daughters of God); pp. 172–4 (The Emperor's Three Widowed Daughters); pp. 353–6 (The Dowries given by the Emperor to his Two Daughters).

[52] *Ballads*, ed. Child, I: 118–41.

harp advises the hanging or drowning of the sister; other versions simply end with the dramatic revelation of the culprit's identity.[53] The convention that the elder sister should marry before the younger sister is disrupted at the start of the 'Twa Sisters', yet the elder's jealous and violent nature explains why she cannot find a husband of her own. '[H]ighly charged feelings between siblings still powerfully entwined, still competing as they did in childhood, still unclear about boundary lines between them', as Klagsbrun notes, are starkly dramatized in this widely circulating ballad.[54]

Erotic rivalry is more subtly nuanced in *Hauksdœla þáttr*, part of the long compilation of contemporary sagas about twelfth- and thirteenth-century Icelandic history, *Sturlunga saga*.[55] Though this tale is related as occurring in an identifiable historical context, it is strongly inflected by folkloric patterns.[56] Two sisters, both called Þóra, live at Þingvellir with their parents; their mother is the daughter of one of the most powerful men in Iceland, while their father's genealogy is more obscure. Þingvellir, the place of the Icelandic assembly, is a potently symbolic site for Icelandic ideas of nationhood and independence and the sisters' future marriages are significant for the course of thirteenth-century Icelandic history. The sisters often do their washing at the river; one day at the water's edge, the elder raises the question of their future marriages. The younger Þóra protests that such matters are already determined by fate, and forces the elder to go first in naming her preferred suitor. The elder Þóra says that she wishes that the high-status chieftain Jón Sigmundarson might ask for her. An unlikely and troubling series of events would have to happen for younger Þóra's wish to come true. Þorvaldr Gizurarson, the high-ranking son of the lawspeaker, is in exile in Norway with his wife Jóra, daughter of one of the Icelandic bishops. Jóra is, however, too closely related to Þorvaldr: the couple are under an anathema and, although the archbishop has declared that they may live together for ten years and then must part, Þorvaldr is known to have declared that he loves Jóra too much ever to renounce her. Young Þóra expresses the hope that Jóra will die and Þorvaldr will return to Iceland and come to woo her. Shocked by her sister's ruthlessness, elder Þóra says that they should drop the subject. But not long afterward Jóra does indeed die; both Jón and Þorvaldr come to Þingvellir and raise the question of marriage. The two sisters share a bed, with the elder next to the bedpost, and the younger close to the partition. The elder Þóra suggests to the younger that they give up their bed to the visitors, and that they should then accept as husband the man

---

[53] Some variants of 'The Twa Sisters' recount that the younger sister survives until she reaches the mill-pool, where the miller steals her jewellery and pushes her under so that she drowns; the revelation of the harp's true identity leads to the execution of the miller, not the sister.

[54] Klagsbrun, *Mixed Feelings*, p. 87.

[55] *Hauksdœla þáttr* in *Sturlunga saga*, ed. Jón Jóhannesson *et al.*, I: 61–3; *Sturlunga saga*, trans. J. H. McGrew and R. G. Thomas, 2 vols (New York, 1970–4), II: 87–9.

[56] See A. Heinrichs, 'Die jüngere und die ältere Þóra: Form und Bedeutung einer Episode in *Hauksdœla þáttr*', *Alvíssmál* 5 (1995), 3–28.

who occupies their usual spot in the bed. She suggests this because she covets Þorvaldr as a husband, though she was neither bold nor heartless enough to express her desire for Jóra's death, and she knows he usually sleeps next to the post. Younger Þóra reiterates that fate has already determined who will marry whom, but concurs with the arrangement. In the event, Þorvaldr gives Jón the choice of where he would like to sleep and *he* chooses to sleep by the post: 'Ok um morgininn eftir hǫfðu þeir uppi bónorð sín, ok fór þat fram, at Þóra in ellri var gift Jóni, en in yngri Þorvaldi' ('And the next morning they brought up their suits, and it happened that the elder Þóra was married to Jón, and the younger to Þorvaldr').[57]

Young Þóra submits to her elder sister, but she knows instinctively that she will get the man she wants, although this depends on the death of Jóra in distant Norway, on Þorvaldr coming to their home with his friend Jón, deciding to make a offer for one of the sisters, and that she should be allotted to him rather than to his friend. The suggestion on the part of the older sister that chance sleeping arrangements might determine the outcome of the wooing journey seems romantic, but as Anne Heinrichs notes, there is a kind of magical thinking at work here – if he lies in her place in the bed, the two of them will in the end be conjoined in bed.[58] The only witnesses to the conversation are the sisters themselves, and thus it is just possible that Þóra the younger may have passed on the tale to the author of *Hauksdœla þáttr*, but it seems rather more likely to be a literary invention.

Þóra the younger's willingness to rely on fate is rewarded when she becomes the mother of Earl Gizurr, the ultimate victor of the civil wars in thirteenth-century Iceland and the first ruler of the country after its submission to the Norwegian crown. Her less fortunate older sister dies in 1203 after only six years of marriage, although her son, Ormr Svínfellingr, was to be a significant player in Icelandic politics. The tale's folkloric inflections dictate that the younger sister should triumph over the older, but there is also psychological realism in the rivalry. Older Þóra is not ambitious enough to aspire to Þorvaldr as a husband, but it also seems plausible that it is not until her younger sister expresses her desire for him that she is impelled to mimic it. Like Helgi's brother Heðinn, discussed in the previous chapter, who swears an oath to have only his brother's lover to wife: 'One wants what the other person wants and mimes that person's desires.'[59] The detail of the sisters amusing themselves by the river when they have their confidential discussion plays perhaps with the 'Two Sisters' ballad motif, evoking a dangerous sisterly jealousy, even as younger Þóra tries to bring the conversation to an end before she admits where her choice would lie. The Norse tradition of the sisters-in-law Brynhildr and Guðrún, who quarrel over the relative precedence of their husbands when bathing in the Rhine, may also

---

[57] *Hauksdœla þáttr*, p. 63; *Sturlunga saga*, trans. McGrew and Thomas, p. 89.
[58] Heinrichs, 'Die jüngere', pp. 15–16.
[59] Mitchell, *Mad Men and Medusas*, p. 25.

influence the scene.⁶⁰ Still, viewed in naturalistic terms, going to a washing-place at a river or stream is one of the few occasions where women can speak privately to one another about intimate matters.

'Sisters always assess each other's partners. A sister may wonder, out of curiosity or anxiety, might my sister's partner have chosen me over her?' suggests Apter.⁶¹ Arthurian narrative makes play with the idea that a man might be deceived into marrying the wrong sister: that the wife's sister might prove more desirable. In an episode in the French *Prose Lancelot* queen Guenièvre gains a half-sister, begotten by her father on his seneschal's wife and apparently identical in appearance to the legitimate queen.⁶² This woman, the 'False Guenièvre', was brought up as Guenièvre's sister, and even accompanied her on her wedding journey, though mysterious information that she was planning to substitute herself for the bride led to her removal from the entourage. She returns from exile and, supported by her associate Bertholai, she claims to be the real queen, who had been whisked away from the marriage bed by unknown conspirators after the wedding night. Now she demands to be restored to her rightful place. Neither Arthur nor his advisors quite know how to handle the matter, although no-one believes the False Guenièvre's story. The imposter manœuvres her way out of submitting to an ordeal, kidnaps and drugs Arthur so that – completely infatuated with her – he no longer cares whether the story is true, and she persuades the barons of Carmelide, Guenièvre's native land, to swear falsely that she is the real Guenièvre. The true queen is sentenced to exile and horrible mutilation: since she was wrongly anointed with chrism at her coronation, the skin touched by the sacred oil must be flayed off. Lancelot fights against three champions at once to prove his beloved's legitimacy, but it is not until, through divine intervention, the two conspirators are stricken by paralysis and die a horrible, lingering death that they confess to their imposture.⁶³

Striking in this story is not simply the ease with which Arthur changes his allegiance from one sister to another – partly accounted for by drugs, but also emblematizing how little sisters are differentiated, except at a moral level – but also Guenièvre's powerlessness in the situation. Although she must realize who the imposter is, and thus be able to give a persuasive explanation for the apparent doubling of queenly claimants, she restricts herself to public denials of the truth of the accusation. Nor is the False Guenièvre is the catspaw of Bertholai, though she relies on him for some strategic advice. The imposter-sister devises her own plan to escape the risk of ordeal, and it is she who knows how to keep Arthur in pharmaceutical and sexual thrall. When, after the confession and death of the two conspirators, Guenièvre returns from the land of Sorelois where she

---

[60] Compare Heinrichs, 'Die jüngere', pp. 24–6, and see chapter seven.
[61] Apter, *Sister Knot*, p. 249; incest laws prevented the marriage of a man with his wife's or former lover's sister, as the discussion of *Lai le Freine* in chapter three notes (p. 78).
[62] *Lancelot*, ed. Micha, I: III; *L-G*, II: 345–8 for the arrival of the False Guenièvre.
[63] For the entire history of the False Guenièvre, her deception of Arthur and the true queen's vindication, see *Lancelot*, ed. Micha, I: VI–IX; *L-G*, II: 362–79.

has sojourned for more than two years with Galehault and, more importantly, with Lancelot, she readily forgives all those who were taken in by her half-sister. But damage has been done to the *Lancelot*-audience's perceptions of Arthur; his gullibility, indecisiveness and lack of fidelity have been demonstrated, and his judgement called into question.[64] This story of the substitute sister speaks at a profound level to sibling anxieties; the new arrival can annihilate the one who was already there and take the sibling's place. For, as Mitchell notes, the sibling can 'par excellence ... threaten uniqueness', a threat which, in the case of medieval sisters is compounded by their social interchangeability.[65] The usurping sister's illegitimacy contributes to her motivation to destroy her sister and take her place; a king's daughter, like the true Guenièvre, she is the product of Leodegrance's adultery with the wife of a man sworn to his service. Conceived in deception, it is hardly surprising that the False Guenièvre should dedicate her life to her half-sister's annihilation and replacement.

Hostility between Brothers and Sisters

Brothers and sisters operate in such different spheres, particularly after marriage, that occasion for rivalry is limited in medieval stories. Where serious hatreds occur it is usually because the relationship is triangulated by the sister's husband, or, more rarely, the brother's wife; such relationships are the subject of chapter seven. In popular literature brothers and sisters tend to aid one another against the machinations of wicked step-sisters and step-mothers.[66] Sisterly hostility towards brothers is restricted largely to the political domain and is relatively rare in medieval texts. In Wolfram von Eschenbach's epic of that name, Willehalm survives a terrible battle against a Saracen army led by his father-in-law in which his sister's young sons Miles and Vivianz are killed.[67] Leaving his wife Gyburg to defend his castle at Orange against the pagans, Willehalm makes his way to Laon – at the opposite end of France from his own lands – expecting to gain military support from his family, and from King Louis, who is married to his sister. When, from the castle window, the queen sees the disguised

---

[64] A reflex of this story is associated with King Pepin in *Valentine and Orson*. A woman unrelated to Pepin's legitimate wife Berthe, but who resembles her physically, is smuggled into the marriage bed on the first night and Berthe is exiled. Later Berthe is restored and Charlemagne is born. The point of Berthe's exile is to produce two half-brothers of dubious legitimacy who persecute both Charlemagne and their cousins, Valentine and Orson. *Valentine and Orson*, ed. Dickson, trans. Watson, p. 11.

[65] Mitchell, *Siblings*, p. xvi; *Mad Men and Medusas*, pp. 10, 132. Contrast the lack of interchangeability between Valentine and Orson, and other male twins and triplets, as discussed in chapter two.

[66] See the Grimm Tales, Tale 47: 'Von dem Machendelboom' ('The Juniper Tree'); Tale 135: 'Die weisse und die schwarze Braut' ('The White Bride and the Black Bride'): Tale 141: 'Das Lämmchen und Fischchen' ('Little Lamb and Little Fish') among others. In J. and W. Grimm, *Kinder- und Hausmärchen*; *Complete Fairy Tales*, trans. Zipes.

[67] See chapter three.

Willehalm approaching, she divines his intentions, comments that he has already brought enough grief to France and orders that the gates be locked against him. When Willehalm eventually gains access to the palace, his brothers embrace him warmly, but the queen remains wary of offering him further resources. Willehalm responds by snatching her crown from her head so that it shatters on the ground; seizing her by her braids, he draws his sword: 'er wolt ir mit dem swerte sîn / daz houbt hân ab geswungen' ('he wanted with his sword to cut off her head').[68] Had their mother not intervened, the queen would have been killed on the spot. Even after his sister has fled to her room, Willehalm continues to rail against her, charging her with marital infidelity and calling her appalling names. Terrified by her brother's behaviour, the queen finally leads her other brothers in begging her husband to aid Willehalm, but, partly because of the insult offered to his wife, Louis at first refuses. The queen has now been recalled to her loyalty to her natal family, 'si sprach nâch swester orden' ('she spoke in a sisterly fashion'), and does not stop pleading with her husband until he accedes.[69] Willehalm's rage against his sister is typical of the epic hero whose unchecked emotions are openly displayed when success in battle is at stake; the narrative shows a limited sympathy for a sister terrorized by her brother's aggression. Although the queen has already lost two sons, including the intensely mourned Vivianz, to her brother's quarrel with his father-in-law, Willehalm still expects her to exhibit solidarity with her birth family and to use her marital relationship with the king to further her brother's interests. Her intercession on Willehalm's behalf is both crucial and finally decisive; the political and religious necessity of defending Willehalm's territory against the Saracen Other is depicted as outweighing her maternal grief and her resentment of her brother's recklessness in seizing Gyburg by force from her husband and father. *Willehalm* thus reproduces the earlier epic pattern in which a sister's children are assimilated to the political interests and military resources of their maternal uncle, and the mother's emotions, when her sons die in battle, are subordinated to the demands of the heroic. The brother's extreme – if only threatened – violence against his sister must be understood as reproducing generic norms.

The False Guenièvre's imposture was motivated as much by a desire for queenly status as by a deep-seated resentment of her legitimate sister: the Arthurian episode centred on fundamental questions of identity rather than equal and contested rights to a kingdom. Historical royal sisters whose rights are infringed might be avenged by punitive expeditions undertaken by their brothers, but these do not often result in reinstatement for the injured wife: *Realpolitik* limits what can be achieved on her behalf.[70] In *Valentine and Orson*,

---

[68] *Willehalm* III.147. 20–1; *Willehalm*, trans. Gibbs and Johnson, p. 82; see also C. Lofmark, *Rennewart in Wolfram's* Willehalm: *A Study of Wolfram von Eschenbach and his Sources* (Cambridge, 1972), pp. 75–6.

[69] *Willehalm*, IV.180.7; *Willehalm*, trans. Gibbs and Johnson, p. 97.

[70] See the instances discussed in chapter one. Froissart notes, for example, how Charles

Sisters and Hostility

Emperor Pepin leaps to the conclusion that his sister is guilty when scandal is falsely alleged against her by the archbishop of Constantinople, whose sexual overtures she had rejected. Even though the report of Bellisent's fate is delivered by her faithful squire who rightly asserts that the archbishop was lying, Pepin retorts:

> 'Of as muche holde I the Emperoure more folysher, because he made not my syster dye, for by the God almighty, if I had her here at this present time, I should neuer reste til that I hadde made her dye an euil death.'[71]

Pepin's readiness to believe the worst of the sister in whom he 'purpensed to haue had once ... in my lyfe Ioye and pleasure', is produced by a generalized misogyny, but his chief regret is the loss of his valuable alliance with the Emperor Alexander, Bellisent's equally intemperate husband. The 'exchange of women' which created homosocial ties between the rulers now threatens to founder on the two brothers-in-law's credulity.[72] When Bellisent's innocence is finally proved through trial by combat, Bellisent's husband kneels to ask his brother-in-law's pardon for his treatment of his sister; they resolve to search together for the lost Bellisent, re-affirming their homosocial bond as stronger than ever.[73] Many chapters and twenty years pass before, through the endeavours of Bellisent's twin sons, Valentine and Orson, the emperor, the empress, their children and her brother are reunited. The narrative focus is on the re-establishment of the nuclear family, however, and Pepin remains a bystander, neither apologizing to his sister for his remarks about her, nor expressly receiving forgiveness from her.[74] When Pepin takes his leave to return to France, accompanied by Orson, Bellisent and her husband weep to see him go, though it seems likely that it is the departure of her son rather than her brother which provokes Bellisent's tears. She has no stake in the 'Ioye and pleasure' which her brother sentimentally ascribed to their sibling bond and their damaged relationship is not visibly repaired.

Even in modern Western society, where the material effects of such preferences are diminishing, sisters often resent a parental preference for sons over daughters.[75] In medieval pseudo-historical texts certain sisters envy their brothers' success and seek to overthrow them, not necessarily because they

---

IV of France offered only limited help to his sister Isabella, queen of Edward II in her struggles against her husband and finally expelled her from France (see chapter one). Jean Froissart, *Chronicles*, trans. G. Brereton (Harmondsworth, 1978), I.40–1.

[71] *Valentine and Orson*, ed. Dixon, p. 35.
[72] See Introduction, p. 12 and compare Rubin, 'The Traffic in Women'; '"Exchange of women" is a shorthand for expressing that the social relations of a kinship system specify that men have certain rights in their female kin, and that women do not have the same rights either to themselves or to their male kin' (p. 77).
[73] *Valentine and Orson*, ed. Dixon, p. 52.
[74] Ibid., p. 202.
[75] See Klagsbrun, *Mixed Feelings*, pp. 105–11, on cross-gender hostility; see also Bank and Kahn, *The Sibling Bond*, pp. 205–17 on favouritism more generally.

believe that they could themselves rule equally well, but in order to place their husbands or lovers on the throne. Rebellious sisters recognize that their gender disqualifies them from wielding sufficient authority to bring their subjects to heel, despite sharing parentage with the usurped brother. In *Hrólfs saga kraka*, Skuld's enmity against her half-brother Hrólfr is exacerbated by his ruse to force her husband to submit to him as his under-king. Hrólfr and Hjǫrvarðr, Skuld's husband, are standing outside a feast one day when Hrólfr removes his belt and swings it around, asking Hjǫrvarðr to hold his sword in the meantime. Hrólfr re-fastens his belt and takes his sword back, pointing out that to hold someone else's sword under such circumstances demonstrates that the holder is inferior to the sword's owner. This sounds like a ceremony which Hrólfr has invented on the spur of the moment (though it may be related to rituals associated with knightly investiture); consequently the humiliated Hjǫrvarðr and his furious wife plot revenge.[76] Thanks to Skuld's magical knowledge, she and her husband prevail in the battle, and Hrólfr and his champions are killed. Their deaths are avenged by the part-animal brothers of the hero Bǫðvarr bjarki, who also falls with his king.[77] The brothers' profound sibling bonds were discussed in chapter two above and contrast markedly with the sustained, if understandable, enmity displayed by Hrólfr's illegitimate, quasi-supernatural half-sister.[78] The resentment and hostility generated by illegitimacy, underpinning the machinations of the False Guenièvre, are equally clear in this narrative, as Skuld uses the magical gifts inherited from her elfwoman mother to usurp and destroy her legitimate (though incestuously conceived) half-brother.

A more sustained power-rivalry than this dispute about the Danish throne is the enchantress Morgan le Fay's animus against her half-brother King Arthur, as evidenced in two related texts. In the Post-Vulgate *Suite de Merlin*, and, based on this source, in Malory's *Morte Darthur*, Morgan mounts a complex bid to seize the throne, using her lover Accolon of Gaul as her proxy. Having manufactured substitutes for Excalibur and its magic scabbard, Morgan gives Accolon the real weapons, entrusted to her keeping by her brother, while she supplies Arthur with the worthless fakes. She engineers a judicial combat between brother and lover which they fight without knowledge of each other's real identities; during the battle she is elsewhere, planning to murder her husband in order to take advantage of Accolon's anticipated victory. Morgan's attack on her husband is thwarted by her son Yvain. Meanwhile the Lady of the Lake intervenes to save Arthur; using magic she forces Accolon to drop the real Excalibur which Arthur is then able to retrieve. Thereafter the two fighters reveal their identities to one another and Accolon explains how his mistress has duped him into fighting against his king. Accolon dies of his wounds and Arthur pursues Morgan, who

---

[76] *Hrólfs saga kraka*, ed. Jónsson I: 93–5; death of Skuld and her husband, I: 105; *Saga of Hrolf Kraki*, trans. Byock, pp. 69–71; death, p. 78.
[77] See chapter two, pp. 63–4.
[78] See *Hrólfs saga kraka*, ed. Jónsson I: 28–9; *Saga of Hrolf Kraki*, trans. Byock, pp. 21–2 for the birth of the 'grimmúðug' ('vicious') Skuld.

escapes his wrath once again by magical means.⁷⁹ This is Morgan's only direct attack on her brother in the two texts; after showing her hand so clearly she can never again return to court. Nevertheless she keeps up a low-level harassment of her brother's knights, an activity compounded by her sexual desire for Lancelot and her dislike of other prominent members of the Round Table. Morgan also plots to reveal the relationship between the queen and Lancelot by a number of indirect – in the event, too indirect – means, although, as I have argued elsewhere, this plot strand is driven by her notable hatred for her sister-in-law Queen Guenevere rather than a dislike of her brother.⁸⁰

Morgan's plan to seize the throne from her brother is remarkably ill-thought through. She has no blood-claim to the throne, being related to Arthur via his mother, and her plan to rule as Accolon's queen seems doomed to failure. '[E]lle en cuidoit bien faire roi, que par anemi que par enchantement que par priiere de haus houmes de la Grant Bretaigne' ('she thought she could make Accolon king, either by the devil's help or by magic or by entreaty of the nobles of Great Britain'), explains the narrator of the *Suite*; the multiplication and over-determination of methods by which Morgan hopes to gain power to power reveals the fundamental impracticability of her scheme.⁸¹ The enchantress's bid for power is rooted in magic and murder rather than honourable combat and political challenge. She finds herself forced to rely on a male agent who quickly reverts to his primary loyalty to his king when faced with the charge of treason. Arthur is young and vigorous and he has a redoubtable ally in the Lady of the Lake, who deploys her powerful feminine magic – acquired from Merlin himself – to counter Morgan's malevolent plotting.⁸² Morgan's political ambition – expressed as a murderous hatred for Arthur – occurs only in these two interdependent texts and contrasts with her original and final role as healer of Arthur after his death. In other Arthurian texts she is more consistently depicted as occupied in persecuting Guenevere, conducting a mischievous ideological enquiry into the nature of chivalry, or, as outlined in chapter three, living a harmonious post-political life in Avalon at her brother's side.⁸³

Murdering the Sister

Brothers very rarely kill their sisters; as discussed in chapter three, the shame of killing a woman usually outweighs considerations of individual or family

---

⁷⁹ *Suite du Roman de Merlin*, ed. G. Roussineau, 2 vols (Geneva, 1996), I: 312–26, II: 327–9, 337–66; L-G, IV: 300–2, 254–9, 261–9, 275–7. Malory, *Le Morte Darthur*, ed. Field, I: 106–22; I: 137–52; Larrington, *King Arthur's Enchantresses*, pp. 33–40.
⁸⁰ Larrington, *King Arthur's Enchantresses*, pp. 40–4.
⁸¹ *Suite*, ed. Roussineau, II: 327; L-G, IV: 369.
⁸² For discussion of the parallels between Morgan and Mordred in Malory, see H. G. Morgan, 'The Role of Morgan le Fay in Malory's *Morte D'Arthur*', *Southern Quarterly* 2 (1963–4), 150–68, and Larrington, *King Arthur's Enchantresses*, pp. 37–8.
⁸³ Larrington, King Arthur's Enchantresses, pp. 47–50.

honour. Exceptions occur in cases of brother–sister incest, or, very rarely in cases where the woman has taken a lover outside marriage.[84] In such cases, as we shall see in chapter seven, the outrage is much more often avenged by the death of the lover.[85] One exception is an unhappy tale related by the Knight of the Tour-Landry, in which a woman leaves her knightly husband to run off with a monk. Pursued by her brothers, the sister is apprehended in bed with her lover. In a strikingly symbolic move the brothers cut off the monk's genitals and throw them in their sister's face before placing both culprits in a stone-freighted sack and casting them into water, where they drown.[86] Here the sister's adulterous behaviour is compounded by her choice of a man vowed to chastity as sexual partner; the brothers' extreme violence reflects the double nature of their sister's transgression.

Although so-called honour-killing of the sister is rare in medieval literature, Arthurian tradition preserves two tales of sister-murder or near murder, both impelled by a fraternal sense of honour. In that often quirky romance *Diu Crône*, Queen Ginover comes close to death at the hands of her brother Gotegrin. Incensed when he learns of the rumours that his sister had a lover before her marriage to Arthur, he abducts her from the court and threatens to kill her, despite her impassioned pleas for mercy and the intercession of his own retinue who are horrified when they learn what he plans to do.[87] Gotegrin carries his sister off deep into the forest, leaving the retinue behind, and is on the point of killing her when the putative lover Gasozein happens to appear. He puts Gotegrin to flight and rescues his former beloved. Ginover's difficulties are not resolved by this intervention. Not only is her position – alone in the forest with her rumoured lover – rendered scandalous, but Gasozein takes the opportunity to make sexual advances to the queen, even attempting to rape her, until prevented, in the nick of time, by the arrival of Gawein. Ginover's masculine associates seem, in this romance, to have questionable notions of appropriate chivalric behaviour; homosocial bonds, as Susann Samples observes, are prioritized over courtesy towards women.[88] Gasozein's problematic passion for the queen is defused when, as noted above, Gawein eventually brokers

---

[84] See J. Rose, 'How do We Write about Honour Killing?', *London Review of Books* (4 November 2009), for a thoughtful discussion of the issues surrounding the murder of women by their families, very often their brothers, in modern Europe.

[85] Compare the story of Lisabetta in *Decameron* IV.5, whose brothers murder their employee, her lover Lorenzo; M. Marcus, 'Cross-Fertilizations: Folklore and Literature in *Decameron* 4.5', *Italica* 66.4 (1989), 383–98; J. Usher, 'Narrative and Descriptive Sequences in the Novella of Lisabetta and the Pot of Basil (*Decameron*, IV.5)', *Italian Studies* 38 (1983), 56–69.

[86] Caxton, *The Book of the Knight of the Tower*, ed. Offord, p. 80.

[87] Thomas, *Diu Crône*, p. 41.

[88] See Samples, 'An Unlikely Hero' and S. Samples, 'The Rape of Ginover in Heinrich von dem Türlin's *Diu Crône*', in *Arthurian Romance and Gender: Selected Proceedings of the XVIIth International Arthurian Congress*, ed. F. Wolfzettel, Internationale Forschungen zur allgemeinen und vergleichenden Literaturwissenschaft 10 (Amsterdam, 1995), pp. 196–205.

his marriage to his own future sister-in-law, Sgoidamur and they retreat to an otherworldly castle.[89] Like King Pepin in *Valentine and Orson*, Ginover's brother is quick to believe in his sister's sexual transgressiveness; without investigating the case in any depth he immediately assumes the worst of his sister. Fraternal policing of a sister's honour is, of course, driven by her value to her birth family as object of exchange between kin groups.[90] No sexual scandal must bring into question the legitimacy of her children; brothers who are quick to avenge their sister's rights, such as those encountered in chapter three (pp. 97–100), are as ready to punish her when she transgresses the aristocratic code of premarital chastity or endangers the homosocial alliance created by her marriage.

In contrast to the murderous Gotegrin and the opportunist Gasozein, Erec, son of Lac in the Post-Vulgate *Queste del Saint Graal*, is a paragon of chivalric honour and truthfulness.[91] His is an astonishing story of sibling-murder, committed not in order to preserve a sister's virtue, but to maintain – under highly questionable circumstances – a brother's honour.[92] As a relatively untried knight, Erec sets off with other knights in search of the missing Lancelot. In this part of his tale, he makes a rash promise, a *don contraignant*, to a certain maiden, who on first sight seems sympathetic. She asks Erec to grant her a boon, asserting with some justice that Round Table knights are notorious liars who regularly deceive maidens, 'ilz en decepvoient assés villainement les damoyseles' ('they deceive maidens quite wickedly').[93] Erec swears that he will never tell a lie, and, the narrator comments approvingly that his truthfulness was indeed a marvellous grace, though the oath's tragic consequence is also anticipated. Later this same girl reappears, leading Erec to a castle where his sister is imprisoned. This prompts a recapitulation of family history, for, as Norris Lacy points out, there is a long tradition of kin-murder in Erec's clan.[94] In the previous generation, Erec's father and uncle had married two sisters. One marriage produced the distinguished Erec and his beautiful sister; the other alliance bred wicked children: three brothers who murdered Erec's father, and a sister. The motives of the girl to whom Erec swore his oath are never made clear, but it seems likely that she is the sister of the three murderous brothers and thus Erec's cousin.[95] She certainly appears to have a score to settle with Erec's branch of the family, and when she announces to the brothers that she has led Erec to them, she seems unnaturally excited: 'Vés cy celluy que vous

---

[89] *Diu Crône*, ed. Felder, lines 11037–12529; *The Crown*, trans. Thomas, pp. 124–39.
[90] Cf. Rubin, 'The Traffic in Women'.
[91] Erec's history is scattered episodically through the Post-Vulgate *Queste*, but has been reconstituted as a single narrative by Cedric Pickford (see n. 1 above).
[92] See F. Wolfzettel, 'Le *Roman d'Erec* en prose du XIIIe siècle: un anti-*Erec et Enide*?', in *The Legacy of Chrétien de Troyes*, ed. N. J. Lacy, D. Kelly and K. Busby, 2 vols (Amsterdam,1988), II: 215–28, and N. J. Lacy, 'The Form of the Prose *Erec*', *Neuphilologische Mitteilungen* 85 (1984), 169–77.
[93] *Erec*, ed. Pickford, p. 82; *L-G*, V: 32. My translation.
[94] Lacy, 'The Form of the Prose *Erec*', p. 175.
[95] As Martha Asher suggests, *L-G*, V: 399, note.

avés tant demandé; or y parra que vous en ferés' ('You see here what you have asked for so long. Now we'll see what you'll do about it').[96]

Erec and his comrade Meraugis swiftly kill the brothers, who are unarmed and taken by surprise. The family's heritage is thus regained and Erec is acclaimed by the castle's retinue. That night, however, he has an ominous dream and at dinner the next day the maiden, now designated by the text as 'la male damoiselle' ('the evil damsel') calls in her boon, demanding that Erec cut off his own sister's head. Deeply upset, Erec begs her to withdraw her request. He asks Meraugis and his servants to kill him instead, reiterating the importance of his earlier promise, but they all refuse, rightly prioritizing their own oaths to Erec over his undertaking to the wicked maiden. Erec's sister offers pathetic pleas for mercy, ineffectually invoking the sacredness of their kin-relation, 'Frere, ayés mercy de moy, et te souviegne de ce que je suis ta seur de pere' ('Brother, have mercy on me and remember that I'm your own sister, of the same father').[97] Erec nevertheless complies with the maiden's demand and beheads his sister with such force that her head flies off more than a lance-length away. As Lacy comments, 'the crime is heinous and the motive absurd'.[98] The girl counters Erec's furious curses by pointing out that if he were not one of the most treacherous knights in the world, he would not have committed such an act 'pour une seule parole que tu m'avoyes acreantee' ('for a simple promise you had made me').[99]

Erec's dilemma points up the failure of his reading of the honour code to accommodate other bases for decision-making, and his inability properly to reckon the primacy of kinship ties.[100] These bonds constitute a higher ethical code than chivalric considerations of personal face and reputation. The *male demoiselle*'s demand articulates a specifically female inquiry into the parameters of male honour behaviour, interrogating the relative value of oaths made to women (in which, as she earlier remarked, knights tend to lie shamelessly), of oaths made to men such as Meraugis within the fictive brotherhood of the Round Table, and the feudal oaths of Erec's retinue, who will not raise their hand against their new lord, These must be weighed against emotions of sibling love and loyalty, and the shame which, Meraugis asserts, Erec will sustain if he murders his sister.[101] As she rides away with Erec's sister's head the *male damoiselle* is immediately struck by divine vengeance in the form of

---

[96] *Erec*, ed. Pickford, p. 157; L-G, V: 399.
[97] *Erec*, ed. Pickford, p. 163; L-G, V: 200.
[98] Lacy, 'The Form of the Prose *Erec*', p. 175.
[99] *Erec*, ed. Pickford, pp. 161–6, here p. 165; L-G, V: 199–201.
[100] Compare chapter three's discussion of sisters' implacable pursuit of vengeance for their brothers and the invocations there of Round Table oaths to pre-empt subsequent promises, especially those made to women.
[101] 'vous estes honis a tous les jours de vostre vie, se vous vostre seur occiés en tel maniere pour une desloyal damoiselle' ('you'll be shamed for the rest of your life if you kill your sister this way for a false maiden'), *Erec*, ed. Pickford, p. 164; L-G, V: 300.

lightning which completely consumes her, with the approbation of onlookers and narrator alike, while the head remains unharmed. Erec's sister, the innocent victim of – or martyr to – the honour code, is thus assimilated to the saint in her corporeal incorruptibility; the woman who manipulates the code for her own vengeance-driven ends is consumed by hellish flame. If Martha Asher is correct in assuming that this is Erec's cousin, the *male damoiselle* has adopted the revenge ethic which drives Perceval's and Yvain's sisters earlier in the Post-Vulgate *Queste* (see chapter three, pp. 94–7), and prosecuted it more successfully; Erec has only just regained his sister when he murders her and her death counterbalances Erec's killing of his three male cousins.

Erec's sister-murder causes him enormous psychological pain from which he never really recovers. His consequent ostracism by a group of noble women is discussed in the next chapter, and by the time he meets his death – like Perceval and Yvain de Cenel, at the hands of Gauvain – he has lost all confidence in himself or his knightly identity within a text which has also come to see the model of chivalry practised in Arthur's court as irredeemable. Erec's long-drawn out tragic fall from promising aspirant in the honour-game to sibling-killer echoes in its melancholy inevitability the 'Tale of Balin' from earlier in the cycle (discussed in chapter two). The values of the Arthurian court embodied in and celebrated by Chrétien's poetic versions of *Yvain* and *Erec* in the twelfth century have indeed, as Friedrich Wolfzettel argues, become 'terrorist and inhumane' in their application here. The absolute value of a knight's sworn word, crucial in a mostly pre-literate society, has become relative, even opportunistic in the Post-Vulgate *Queste*. Tragic Erec is a heroic exception; yet even though his resistance to oath-breaking is at first lauded by the narrator, when he is caught in a double-bind by the cunning *male damoiselle* it causes his death.[102] Erec's murder has little to do with the psychological dynamics of the brother–sister relationship. Rather it serves to focus attention on the political and ethical implications of an individual sibling's actions within the context of the kin-group and within the larger social institution of chivalry: one which depends on repressing the interests of the family. Here we find, as Judith Butler posits, 'kinship figured at the limit of ... "the ethical order"', pointing up how the failure of the Arthurian ethical order to accommodate kinship – specifically sibling – bonds impels the Round Table towards its tragic ending.[103]

Conclusion

As between brothers, conflict between sisters in medieval texts is driven largely by an underlying competitiveness, expressed through quarrels about inheritance and sexual rivalry. Battles for political power are suppressed by women's general

---

[102] Though Gauvain's attack is the immediate cause of Erec's death, its ultimate cause is the sin of killing his sister, as Lacy argues, 'The Form of the Prose *Erec*', p. 174.
[103] Butler, *Antigone's Claim*, p. 3.

incapacity to rule in their own right, and thus the struggles for rule, explored mainly in legendary histories such as Saxo's, are resolved to the detriment of female royal claimants. The sister-stories analysed here uncover the kinds of emotional dilemmas which reflect aristocratic women's restricted agency when marriage arrangements are being made for them, and the frustration and anger which this generates. Sisters can behave as ruthlessly as their brothers when property interests are at stake; the social norm which impels brothers to make provision for their sisters' dowries seems on occasion to be disregarded by sisters when they gain sole possession of their inheritances. On a psychological level, the interchangeability of sisters, noted in chapter three, works to unsettle the sisterly bond in the erotic domain; the competition between them becomes explicit when suitors are especially desirable or if there are not enough of them for each marriageable young woman. The ease with which one sister can be substituted for another encourages criminal imposture in the case of the False Guenièvre, offering a notable contrast to the happily altruistic sisterly sacrifices explored in chapter three.

Sisters fear their annihilation by a sibling: psychic annihilation through a sister's usurpation is more likely than physical attack by one sister on another. Brothers have less to fear from their sisters: a sister's political threat can usually be countered, except in the kinds of narratives where sibling and affinal rivalries multiply to involve whole lineages, the focus of chapter seven. Brothers' readiness to defend their sisters' interests after marriage are generally subordinated to the wider interests of the patriarchy; the maintenance of homosocial bonds is prioritized over a sister's well-being and they can be quick to side with her husband.[104] The asymmetry of the brother–sister bond, discussed in chapter three, is apparent in cross-sex sibling conflict. Unless marriage alliances are at stake, as Harriet Martineau observes, 'sisters can never be to brothers ... objects of engrossing and devoted expression'.[105] Although brothers may connive in husbands' violence towards their sisters, they rarely raise a hand against them; when Erec breaches this social taboo he is doomed to become a social outcast. The principal circumstance in which a brother is likely to inflict murderous violence on his sister, in which one or both siblings are prone to committing suicide, is brother–sister incest. Combining the powerful sibling emotions of passionate love and hatred, and the imperatives of sexual desire, incest is the subject of the next chapter.

---

[104] Cf. L. Davidoff, 'The Sibling Relationship and Sibling Incest in Historical Context', in *Sibling Relationships*, ed. Coles, pp. 17–47 (p. 21).
[105] H. Martineau, *Autobiography*, 3 vols (London, 1877), I: 99, cited from Davidoff, 'The Sibling Relationship', p. 22.

6

'The king's dochter gaes wi child to her brither': Sibling Incest

Introduction

Why should not brothers and sisters marry each other?[1] Clearly the children of Adam and Eve must have had little choice in the matter of mates, as Augustine makes clear in his most focused discussion of sibling relationships, in *De civitate Dei* (*The City of God*). Augustine observes that at the beginning of human history men must have married their sisters:

> nec essent ulli homines, nisi qui ex illis duobus nati fuissent: uiri sorores suas coniuges acceperunt; quod profecto quanto est antiquius conpellente necessitate, tanto postea factum est damnabilius religione prohibente.[2]

> ('as there were no human beings, except those who had been born of these two [sc. Adam and Eve], men took their sisters for wives – an act which was as certainly dictated by necessity in these ancient days as afterwards it was condemned by the prohibitions of religion.')[3]

Once a larger population came into existence, however, brothers were enjoined to look elsewhere for wives, for, Augustine argues, one of the goods of marriage is to form new alliances, to create friendship and affection between different families. Thus to have a father and a father-in-law as one and the same person, as Adam's children did, is to lose the opportunity to bring another man into a close kin relationship. Lévi-Strauss appositely notes how the Arapesh tribe explained to Margaret Mead that a man must marry another man's sister, and give his sister in marriage, so as to acquire brothers-in-law, otherwise 'with whom will you hunt, with whom will you garden, whom will you go to visit?'[4] Augustine proposes – perhaps thinking of Egyptian royal marriage customs or Greek myth – that although other religions permit brother–sister marriage,

---

[1] This chapter draws on the definitive account of medieval incest in literature: Archibald, *Incest and the Medieval Imagination*.
[2] Augustine, *De civitate Dei* XV.16. http://www.thelatinlibrary.com/augustine/civ15.shtml
[3] Translation: http://www.newadvent.org/fathers/120115.htm
[4] Lévi-Strauss, *Elementary Structures of Kinship*, p 485, citing Mead, *Sex and Temperament in Three Primitive Societies*, p. 84. Cf. p. 12 above.

in practice it is shunned:

> etiam quia nescio quo modo inest humanae ueracundiae quiddam naturale atque laudibile, ut, cui debet causa propinquitatis reuerendum honorem, ad ea contineat.
>
> ('there is in human nature I know not what natural and praiseworthy shamefacedness which restrains us from desiring that connection . . . with any one to whom consanguinity bids us render respect.')[5]

Although 'human nature', as Augustine opines, generally does shrink from brother–sister incest (and still more from same-sex incest), nevertheless medieval writers treat forbidden love between siblings, and not just as occurring problematically in the book of Genesis. In some instances the siblings are unaware of their relationship until the deed is committed or a strong relationship is formed; sometimes one sib may be aware of the bond, while the other is not. Rare are siblings who deliberately choose to have sexual relationships with each other in full knowledge of their kin-relation. Such liaisons tend to occur when children are orphaned and thrown back on one another's company: high social status means that they are not subject to close adult supervision. Deliberately incestuous siblings are also to be found in ballads, where, as earlier chapters have shown, extreme behaviour in family relationships is a recurrent theme. Bank and Kahn usefully distinguish between 'power-oriented incest' and 'nurturing incest' within sibling sexual relationships; the first is 'sadistic, exploitative and coercive', while the second can be characterized by 'erotic pleasure, loyalty, love, and compassion . . . a welcome island of refuge in an ocean of troubled and despairing family relationships'.[6] Both types of incest are visible in medieval literature: moreover, what may begin in nurturing can end in murder. Conversely, coercive seduction or outright rape tends to occur outside the domestic setting – indeed often out in the forest – when the brother fails to recognize his long-lost sister. Death is the only possible recourse in such disastrous circumstances.

Incest narratives are not only about sexual transgression: they also speak to deep-rooted concerns about the emergence of young people into adulthood, embarking on life outside the family group. One kind of incest narrative thus reflects social anxiety about the return of the adult son to the family: can he adapt his new sense of himself and redefine his role among the sibling cohort? His siblings will also have changed and grown while he has been away; what might their impact be upon the returning brother? In the second type of narrative, sibling pairs (often those who have undergone some kind of trauma) avoid the risky and unfamiliar, turning away from the social imperative of exogamy, by permitting free rein to the polymorphous desires of infancy. While the sexual relationship with the sibling is not necessarily coercive, its outcome is frequently catastrophic.

[5] Augustine, *De civitate Dei* XV.16; *City of God* XV.16.
[6] Bank and Kahn, *The Sibling Bond*, p. 178.

Unwitting Incest

Orally transmitted traditional poetry foregrounds the tragic theme of siblings who have been separated for a long time and thus fail to recognize one another. The motif acknowledges the understanding, now well supported by psychological research, that long-separated siblings may have difficulty in distinguishing the mutual attraction produced by shared, inherited traits from 'normal' sexual desire.[7] Medieval romance authors often suggest that unwitting siblings may feel strong affect in their dealings with one another because, although they do not know it, they share blood; this 'knowledge of the body' conditions their behaviour at some instinctual level. Thus in Malory's 'Tale of Sir Gareth', Gawain is kind to his unrecognized and disguised brother, but is given no moral credit for it by the author: 'that proffer com of his bloode, for he was nere kyn to hym than he wyste off'. His solicitude for the unknown kitchen-boy is contrasted with Lancelot's care for Gareth, ascribed to the great knight's magnanimous nature: 'but that sir Launcelot ded was of his grete jantylnesse and curtesy'.[8] So too, in Wolfram's *Willehalm*, Gyburg is drawn to be kind to Rennewart, her unrecognized brother: 'der vrouwen tet ir herze kuont / daz si niht erfuor wan lange sidr' ('the lady's heart was telling her something which she did not find out until a long time later'). Rennewart reciprocates her warm feelings because, he explains, she reminds him of the sister he had loved in his earliest childhood, 'man gap etswâ ze swester mir . . . eteslîcher mîner swester schîn / möht ir wol in der jugende tragn' ('I had a sister at one time . . . you must have looked like one of my sisters when you were young').[9] These intuitions of kinship are likely to be rooted in unconsciously detected physical and psychological similarities; the instinctive attraction is enough to initiate the establishment of affective bonds, but the attraction stops short of sexual expression. In both these instances sibling warmth is somewhat inhibited by class difference: both brothers are employed in the court kitchens.

In Irish heroic saga the youthful Cú Chulainn's battle-fury can only be assuaged on his return home by plunging him into cold baths and having women show him their bared breasts; this neutralizes a warrior arousal which would otherwise endanger the men of Ulster. His testosterone-fuelled battle-frenzy must be 'earthed', lest he damage his own community through indiscriminate violence.[10] Similarly, it is the young man who has been away establishing

---

[7] On genetic sexual attraction see M. Greenberg and R. Littlewood, 'Post-adoption Incest and Phenotypic Matching: Experience, Social Meanings and Biosocial Implications', *British Journal of Medical Psychology* 68 (1995), 29–44. See also Greenberg's Hilda Lewis Memorial Lecture, 'Post-Adoption Reunion – Are We Entering Uncharted Territory?', *Adoption and Fostering* 17 (1993), 5–15.
[8] Malory, *Le Morte Darthur*, ed. Field, I: 225.
[9] *Willehalm* VI.391. 2–3; VI.392. 10, 28–9; *Willehalm*, trans. Gibbs and Johnson, p. 148; p. 148–9. See also chapter three.
[10] *Táin Bó Cualaigne*, ed. P. Ó Fiannachta (Dublin, 1966), p. 1; *The Tain*, trans. T. Kinsella

his heroic reputation, and who returns unannounced, who is in the greatest danger of committing inadvertent incest. The hero is emotionally aroused as he approaches his home, an arousal which manifests itself as uninhibited sexual desire. In the Finnish *Kalevala* tale of Kullervo, the hero is sold as a slave to the craftsman Ilmarinen by his uncle Untamo, who fears the young man may eventually avenge the death of his father on him.[11] Kullervo runs away from Ilmarinen's home after engineering the death of his wife and discovers that, in fact, his family are still alive.[12] His sister, however, had departed on a berrying expedition some years previously and had never returned. Useless at jobs around the home, Kullervo is sent to deliver the family's taxes, trying unsuccessfully to seduce the maidens he meets on his way. Having managed for once to accomplish a mission successfully, Kullervo returns with his sleigh unaccountably full of the kinds of riches to take a girl's fancy, 'gold-edged stockings, silver-tipped belts'.[13] With them he seduces a maiden whom he meets in the woods. Only afterwards does she enquire after his descent; Kullervo replies: 'I am not of a great clan, neither great nor small / I am just in between, humble son of Kalervo'. The girl reveals her own identity: 'I am not of a great clan, neither great nor small / I am just in between, humble daughter of Kalervo'.[14] She flings herself from the sleigh into a river and drowns.

Kullervo weeps violently; when he returns home he reproaches his mother for not killing him at birth, and threatens suicide. His parents die while he is taking vengeance on his uncle; bereft of kinsmen he wanders in the forest with only a dog for company. Finally he stumbles upon the accursed clearing where he seduced his sister, where no 'young grass had sprung up, no heather bloom come out / grown up in that spot in that evil place'.[15] Here he plunges his sword into his chest, bringing about 'the death of the luckless one'. The seer Väinämöinen delivers the final verdict on the unfortunate Kullervo: the boy had been 'reared the wrong way', and thus could not 'acquire the mind of a man'.[16]

Kullervo's accidental incest is tightly bound up with larger indications of family dysfunction. The previous generation's fraternal strife maroons the child at his uncle's farm as a slave. Untamo tries to kill him on three occasions, but the boy always survives and grows strong. Given the opportunity to learn a craft with Ilmarinen, he is the victim of a prank by the smith's wife; he sabotages his chances in a new environment when he murders her in reprisal. When Kullervo is finally reunited with his family, it is too late; he has no skills and

(Oxford, 1969), pp. 91–2.

[11] Kullervo is the son of Kalervo, whose murder by his brother was discussed in chapter four.

[12] *Kalevala*, runo 33, online at http://runeberg.org/kalevala/33.html; *The Kalevala*, trans. Magoun, Poems 33–6. That the family are all murdered in an earlier *runo* and are alive and well in another is typical of orally transmitted poetry.

[13] *Kalevala*, runo 35; *Kalevala*, trans. Magoun, Poem 35, p. 247.

[14] Ibid., p. 248.

[15] *Kalevala*, runo 36; *Kalevala*, Poem 36, p. 255.

[16] *Kalevala*, Poem 36, p. 255.

will not listen to advice, and he allows his uncontrolled sexuality to ruin his successful homecoming after delivering the taxes. Thereafter he is alienated from his kin, and loses them all; he revives the old vendetta with Untamo, but vengeance brings no joy. The family's inherited violence culminates in Kullervo's transgression against crucial social and sexual boundaries. He is indeed 'luckless', but as Väinämöinen observes, his upbringing has taught him neither to control his strength nor to rein in his desires. The unrestrained primal drives of childhood disastrously impel Kullervo still in adulthood; his dysfunctional kin-group and an ill-luck which he brings on himself contribute to his doom.

Unwitting incest is a significant theme in traditional literature: a number of ballads, some recorded by Child, follow the Kullervo plot in which the young man's long absence has made it impossible for the siblings to recognize one another and a sexual encounter takes place at a short distance from home.[17] In Child Ballad 50, 'The Bonnie Hind', for example, a maiden willingly yields up her virginity to a 'brisk young squire' encountered out in the woods. Afterwards she accepts his gift of a silver comb, asking his name and whether he is a courtier. The squire reveals that he has just come from sea-faring, and that he is the son of Lord Randal. The girl, Lord Randal's daughter, had not known that she had a brother; taking out her knife, she stabs herself. Jock, the brother, buries her under the holly tree and goes home to meet his father, lamenting for the 'bonnie hind / beneath yon hollin tree'.[18] His father cannot understand his sorrow – there are many more fine deer in the park, and he may take three of the silver-shod ones. Still Jock cannot stop grieving; thinking to comfort him, his father tells him to visit his sister's bower, for when he sees her loveliness he will no longer fret for the 'bonny hind'. The ballad as preserved ends on this note of tragic irony.

Here the double crime of incest and suicide, too horrible for the brother to admit except through euphemism, is treated metaphorically. Child Ballad 16, 'Sheath and Knife', discussed below, becomes similarly obscure when the brother tries to confess to his mother what he has done.[19] In Child Ballad 14, 'Babylon or the Bonnie Banks o Fordie', an outlaw, 'a banisht man', meets successively three sisters who dwell in the woods. The first two, given the choice of wedding the outlaw or being killed by him, prefer to die; the third sister says that she will take neither choice, for she knows that her brother too haunts these woods as a 'banisht man'. Realizing he has murdered his own sisters, the outlaw turns his knife on himself. Some variants of the ballad depict the girls' other brothers riding up and killing the robber without acknowledging their relationship to him, but generally the combination of incestuous desire (even if not fully

---

[17] See P. Brewster, *The Incest Theme in Folksong*, Folklore Fellowship Communications 212 (Helsinki, 1972), for further international analogues to the Kullervo story.
[18] *Ballads*, ed. Child, I: 444–7.
[19] Ibid., I: 185–7.

acted on) and murder can only be punished by the death of the perpetrator.[20] In Child Ballad 52, 'The King's Dochter Lady Jean', a princess goes out to the greenwood and meets a young man to whom she loses her virginity. Afterwards she learns he is her brother, who has been long away at sea. In version A she stabs herself and staggers home to die; her brother follows her and dies in her arms. In version B the brother stabs her, while in other versions both siblings die of grief.[21] Sibling sexuality, as Juliet Mitchell argues, is closely bound up with violence; the taboo is intimately allied with self-violence and its rupture is unsurvivable.[22] These ballads, like those employing the elf-knight topos (such as Child 2, 'The Elfin Knight' and Child 4, 'Lady Isabel and the Elf-Knight'), also serve to warn young women against sexual adventuring, alerting them to the dangers that threaten when they venture beyond the home and roam alone in the forest. Extreme outcomes – incest and murder – reinforce the moral imperative. These ballads also address family and community anxieties about the now-adult young man who returns to his family, raising questions about whether the incomer can be re-integrated into his kin-group, and how his new status will be negotiated with his siblings. Although principles of filial obedience and respect remain constant, the other brothers and sisters may experience their sibling as changed – even as unrecognizable – and it may be impossible to reassimilate him.

Incest between long-separated siblings is narrowly avoided in *Decameron* V.5.[23] Giacomino, living in the Marche region, becomes the guardian of a young girl, left in his charge by his dying friend. When Agnesa is old enough to marry they move to Faenza. There two gallants quarrel over the girl; since nothing is known of her ancestry neither can obtain the permission of their relatives to woo her. After an open brawl between the two lovers, they are imprisoned. Their families visit Giacomino to ask for clemency, whereupon he narrates Agnesa's history. When his now-dead friend looted Faenza, he stole Agnesa away. One man present realizes that this must be his lost daughter, a suspicion confirmed by a little scar above her ear. Since Agnesa is thus revealed to be the sister of Giannole, one of her suitors (and indeed the one for whom she felt no particular love and who had attempted to abduct her), she marries the preferred Minghino amid great rejoicing on the part of her rediscovered family. As in the cases of Gareth and Gawain, and Gyburg and Rennewart, shared similarities with an unrecognized sibling are construed as sympathetic. Giannole perceives the bond as sexual attraction, while Agnesa's instincts prove the truth of Augustine's dictum about the natural abhorrence of sibling incest. The warfare endemic to medieval Italy destroys family bonds – for it was during the sack of Faenza by the emperor Frederick II that Agnesa was separated from her natal family – and it prevents a clear understanding of who one's kindred really are

---

[20] Ibid., I: 170–7.
[21] Ibid., I: 450–4.
[22] Mitchell, *Siblings*, p. 26.
[23] Giovanni Boccaccio, *Decameron* V.3.

Sibling Incest

and where one belongs.[24] The incest so narrowly avoided is symptomatic of a wider social disruption.[25]

Doubling, incest and the multiplication of lateral relations is typical of the Welsh *Mabinogi* tales, dating back perhaps to the eleventh century. The *Mabinogion* treats important ethical questions on a mythic level: though they occur within a family context, kin-group interactions both figure and directly impact upon political relations between Welsh kingdoms. Sworn-brother loyalties, fraternal jealousy and affinal strife feature strongly in the Second Branch (discussed in the next chapter, pp. 193–4). In the Fourth Branch, two brothers, Gwydion and Gilfaethwy, are punished for conspiracy to rape, and the commission of the rape itself.[26] Their outraged magician-uncle Math acts against them, transforming them not only into beasts, but into animal sexual partners. Gilfaethwy becomes a hind and Gwydion a stag. The animal pair depart to the woods, returning to court each year with a single offspring. The men's son is granted human shape while the parents exchange sexes and change species: from deer to boar and from boar to wolf. Gilfaethwy – the rapist – is made female twice, Gwydion once. When the three years of their punishment is up, Math restores them to human form. The punishment of Gilfaethwy and Gwydion is undoubtedly bizarre; that two males should be transformed into a male/female pair of animals is a plot development for which no exact analogues have been adduced. The brothers seem to become totally beast-like, subject solely to instinct in their pairing and mating; they do not apparently retain their rationality nor any clear signs of self-consciousness about their behaviour. Whether the two animal-brothers can be understood as committing incest is thus debateable. Their punishment is social shame: both the loss of human identity and, for the temporarily female animal, the sexual shame of being penetrated by a male partner.[27]

Incest typically ends in death or exile. Yet, after the men finally return to human form, Gilfaethwy disappears from the story while Gwydion is restored to his uncle's favour: Math asks him for help in finding a new virgin to hold his feet.[28] The previous holder of the office had been Gilfaethwy's rape victim. Gwydion's sister Aranrhod is put forward, but she fails Math's virginity test: as she steps over his magic staff she drops first a large blond-haired boy – Dylan, later god of the sea – and then a second little creature. Gwydion nurtures this little creature which matures into a tall, strong boy. Aranrhod is consistently

---

[24] Compare the story of Andreuccio (*Decameron* II.5), discussed in chapter three.
[25] Archibald is no doubt correct to link this plot with late classical New Comedy: Archibald, *Incest and the Medieval Imagination*, pp. 193–4, n. 4.
[26] 'Math uab Mathonwy' in *Pedeir Keinc y Mabinogi*, ed. I. Williams (Cardiff, 1930), pp. 67–92; 'Math son of Mathonwy', in *The Mabinogi and Other Medieval Welsh Texts*, trans. P. K. Ford (Berkeley and Los Angeles, 1977), pp. 89–110.
[27] See S. L. Higley, 'Dirty Magic: Seiðr, Science and the Parturating Man in Medieval Norse and Welsh Literature', *Essays in Medieval Studies* 11 (1994), 137–45.
[28] Math is subject to a *geis* (an idiosyncratic taboo, either of obligation or prohibition) which requires him to rest his feet in a virgin's lap except in times of war.

hostile to this child of an unknown father; he eventually gains the name 'Lleu'. Gwydion's love and care for this boy may be purely that of a brother for his sister's son, but the implication that the child was conceived under circumstances which left Aranrhod unaware of her condition points towards incestuous circumstances.[29] Gwydion's concern for his sister's son is paralleled by other maternal uncles whose avuncular patronage disguises what is actually paternal investment in an unacknowledged, incestuously conceived son's fortunes. While Gilfaethwy's sexual trangression is the rape of Math's former foot-holder, his brother and double Gwydion seems also to have had transgressive sex: with his sister. The Fourth Branch ostensibly examines sexual violence and deception, and their procreative outcomes: the brothers' animal children develop into fine warriors, but the extraordinary nature of Aranrhod's twins signals the presence of the incest motif.

Begetting a Hero

Incestuous coupling, whether unwitting, but later discovered, as in the case of the legend of Gregorius (discussed below), or whether deliberately undertaken by one or both siblings, often results in the birth of a remarkable child. Lleu, the son of Aranrhod, and very likely Gwydion, grows up with his uncle's help to be a impressively strong warrior and he succeeds his maternal great-uncle Math as lord of Gwynedd. Analogous to the story of Lleu's curious conception and birth, but functioning on a more evidently mythic level, is the 'Compert con Culainn', the conception and birth story of the Irish hero, Cú Chulainn. The tale exists in two different traditions; the older one may date back to the ninth century. Cú Chulainn's mother Deichtine would often act as charioteer for her brother Conchobar, the high king of Ulster.[30] In a complicated

---

[29] See among others C. W. Sullivan III, 'Inheritance and Lordship in Math', in *The Mabinogi: A Book of Essays*, ed. C. W. Sullivan, III (New York and London, 1996), 347–66; R. Valente, 'Gwydion and Aranrhod: Crossing the Borders of Gender in Math', *Bulletin of the Board of Celtic Studies* 35 (1988), 1–9; P.-Y. Lambert, 'Magie et pouvoir dans la quatrième branche du Mabinogi', *Studia Celtica* 28 (1994), 97–107; A.Welsh, 'Doubling and Incest in the Mabinogi', *Speculum* 65 (1990), 344–62.

[30] As noted by T. Ó Concheanainn, 'The Textual Tradition of *Compert con Culainn*', *Essays in Honour of Brian Ó Cuív, Celtica* 21 (1990), 441–55 (p. 444, n. 15), there are two conflicting traditions about the relationship between Deichtine and Conchobar. She is either his daughter or his sister, and hence Cú Chulainn is the king's grandson or nephew. Given the importance of the sister's son in Celtic (as in other medieval literatures), it seems likely that Deichtine is Conchobar's sister. See T. Ó Cathasaigh, 'The Sister's Son in Early Irish Literature', *Peritia* 5 (1986), 128–60 (pp. 136–7); also T. Ó Concheanainn, 'A Connacht Medieval Literary Heritage: Text Derived from Cín Drommo Snechtain through Leabhar na hUidhre', *Cambridge Medieval Celtic Studies* 16 (1988), 1–40 (pp. 27–30). Here Ó Concheanainn argues that the understanding of Dechtine/Dechtire as Conchobar's daughter is the result of earlier scholars concluding that she seems to be too young to be his sister.

story, summarized here according to the *Leabhar na hUidre* version, Deichtine, her brother and a host of Ulstermen go out hunting some marvellous birds. Overtaken by a snowstorm, they seek shelter in a house where a woman is in labour. A boy is born and Deichtine takes charge of him. At daybreak the house disappears, and they return to the High King's seat at Emain. The boy later dies. Still lamenting her fosterling's death, Deichtine drinks from a copper bowl; in it is a small creature which keeps jumping towards her lips and which she eventually swallows.[31] That night the god Lugh appears to her in a dream and reveals that he has impregnated her. The first boy was his child and now he is in her womb. The pregnancy of the king's unmarried sister is a scandal; the Ulstermen suspect Conchobar of being the father since the siblings would often sleep in the same chamber. Deichtine is married off to a certain Sualdaim, but the pregnancy miscarries. In due time she gives birth to a boy, Sétanta, who is reared by another of Conchobar's sisters, Finnchoem.[32]

In the second, later, version of the story, Deichtire (as she is called here) has left Ulster with fifty maidens for three years. They return in bird form and are pursued by the Ulstermen. They shelter for the night in a small house; one of the Ulstermen, Bricriu, goes out in the night and finds a big house full of folk, including Deichtire, who is said to be the beautiful wife of the master of the house. Bricriu returns and relates the adventure to Conchobar without mentioning the beautiful woman's identity. Conchobar sends for the beautiful woman to sleep with him; when she arrives she anounces that she is about to give birth and the next day a child was found on Conchobar's breast. The boy Sétanta is adopted by Finnchoem at Conchobar's command. Later in the story cycle, as related in the *Táin*, Sétanta is renamed 'Cú Chulainn' ('the Hound of Culann') after his first great feat, slaying a monstrous dog.[33]

It is difficult to unpick these closely interwoven traditions of the hero's birth. Clearly Deichtine is Sétanta's mother, whether via the triple conception of the *Leabhar na hUidre* or the single birth in the otherworld house. The boy's paternity is ascribed to the god Lugh, whose name is cognate with Lleu, that Welsh product of a mysterious conception in the Fourth Branch of the Mabinogi, discussed above. Nevertheless, the consistent presence of Deichtine's brother at the otherworld locale in which Deichtine acquires the first avatar of her son, or in which he is born, is clearly significant. The two versions deal differently with the problematic and potentially scandalous pregnancy: version I moots Conchobar's paternity, only to erase it through the termination, while version II passes over the incestuous possibilities in silence.

Cú Chulainn would not be alone among sister's-son figures who are also the products of incest: Mordred, considered below, was transformed from Arthur's

---

[31] The similarity to the prematurely born Lleu is striking.
[32] *Compert Con Culainn and Other Stories*, ed. A. G. van Hamel, Mediaeval and Modern Irish Series 3 (Dublin, 1933), pp. 3–8; trans. C.-J. Guyonvarc'h, 'La conception de Cúchulainn', *Ogam* 17 (1965), pp. 363–91.
[33] Summarized from Ó Concheanainn, 'The Textual Tradition'.

nephew into his incestuously conceived son by the early thirteenth century. The Old Norse version of the life of Charlemagne, *Karlamagnús saga*, preserves the tradition that Rollant (the hero Roland), elsewhere Charlemagne's nephew, is also his son.[34] After his coronation in Rome, Karlamagnús returns home to Aix and, finding his sister Gilem there, 'leiddi hana í svefnhǫll sína, ok svaf hann hjá henni, svá at hann lagði ást við hana, til þess er lag þeirra varð' ('he took her into his sleeping quarters and he slept with her, and as he felt love for her so they lay together').[35] Like Deichtine, who habitually sleeps with her brother without being his regular sexual partner, the saga implies that Gilem would often join Karlamagnús in his bed-space, but that, on this one occasion, he felt and yielded to his sexual desire for her. This seems to be an unexpected one-off occurrence within the sibling relationship: Karlamagnús's enhanced sense of his own masculine power bestowed by the coronation ceremony produces inappropriate sexual arousal when he returns home.

The emotional intimacy of the relationship between Karlamagnús and Gilem is demonstrated in other ways. Early in the saga Karlamagnús entrusts evidence of a plot against him – a bloody glove – to Gilem.[36] When Renfrei and his co-conspirators are arrested and charged, Gilem is asked to bring out the glove as proof.[37] Karlamagnús's decision to place this crucial item in his sister's keeping parallels the confidence misguidedly placed by Arthur in Morgan le Fay in the Post-Vulgate *Suite de Merlin* (as discussed in chapter five). Sisters, more so than wives, are thought to have their brothers' interests close to their hearts, particularly when they are unwed and have not forged affective ties with a husband and his family.[38] Moreover, although Gilem is the older sister, it is her younger sister Belisent who is married first: she weds Reinbald the Frisian. Karlamagnús prefers to keep his most beloved sister by his side, just as the historical Charlemagne kept his unmarried daughters about him.[39] Gilem's eventual marriage is necessitated by her pregnancy.[40]

After the incestuous encounter, Karlamagnús goes to mass, but omits to confess his offence. The angel Gabriel lays a letter on the mass-paten, and St Egidius (St Giles), the emperor's confessor, reads it to him: Karlamagnús's sin and

[34] *Karlamagnús saga ok kappa hans: Fortællinger om keiser Karl Magnus og kappa hans*, ed. C. R. Unger (Christiania [Oslo], 1860); *Karlamagnús saga: The Saga of Charlemagne and his Heroes*, trans. C. B. Hieatt, 3 vols (Toronto, 1975–80).
[35] *Karlamagnús saga*, ed. Unger, pp. 31–3. *Saga of Charlemagne*, trans. Hieatt, I: 117–18.
[36] *Karlamagnús saga*, ed. Unger, ch. 1; *Saga of Charlemagne*, trans. Hieatt, I: 58–61.
[37] *Karlamagnús saga*, ed. Unger, chs. 10, 23; *Saga of Charlemagne*, trans. Hieatt, I: 79, 98–9.
[38] Arthur entrusts his magic scabbard of invulnerability to his sister rather than to his wife; this enables Morgan to manufacture a fake version which she uses in her plot against him. See Larrington, *King Arthur's Enchantresses*, pp. 33–40.
[39] J. L. Nelson, 'Women at the Court of Charlemagne: A Case of Monstrous Regiment?', in *Medieval Queenship*, ed. J. C. Parsons (New York, 1993), pp. 43–62.
[40] Although in ch. 26 Reinbald apparently asks for Gilem as his wife (according to MS AM 180c fo.), in ch. 33 his wife is identified as Belisent, as in the other manuscripts (see *Saga of Charlemagne*, trans. Hieatt, I: 103).

Gilem's pregnancy is revealed.⁴¹ Karlamagnús now confesses his transgression – how could he not? – and, in obedience to the dictates of the letter, he marries off Gilem and makes her husband duke of Brittany. Young Rollant is fostered by canons and taught to read and write; at the age of seven he is brought before the emperor, who asks if he knows who he is. When Rollant identifies him as his maternal uncle: 'móðurbróðir minn', Karlamagnús laughs. The answer seems to have persuaded his father that any scandal has died down; hereafter he is persistently identified as Karlamagnús's 'systursonr' ('sister's son') and his heroic career flourishes.⁴²

The circumstances of the incest are only made clear in the Norse tradition, but intimations of unusual tensions in the relationship between Roland, Charlemagne and Roland's stepfather Ganelon are already apparent in the *Chanson de Roland*. 'In retaining the evidence, ("stepfather", "nephew") for the blood ties which bind Charlemagne, Roland, and Ganelon, the author cannot avoid evoking other aspects of these ties which are best forgotten, hence the suppression of the wife/mother/sister's very name', argues Richard Serrano.⁴³ In the *Chanson*, the existence of the woman who unites the three men is effaced, a disappearance which gestures towards a fourth role – that of lover – which cannot be uttered. In *Ronsasvals*, a Provençal fragment, Charlemagne admits he is Roland's father as he laments over his son's corpse: 'per lo mieu peccat gran / De ma seror... Qu'ieu soy tos payres, tos oncles eyssamant' ('through my very great sin / with my sister ... That I am both your father, and your uncle') (lines 1623–5).⁴⁴ Miranda Griffin links Charlemagne's incest, left obscure in the surviving texts predating *Karlamagnús saga*, with that of Arthur and argues that rumours of an incestuous scandal circulating about Roland's birth may have been grafted onto Arthurian tradition.⁴⁵

The occasion of Mordred's conception varies considerably.⁴⁶ Griffin traces the first reference to the scandal of Mordred's origin in French tradition in the

---

⁴¹ The story of the incomplete confession originally occurs in the tenth-century *Vita Aegidii*, told of Charlemagne's grandfather, Charles Martel, and in the twelfth-century *La vie de saint Gilles*, where Charlemagne is again the culprit. See M. Griffin, 'Writing out the Incest: Arthur, Charlemagne and the Spectre of Incest', *Neophilologus* 88 (2004), 499–519 (pp. 504–5).

⁴² See S. Martinet, 'Le péché de Charlemagne, Gisèle, Roland et Ganelon', in *Amour, mariage et transgressions au Moyen Age: Actes du Colloque des 24, 25, 26 et 27 mars 1983*, ed. D. Buschinger and A. Crépin (Göppingen, 1984), pp. 9–16 for the argument that there may be some historical basis for both the incest and Roland's paternity.

⁴³ R. Serrano, 'No Place for a Lady in the "Song of Roland"', *Pacific Coast Philology* 27 (1992), 110–16 (p. 110); see also R. Lejeune, 'Le péché de Charlemagne et la Chanson de Roland', in *Studia Philologica: Homenaje ofrecido a Dámaso Alonso*, 3 vols (Madrid, 1961), II: 339– 371.

⁴⁴ Martinet, 'Le péché', p. 9; see also S. Hafner, 'Charlemagne's Unspeakable Sin', *Modern Language Studies*, 32 (2002), 1–14 (p. 4, n. 10).

⁴⁵ Griffin, 'Writing out the Incest'.

⁴⁶ For a full discussion of Mordred's conception and its ramifications, see Larrington, *King Arthur's Enchantresses*, pp. 127–35.

Lancelot, revealed via another mysterious letter, this time clutched in the hand of a hermit encountered by Lancelot and Mordred.[47] The circumstances by which the union between Arthur and his half-sister came about are not outlined there; in the Vulgate *Estoire de Merlin*, which provides the first explanation of Arthur's sexual encounter with his sister, Mordred is conceived in a kind of 'bed-trick'.[48] Arthur takes Lot's place in his sister's bed without knowing yet that she *is* his sister. The Vulgate cycle makes no further reference to the incest and there is no scene in which Arthur is confronted with the horror of his unwitting trespass. Unlike Charlemagne, however obliquely expressed his confession might be in the versions of the story predating *Karlamagnús saga*, Arthur does not admit his paternity until Mordred's usurpation – to the astonishment of his nobles.[49] Arthur's incest is handled very differently in the Post-Vulgate *Suite de Merlin*. Here the queen of Orkney comes on a formal visit to the court; both she and Arthur are ignorant of their kinship, and they begin an adulterous affair. The narrative voice immediately announces the disaster which will ensue: 'Adont conut li freres carneument sa serour et porta la dame chelui qui puissedi le traist a mort et mist a destruction et a martyre la terre' ('Thus the brother knew his sister carnally, and the lady carried the one who later betrayed and killed his father and put the land to torture and destruction').[50] After the queen returns to Orkney, Arthur has prophetic nightmares, and shortly afterwards he encounters the monstrous Questing Beast, whose history is related below. Merlin subsequently reveals the incest to him: Arthur is prevented from destroying all May-born male babies in order to eliminate Mordred, and Jesus takes charge of their fates, safely conducting the boat in which they are set adrift to the land of King Orians, where they are reared in the Castle of Boys.[51] Mordred himself is lost at sea on the journey from Orkney to London. Rescued by a fisherman, he is fostered by King Nabur and acquires the prominent knight Sagremor as his brother.[52]

In the Vulgate version, Arthur's confession to her about their sexual encounter converts his sister into a partisan for his bid for the throne; in the Post-Vulgate Cycle in contrast the queen of Orkney becomes his enemy when her son is lost, and she supports her husband in his abortive rebellion against her brother. Malory's treatment of the incest, although based on the Post-Vulgate *Suite*, is

---

[47] *Lancelot*, ed. Micha, V: 219–24; *L-G*, III: 360–1.
[48] *The Vulgate Version of the Arthurian Romances*, ed. H. O. Sommer, 8 vols (Washington DC, 1908–16), II: 128–9; *L-G*, I: 337. See more generally W. Doniger, *The Bedtrick: Tales of Sex and Masquerade* (Chicago, 2000), though she does not discuss Arthurian cases.
[49] *La Mort le Roi Artu*, ed. Frappier, p. 211; *L-G*, IV: 311.
[50] *Suite du Roman de Merlin*, ed. Roussineau, I: 2; *L-G*, IV: 367
[51] *Suite du Roman de Merlin*, ed. Roussineau, I: 64–5; *L-G*, IV: 383–5.
[52] *Suite du Roman de Merlin*, ed. Roussineau, I: 56–64; *L-G*, IV: 370–1. In the Post-Vulgate Cycle's account of the final battle, Mordred kills his foster-brother just before he confronts his father, a textual move which draws attention to the seriousness of the rupturing of the foster-brother bond.

Sibling Incest

somewhat differently inflected.[53] Here the queen comes to Arthur's court on a spying mission for her husband and the affair follows. That she is apparently deceiving Arthur as to the real purpose of her visit and deceiving her husband in her adultery is suggestive; it is scarcely surprising that the child who results from the liaison should be the worst of traitors. In a Massacre of the Innocents, Malory's Arthur sets the May-born babies adrift; the boat founders and all are lost.[54] Mordred is not among them; having survived an earlier shipwreck en route to London he eventually arrives at the court without fanfare.

The Vulgate cycle does not develop the theme of incest. Mordred's revolt against his father is motivated by political opportunism and a sudden and astonishing passion for his father's wife Guenevere: the traitor's scandalous origins are incidental. The fragmentary state of the Post-Vulgate Cycle makes it less easy to judge the incestuous encounter's significance for the rest of the Cycle's themes at the point at which it occurs. Nevertheless, the Post-Vulgate version of the *Queste del Saint Graal*, as discussed below, concludes with the death of the Questing Beast, and the long-postponed rehearsal of the monster's incest-framed origin, while the Cycle as a whole culminates in the murderous confrontation of Arthur with the product of his own incest.[55] As Judith Butler notes of the Oedipus cycle, the Post-Vulgate cycle is thoroughly 'steeped in incestuous legacies'; these figure the gradual collapse of the chivalric world in the recurrent disruption of sexual taboo within the family.[56] Arthur, himself a product of a problematic conception, acts in ignorance when he sleeps with his sister, but he is always aware that she is another man's wife: his failure to rein in his desires unsettles the realm as his kingship begins.[57]

Mordred is not an especially heroic knight; both in the Post-Vulgate tradition and Malory his chivalric failures are commented upon. Lleu, Cú Chulainn and Roland, in contrast, are all remarkable if flawed heroes, begotten in incestuous encounters which later-medieval literary traditions treated in complicated ways. Their incestuous origins are suppressed to the extent that the paternity of the

---

[53] Malory, *Morte Darthur*, ed. Field, I: 33–4; Merlin's prophecy, Malory, *Morte Darthur*, ed. Field, I: 36; death of children, *Morte Darthur* I: 46. See also H. Cooper, *The English Romance in Time* (Oxford, 2004), 376–7.

[54] On the absence of any recognition scene between Mordred and his father, see E. Archibald, 'Comedy and Tragedy in Some Arthurian Recognition Scenes', in *Comedy in Arthurian Literature*, ed. K. Busby and R. Dalrymple, *Arthurian Literature* 19 (Cambridge, 2003), 1–16.

[55] See L. R. Muir, 'The Questing Beast: Its Origin and Development', *Orpheus* 4 (1957), 24–32, W. A. Nitze, 'The Beste Glatissante in Arthurian Romance', *Zeitschrift für romanische Philologie* 56 (1936), 409–18, and now D. Armstrong and K. Hodges, *Mapping Malory: Regional Identities and National Geographies in* Le Morte Darthur (New York, 2014), pp. 157–72.

[56] Butler, *Antigone's Claim*, p. 2.

[57] See R. Morris, 'Uther and Ygerne: A Study in Uncourtly Love', *Arthurian Literature* 4, (1985), 70–92, and M. V. Guerin, 'The King's Sin: The Origins of the David-Arthur Parallel', in *The Passing of Arthur: New Essays in Arthurian Tradition*, ed. C. Baswell and W. Sharpe (New York, 1998), 15–30.

two Celtic heroes cannot be determined for certain; the scandal of Roland's conception only emerges clearly centuries after Charlemagne's death and in rather distant cultural ambits. None of the sibling pairs involved in these three stories intended to produce a child; Deichtine's instinct to get rid of the baby who might be regarded as Conchobar's offspring is thwarted by Lugh's intention that his son shall indeed be born. Aranrot would scarcely have undertaken a public virginity test if she had any inkling that she was pregnant, while, in *Karlamagnús saga*, Gilem's emotional situation remains unexplored.

In one tradition, however, the birth of the heroic child is the planned outcome of deliberately undertaken incest. In the probably mid-thirteenth-century *Vǫlsunga saga*, which relates a complex story of revenge not attested elsewhere in medieval Scandinavia, a sister purposely has intercourse with her brother in order to breed a son brave enough to take revenge on her natal clan's enemy, her own hated husband.[58] Signý and Sigmundr are twins. Signý is unwillingly married to King Siggeir of Gautland, who later murders her father Vǫlsungr and all her brothers, with the exception of Sigmundr. Signý despairs of her despised husband fathering a son who might be both courageous and motivated enough to join Sigmundr in vengeance: two children fail the test she and Sigmundr set to gauge their mettle and are murdered by their uncle. Finally, Signý exchanges outer appearances with a sorceress and sleeps three nights with her unwitting brother: thus she conceives Sinfjǫtli, a strong and uncompromising son. When he is grown, she sews his clothes onto his flesh and then tears them off. When asked if this was painful, Sinfjǫtli proudly compares himself to his double grandfather: 'Lítit mundi slíkt sárt þykkja Vǫlsungi' ('this pain would seem slight to Vǫlsungr').[59] He triumphantly passes Sigmundr's test also. In the course of their vengeance attack, Sigmundr refuses to slay his sister's children but Sinfjǫtli does not shrink from murdering his two little half-siblings when they betray his presence to their father. When Siggeir's hall is alight, and all within it about to perish, Signý reveals the truth to her brother and her son:

> ek fór í skóg til þín í vǫlvulíki og er Sinfjǫtli okkarr son. Hefir hann af því mikit kapp at hann er bæði sonarsonr ok dóttursonr Vǫlsungs konungs.

> ('I came to you in the forest in the shape of a seeress and Sinfjǫtli is our son. He is so heroic because he is both son's son and daughter's son of King Vǫlsungr.')[60]

Signý declares that she has done so much to bring about revenge that she can live no longer, and she returns to die in the flames with her loathed husband.

Signý's deliberate breeding of a revenger, one so alienated from those he believes to be his paternal kindred that he kills his tiny half-siblings without a moment's hesitation, is unique among medieval narratives and its details

---

[58] *Vǫlsunga saga*, ed. and trans. Finch.
[59] Ibid., ch. 7, p. 10.
[60] Ibid., ch. 8, pp. 13–14.

Sibling Incest

are not attested elsewhere in Norse tradition. Signý's logic, voiced only in her final revelation, makes explicit the understanding of heritable traits and their intensification through inbreeding which implicitly underpins the other 'conception of a hero' incest-stories. Nevertheless, once the incest is acknowledged, like the luckless heroines who unknowingly have sex with their brothers, suicide is her only option. While Signý cannot envisage a normal existence alongside her brother/lover and her son, Sigmundr's ignorance of Signý's machinations permits him finally to lead a normal family life. He marries a woman called Borghildr and has two sons with her. Sinfjǫtli models an exemplary fraternal bond with his younger brother Helgi, loyally serving him as a military commander until his stepmother poisons him in revenge for the death of her own brother, slain by Sinfjǫtli in a contest over a woman. Sinfjǫtli thus partially undoes his earlier murder of his half-siblings through his loyal fraternal service, though, in a formal challenge before battle, an enemy warrior Guðmundr throws his fratricide in his face.[61] Like Rollant, Sinfjǫtli dies before he fathers children. Cú Chulainn kills his only son, while in those texts where Mordred does have offspring the survivors of the Arthurian cataclysm make sure to exterminate them.[62] The child born of incest cannot be fully incorporated into a lineage and thus he tends to die young and without issue.

Doubt or scandal surrounding the birth of such a hero temporarily recedes in the face of his exceptional qualities, and since the sister's-son relationship is a privileged one in a number of early Western European societies, the incestuous father is able to cloak his nephew's origins in secrecy and avoid open condemnation. The mothers too conceal their pregnancies through marriage to another man and, in the case of Dechtine, brazen out the rumours. In the Post-Vulgate Cycle, Mordred's mother, the queen of Orkney, dies at the hands of another of her sons. Her death is closely bound up with considerations of family honour, but Mordred's true paternity has not yet become clear.[63] Signý's suicide, like the deaths of the ballad-heroines, confirms that the scandal of incest is so damaging to a woman's sense of personal honour that it cannot be survived once it is publicly acknowledged.

Deliberate Incest

As the cleric John Mirk warned (see chapter one, p. 26), it is children who share a bed beyond the age of seven, often those who are orphaned or left to their

---

[61] See Larrington, 'Sibling Drama', pp. 169–87.
[62] *Aided Óenfir Aífe*, in *Compert Con Culainn*, ed. van Hamel, pp. 9–15; trans. C.-J. Guyonvarc'h, 'La mort du fils unique d'Aífe', *Ogam* 9 (1957), 115–21; and E. D. Kennedy, 'Mordred's Sons', in *The Arthurian Way of Death*, ed. K. Cherewatuk and K. S. Whetter, Arthurian Studies 74(Cambridge, 2009), pp. 33–49.
[63] On the queen of Orkney's death, see Larrington, *King Arthur's Enchantresses*, pp. 136–41.

own devices, who are most likely to begin a sexual relationship.[64] 'Sibling incest and parental abandonment seem to go hand-in-hand', notes Prophecy Coles; incest thus becomes a refuge from a dangerous or incompletely understood world.[65] Mitchell asks: 'Repeated trauma leaves too little of the self – can the sibling replenish it?'[66] Crisis in the nuclear family is thus a harbinger of sibling sexual experimentation. Deliberate sibling incest functions also as an extreme manifestation of failure to achieve identity differentiation (as discussed in chapter four). Not only must a sibling distinguish him- or herself from other siblings, he or she must also achieve an adult identity, primarily – especially in romance – by finding and marrying an appropriate object of heterosexual desire, a spouse from outside the kin-group, who enables the creation of a new exogamic alliance and an independent household.[67] For the siblings discussed below, extreme endogamous desire means that their emerging heterosexual impulses are not directed beyond the family group. Through adult failure and absence these inward-gazing siblings turn to one another in narcissistic, sometimes coercive, sibling sexual experimentation.

From a medieval moral perspective, both parental neglect and overindulgence provide opportunity for children to go morally astray – as in the Knight of the Tour-Landry's story of the spoiled sister who ended up losing an eye, recounted in chapter five. In a widespread story, an example of which occurs in the *Gesta Romanorum* (story 71), a *nouveau riche* couple have a son and a daughter whom they spoil with rich food and fine clothes. They are allowed to share a bed too long, with the result that the girl becomes pregnant.[68] Rather than confess their crime they run away together, but, out in the forest, the sister goes into labour. The brother is impatient that her travails are preventing him from reaching the safety of a town; drawing his sword, he kills both mother and child. In the city the brother makes his fortune, marries and prospers until he falls fatally ill. Sending for a priest, the murderer confesses his history, receives absolution and dies. At his funeral a heavenly voice is heard, noting with what difficulty this soul had been won.[69] As in the story of Gregorius, discussed below,

---

[64] See V. R. Wiehe, *Sibling Abuse: Hidden Physical, Emotional and Sexual Trauma*, 2nd edn (Thousand Oaks CA and London, 1997), 'the absence of privacy in sleeping arrangments . . . may also increase a victim's vulnerability', pp. 131–2. C. Dinshaw, *Getting Medieval: Sexualities and Communities, Pre- and Postmodern* (Durham NC and London, 1999), 10–11, argues that the sexual activity feared by Mirk could equally occur between same-sex siblings or other less closely related children who continue to share a bed.

[65] Coles, *The Importance of Sibling Relationships*, p. 65.

[66] Mitchell, *Siblings*, p. 65.

[67] That Signý and Sigmundr are twins is no coincidence; that it is the woman who takes the incestuous initiative is unusual (but see the story of Ypomenés's daughter, below).

[68] *Early English Versions of the Gesta Romanorum*, ed. Herrtage, pp. 388–90. Pregnancy also provokes the crisis in modern psychoanalytical treatment of incest: 'it is only when sibling conception actually occurs that the patient's horror and fear of monstrous progeny break in and the clinician becomes worried too', Mitchell, *Sibings*, p. 40.

[69] *Gesta Romanorum*, ed. Herrtage, pp. 388–90.

the worst of crimes, incest and murder, are deployed as sensational precursors to moral instruction, specifically about the key sacrament in the later-medieval period: penance.

The *Gesta Romanorum* story recalls the stark treatment of consensual incest in the ballads. In 'Sheath and Knife' (Child Ballad 16), the rumour is noised abroad 'that the king's dochter gaes wi child to her brither'.[70] The brother takes his sister out to the deer-park (compare the imagery of Child Ballad 50, 'The Bonnie Hind', above p. 159) and she asks him to shoot her with his bow when she cries out at the climax of her labour. He does as she asks, buries both sister and baby and returns to his father's court. The young man is heartbroken, but can only speak in coded metaphorical terms about his sorrow: he has lost his knife (the baby) but worse, he has lost his beloved sister, the sheath that the knife was in. His father or mother cannot understand his melancholy, and, like the father in 'The Bonnie Hind', they offer uselessly practical alternatives: there are cowpers (merchants) in Fife who can replace what he has lost. The parents cannot grasp the literally unspeakable nature of the bereft brother's crime.

Medieval sibling incest always contains death, whether that of the perpetrators or via the conception of a ruthless killer like Sinfjǫtli, or the parricide Mordred.[71] In Child Ballad 51, 'Lizzie Wan', the protagonist tells her father that she is pregnant by her brother Geordie and then reveals this confession to him. Geordie kills his sister and tells his mother that the blood is his greyhound's; when she does not believe him, he admits what he has done. Rather than face his father he declares that he will drown himself.[72] The incest motif need not always be explicit: in 'The Cruel Brother' (Child Ballad 11), a marriage is agreed between a knight, the bride and her family, but, crucially, the bridegroom 'forgot to spiek to her brother John'.[73] On the wedding day the family take their leave of the bride and brother John lifts her up onto her horse. As she leans down to kiss him, he quietly stabs her with his knife 'baith lang and sharp'. The best man notices the dying girl's pallor during the bridal journey; she dismounts and makes her will. To her parents and sisters she bequeaths her most precious possessions, but to brother John is left 'the gallows-tree to hang him on'. The ballad's typically elliptical style leaves open questions of motivation: but the final kiss and the phallic knife certainly suggest an incestuous impulse – the jealous instinct that if the brother may not enjoy his sister, no-one will.

In one version of 'Brown Robyn's Confession' (Child Ballad 57), Brown Robyn and his men go to sea, but they cannot see the sun, moon or stars.[74] Believing that they must have some accursed man among them, they cast lots to see who should be thrown overboard. The lot falls on Robyn himself: he is scarcely surprised to be selected, for he has begotten two children on his mother and five

---

[70] *Ballads*, ed. Child, I: 185–7.
[71] Mitchell, *Siblings*, p. 81.
[72] *Ballads*, ed. Child, I: 448–9.
[73] Ibid., I: 141–51.
[74] Ibid., II: 13–16.

on his sister. Having confessed, he asks to be thrown in the sea, yet the Virgin appears in order to save him. '[F]or your fair confession you've made upon the sea', she tells him, he can choose whether to return to his ship or depart with her for heaven. Since revealed incest is not survivable, Robyn chooses the second option. As in the *Gesta Romanorum* tale, incest (coupled with parricide in some versions of this ballad) functions as the worst sin imaginable; nevertheless the perpetrator can still achieve salvation through his freely made confession and the boundlessness of divine mercy.

Brother–sister incest forms the opening episode in the so-called 'double incest' narrative. In another *Gesta Romanorum* tale, a dying Roman emperor bequeaths his throne to his son and his chattels to his daughter, charging his son with arranging his sister's marriage.[75] The siblings are preternaturally close, eating out of a single dish and sleeping in the same chamber, though in separate beds: circumstances typical of 'nurturance-oriented incest'.[76] One night the young emperor is overcome with an extraordinary desire for his sister and he calls out to her, 'Awake, sister, for þer is com vpon me swiche a temptacion, þat but yf I lye be yowe, I am but dede'.[77] The sister protests, reminding him of his father's dying request and her own marriage prospects, but in the end 'of hir boþe assent' they lie together.

Inevitably the sister becomes pregnant; having taken refuge with a kindly knight she gives birth. The child is placed in a barrel along with recognition tokens and tablets relating his origins, then thrown into the sea. The incestuous brother dies while on pilgrimage; his sister rules in his stead, but Rome is besieged by a duke who wishes to marry her. Meanwhile the boy grows up, learns from the tablets that he is the fruit of incest, and decides to go on pilgrimage to the Holy Land. Journeying via Rome, he overcomes the besieger and marries the beleaguered lady, his unknown mother. Every day he re-reads his origin story and weeps; when a damsel tells the empress of her husband's secret sorrow, she finds the tablets. Confronting her husband privately and revealing her identity, the empress and her husband send for a priest and make a full confession; they then fall dead and go straight to heaven.

This version of the legend foregrounds the social significance of the emperor's failure to follow his father's final instruction to see to his sister's future: the old emperor's only regret as he prepares for death is 'that I have not marrijd my dowter'.[78] The young emperor refrains from marrying his sister outside the family because he wishes (like Karlamagnús) to keep her for himself, even though, as he proposes incest to her, the girl reminds him that their father charged him with attending to her 'matrimony'. The dysfunctionality and

---

[75] Cf. Wiehe, *Sibling Abuse*, 'when parents are physically or psychologically absent, such as through death, divorce, illness . . . the likelihood of sexual abuse increases', p. 131. *Gesta Romanorum*, ed. Herrtage, pp. 250–63.
[76] Bank and Kahn, *The Sibling Bond*, p. 178.
[77] *Gesta Romanorum*, ed. Herrtage, p. 250.
[78] Ibid., p. 250.

inwardness of the first sibling-couple results in the second tragedy; the sister is willing to marry the outsider who has saved her from the besieging duke, only to find that exogamy too fails her. Extreme sinfulness once again offers an occasion for God to demonstrate the power of contrition and penance to bring the greatest possible grace.[79]

The double incest narrative becomes attached to the biography of the legendary Pope Gregory.[80] In *Gregorius*, the early-thirteenth-century German hagiographical romance by Hartmann von Aue, the orphaned son of the Duke of Aquitaine is similarly charged by his dying father to take care of his younger sister and to arrange her marriage: 'daz dû dich wol an ir bewarst / und ir bruoderlîchen mite varst' ('that you take good care of her and treat her in a brotherly way').[81] Despite this injunction the young man is prompted by the devil to climb into his sister's bed and make love to her. The girl is aware of the likely consequences; even as she asks her brother, 'waz diutet diz ringen?' ('What is this tussling all about?'), she realizes that if she cries out they will both be disgraced, but if she keeps quiet then the devil will get his way – and she will become – horrifyingly – 'mînes bruoder brût' ('[her] brother's bride').[82] Although that very night is the one in which she becomes pregnant, they become habitual lovers. When the girl reveals her pregnancy her brother is plunged into misery. Their story follows the same pattern found in the *Gesta Romanorum* tale until the revelation of the mother's marriage to her son. Hartmann's Gregorius undertakes spectacularly ascetic penance, chaining himself to a crag and lamenting his sins for seventeen years, until, through God's grace, he is chosen as pope. The devil is figured as instrumental in urging Gregorius's father to the rape of his sister:

> an sîner swester minne
> sô riet er im ze verre
> unz daz der juncherre
> verkêrte sîne triuwe guot
> ûf einen valschen muot[83]

('he advised him to go too far in the love of his sister, to the point that the young lord turned his good devotion into a wrong way of thinking').

---

[79] See Archibald's thoughtful discussion of Gregorius and related stories in *Incest and the Medieval Imagination*, pp. 111–24.

[80] Not to be confused with Pope Gregory the Great.

[81] Hartmann von Aue, *Gregorius, Der Arme Heinrich und Iwein*, ed. and trans. V. Mertens. (Frankfurt-am-Main, 2004), lines 261–2. See also *Arthurian Romances, Tales and Lyric Poetry: The Complete Works of Hartmann von Aue*, trans. F. Tobin, K. Vivian and R. Lawson (University Park PA, 2001), pp. 165–214. For a full account of the Gregorius legend, see B. Murdoch, *Gregorius: An Incestuous Saint in Medieval Europe and Beyond* (Oxford, 2012), particularly pp. 24–7, which discuss the sin of Gregorius's parents in relation to Adam and Eve.

[82] *Gregorius*, ed. Mertens, line 384; *Arthurian Romances*, p. 172. Sexual ignorance also contributes to sibling sexual abuse, see Wiehe, *Sibling Abuse*, p. 132.

[83] *Gregorius*, ed. Mertens, lines 318–21.

Yet Hartmann notes that other factors are involved:

> diu minne
> diu im verriet die sinne,
> daz ander sîner swester schœne,
> daz dritte des tiuvels hœne,
> daz vierde was sîn kintheit

('love which betrayed his mind, the second his sister's beauty, the third the devil's malice and the fourth his childish innocence').[84]

Every man should take warning by this and not be too intimate with his sister or any other close relative, Hartmann warns. As churchmen feared (discussed in chapters one and three), proximity to any woman, even a blood-relative, could prompt sexual desire.[85] Absent from the *Gesta Romanorum* version, where natural sexual urges and a lack of supervision prompt the emperor to act on his desire for his sister, the devil's agency is only one of the factors involved in Hartmann's analysis of illicit sibling passion. Normal love for a sister 'triuwe guot' becomes perverted into 'valschen muot' ('a wrong way of thinking'). Further demonic involvement in non-consensual sibling incest episodes is discussed below.

Among the classical stories inherited by medieval authors was the tale of Canace and Machaire (Canacis and Macharius) from Ovid's *Heroides*.[86] Gower's *Confessio Amantis*, Book III, dealing with the symptoms of Wrath, under the heading of Melancolie, narrates a version of their legend. Machaire and Canace ill-advisedly share a chamber until they grow 'into the youthe of lusti age, / When kinde assaileth the corage / With love'.[87] Cupid urges Machaire to kiss his sister; Nature teaches the couple what to do next, and before too long Canace is pregnant. Machaire leaves the court to avoid suspicion, while Canace bears the child. Their father Eolus's rage is glossed by Genius as Melancolie; instead of turning inward in depression, Eolus's distemper manifests itself as fury. Despite Canace's pleas for mercy, Eolus sends her a naked sword, intimating that she should kill herself. Before her death, Canace composes a letter to Machaire in which she elaborates the fundamental paradox that her brother should be her lover through a series of other paradoxes:

---

[84] *Gregorius*, ed. Mertens, lines 323–7.

[85] *Gregorius*, ed. Mertens, lines 415–27; *Arthurian Romances*, p. 172. Cf. Thomas Aquinas's discussion in *Summa Theologiae*, Second Part of Second Part, Question 154, article 9, available at: http://www.corpusthomisticum.org/sth3146.html; trans. http://www.newadvent.org/summa/3154.htm#article9.

[86] Ovid, *Heroides and Amores*, ed. and trans. G. Showerman, Loeb Classical Library 41 (London, 1931), Book 11. For Chaucer's approach to and avoidance of Canace's story, see E. Scala, 'Canacee and the Chaucer Canon: Incest and Other Unnarratables', *Chaucer Review* 30 (1995), 15–39.

[87] John Gower, *Confessio Amantis*, ed. R. A. Peck et al., 3 vols (Kalamazoo, 2003), vol. II, III.153–5.

> O thou my sorwe and my gladnesse ...
> O my wanhope and al my trust ...
> O thou my frend, o thou my fo
> O thou my love, o thou myn hate
> For thee mot I be ded algate.[88]

Finally she falls on the sword.[89] On Eolus's orders the child is exposed in the forest, probably to be devoured by wild animals. Unlike Gregorius, set adrift in his barrel, there is no suggestion that the baby might be rescued; his fate parallels that of those incest-begotten babies of ballad who die along with their mother in the forest.

Gower does not moralize about this incest; the young people's desire is analysed as entirely natural, given the proximity in which they live and Eolus's failure of supervision. Elizabeth Archibald is surely right to read both this account and John Lydgate's expanded version as being chiefly about the power of love – turned narcissistically inward – rather than the psychology of anger.[90] Nor is the baby monstrous: Lydgate emphasizes that the siblings' child 'excellid in fauour and fairnesse; / For lik to hym off beute was non other'.[91] As Archibald notes, medieval theories of heritability do not imagine the offspring of incest as deformed, rather, as Signý calculated when deliberately conceiving an avenger by her brother, the desirable traits in the sibling parents are intensified.[92] Lydgate's retelling of the tale in *The Fall of Princes* closes down the question of the child's survival, left a little open by Gower. After Canace's death the baby is ordered 'Off cruel houndis in haste for to be rent / And be deuoured'; the child's attractiveness intensifies the tragedy and horror.[93]

The dog, at some fundamental imaginative level, signifies incest for medieval audiences, perhaps because the animals are traditionally thought to be notoriously unchoosy about whom they mate with. The Questing Beast, a monstrous creature who utters 'the greatest barking in the world' and who, in various texts, moves through the Arthurian world, pursued by the lineage of King Pellinor, is intimately linked both with the canine and with incest. In the Post-Vulgate Cycle the creature makes its first mysterious appearance after Arthur has incestuously begotten Mordred.[94] Only after the Beast has been killed by Palamedes does King Pellehan, a Grail-king-turned-hermit, narrate the monster's history to the listening Grail heroes.[95] King Ypomenés, he relates,

---

[88] Gower, *Confessio*, vol. II, Bk III.279–86.
[89] See M. Nolan, 'Lydgate's Literary History: Chaucer, Gower, and Canacee', *Studies in the Age of Chaucer* 27 (2005), 59–92.
[90] Archibald, *Incest and the Medieval Imagination*, pp. 79–85.
[91] John Lydgate, *Fall of Princes*, ed. H. Bergen, 4 vols, EETS ES 121–4 (London, 1924–7), I: 193–9 (p. 194).
[92] Archibald, *Incest and the Medieval Imagination*, p. 84. Cf. also the case of Adonis, p. 58.
[93] Lydgate, *Fall of Princes*, I: 198.
[94] *La Suite du Roman de Merlin*, ed. Roussineau, I: 3–5.
[95] *La version Post-Vulgate*, ed. Bogdanow, III: 351–66; *L-G*, V: 383–5. See also F. Bogdanow,

once had a son and a daughter; the young man was virtuous and loved religion, the young woman was intelligent and studied the seven arts, in particular necromancy. The sister falls in love with her brother and confesses her desire to him. Appalled, he rejects her and threatens to have her burned if she ever approaches him in such a way again. On the verge of suicide – the usual female fate *after* incestuous intercourse – the girl is comforted by a demon, who offers to help her obtain her brother if she will sleep with him. The girl consents; after she and the demon have made love she forgets her passion for her brother. Later the demon persuades her to accuse her brother of rape, both avenging her previous rejection and accounting for the girl's pregnancy with the demon's offspring. Consequently Ypomenés has his son thrown to ravenous dogs; he dies cursing his sister and prophesying that she will give birth to a terrible beast. As she has given him to the dogs, so her child will contain within its belly dogs who bark constantly. When the monstrous baby is born, the truth is revealed, the girl is executed by her father, and the Questing Beast (*la Bête Glatissante*) escapes into the forest, where it remains in a constant state of flight across the Arthurian landscape. When the Beast is finally cornered and killed in a lake the water begins to boil: it will continue boiling until the end of the world as a sign of the demonic presence within it.[96] The genesis of the Beast has been traced to classical sources, in particular the legend of Scylla, metamorphosed by Circe into a monster with multiple dog-heads.[97] This seems highly probable: an Ovidian connection would account both for the metamorphosis and for the unusual initiation of the incestuous approach by the woman.[98] In almost all the other deliberate sibling incest stories in the medieval period, as we have seen, the (older) brother is the one who takes the sexual initiative, whether assailed by Cupid or encouraged by the devil to seduce or coerce his sister.[99] Ypomenés's daughter is already dangerously involved in necromancy when her desire for her brother manifests itself.[100] She has declared her feelings, been repulsed

---

The Romance of the Grail: A Study of the Structure and Genesis of a Thirteenth-Century Arthurian Prose Romance (Manchester and New York, 1966), pp. 124–6; also Archibald, *Incest and the Medieval Imagination*, pp. 196–8; C. Batt, *Malory's* Morte Darthur: *Remaking Arthurian Tradition* (New York and Basingstoke, 2002), pp. 124–9 for a thoughtful account of the different Questing Beasts in Paris, BNF MS fr. 112, and Malory, and Armstrong and Hodges, *Mapping Malory*, pp. 157–72.

[96] See further, Muir, 'The Questing Beast' and A. L. Furtado, 'The Questing Beast as Emblem of the Ruin of Logres in the "Post-Vulgate"', *Arthuriana* 9.3 (1999), 27–48.

[97] Furtado, 'Questing Beast', pp. 31–6.

[98] Compare the stories of Myrrha's incestuous relationship with her father, and Byblis's passion for her brother in Books 9 and 10 of the *Metamorphoses*; see B. R. Nagle, 'Byblis and Myrrha: Two Incest Narratives in the "Metamorphoses"', *The Classical Journal* 79 (1983), 301–15.

[99] Cicirelli, *Sibling Relationships*, pp. 170–5, Klagsbrun, *Mixed Feelings*, pp. 219–22, and Bank's and Kahn's 'power-oriented incest', *The Sibling Bond*, p. 178, the older brother is most frequently the initiator.

[100] For demonic magic (necromancy) see C. Saunders, *Magic and the Supernatural in Medieval English Romance* (Cambridge, 2010), pp. 109–16, and Larrington, *King Arthur's Enchantresses*, pp. 9–11; pp. 23–7.

Sibling Incest

and has fallen victim to the sin of despair when the demon appears to distract her from her unlawful passion. Female curiosity, forbidden desire, diabolical opportunity and irredeemable sin are logically linked in a chain of cause and effect. The demon alleviates her misery, but also drags her deeper into sin, ensnaring her soul and writing her unnatural desire on the monstrous body of their child. While diabolical prompting leads to the incestuous conception of Gregorius, here the girl's education exposes her to unholy, necromantic knowledge, which, the narrative implies, troubles the natural instinct to repress sexual desire for a sibling.

In contrast to the sinister lake into which the Beast finally sinks, the Spring of the Virgin, mentioned earlier in the Post-Vulgate *Queste*, comes into existence when a girl narrowly escapes rape by her own brother. Lost in the forest, a squire is persuaded by a demon to believe that his sister Aglinde is in fact a foundling. The demon claims that she is his own daughter, stolen from him by the queen, the siblings' mother. Nabor, the squire, is convinced by this slander and grieves to learn that his sister is not his sister after all.[101] The demon promises to guide the youth home if he will entice Aglinde into the forest, claiming he wants to recover his abducted child. Starving and disoriented, Nabor agrees, and later he fulfils his promise. As they ride along towards the woods, the young man gazes at his sister.

> Lors se commença a pourpenser que moult seroit mauvaiz et recreant s'il n'acomplissoit son desir de si belle damoiselle com est ceste, qu'il ne luy appartient fors de nourriture.
>
> ('Then he began to consider that it would be very bad and cowardly if he could not satisfy his desire for such a beautiful girl as this one, and that he was not related to her save through their upbringing.')[102]

Persuaded that they are not kin, and that the girl will shortly disappear with her pretended father, Nabor murders Aglinde's tutor, and threatens to kill her if she will not lie with him. When Aglinde prays to be delivered from this unlooked-for assault on her chastity, her brother immediately drops dead. Aglinde prophesies that the spring where the demon first appeared would henceforth be called the Spring of the Virgin. Any knight who came there who was not a virgin would be paralysed unless a woman chose to help him; the custom would prevail until Galahad arrived at the Spring. This unusual emphasis on male chastity is produced by the Grail context with its ideological preoccupation with chastity for both sexes.

The Spring's history is related in connection with Erec, whose murder of his sister we learned about in chapter five. After his sister-killing, Erec inadvertently

---

[101] Compare the story of *Richars li biaus*, discussed in chapter eight; cf. Archibald, *Incest and the Medieval Imagination*, pp. 195–6.

[102] The tale of Aglinde and her brother: *Erec: Roman arthurien en prose*, ed. Pickford, pp. 185–94; *L-G*, V: 305–7; quotation from *Erec*, ed. Pickford, p. 192; my translation.

rests by the Spring and becomes immobilized, his powerlessness and paralysis a wonderfully apt figuration of the castration anxiety adduced by Mitchell as the fraternal parallel to the sister's fear of annihilation by her brother.[103] Erec is on the verge of death when he is rescued by a group of ladies; they curse the motionless knight when they recognize him as the recent sister-murderer. Erec explains his honour-driven rationale for killing his sister, but the women make no reply and silently watch him ride away. Erec's sister-murder is thus juxtaposed with the incestuously motivated assault on Aglinde, drawing attention to the underlying common elements: a brother who fails to honour his sister's autonomy and personhood in pursuit of his own ends. The squire's sexual attack also confirms the clerical misogynist suspicion of women's bodies, suggesting that it is only the incest taboo which prevents brothers from acting on their desire for their sisters.

The two fraternal assaults on innocent sisters, motivated by rash promises given under duress to a demon or a demon-like vengeful cousin, link these two Post-Vulgate episodes, and they also chime with the inverted incest-story of Ypomenés's daughter. In the story of Aglinde and her brother, the demon does not prompt Nabor to incest. Once Nabor has consented to cooperate with the demon by betraying his sister's trust, further wicked desires press in on him. Nabor is under no illusion as to the sinfulness of what he has sworn to do: lying to his sister to draw her into the forest and into the demon's clutches. One sin leads all too quickly to another; having persuaded himself that his sister is not his sister, he can contemplate murder and rape without inhibition. The demon does not need to reappear for he has easily gained the young man's soul; he has no purchase on Aglinde's virgin body, however, once she calls on God for protection.

These two tales – like the *Gregorius* and *Gesta Romanorum* stories – recognize adolescent sexual desire as capable of taking an incestuous turn when children's behaviour is unregulated. Childish sex play becomes a furtive and powerful passion: propinquity – the natural closeness of brother and sister within the nuclear family, especially within a sibling unit which has been orphaned or placed under traumatic pressure – offers occasion for the noble children to express reciprocal forbidden desire. Incestuous rape, 'power-oriented incest' in Bank's and Kahn's terms, is relatively infrequent in medieval story, though coercive and abusive elements certainly seem to play a part in the fraternal solicitation to incest. Abuse of sibling power at its most extreme results in the murder of the incestuous female partner, the resulting offspring and often the perpetrator himself. These are families in crisis, turning unhealthily inwards, failing to grasp the importance of exchange and exogamy in maintaining a functional social dynamic.[104] The consequences of the siblings' narcissistic

---

[103] Mitchell, *Siblings*, p. 3.
[104] See D. Finkelhor, 'Sex among Siblings: A Survey on Prevalence, Variety, and Effect', *Archives of Sexual Behavior* 9 (1980), 171–94, for an overview of childhood sibling sexual relations as being capable of positive and negative effects; finding summarized, p.

identification of another sibling as object of desire bring death not only to the perpetrators, but also to their offspring. The repercussions of deliberate incest are strictly enforced within the family; the kin-group polices itself for fear of social stigma and the resulting children – whether monstrous or beautiful – are exposed in the forest or set adrift on the ocean. In hagiographic and other moral tales, however, the sibling-incest episode highlights the possibility of redemption when contrition for even the worst of crimes is truly felt.

Conclusion

Medieval sibling incest is not a frequent narrative topos, but its outcome is almost always tragic. Even when its product is a hero, the man will die young and without offspring; incest precipitates a disastrous dead-end for a lineage.[105] Unwitting incest tends to occur in the European ballad or other oral traditions; its male perpetrators are often criminals, outcasts or exiles, whose social exclusion alienates them from normal sexual mores. Their debauching of their sisters is a shameful deed, a punishment for their ungoverned sexual drives; it usually results in the mortal sin of suicide, and the inevitable death of the female innocent. The returning hero, the young man who has established a new adult identity for himself, will fail to reintegrate himself into his original family structure if he cannot control his impulses. A primary entailment of adulthood for the young man is obtaining an appropriate sexual partner and establishing a new family unit; if he has not achieved this, his return home signals that the transition to adult status is incomplete. Sibling affection, essential human drives and adult desire combine to thwart the triumphant return through a catastrophic failure of mature self-regulation.

Mirk's observations about cross-sex bed-sharing in later childhood offer a stark warning about the dangers of propinquity. In lower-class familes, as Kathryn Gravdal suggests, incestuous pregnancies might be easier to disguise or terminate, or the child might simply be absorbed among the other youngsters in the family.[106] Though clerical writers seem to be thinking of more ordinary families than the noble children who fall into incest in the stories discussed above, it is precisely in the aristocratic milieu where the obsession with lineage demands that female chastity come under particular surveillance. Nurturance-oriented incest occurs when children are orphaned and left to their own devices: when the family becomes dysfunctional. Such incest figures a failure in the young people to develop adult heterosexual identities in which desire is properly directed outside the family group. The turn inwards, whether prompted by narcissism, fear of the unknown, Cupid or the devil, brings disaster both to the individuals involved and to the lineage. Incest deliberately undertaken with the

191.
[105] Kennedy, 'Mordred's Sons'.
[106] Gravdal, 'Confessing Incest'.

aim of breeding a hero, with doubled ancestry and genetic traits, is rare indeed; heroic legendary tradition nevertheless understands incest as conducive to the conception of a remarkable child.

Medieval families must make alliances through the exchange of women: the lineage must be continued through exogamic couple formation. And yet, if sibling sexuality is unnatural, even catastrophic if expressed within the family, the negotiation of sibling relations after marriage, the establishment of new identities as husband and wife, and the management of new affinal ties are not without risk. As the next chapter shows, marriage brings new crises and new benefits to sibling relations across different medieval genres.

7

'So wil ich dir ce wibe mine swester gebn':[1]
When Siblings Marry

Introduction

Sibling closeness fluctuates at different stages of life. A brother's or sister's marriage entails a radical redefinition of relationships, both for the one who weds and for the other siblings.[2] Affines (relations by marriage) very often belong to the same age-cohort as the new spouses' siblings, and thus they may feel themselves to be in competition, with same-sex in-laws in particular. Francine Klagsbrun suggests:

> What is re-awakened when a sib-in-law appears on the scene is the very old perception of being dethroned, as they had once been when a new-born sibling entered their lives back in childhood. And what they lose, as they lost then, is the exuberance of being in charge, in control, at the center.[3]

Juliet Mitchell's psychoanalytic investigations predict that sibling bonds formed in childhood will condition later marital and affinal relationships, and thus fierce rivalry and inappropriate sexual feelings as well as warm loyalty and generosity can mark affinal ties, just as they colour sibling interactions.[4] Anthropologists attend closely to in-laws, although the earlier fundamental assumption that the subject is male has tended to exclude or underestimate the

---

[1] 'Then I will give you my sister as wife', *Das Nibelungenlied* (Bibliotheca Augustana), based on the edition of K. Bartsch (Leipzig 1870–80, ed. H. Reichert), Aventiure 6, st. 334. http://www.hs-augsburg.de/~harsch/germanica/Chronologie/12Jh/Nibelungen/nib_intr.html
[2] See Allen, 'Sibling Solidarity', p. 181; Connidis, 'Life Transitions'.
[3] Klagsbrun, *Mixed Feelings*, pp. 264–7. Little detailed psychological research has been carried out on affinal relationships. Three very different exceptions are: C. G. Yoshimura, 'The Experience and Communication of Envy among Siblings, Siblings-in-Law, and Spouses', *Journal of Social and Personal Relationships* 27(8) (2010), 1075–88; K. Floyd and M. C. Morr, 'Human Affection Exchange: VII. Affectionate Communication in the Sibling/Spouse/Sibling-in-Law Triad', *Communications Quarterly* 51 (2003), 247–61; S. Kemp and F. Hunt, 'Exploring the Psychology of Inheritances', *Zeitschrift für Sozialpsychologie* 32 (2001), 171–9.
[4] See Mitchell, *Mad Men and Medusas*, p. 40. Compare also E. Morley, 'The Influence of Sibling Relationships on Couple Choice and Development', in *Sibling Relationships*, ed. Coles (London, 2006), pp. 197–224.

female subject in in kin and family analyses and in the 'exchange of women'.[5] Feminist anthropologists have now redressed this imbalance, increasingly focus on female perspective and agency in narratives told about affinal relationships.[6]

'[M]arriages are not always so simply activities to make peace', observes Gayle Rubin, 'Marriages may be highly competitive, and there are plenty of affines who fight each other.'[7] In the medieval literary imagination, the affinal relationship productive of the most dramatic narratives is that between a woman's brother(s) and her husband: an alliance previously perceived by the bride's family as advantageous can suddenly turn sour. For, as argued earlier, successful fraternal relationships are predicated on managing difference; yet considerations of status mean that a sister is likely to gain a husband who belongs to the same social stratum as her brother. Brothers-in-law are expected to form mutual homosocial bonds, sealed by the 'exchange of women'; their reciprocal relationship is guaranteed by a woman who is a legitimate object of desire for one participant, and tabooed for the other. The similarities between husband and brother invite (often explicit) comparison: envy, rivalry and insecurity can be the outcome. Thus the homosocial bond can founder on unresolved masculine tensions generated by perceived differential elements in relative status. The woman or women involved in the exchange are often the agents who identify these elements, opening up areas of contestation when they speak from their own perspective. 'The difference women make cannot be eradicated, but survives in the form of a "counternarrative"', observes Sarah Kay.[8] Although wives and sisters work hard to keep the peace between husbands and brothers – the primary function of the peace-weaver marriage – in some of the most powerful medieval narratives of affinal conflict it is precisely that female 'counternarrative' which precipitates crisis.

Chapter one noted the pattern in some rural communities for pairs of brothers to marry pairs of sisters, allowing a merger of family property. The pragmatic reasons for such marriages are obvious, but so too is the danger that married couples living at close quarters with their siblings will escalate the resulting psychological tensions into open conflict. Proximity then is one risk factor; other socio-historical issues which can ramify affinal psychology are those of dowry, rank and power, and agency. What property has been settled on the

---

[5] Cf. Lévi-Strauss, *Elementary Structures of Kinship*, p. 115: 'the woman figures only as one of the objects in the exchange, not as one of the partners between whom the exchange takes place', and see, for example, T. Moi's review of Girard, 'The Missing Mother: The Oedipal Rivalries of René Girard', *Diacritics* 12 (1982), 21–31.

[6] For feminist redefinitions of anthropology see *Toward an Anthropology of Women*, ed. R. R. Reiter (New York, 1975); *Woman, Culture and Society*, ed. M. Z. Rosaldo and L. Lamphere (Stanford CA, 1974); *Sexual Meanings: The Cultural Construction of Gender and Sexuality*, ed. S. Ortner and H. Whitehead (Cambridge, 1981); H. Moore, *Feminism and Anthropology* (Cambridge, 1988) and the key articles reprinted in *Feminist Anthropology: A Reader*, ed. E. Lewin (Oxford, 2006).

[7] Rubin, 'The Traffic in Women', p. 173.

[8] Sarah Kay, *The* Chansons de Geste *in the Age of Romance* (Oxford, 1995), p. 147;

bride and what resources does the groom have at his disposal? Who wields more official and unofficial power within the new relationships? And, most significantly, how much agency has been granted to the woman or women who have been exchanged?[9] The relationships between brothers-in-law are subject both to the psychological tensions of fraternity and to social anxiety about differential status, power and resources that develops gradually after the marriage. Brothers can also exert a positive influence, policing their sisters' marriages when marital crises occur and intervening to recuperate the woman's reputation or to chastise her husband's cruelty. The relationship of sisters-in-law comes less frequently under scrutiny in medieval tales, but it also offers the potentiality both for conflict and for mutual support. Husbands' dealings with their wives' sisters likewise generate sexual intrigue; again sibling proximity is dangerous to harmony in the married couple's relationship. Finally, this chapter briefly considers sisters' sons; these stand in a special relationship to their maternal uncles and they have a significant role to play in the maintenance or collapse of the homosocial bonds between male affines.

Brothers and their Brothers-in-Law

Legal documents from thirteenth-century Genoa preserve some details of the Embrone/Pevere case in the 1220s, that 'long story of high politics and revenge', as Epstein calls it (see chapter one, pp. 35–6). The case provides a historically attested example of the failure of an attempt to manage a feud by marrying a young woman to a prominent male member of an opposing clan.[10] Prevalent in the vendetta politics of Italian cities, but equally typical of Germanic and Scandinavian heroic legend, the husband killed by the brother or the brother killed by the husband places the sister/wife in a conflicted and tragic position. One of the oldest surviving literary accounts of feud, the 'Finnesburh Episode', the lay recited in Heorot after Beowulf's victory over Grendel, chronicles the climax of a longstanding hostility between the Frisians and the Danes.[11] From an independently preserved poem, *The Finnesburh Fragment*, an Anglo-Saxon audience might learn how the feud had reignited during the visit of the Danish warrior Hnæf to his sister Hildeburh and her husband Finn, lord of the Frisians.[12] Since the poem is fragmentary it is not possible to determine what provokes the attack of the Frisians on the hall where the Danes are lodged; by the end of the battle, however, as the inset lay in *Beowulf* relates, Hildeburh's brother Hnæf lies on the funeral pyre alongside his nephew, his sister's son. The maternal nephew is strikingly ill-fated in such peace-weaving narratives, as we shall see

---

[9] Married sisters, as noted in chapter one, p. 34, continued to retain some rights in their natal families; see Lett, 'Liens adelphiques'.
[10] Epstein, 'The Medieval Family', p. 153.
[11] *Klaeber's Beowulf*, ed. Fulk *et al.*, lines 1071–1159a.
[12] Edited in *Klaeber's Beowulf*, pp. 283–5.

below, for the child incarnates the accord sealed by the exchange of his mother to the hostile group and the breakdown of peace usually entails his death.[13] Despite Hildeburh's attempt to render equivalent the deaths of brother and son by cremating them on the same pyre, at the end of the *Beowulf* lay the uneasy accord existing between the two sides through the winter melts away along with the sea-ice that has kept the Danes trapped in Frisia. The Frisian hall is reddened with blood, 'feonda feorum, swilce Fin slægen' ('with the lives of enemies, likewise Finn slain') (line 1152) and the widowed and sonless queen is carried off back to the homeland she left many years before. Hildeburh has very limited agency in the lay; her symbolic mediation between the tribes fails, while the poem affords no sense of her own perception of her conflicted situation.

Early medieval heroic legend represents the hero–sister–affine relationship as triangular. Where the marriage of the hero follows killing within the bride's family, the oaths sworn between husband and affines are particularly prone to rupture. In the eddic poem *Helgakviða Hundingsbana II*, Helgi slays most of Sigrún's male kindred and her undesired suitor in order to win her hand. When Sigrún's brother Dagr later reneges on the oath he had sworn to Helgi, Sigrún curses him.[14] Dagr is alarmed and astonished that his sister should side with her (freely chosen) husband against her remaining blood relative: 'Œr ertu, systir, oc ervita / er þú brœðr þínom biðr forscapa' ('You're mad, sister! you're out of your wits that you wish this evil fate on your brother').[15] This female conflict of loyalties between lover and brother is revisited and complicated in other heroic eddic poems.

The triangularity of the topos can be complicated by doubling roles and introducing parallel social bonds to the central affinal tie. The most complex medieval narrative of brother-in-law conflict, preserved in differing versions in both Old Icelandic and Middle High German, concerns the lord of Worms on the Rhine, his wife and his brothers, their sister and her husband. The roles of brother, brother-in-law and conflicted woman are all doubled within the core narrative's structure; among the affines oath-taking and breaking, sexual and other kinds of loyalty and disloyalty, and vengeance all recur. Poems preserved in the *Poetic Edda*, and the prose *Vǫlsunga saga*, tell the story of Gunnarr of Worms and his siblings.[16] Another version of the story in *Þiðreks saga af Bern*, composed in Old Norse but deriving primarily from German tradition, probably also originates in mid-thirteenth-century Norway.[17] The southern German tradition is

---

[13] See Larrington, '"I have long desired to cure you"', p. 146.
[14] See Larrington, 'Sibling Drama'.
[15] *Helgakviða Hundingsbana II*, v. 34.1–4, in *Edda*, ed. Neckel and Kuhn; *Edda*, trans. Larrington. See also Cicirelli, *Sibling Relationships*, p. 62, where he notes how dislike of a spouse provokes crisis among a sibling group.
[16] See primarily the poems *Brot af Sigurðarkviða*, *Sigurðarkviða in skamma* and *Helreið Brynhildar* in *Edda*, ed. Neckel and Kuhn, trans. as *Fragment of a Poem about Sigurd*, *A Short Poem about Sigurd* and *Brynhild's Ride to Hell* in *Edda*, trans. Larrington.
[17] *Þiðreks saga af Bern*, ed. Guðni Jónsson, 2 vols (Reykjavík, 1951–4); translation, E. Haymes, *The Saga of Thidrek of Bern* (New York and London, 1988).

found in the various recensions of the *Nibelungenlied*, composed probably by an Austrian poet around 1200.[18] Both traditions share the theme of warm friendship between warriors of broadly equal rank, sealed by the outsider's marriage to a sister, and they trace how that friendship is destroyed, ostensibly by a quarrel between sisters-in-law, but fundamentally by jealousies over wealth, martial prowess and sexual honour. The repercussions of the outsider's murder – the sister's decision to forgive her brothers, unwillingly to marry again and to avenge her new husband's slaying of her brothers, or to avenge her husband's death on her brothers and their associates – distinguish the northern and southern traditions. All three versions – *Vǫlsunga saga*, *Das Nibelungenlied* and *Þiðreks saga* – look back on epic-heroic values from a perspective shaped by new courtly mores. In particular, they incorporate female figures with independent subjectivities, an innovation which reflects the rising influence of the romance genre on older heroic material.[19]

In both traditions the outsider hero comes to a group of noble siblings and is accepted by its men – particularly by the eldest brother Gunnarr/Gunther – as a useful ally, a valuable brother-in-law. In Norse he also becomes a fictive sibling: a sworn-brother. The hero willingly betroths himself to the sister (Guðrún / Kriemhilt) who is enthusiastic about the marriage. Sigurðr/Sivrit is then invited by Gunnarr/Gunther to demonstrate his homosocial loyalty to his new quasi-fraternity by participating in a wooing mission to Brynhildr/Prünhilt. In the *Nibelungenlied* it is at this point that Gunther agrees that Sifrit may marry Kriemhilt: 'so wil ich dir ce wibe mine swester gebn' ('so I will give you my sister to wife').[20] The men regard the deception involved in winning Brynhildr/Prünhilt for Gunnarr/Gunther as morally permissible, indeed necessary, and the bride is brought to Worms.[21] A quarrel between the two sisters-in-law (private in *Vǫlsunga saga*, public in *Das Nibelungenlied*) reveals to the victim the extent of her deception and she forces her husband to recuperate the situation by eliminating Sigurðr/Sivrit, despite the multiple homosocial obligations which bind the hero to his wife's brothers.

In the second movement of the story, the traditions diverge. In Norse, Sigurðr's wife refrains from vengeance for him and is persuaded to marry again. She is exchanged to Atli, king of the Huns and Brynhildr's brother. When Atli murders her brothers in a bid to seize Sigurðr's gold-hoard, Guðrún avenges them on

---

[18] *Das Nibelungenlied* (Bibliotheca Augustana), http://www.hs-augsburg.de/~harsch/germanica/Chronologie/12Jh/Nibelungen/; *The Nibelungenlied: The Lay of the Nibelungs*, trans. C. Edwards (Oxford, 2010).
[19] See J. C. Frakes, *Brides and Doom: Gender, Property, and Power in Medieval German Women's Epic* (Philadelphia, 1994) and also C. Larrington, '*Vǫlsunga saga* and *Ragnars saga* and Romance in Old Norse: Revisiting the Relationship', in *The Legendary Sagas: Origins and Development*, ed. Ármann Jakobsson, A. Lassen and A. Ney (Reykjavík, 2012), pp. 251–70.
[20] *Das Nibelungenlied*, Aventiure 6, st. 334.
[21] Frakes, *Brides and Doom*, p. 67, n. 47 notes that 'the brideprice – as it were – [is] Siegfried's aid in defrauding Brünhild'.

him, first by killing his sons and feeding them to him, then by murdering him and burning down his hall.[22] In the southern tradition (also employed in *Þiðreks saga*), Kriemhilt's marriage to Etzel facilitates her vengeance on her brothers; she invites them and her particular enemy, the magnate Hagen von Troenich to visit, ensures that conflict breaks out and brings about the deaths of everyone whom she blames for Sivrit's murder.

The tangled destinies of Sigurðr/Sivrit, Brynhildr/Prünhilt, Guðrún/Kriemhilt and her other siblings evidence strong, genuine affection between sister and brothers, even if the sister's desires are consistently sacrificed to the brothers' interests. The fraternal group decides that it would be advantageous to retain the impressive newcomer at the court as an ally by marrying him to their sister. In *Vǫlsunga saga* Sigurðr seems pleased, perhaps as an only child, to acquire a whole set of affines at a stroke, but he lacks the instinctive understanding of sibling jealousies and disloyalties with which he would have been equipped had he grown up with brothers and sisters.[23] The disastrous outcome of his affinal relationship is predicated on his lack of territorial ambition on his own account and the consequent uxorilocality of his marriage. Had he not 'squander[ed] the sanctity of kingship which had been bestowed on him', as Carola Gottzman has suggested, Sigurðr might have claimed back his father's kingdom from the sons of Hundingr and settled down with his wife within the heroic ambit of his ancestral lands.[24] Far from the courtly intrigues of the Gjúkungs' palace on the Rhine, he could have avoided being drawn into the sexual and political rivalries stirred up by his sister-in-law.[25] Similarly, Sivrit's marriage to Kriemhilt is successful as long as he stays away from the toxic intrigues of Worms; only when the couple come there on a visit does the alliance founder. Proximity is not the only cause of contention. Sivrit's superior strength and possession of a vast treasure hoard also provokes insecurity and avarice among his wife's relatives and in their retainer, Hagen; in Norse tradition the economic motive only becomes crucial after Sigurðr's death.[26] Of sovereign importance, however, is the bad faith of the homosocial pair, Sigurðr/Sivrit and Gunnarr/Gunther, with regard to Brynhildr/Prünhilt: bad faith exhibited towards women is, as we shall see in chapter eight, typical of sworn-brother relationships, and here it forms a vital component of the story's catastrophe.

[22] See *Atlakviða* and *Atlamál* in *Edda*, ed. Neckel and Kuhn; *The Poem of Atli* and *The Greenlandic Lay of Atli* in *Edda*, trans. Larrington.

[23] See Larrington, 'Sibling Drama'.

[24] Carola Gottzmann, "*Vǫlsunga saga*: Legendary History and Textual Analysis," in *Preprints of the 4th International Saga Conference* (Munich, 1979), I: (articles individually paginated) (p. 8).

[25] On the courtly versus the heroic in the sagas of MS NKS 1824 b 4to, see Larrington, '*Vǫlsunga saga* and *Ragnars saga*'.

[26] See Frakes, *Brides and Doom*, pp. 64–95 on the importance of treasure both to Prünhilt and Kriemhilt; see also A. Cowell, *The Medieval Warrior Aristocracy: Gifts, Violence, Performance and the Sacred* (Cambridge, 2007), pp. 134–52 for an acute reading of the *Nibelungenlied* in terms of the circulation of treasure and of women.

Brynhildr's fury at her situation is intensified by her general unwillingness to marry; her brother Atli coerces her into accepting her suitor by threatening to withhold her paternal inheritance.²⁷ Prünhilt is queen of Iceland, wielding sovereignty in her own right and thus capable of exchanging herself; she establishes strict conditions under which she will enter into marriage.²⁸ Nevertheless, both queens and sisters *must* be married; not only is the independence of an unwed warrior-woman like Brynhildr a threat to established patriarchal order, the fraternity's postponement of their exchange of Guðrún would deprive them of a brother-in-law who would support them in political and military confrontations.²⁹ Both Brynhildr and Prünhilt consent – not without some misgivings about both process and outcome – to marry the man who they believe has won them. It is not until their sister-in-law reveals the truth – that the brothers-in-law had exchanged appearances and that consequently Sigurðr/Sivrit had spent a crucial period of time in apparent sexual intimacy with his now sister-in-law – that Brynhildr / Prünhilt is possessed of the facts and thus enabled to construct a 'counter-narrative' which will disrupt the homosocial unity of the affines.

Brynhildr's charge that Sigurðr had slept with her after crossing the flames, Prünhilt's belief that Sivrit took her virginity, strike to the heart of their husbands' sexual honour.³⁰ Brynhildr knows that the narrative which she relates to Gunnarr is untrue, for Sigurðr had laid a drawn sword between them. Her demand for vengeance is partly driven by rage that Sigurðr broke his earlier oaths to her in marrying another woman, but, primarily, because he thus transformed her into an oath-breaker: for she had sworn to marry only the man who crossed the flame-wall.³¹ Like the poet of the *Nibelungenlied*, Prünhilt does not make explicit what transpired in the bridal chamber, but Kriemhilt's public accusation irrevocably shames Gunther and his queen:

---

²⁷ *Guðrúnarkviða* I, vv. 25–6; *Sigurðarkviða in skamma*, v. 36, in *Edda*, ed. Neckel and Kuhn; *First Poem of Gudrun*, vv. 25–6, and *Short Poem about Sigurd*, v. 36 in *Edda*, trans. Larrington. Cf. *Vǫlsunga saga*, ed. Finch, pp. 59–60, where Atli's threat is ameliorated into a strong suggestion.

²⁸ See E. Tennant, 'Prescriptions and Performatives in Imagined Cultures: Gender Dynamics in Nibelungenlied Adventure 11', in *Mittelalter: Neue Wege durch einen alten Kontinent*, ed. J.-D. Müller and H. Wenzel (Stuttgart, 1999), pp. 273–316, and K. Starkey, 'Performative Emotion and the Politics of Gender in the *Nibelungenlied*', in *Women and Medieval Epic: Gender, Genre and the Limits of Masculinity*, ed. S. Poor and J. K. Schulman. (London and New York, 2007), pp. 253–71.

²⁹ *Sigurðarkviða in skamma / Short Poem about Sigurd*, v. 18; *Vǫlsunga saga*, ed. Finch, p. 57.

³⁰ *Vǫlsunga saga*, chs. 29–30; *Das Nibelungenlied*, Aventiure 10.

³¹ In *Vǫlsunga saga* Brynhildr had in fact had a sexual relationship with and borne a child to Sigurðr, before the administration of *óminnisǫl* (ale of forgetfulness) caused him to forget his prior betrothal and agree to marry Guðrún. See chs. 21, 24 and 27, and see also Jóhanna K. Friðriksdóttir, '"Gerðit hon . . . sem konor aðrar": Women and Subversion in Eddic Heroic Poetry', in *Revisiting the Poetic Edda*, ed. Acker and Larrington, pp. 117–35.

> den dinen schœnen lip
> den minnet erste sifrit / der min vil liber man /
> ia ne was ez niht min brvder / der dir den magtvm
> angewan

('for it was Sifrit who first made love to your beautiful body, my beloved husband, it was not my brother who took your virginity').[32]

In the Norse tradition, Gunnarr's weakness, Hǫgni's counsel and Brynhildr's potent rage come together; Guttormr, the youngest brother who had not sworn oaths to Sigurðr, is sent to murder him. For Prünhilt, Gunther and his powerful vassal Hagen, Sivrit's death is the only possible solution to Gunther's shame and Prünhilt's outrage: 'ez hat geraten Prvennhilt daz ez hat Hagen getan' ('Prünhilt planned this and Hagen has brought it about') the grief-stricken Kriemhilt recognizes when she finds her husband's corpse.[33] If Gunnarr/Gunther's public face is to be restored and his marriage rescued, Sigurðr/Sivrit must die: 'the brother-in-law, then, becomes the sacrificial substitute for the brother as hostile object', as Girard observes.[34] Girard's concept of 'mimetic desire', discussed in chapter four, is also relevant here. For Sivrit must desire Prünhilt in order to deflower her for Gunther, while Sigurðr recovers from the potion of forgetfulness administered by his mother-in-law and re-experiences his former desire for Brynhildr. From the fraternity's perspective this converts the once valued brother-in-law into a 'monstrous double' and motivates his elimination.[35]

The brothers-in-law Sigurðr and Sivrit thus become disposable as far as their wife's kindred are concerned: not because they cease to be highly effective military allies, but because profound anxieties about sexual honour and relative status are provoked when the two women at the heart of the nexus publicly and privately voice their counter-narratives. Or, more precisely: when Guðrún/Kriemhilt divulges the shocking truth of female betrayal that underpinned the men's friendship, which is adapted and relayed by Brynhildr/Prünhilt. The men's anxieties are mitigated through their oath-breaking violence. One hero is killed in bed, the other's corpse is abandoned outside his wife's chamber-door, clearly marking the crisis of masculinity and sexual potency at stake in the first act of the narrative.[36]

In the story's second act, the women's motivations diverge. Despite her brothers' treatment of her first husband, Guðrún's loyalty to Gunnarr and Hǫgni is absolute, transcending not only the weak emotional ties she has to her second husband, but also the powerful imperatives of motherhood. She pointedly prioritizes sibling blood-bonds over marital obligations; indeed she decides to erase her status as an exchanged woman, given to Atli in reparation

---

[32] *Das Nibelungenlied*, Aventiure 14, v. 840; see also Frakes, *Brides and Doom*, pp. 117–22.
[33] *Das Nibelungenlied*, Aventiure 17, str. 1010 (my translation).
[34] Girard, *Violence and the Sacred*, p. 295.
[35] Ibid., pp. 154–8; 169–71.
[36] *Das Nibelungenlied*, Aventiure 17.

for the loss of his sister, by destroying the very products of the new alliance. These are her children, whom she sacrifices in an open challenge to patriliny.[37] The sibling bond proves stronger than the marital bond. Atli's hatred for his brothers-in-law is motivated by avarice; the men's treatment of his sister is largely irrelevant once he has secured Guðrún in exchange for the woman he gave to the Gjúkungs.[38]

Kriemhilt's principal affective bond was forged once and for all with her beloved Sivrit. Twenty years or more after his death she still weeps for him every morning. Her relationship with Gunther, notionally repaired by a formal greeting ritual after Sivrit's death, is never properly restored, for she has a clear view of Gunther's readiness to allow Hagen to break oaths and act treacherously as long as he serves the king's interests, both in the killing of Sivrit and the confiscation of his treasure. Kriemhilt's rage against the brothers whom she loved so much before her husband's death is fuelled by Hagen's provocations and Gunther's weakness in restraining him. Etzel is ineffectual in preventing his wife from prosecuting her long-nurtured vengeance not only on Gunther and Hagen, but also on her other beloved brothers, Giselher and Gernot, who refuse to save their lives by surrendering Hagen to her.[39] The loyalty of the kin-group is extended neither to its female members nor its incomers. Hagen is more highly valued than Sivrit, and Prünhilt's injured feelings are a mere pretext for Hagen to pursue his long-term plan for Gunther to seize political power over the kingdoms under Sivrit's aegis and to acquire the Nibelunc hoard. Prünhilt's disappearance from the *Nibelungenlied*, in strong contrast to her emotionally ambiguous expressions of triumph and sorrow and her final suicide in Old Norse tradition, points up her final irrelevance to the deadly battle between Kriemhilt, her siblings and Hagen.[40]

The legend of the Gjúkung siblings, in particular the relative loyalties of Guðrún to her brothers and to Atli, forms an important intertext for the Icelandic *Gísla saga*, a saga probably dating from the mid-thirteenth century.[41] Gísli's assiduous policing of his sister's premarital reputation was discussed in chapter three. Later in the saga, Gísli, his sister Þórdís and his brother Þorkell emigrate to Iceland. All three siblings marry, and the two brothers, Þórdís's husband Þorgrímr, and Vésteinn, the brother of Gísli's wife, agree to become sworn-

[37] See Larrington, '"I have long desired"', and Rubin, 'The Traffic in Women'.
[38] See J. Quinn, 'The Endless Triangles of Eddic Tragedy: Reading *Oddrúnargrátr*', in *Studi anglo-norreni in onore di John S. McKinnell*, ed. M. E. Ruggerini (Cagliari, 2009), pp. 304–26.
[39] See S. B. Pafenberg, 'The Spindle and the Sword: Gender, Sex, and Heroism in the "Nibelungenlied" and the "Kudrun"', *Germanic Review* 70 (1995), 106–15 (p. 110).
[40] Kriemhilt's conflict with her brothers over the death of her husband was well enough known in northern Europe for Saxo Grammaticus (*GD* XIII.6.7) to relate a story in which Knut of Jutland is indirectly warned through the performance of a song about 'Grimilda and her brothers' that his brother-in-law King Magnus intends to murder him. See Aurell, 'Rompre la concorde', p. 9.
[41] *Gísla saga*, in *Vestfirðinga sögur*, ed. Björn K. Þórólfsson and Guðni Jónsson, ÍF 7 (Reykjavík, 1953).

brothers. This fictive kinship arrangement reveals itself to be over-extended; although each of the parties is willing to reinforce his *own* brother-in-law bond with a sworn-brother oath, Þorgrímr sees no reason to bind himself to Vésteinn, his brother-in-law's brother-in-law, and the oath-taking fails acrimoniously. The rest of the saga deals with the repercussions from the abortive ceremony. 'With this constellation of siblings, spouses and in-laws the saga has made the innermost circle of the Icelandic kinship system into the subject of its narrative', observes Preben Meulengracht Sørensen.[42]

Later, Þorkell overhears a conversation between his wife Ásgerðr and Gísli's wife Auðr in which Ásgerðr acknowledges her desire for Vésteinn. Consequently Vésteinn is murdered, most likely by Þórgrímr.[43] Gísli murders Þórgrímr in revenge; his sister betrays his crime to her new husband (Bǫrkr, Þórgrímr's brother), and Gísli is outlawed. Þorkell refuses to offer his brother more than a modicum of help, justifying his lack of fraternal loyalty by citing his bonds to the dead man: 'drepinn er Þorgrímr, mágr minn ok félagi ok virðavinr' ('Þorgrímr, my brother-in-law, my partner and my good friend has been killed').[44] Gísli is finally killed by an agent paid by his new brother-in-law Bǫrkr. When the news is brought to Bǫrkr and Þórdís, Bǫrkr celebrates while Þórdís refuses to rejoice; later in the scene she attacks and injures Gísli's killer and then declares herself divorced from Bǫrkr.[45]

Gísla saga is one of the few surviving sagas which foregrounds jealousy and masculine honour as intrinsically bound up with female sexual behaviour. Sexual honour and sibling relations are closely woven together; although Vésteinn was far away in England when Ásgerðr's feelings about him were made known to her husband, Þorkell's reaction to the revelation is to sever himself from his brother and to attach himself to his new friend and sworn-brother Þorgrímr, his sister's husband. Alienation between brothers, mainly generated by Þorkell, is balanced by warm affection towards brothers-in-law: Gísli is Vésteinn's blood-brother and travelling companion as well as his brother-in-law, and his powerful love for his wife is bound up with his strong attachment to her brother. Likewise Þorkell chooses his brother-in-law over his brother, both when Þorgrímr is alive and after his death.[46] The paradigm within which the chosen sworn-brother becomes emotionally closer than the blood-brother, the

---

[42] P. M. Sørensen, 'Murder in Marital Bed: An Attempt at Understanding a Crucial Scene in *Gísla saga*', in *Structure and Meaning in Old Norse Literature*, ed. J. Lindow, L. Lönnroth and G. W. Weber, Viking Collection 3 (Odense, 1986), pp. 235–63 (p. 243).

[43] The E version of the saga (AM 556 a, 4to) takes pains to conceal the identity of Vésteinn's killer, while the Y version (NKS 1181, fol. / AM 149, fol.) directly ascribes the murder to Þorgrímr, as does *Eyrbyggja saga*, ed. Matthías Þorðarson, ÍF 4 (Reykjavík, 1935), p. 20.

[44] *Gísla saga*, ed. Björn K. Þórólfsson and Guðni Jónsson, p. 63.

[45] Ibid., pp. 116–17.

[46] Earlier, in the short text of the saga, Gísli's killing of Þórdís's suitor, Þorkell's friend, is said irreparably to have damaged relations between them: 'aldri varð síðan jafnblítt með þeim brœðrum' ('the brothers were never again on such good terms'), ibid., p. 8.

focus of the next chapter, troubles the ideology of family, particularly fraternal, loyalty which usually underlies the Icelandic family sagas.[47] Gísli and his siblings are, significantly, recent immigrants to the Westfjords and the sibling tragedy is precipitated by Gísli's anxiety to form strong, new, homosocial bonds in the unfamiliar environment: swearing brotherhood and exchanging women with Þorgrímr, an established *góði* ('chieftain'), and with Vésteinn. Future conflict is anticipated by the collapse of the sworn-brotherhood ceremony and Þorkell's sexual insecurity is merely the catalyst for the final rupture between siblings, affines and friends.

Ásgerðr and Auðr's conversation, overheard by Þorkell, functions as a 'counter-narrative' here, setting up an alternative weft of female desire which threatens the multiple vectors of the men's homosocial network; all the deaths in the following chapters of the saga result from Ásgerðr's admission of her preference for Vésteinn over her husband Þorkell.[48] Absent from this scene, Þórdís discloses very little about her own feelings, but when she interprets and then reveals the import of the verse in which her brother admits his slaying of her husband, her utterance is decisive. Seizing agency for herself (for she cannot be unaware of the consequences of her action), she apparently chooses her dead husband over her living brother. That Þórdís is carrying her dead husband's child is surely significant; her pregnancy may impel her to seek resolution of the feud now, rather than live with the knowledge that her unborn son – the charismatic and unscrupulous Snorri *góði* – will be obligated to take revenge on his maternal uncle when he grows up.[49] In response to the news of Þórdís's revelation, Gísli composes another verse, bitterly reproaching his sister for her disloyalty and contrasting her with Guðrún Gjúkadóttir who placed vengeance for her brothers above her marital bond with Atli. The comparison is more apposite than Gísli acknowledges, for just as Guðrún's brothers killed her first husband, so Gísli had killed Þórdís's first suitor (above, p. 85).

The spareness of saga narrative, and the very little that Þórdís herself says, has encouraged a wide range of interpretations of her motivation. Conceivably she is tired of Gísli's interference in her life – 'he had killed her first love and she remembered it', as Anne Holtsmark romantically frames Þórdís's feelings.[50] Whether Gísli harbours an unconscious sexual jealousy of his sister's lovers is a matter of debate; certainly the scene in which Gísli kills Þorgrímr, creeping at

---

[47] Compare Meulengracht Sørensen, 'Murder in Marital Bed', p. 246: 'The obligations inherent in sworn-brotherhood are of the same sort as those between brothers-in-law, but are stronger as a marriage and hence the in-law relationship can be dissolved, while the same is not true of sworn-brotherhood.'

[48] Auðr also admits having had feelings in the past for Þorgrímr, but since her marriage she has only loved Gísli, and she remains outstandingly loyal to him throughout the saga.

[49] See Vésteinn Ólason, 'Gísli Súrsson – A Flawless or Flawed Hero?' in *Die Aktualität der Saga: Festschrift für Hans Schottmann*, ed. S. Toftgaard Andersen (Berlin, New York, 1999), pp. 163–75 (p. 170).

[50] A. Holtsmark, *Studies in the Gísla saga*, Studia Norvegica 6 (Oslo, 1951), p. 33.

night into the farmhouse, sliding open the couple's bedcloset, and first touching his sister's breast with his cold hands, is disturbingly ambiguous. The narrative's apparent interest in the consequent sexual activity within the marriage-bed, witnessed, even triggered, by Gísli has provoked speculation about the brother's suppressed feelings for his sister. The possibility of a fundamentally sexual jealousy as a factor in brother-in-law killings cannot be ruled out entirely: the ballad 'The Cruel Brother', discussed in the previous chapter, certainly invites such a Freudian interpretation. However Gísli's placing his hand on his sister's breast is at least as likely, as Vésteinn Ólason argues, to be a practical detail. It allows him to ascertain in the dark who is sleeping where in the bed-closet, and Gísli's second touch persuades Þorgrímr to turn towards his wife and thus present his chest to his waiting killer.[51]

The brother-in-law who breaches the oaths made between a kin-group and an incomer – or who ostentatiously refuses to swear such oaths in the first place – and the unsettling questions that the affinal-triangle topos raise about the fundamental loyalties of women towards brother and husband are good for the heroic-epic narratives of northern Europe to think with. Icelandic social organization depended on alliances forged through in-law and fostering bonds to constitute power blocs capable of delivering success in law-suits at the *Alþingi* and in armed expeditions against common enemies. In Continental Germanic literature, the tension between brothers-in-law is often a function of already existing hostility between feuding groups, where the exchange of a woman in the peace-weaver role between groups may only be temporarily effective: 'Oft seldan hwær / æfter leodhryre   lytle hwile / bongar bugeð,   þeah seo bryd duge' ('Seldom after the death of a man does the slaughtering spear rest for long, however excellent the bride may be'), as Beowulf sagely comments.[52]

Changing social conditions – most importantly the geographical and social mobility of the merchant classes concomitant with the growth of urbanism – transform the circumstances, if not the fundamental motives, of brother-in-law conflict. Caesarius of Heisterbach relates an exemplum about a certain Bernard of Munster who squanders his fortune and becomes a dependent of his sister and brother-in-law. Bernard comes to believe that his brother-in-law had swindled him when buying his house from him and strikes him down with an axe, significantly in the market-place, the mercantile heart of the medieval German city.[53] This tale illustrates the shift from aristocratic feud and the cross-generational legacy of remembered wrongs to plainly economic motives for affinal violence. Despite the move from the court to the city, from the noblity to the bourgeoisie, brother and brother-in-law rivalry remains highly productive in later-medieval narratives.

---

[51] Vésteinn Ólason, 'Morð í rekkju hjóna', in *Sagnaþing helgað Jónasi Kristjánssyni, sjötungum. 10 apríl 1994*, ed. Gísli Sigurðsson, Guðrún Kvaran and Sigurgeir Steingrímsson (Reykjavík, 1994), pp. 823–8.
[52] *Beowulf*, ed. Fulk *et al.*, lines 2029b-31.
[53] Caesarius of Heisterbach, *Dialogue on Miracles*, ed. Scott and Bland, II.xi.liv, pp. 280–1.

Policing the Marriage

The proximity of married siblings within urban environments facilitates, as noted in chapter one, their continuing interaction after marriage. Although, as in the Pevere/Embrone case, fraternal intervention may end in the husband's death, the interventions of brothers or brothers-in-law in a sibling's marriage need not always be detrimental to the sister's or her husband's interests. Royal brothers are liable to defend their sister's rights in cases of marital breakdown; as discussed in chapter one (p. 36) the repudiation of a woman exchanged to seal an alliance signals the probable collapse of that alliance, irrespective of the personal emotions involved.

Politics, questions of face and honour, and strong emotions combine in the Welsh-Irish affinal conflict depicted in the Second Branch of the *Mabinogi*.[54] Matholwch, king of Ireland, comes to visit Bendigeidfran ('Bran the Blessed'), king of Britain. Bran has two half-brothers, Nisien and Efnisien, obvious doubles. Nisien is a peacemaker, but as for Efnisien: '[y] llal a barei ymlad y rwng y deu uroder, ban uei uwyaf yd ymgerynt' ('[he] could incite his two brothers to fight when they were most affectionate').[55] Matholwch seeks the hand of Branwen, Bran's full sister, and half-sister to Nisien and Efnisien, and she is granted to him. Efnisien is absent, and cannot be consulted. When he returns to court to find the wedding feast underway he is furious and takes revenge by maiming the king's horses. Matholwch is appeased only with the gift of a cauldron which brings the dead back to life. The relationship between the in-laws apparently repaired, the king and his bride return to Ireland, where she gives birth to a son, Gwern.

Matholwch cannot forget the insulting treatment he received in Wales and begins to abuse Branwen. She succeeds in taming a bird to send word of her plight to her brother, and Bran and his men come to avenge her. Matholwch hastily offers terms: he will invest Gwern – Bran's sister's son – with the kingship. Bran is persuaded to attend a peace council. Once Gwern has become king, he walks round the hall to greet each of his uncles in turn, but he shrinks from Efnisien. Enraged, the uncle seizes his nephew and hurls him into the fire. Battle breaks out anew, and only the death of Efnisien, which destroys the magical cauldron, brings an end to the fighting. Branwen dies of grief, while only seven British warriors live to return to Britain.

Here the failure to consult the half-brother, the son of a different father, about his sister's match and its repercussions offer a *casus belli* for the Irish and the Welsh. Efnisien is calculating in the scale of insult he offers to the visitors, knowing that his kinship with the king will protect him from direct reprisals. The strife between in-laws in this tale figures wider tensions between the Welsh and

---

[54] 'Branwen uerch Lyr', in *Pedeir Keinc y Mabinogi*, ed. Williams, pp. 29–48; 'Branwen, Daughter of Llŷr', in *The Mabinogi*, trans. Ford, pp. 57–72.
[55] 'Branwen', ed. Williams, p. 29; 'Branwen', trans. Ford, p. 59.

the Irish; Efnisien's provocative behaviour is motivated by a political objection to an alliance with the Irish king, but, as is typical of heroic literature, he also feels that his personal honour has been affronted.[56] Warrior honour is always performative in Judith Butler's sense; a perceived infringement must be reacted to with violence if face is to be maintained.[57] The sister (and the cauldron) are exchanged to establish political ties that are underpinned by personal bonds. Gwern, as sister's child, will embody the new alliance in the royal lineage while the cauldron guarantees Ireland's sacred supremacy in its capacity to revivify the dead.[58] Branwen's mistreatment functions to save Matholwch's face among his own people; their collective honour has been repaired neither by the gift nor the marriage. The Irish king does not intend a direct challenge to Bran; he relies on Branwen's inability to communicate her suffering to her distant natal family. When she ingeniously teaches a starling both to speak and to bear a letter to Wales relaying her mistreatment, Bran is prompt to respond, both to his sister's personal plight ('he grieved to learn of the punishment on Branwen') and to the threat to the alliance which her humiliation figures.[59] The ruptured bonds could have been renewed and strengthened through the investiture of Gwern in whose veins British and Irish blood mingle, but Efnisien's nihilistic act destroys the fruit of the marriage, wrecks the peace deal and leads to his own and his sister's deaths. In detecting Irish treason in Matholwch's hall and through his final self-sacrifice which destroys the cauldron, Efnisien actively chooses to subordinate his individualism for the good of the group to which he belongs; but when he rejects his role as as brother-in-law and as maternal uncle his provocation precipitates the ultimate failure of the exchange, the marriage and the alliance.

In later-medieval urban communities, particularly in classes below the nobility, the natal family and the in-laws often lived close enough for the brothers to police their sisters' honour after marriage, or for a sister to invoke their assistance in chastising a cruel husband. Class is crucial to the dynamic of these stories; the tension between gentle birth and the new fortunes amassed by enterprising tradesmen in Italian cities complicates women's expectations of the kind of marriages their brothers will arrange for them, and their behaviour within those marriages. Women who are unfaithful to low-status husbands are viewed surprisingly sympathetically by the narrators of some *Decameron* stories.

---

[56] D. Wyatt, *Slaves and Warriors in Medieval Britain and Ireland, 800–1200* (Leiden, 2009), pp. 90–1. See also for Irish sources and analogues, P. Sims-Williams, *Irish Influence on Medieval Welsh Literature* (Oxford, 2011).

[57] J. Butler, *Gender Trouble: Feminism and the Subversion of Identity* (New York and London, 1999), p. 190: 'gender is an identity tenuously constituted in time ... through a *stylized repetition of acts*' (her italics); see also D. Hadley, 'Introduction: Medieval Masculinities' in *Masculinity in Medieval Europe*, ed. D. M. Hadley (London, 1999), pp. 1–18 (p. 14).

[58] On gift-exchange and the exchange of women, see Cowell, *The Medieval Warrior Aristocracy*, chapter one.

[59] 'Branwen', ed. Williams, p. 38; 'Branwen', trans. Ford, p. 65.

When Siblings Marry

The urban context of Boccaccio's tales facilitates fraternal intervention to keep the peace in a troubled marriage, for brothers can be alerted to sisterly mistreatment within hours of its occurrence. In one such story (VII.8), a husband, Arriguccio, discovers that his wife's lover is in the habit of visiting her while Arriguccio is sound asleep, alerting her to his presence outside by tugging on a thread attached to her toe.[60] He confronts the lover, who takes to his heels, while the wife quickly substitutes her maid for herself in the dark bedroom, promising her a fine reward for putting up with whatever happens. Arriguccio returns home, beats his bed-partner soundly and cuts off all her hair. Then he announces that he will fetch his wife's brothers and ask them to deal with her as they see fit. The wife treats the maid's injuries and installs her elsewhere; when the brothers arrive, intending to chastise her, the wife's calm demeanour, lack of injuries, and most tellingly, her uncut hair – a widely recognized symbol of female sexual honour – persuade them that Arriguccio has been out carousing, fallen into bed with some other woman and made a catastrophic error. Their mother, who has accompanied the brothers, volubly blames them for having bestowed their sister on an ignoble husband, a 'mercatantuolo di quattro denari' ('petty tuppeny-ha'penny trader'), simply on account of his wealth.[61] The brothers threaten their brother-in-law, warning that he will not be forgiven a second time for disrespecting their sister. Terrified and bewildered, Arriguccio henceforth leaves his wife in peace, and she enjoys further undisturbed rendezvous with her lover.

In *Decameron* III.3, a woman who feels that she has married beneath her in wedding a wealthy wool-merchant, employs a friar to act as an unwitting go-between to a particular young nobleman.[62] The lady's complaints to the friar about the young man's attentions cause the friar to rebuke his friend, thus planting the idea of the relationship in his mind. At several points in the tale, the lady and the friar warn the lover that she may be forced to complain to her brothers about his behaviour; but tellingly she makes no threat to involve her low-born husband. The nobleman understands the code and initiates the affair.

These fabliau-type tales show how the sister retains her class status even after marrying down. Like her daughter, the mother in the tale of Arriguccio and his wife resents her sons' acceptance of a bourgeois if wealthy son-in-law. The difference in rank between husband and wife in the second story apparently legitimizes the woman's adultery. This lady's noble would-be lover is expected to recognize the code by which she transmits her continuing affiliations with her birth family: when she threatens to appeal to her brothers for protection. Her implication is that the merchant husband could not understand the ethics of personal honour and of public and private behaviour which high-ranking men can be assumed to share. The unfortunate husband is excluded in and from his wife's discourse; the tale ends with the lovers in bed together, making fun

---

[60] Boccaccio, *Decameron* VII.8; trans. Waldman, pp. 450–7.
[61] *Decameron* VII.8.48; my translation.
[62] Boccaccio, *Decameron* III.3.

of the implements of the wool-trade which underwrite the prosperity that the lady enjoys.[63] Tragic and violent possibilities, despite these comic endings, are also thinkable within the town setting; the brothers in Tale VII.8 might easily have killed their sister, had she not persuaded them that her low-born husband was capable of idiotic drunkenness and brutality and had they not, perhaps, a bad conscience about the quality of husband they had found for her.

Husband's Brothers and Wife's Sisters

Whether the married couple live close to the wife's or the husband's kindred is crucial to affinal relations. Had Sivrit not returned from Xanten to visit his wife's brothers, the Quarrel of the Queens in the *Nibelungenlied* would have been avoided: keeping out of the in-laws' way is conducive to better relations. In virilocal societies, the husband's brother may well still be present in the parental or fraternal home when his sibling marries. The sexual attraction of a wife for her husband's brother causes conflict which, as in the Amleth story and the tale of Yngvi, Álfr and his wife (discussed in chapter four), culminates in fratricide.[64] Conversely, a man's sexual interest in his brother's wife may go unreciprocated; his persecution of his sister-in-law, her sufferings and eventual vindication are a popular theme in a group of European texts relating the story of the empress of Rome.[65] The earliest of these is the Crescentia-legend found in the *Kaiserchronik* from Regensburg around 1150. Here, significantly, the brothers are twins, both named Dietrich.[66] Other influential versions of this tale are found in the *Miracles de Notre Dame* of Gautier de Coinci and in Christine de Pizan's *Le Livre de la Cité des Dames*.[67] The broad plot reappears in the French and English romances of Florence de Rome, while a condensed version is also to be found in the *Gesta Romanorum*.[68]

In the early versions of the tale (and, as summarized here from the *Gesta Romanorum*), the empress is left in charge of the kingdom in her husband's absence, while his brother takes on the role of steward. The empress is propositioned by her brother-in-law and rejects him; she has him cast into

---

[63] *Decameron* III.3.53: 'biasimando i lucignoli e' pettini e gli scardassi' ('passing rude comments on [such objects and utensils of the wool trade] as slubs, combs and cards'), trans. Waldman, p. 190.

[64] See chapter four, p. 122.

[65] N. B. Black, *Medieval Narratives of Accused Queens* (Gainsville FL, 2003).

[66] See *Die Crescentialegende in der deutschen Dichtung des Mittelalters*, ed. K. Baasch (Stuttgart, 1968), lines 11365–9; the Crescentia-legend from the Middle High German *Deutsche Kaiserchronik eines Regensburger Geistlichen*, ed. E. Schröder (Hannover, 1892).

[67] See Black, *Medieval Narratives*, pp. 20–36 on Gautier, and pp. 151–2 for Christine de Pizan.

[68] *Florence de Rome: chanson d'aventure du premier quart du XIIIe siècle*, ed. A. Wallensköld, 2 vols, SATF (Paris, 1907–9); *Le Bone Florence of Rome*, ed. C. F. Heffernan (Manchester, 1976); *Gesta Romanorum: or Entertaining Moral Stories*, trans. C. Swann (London, 1824), pp. cxiv–cxxxii.

prison, but when he repents she permits his release. The villain renews his assault on the empress in the forest; threatening her with rape and violence, he finally hangs her by her hair in a tree and abandons her, afterwards claiming that she has been kidnapped. The empress undergoes various picaresque adventures – in Gautier she is frequently succoured by the Virgin Mary – until finally she is granted healing powers through divine agency. All those who have wronged her, including the emperor's wicked brother, find themselves afflicted by disease. The villain contracts leprosy and is compelled to make a full confession of his sins before he can be cured.[69] The empress reveals her identity and is restored to her husband; in the hagiographical versions (sc. *Crescentia*-legend, *Miracles*) she retreats to a convent instead.

The empress's authority is demonstrated by her imprisonment of her brother-in-law: 'an assertive act, a turning of the world of power and gender relations upside down, an act for which she later pays dearly', notes Nancy Black.[70] At first sight the brother-in-law's villainy appears to be driven solely by sexual desire, but a medieval audience would note that a political motive most likely underlies the attempted seduction. Usurpers, from Merovingian kings to Amleth's murderous uncle to Mordred, marry the wives of their predecessor as a matter of policy.[71] Where the queen holds the keys to the treasury as part of her household responsibilities, her cooperation is needed if the new king is to gain access to the resources required to bribe magnates to accept his sovereignty. Moreover, the queen was regarded as providing stability and continuity; she and her kinsmen were likely to be significant in the politics of régime change. The usurpation motive as underlying the brother-in-law's sexual predation is highlighted in the French and English romances of *Florence de/of Rome*. In this tradition the plot is complicated by the presence of three suitors: in English, Garcy, the elderly emperor of Constantinople, and the two sons of the king of Hungary. Florence seems destined to end up first with one, then the other brother as their fortunes fluctuate in the battle against Garcy and his army. Mylys is cowardly where Emere is brave; the barons of Rome advise Florence to marry Mylys when Emere has been captured and the city is under siege. The marriage is forestalled when Emere is released and the wedding with Florence takes place. But Mylys takes advantage of Emere's subsequent departure to attack Constantinople and terminate Garcy's interest in his wife; he stages a coup, assuring those in his conspiracy: 'Thys herytage to me wyll falle / My

---

[69] On the French romance of *Florence* see Kay, *The Chansons de Geste*, pp. 157–9. Kay comments astutely on the fact that the virtuous brother Esmeré is also diseased (in the head rather than in the lower parts where the wicked Milon is afflicted). Although Esmeré needs also to be in pain in order to encounter his wife as healer, his condition indicates that 'The "brotherhood" is entirely corrupted; only the "sisterhood" of the convent can return it to humanity', p. 159.

[70] Black, *Medieval Narratives*, p. 188.

[71] On early-medieval usurpers see P. Stafford, *Queens, Concubines and Dowagers: the King's Wife in the Early Middle Ages* (London, 1983), p. 50. The usurper's strategy does not change much in later chronicles.

brodur comyþ neuyr agayne / I wyll wedde the yonge bryde'.[72] Mylys abducts and brutalizes Florence in a sequence strongly inflected by hagiographical conventions. He strips and beats her, but his attempts at rape are thwarted by Florence's prayers and his desire vanishes. Once he has abandoned her, her fate unfolds much as in the *Gesta Romanorum*; a series of evil-doers are afflicted by illness and Florence heals them as they confess their sins in her husband's presence.

In contrast to the narratives explored in chapter four, where brotherly competition over a woman is figured as exemplifying disloyalty and sibling envy, and the conflict is compounded by the woman's reciprocal interest in her brother-in-law, in this tradition the focus is on the interaction between the brother-in-law and Florence. Significantly, when an exchange of fiancés is mooted she absolutely refuses, refuting the barons' proposition that the brothers are interchangeable and that Mylys would do just as well as Emere both as a husband and as a ruler. The empress's insistence on being her own person, even if her husband is dead (as the brother-in-law sometimes claims) establishes her as possessing an independent subjectivity. She refuses to be swayed by claims about political stability or fraternal substitutability, nor will she subordinate her desire to the apparent good of the realm. Although the brother-in-law exploits her goodness and compassion to trick her into releasing him from prison, relying on her not to disrupt fraternal relations by revealing his behaviour to her husband, that same compassion – now externalized as the power to heal – is instrumental in her restoration to her rightful place.

Just as men cannot always restrain themselves from trying to seduce their brothers' wives, so husbands become attracted to their wives' sisters. Sisters' interchangeability was discussed in chapter three, where a woman about to be cast aside for a higher-born bride is revealed to be the bride's lost sister. Unlike the lustful brother-in-law, who, thanks to virilocal marriage, may see a great deal of his brother's wife, a husband is less likely to come into contact with his wife's sister, since she will very likely live elsewhere. In the twelfth-century French poem *Philomena*, probably composed by Chrétien de Troyes, and deriving from Ovid's version of the classical myth, Tereus, king of Thrace, goes to Athens to fetch his sister-in-law Philomena from her father Pandion, so that she may visit her sister Progné.[73] He is stunned by Philomena's beauty; while the text does not comment on Progné's appearance, we might suspect that part of Philomena's attraction is that, in Updike's phrase, she represents another 'throw of the dice': a younger and lovelier version of the wife who has already endured five years of an ill-fated marriage and borne Tereus a son.[74]

Pandion is reluctant to let his daughter go, but Tereus presses Progné's longing to see her sister as a counter-argument. Weeping, he claims that Progné has

---

[72] *Bone Florence de Rome*, ed. Heffernan, lines 1067–9.
[73] *Philomena*, ed. C. de Boer, trans. O. Collet, in *Chrétien de Troyes: Romans*, ed. Zink, pp. 1229–67.
[74] See chapter four, p. 121 for Gertrude's comment on Claudius.

threatened to withdraw her love from him should he return without Philomena: a rhetorical invocation of the strong sisterly bond which will rebound upon him. Philomena has no brother to protect her, only a weak and doting father who cannot see through Tereus's false emotional display. During the rape scene, Philomena reminds her brother-in-law to no avail of her relationship to his wife, 'ma seror ... vostre leal espose' ('my sister ... your loyal wife').[75] These sisters are manifestly not interchangable: Tereus has no intention of replacing Progné with her sister, rather Philomena supplements her sister in the rapist's sexual economy, forced into a degraded and violent union with him.[76]

Though she lacks a brother, Philomena has sisters who help her. First, these are notional sisters: the *vilainne* ('peasant woman') and her daughter who tend the mutilated girl and help her create the tapestry which communicates the horror of her plight to Progné. Second is Progné herself, sister and rescuer.[77] Progné's first words, as she enters the cottage where Philomena is captive, reiterate the sibling tie: 'Philomena, suer, ou es tu? / Je suis ta suer. Ne dote pas!' ('Philomena, sister, where are you? I am your sister. Don't be afraid!')[78] The sisters' long-anticipated reunion culminates in their murder of Tereus's son Itys; his flesh is fed to the evil-doer and the protagonists all metamorphose into birds.

The sacrificial dimensions of child-killing and cannibalism, the destruction of the lineage and the macabre reincorporation of the child's flesh into his father's body, signal that Tereus's crime has erased all bonds between husband and wife. The sisters' murderous solidarity in killing Itys flags up the husband's original distortion of normative kin-relations. As E. Jane Burns notes,

> Progne's act, cast as a message to her savage husband, might read less as a mother's senselessly brutal infanticide than a move on the part of a complicitous procreator to take back the child she gave in birth. It is almost as if, in killing Itys, Progne unravels the threads of time, reversing the course of past events to a moment before the birth of her child, a moment perhaps even before her marriage.[79]

Following tragic rather than romance conventions, with a strong emphasis on horror and pathos, *Philomena*, like the Second Branch of the *Mabinogi*, culminates in the death of the sister's son. The human ties of flesh: its gestation, autonomy and final re-incorporation are resolved by the transformation into bird-form, when the protagonists become no longer kindred, no longer human. Although the poem insistently focuses on the family: the emotional dependence of old age, the perversion of love in Tereus's furious lust for his sister-in-law and, above all,

---

[75] *Philomena*, ed. de Boer, lines 784–5.
[76] See N. A. Jones, 'The Daughter's Text and the Thread of Lineage in the Old French *Philomena*', in Representing Rape in Medieval and Early Modern Literature, ed. E. Robertson and C. K. Rose (New York, 2001, pp. 161–87 (p. 180).
[77] Jones, 'The Daughter's Text'.
[78] *Philomena*, ed. de Boer, lines 1264–5.
[79] E. J. Burns, 'Raping Men: What's motherhood got to do with it?', in *Representing Rape*, ed. Robertson and Rose, pp. 127–60 (p. 151).

the powerful bonds of sisterhood, a political dimension is also understood. Not only is the marriage undone, the murder makes impossible even reversion to the *status ante quo* and the downfall of two mighty kingdoms and two lineages – of Thrace and of Athens – is presaged. The sacrificial murder – like Guðrún's killing and cannibalizing of her sons in the eddic tradition – is a rejection of patriliny. Once the marital bond has been fractured by affinal violence, sibling solidarity outweighs even the blood-tie between a mother and her son.

Sisters-in-Law

A brother's marriage means that a sister acquires a new sister, a bond prone both to the solidarity and the powerful jealousies inherent in sister-relationships. Since the new sister has not grown up with her in-law, the strategies that sisters normally evolve for managing their relationship and their bonds with their brothers are not necessarily available to them, and discord between women frequently escalates into a deadly feud which claims mutiple lives on both sides. The conflict between Doña Lambra and her husband's nephews in the Spanish *Los Siete Infantes de Lara* tradition is triggered by an exchange of insults between sisters-in-law in the ballad sequences derived from the legend. When Doña Sancha praises her seven sons for their exploits in the tournament at her brother's wedding, the new bride, Doña Lambra, turns her sister-in-law's pride in her offspring into an insult, accusing her husband's sister of having borne so many sons 'como puerca en muladar' ('like a sow in the mud').[80] Sancha's youngest son Gonzalo springs to his mother's defence, threatening to cut the skirts off Lambra and her ladies: for short skirts are a sign of loose morals. The implications of promiscuity are elaborated when Gonzalo kills the bride's cousin during the feast: it seems that he was Lambra's lover. Gonzalo's move thus exacerbates the quarrel; there are further ramifications when Doña Lambra sends a servant to throw blood over Gonzales, promising the young man protection, but the Infantes pursue and kill their opponent, even though he hides under Lambra's skirts.[81] As with Guðrún/Kriemhilt and Brynhildr/Prünhilt, psychological warfare and its open expression draws on the domain of women's sexual and reproductive lives: sexual desire, sexual honour, and maternal fecundity. The sisters-in-law deploy their knowledge of the other's intimate secrets as a weapon in their conflicts, making public what should be private and making women's business into men's. For such women, speaking out becomes 'a political act, but that potentially political nature of the case is not opened up until the politically responsible, male parties become involved',

---

[80] '¡Ay Dios qué buen callero!', in *Romancero tradicional de las lenguas hispánicas*, ed. R. Menéndez Pidal *et al.* 3 vols (Madrid, 1963), II: 105; Cf. C. Bluestine, 'The Power of Blood in the Siete Infantes de Lara', *Hispanic Review* 50 (1982), 201–17 (p. 203).

[81] See Bluestine, 'The Power of Blood', pp. 204–7.

as Frakes observes.[82] In contradistinction to the 'peace-weaver' model of conflict resolution, here the marriage actually generates feud between previously friendly kindreds. Doña Lambra and Doña Sancha's public voicing of insult escalates the quarrel to the level of family feud, whose culmination is discussed further below (pp. 203–4)

Sister-in-law relationships need not always be hostile. In the probably thirteenth-century Austro-German poem *Kudrun*, the eponymous heroine secures for her brother a match which acknowledges friendship between women, serves the *Realpolitik* of her fictional world, and brings her brother personal satisfaction.[83] Kudrûn, daughter of King Hegel of Ireland, attracts three suitors: Sivrit, king of the Moors, Hartmuot of Normandy and Herwic of Zeeland. Once she is promised to Herwic, the infuriated Sivrit makes war upon him, while Hartmuot takes advantage of the situation to abduct Kudrûn. An expedition led by Hegel and his son Ortwin to recover the lost princess ends in disaster. Kudrûn refuses to marry Hartmuot and his vengeful mother Gerlint forces her to become a washerwoman; only her faithful companion Hildeburc offers her support and comfort. But Hartmuot's sister Ortrûn, enlisted by her brother to persuade Kudrûn to marry him, is always kind to the unhappy princess. Finally – after an interval of fourteen years – Herwic and Ortwin attack Hartmuot and his father Ludewic. Ludewic is killed and Hartmuot and his sister are captured. The prisoners are brought back to Ireland, where Kudrûn makes peace, contriving to bring about reconciliation between all the men involved by proposing that Hartmuot marry the lower-status Hildeburc, while Herwic's unnamed sister is bestowed on Sivrit, who had also participated in the rescue. Kudrûn also persuades her brother Ortwin to marry the kindly Ortrûn. Thus Kudrûn and Ortrûn do indeed becomes sisters-in-law, but by dint of Ortrûn marrying Kudrûn's noble brother, rather than Kudrûn being compelled to marry her abductor. As Brian Murdoch notes, *Kudrun* ends with the poem's various dynasties being strengthened by new marriages, and the rivalry of the princes is ended by Kudrûn's diplomacy.[84]

This satisfactory resolution of sibling loyalties and marital ambitions contrasts with the death and desolation at the end of the *Nibelungenlied*, to which *Kudrun*, composed in the same region of Bavaria-Austria, is in part a response. It might be argued that the poem finally offers some courtly alternatives to the epic ethos of the *Nibelungenlied*; Hartmuot's adherence to courtly values allows Kudrûn to maintain her chastity, in marked contrast to Prünhilt's fate.[85] Nevertheless, the poem does not fully assimilate romance values; Kudrûn's *suone* or reconciliation-plan takes remarkably little notice of questions of consent.[86] Consequently,

---

[82] Frakes, *Brides and Doom*, p. 119.
[83] *Kudrun*, ed. R. Wisniewski, 2nd edn (Stuttgart, 1969).
[84] *Kudrun*, transl and intro. B. Murdoch (London, 1987), pp. xvi–xvii; cf. Pafenberg, 'The Spindle and the Sword', p. 113, on Kudrun's politics of 'compassion and diplomacy'.
[85] Pafenberg, 'The Spindle and the Sword', p. 112.
[86] Frakes, *Brides and Doom*, p. 248: 'the poem is not sufficiently implicated in romance conventions that the marriages can function as present evidence of future happiness'.

'des nam Herwîges swester wunder' ('Herwig's sister was greatly surprised at this') when told of her proposed marriage to the king of the Moors, and she is by no means willing. 'Doch lobete si in trâge, als dicke ein maget tuot' ('she did, however, show some reluctance, as young women often do'), notes the narrator, obfuscating the girl's unenthusiastic reaction by re-interpreting it as merely a conventional performance of courtly *danger*.[87] The marriages are 'obviously politically motivated and have less emotional basis or promise of potential affection even than is customary', comments Frakes pessimistically; female solidarity is swiftly subordinated to political pragmatism.[88] Kudrûn herself assumes both authority and agency in organizing the marriages; her aim is to maintain the just-recovered Heteling superiority and to cement the ties between the allies and the peace with the enemy, not to procure love-matches.[89] She effects her aims through the exchange of women, but their status is now properly calibrated with the relative standing of the men. Female hypergamy means that Ortwin can raise Ortrûn to his level on marriage; Hartmuot's enforced wedding to the non-royal (and ageing) Hildeburc, by contrast, is 'a deserved comeuppance'.[90] Neither Kudrûn (nor *Kudrun*) can imagine women seizing or being granted autonomy in the exchange process, not even when a woman is the authorizing figure, though the existing warmth of the bond between Kudrûn and Ortrûn (along with the new couple's chiming names) promises well for Ortwin's marriage.

Sisters' Sons

The sister's son is culturally marked in medieval narrative, a figure who, in some contexts, can be as important to his maternal uncle as his own son. As Martin Aurell has pointed out, historically there tends to be little strife between men and their maternal uncles; hypergamy implies that the sister's husband may well be more powerful than her brother, and his patronage is welcomed.[91] Paternal uncles, who usually stand to inherit if the nephew dies, are more consistently wicked in medieval literature, and indeed medieval history.[92] The fortunes of sister-sons tend to vary by genre; in Saxo's pseudo-historical account Harald hilditǫnn ('battle-tooth'), king of Denmark, keeps a watchful eye on the fortunes of his sisters' children. When as a small child Ring inherits Sweden, his uncle confirms him in the succession and appoints guardians for him. Oli, son of the formidable Sivard and another of Harald's sisters, and a remarkable hero in his own right, enters Harald's service and wins the princess

---

[87] *Kudrun*, ed. Wisniewski, sts. 1662, 1665; *Kudrun*, trans. Murdoch, pp. 147, 148.
[88] Frakes, *Brides and Doom*, pp. 242–3.
[89] W. McConnell, *The Epic of Kudrun: A Critical Commentary* (Göppingen, 1988), p. 85.
[90] Frakes, *Brides and Doom*, p. 263.
[91] Aurell, 'Rompre la concorde familiale', p. 21.
[92] See Lecuppre, 'L'oncle usurpateur' on Richard III and various other murderous paternal uncles, and also chapter one, pp. 38–9.

of Värmland as his bride. He also becomes Harald's chief naval commander. The two kings' exemplary relationship enables Harald and his sister-sons to assert their dominion over the whole of southern Scandinavia until Bruni, an Odinic troublemaking figure, sows dissension between Harald and Ring. When the uncle and nephew clash at the Battle of Bravalla, Ring is victorious, but he treats his uncle's body with great respect, ensuring an honourable and rich funeral.[93] Peaceable relations between the uncle and his sisters' sons are conditional on the younger men fulfilling distinct social roles. Ring's mother married into a different kingdom, removing her son from competition for the Danish throne, while Oli's mother had married a hero, but not a man of royal rank. The alliances formed by the maternal marriages shape the sons' destinies, removing them from direct competition with their uncle until Ring and Harald finally square up to one another. Saxo over-determines the causes of the great confrontation at Bravalla in which Harald is slain by Bruni, acting as his charioteer. The battle is instigated by Bruni's trouble-making, Odin's habitual duplicity when it comes to granting victory to the opponents of his former favourites, and by the desire of Harald, now elderly and blind, to die fighting rather than in his bed. The rupture between uncle and maternal nephew must accommodate both Harald's powerful reputation and Ring's nobility, particularly in triumph: 'Tali parentationis cura iustis avunculo persolutis, Danorum sibi favorem conscivit odiumque hostium ad gratiam deflexit' ('by carefully performing the due obsequies for his uncle, Ring won the Danes' goodwill and turned inimical hatred into friendship'), Saxo comments approvingly.[94]

Maternal uncles are not always as well disposed towards their nephews as Harald initially was to Ring. As noted above, when the tensions, which had been temporarily resolved by a sister's marriage to a member of an enemy group, boil up again, the sister's son is often both catalyst and victim and his death inaugurates a new stage in the feud. Thus in *Beowulf* Hildeburh's son dies fighting against his uncle Hnæf, though Hnæf may not have killed him personally. Efnisien provocatively murders Branwen's son Gwern in order to sabotage the peace agreement about to be concluded between the Welsh and the Irish in the Second Branch of the *Mabinogi*. In the legend of *Los Siete Infantes de Lara*, Ruy Veláquez brings about the death of all seven of his sister Doña Sancha's children, though he does not directly shed their blood.[95] The legend is based on actual events from the last part of the tenth century; Ruy allies himself with with Muslim invaders in order to destroy his nephews, choosing to become a traitor in order to achieve vengeance for the insults offered to his wife. The Siete Infantes are betrayed by Ruy to Almanzor, the leader of the Moors who have

---

[93] Saxo, *GD*, VII–VIII; Saxo, *HD*, pp. 228–33; 238–46.
[94] Saxo, *GD*, VIII.5.1; Saxo, *HD*, pp. 243–4.
[95] See above, p. 200; Bluestine, 'The Power of Blood'; R. Menéndez Pidal, *La leyenda de los Infantes de Lara*, 3rd. edn (Madrid, 1971); T. A. Lathrop, *The Legend of the* Siete Infantes de Lara (Chapel Hill NC, 1972). For the ballad traditions, see *Romancero tradicional de las lenguas hispánicas*, ed. Menéndez Pidal *et al.* II: 97–160.

invaded northern Spain; they are ambushed, captured and die martyrs' deaths. Doña Sancha's husband and father of the Infantes, Gonzalo Gustioz, survives his sons. Imprisoned, he begets another son, Mudarra, on a Moorish princess, his captor's daughter. Vengeance is long-delayed: Mudarra, half-brother to the seven Infantes, must first grow to adulthood before Ruy is brought to justice. Sancha had earlier dreamed of drinking her brother's blood, signalling the final sundering of sibling bonds, if also encoding a disturbing allusion to the sacrament; finally her desire for vengeance is fulfilled.[96] In the *Siete Infantes* tales, the deaths of the seven sister-sons are consequent on the women's quarrel, exacerbated by the arrogance of Gonzalo, the youngest nephew. The two brothers-in-law become embroiled in a sisters-in-law's domestic conflict which, like the *Nibelungenlied*'s 'Quarrel of the Queens', moves out into public space and develops into a political power struggle.

Sister-sons also die in the sibling-affine conflicts of the Gjúkungs and the Nibelungs. In *Vǫlsunga saga*, Guðrún's infant son Sigmundr is killed at the same time as his father on the orders of his maternal uncle, but his slaying does not register as significant in comparison with the ramifications of his father's death. While in the *Nibelungenlied*, it is the unrelated Hagen who brutally kills the son of Etzel and Kriemhilt, *Þiðreks saga* adapts this scene in order to precipitate Grímhildr's vengeance on her brothers. She and her ageing husband Atli invite her brothers – including Hǫgni – to visit the Huns; as maternal uncles to the couple's son Aldrian they are to advise on the transfer of power between father and son.[97] At a feast Grímhildr sends Aldrian to provoke Hǫgni, challenging him to snatch his uncle's food from his plate and punch him in the face. Aldrian does as his mother bids; 'en þat hǫgg varð meira en ván væri at af svá ungum manni' ('and that blow turned out to be greater than might be expected from such a young man').[98] Hǫgni seizes the boy by the hair, slices off his head and hurls it at Grímhildr, striking her breast. Battle is now freely joined between the Burgundians and the Huns, ending in the deaths of all four brothers and of Grímhildr herself.[99] Thus in epic and other heroic genres the death of the sister's son definitively destroys the alliance inaugurated by her marriage; hope of peace and the continuation of the lineage incarnated in the child are symbolically extinguished before conflict between affines is (re)-ignited.

In mythic-heroic story, in romance and the somewhat anomalous *Karlamagnús saga* (as noted in the previous chapter), Cú Chulainn, Sinfjǫtli, Rollant and

---

[96] See Lathrop, *The Legend*, pp. 139–40, for Sancha's prophetic dream of drinking her brother's blood; p. 165 for the dream's fulfilment. Cf. Bluestine, 'Power of Blood', pp. 215–16, who notes the Christ-like presentation of Ruy when he is executed.

[97] *Þiðreks saga*, ed. Guðni Jónsson, II: 488. Compare the transfer of power between Matholwch and his son Gwern in the Second Branch.

[98] Ibid., II: 512.

[99] Depicted as even more diabolical than Kriemhilt, Grímhildr seizes a lighted brand from the fire and thrusts it in the mouths of Gernoz and Gíslher to make sure that they are dead. Gernoz has already perished, but Gíslher dies from this maltreatment. This action provokes the hero Þiðrekr to cut Grímhildr in two with his sword.

Mordred, incestuously conceived sons, pass as maternal nephews. Favoured and promoted by their father-uncles who take advantage of the traditional closeness of sister-son relationships to disguise the truth of their paternity, these heroes usually offer unstinting loyalty to their uncles and lords. Mordred is the exception; neither particularly heroic and finally a usurper and parricide, he shatters the sister-son / actual son model through his designs on his uncle-father's wife and his treacherous bid for the throne. If, as Miranda Griffin has argued, the conversion of Mordred from sister-son in Geoffrey of Monmouth to incestuous son in the Vulgate derives from the Charlemagne legend, Mordred is certainly no Roland.[100] His treachery is marked as doubly deviant when measured against the loyalty of his brother Gawain, and in comparison with the other incest-born heroes discussed in chapter six.

Madeleine Blaess has noticed the multiplication of often-nameless Arthurian sisters in the early stages of the legend.[101] Tradition freely invents sisters for Arthur in order to emphasize the sister-son status of various heroes within Arthur's following. In later romance (the Vulgate, the Post-Vulgate and their derivatives) Arthur's sisters are reduced to three, and two – Morgan le Fay and the queen of Orkney – acquire more significant roles. Arthur's nephews, Gauvain/Gawain, Agravain, and Gaheriet and the youngest son of Lot of Lothian and Orkney, variously Guerrhes or Gareth, along with Yvain, the son of Morgan le Fay, are among Arthur's most prominent knights. When they reach maturity, they join Arthur at Camelot, intent on parlaying their privileged relationship with the king into individual reputations for honour. In the Vulgate *Merlin*, Arthur's half-sisters succeed in persuading their sons to support their uncle's claim to the throne despite the opposition of the women's husbands, Lot and Uriens.[102] Gauvain thus finds himself in a tense confrontation with his father after fighting on his uncle's side.[103] In *Sir Gawain and the Green Knight*, Gawain mock-modestly calls attention to his sister-son status when claiming the adventure; his loss to the court would be unimportant since he has no merit, except that: 'as much as 3e ar myn em I am only to prayse, / No bounté bot your blod I in my bodé knowe' ('I only deserve praise because you are my uncle / I know of no goodness in my body but your blood').[104] By the end of the poem, of course, Gawain has learned that his uncle's noble blood also flows in the veins of his aunt, Morgan le Fay, and that his own nature consequently contains both 'trecherye' and 'trawþe'.[105]

[100] See Griffin, 'Writing out the Incest'.
[101] M. Blaess, 'Arthur's Sisters', *Bibliographic Bulletin of the International Arthurian Society* 8 (1956), 69–77.
[102] *Vulgate Version*, ed. Sommer, 130; L-G, I: 338. See also Larrington, *King Arthur's Enchantresses*, pp. 124–7.
[103] *Vulgate Version*, ed. Sommer, II: 315–19 (p. 319); L-G, I: 342–4 (p. 344).
[104] *Sir Gawain and the Green Knight*, ed. J. R. R. Tolkien and E. V. Gordon, 2nd edn, rev. N. Davis (Oxford, 1967), lines 356–7.
[105] *Sir Gawain and the Green Knight*, ed. Tolkien, Gordon and Davis, lines 2383, 2287; see also C. Larrington, 'The Enchantress, the Knight and the Cleric: Authorial Surrogates

Nevertheless, Gawain amply fulfils the idealized sister-son role. Remaining by Arthur's side until his death, he both supports Arthur and exploits his uncle's loyalty and his vulnerability in pursuit of his blood-feud with Lancelot. Gawain's death at the hands of his (half?)-brother Mordred, that 'false fostered fode' in the *Alliterative Morte Arthure* forms a fitting climax to the poem's narrative of faithful and treacherous sister-sons.[106]

Even if they have not seen their sisters for many years, brothers in family romances are willing to help their nephews. In *Parzival* the hero is given useful advice and trained in knightly skills by Gornemanz, his mother's brother; the hermit Trevrizent who hears his confession on Good Friday and sets him back on the way to salvation is also a maternal uncle, as indeed is the suffering Grail King Anfortas. *Parzival* is highly structured by its kin networks; sibling relations and concomitant bonds of cousinship are gradually revealed over the course of the romance, tying together the two clans of Arthur's house and the lineage of the Grail.[107] However positive the bond between maternal uncles and their nephews, in the next generation rivalry frequently springs up between sister's son and brother's son.[108] So Ither the Red Knight, slain by Parzival in his first joust, is revealed to be the son of Uther Pendragon's sister, and thus Arthur's father's sister's son. Ither came to the Round Table to claim his inheritance (the land of Bertâne), seized a cup as symbol of his claim and accidentally spilled wine over Ginover.[109] Although Parzival's killing is widely regretted by ladies, especially Ginover, and is strongly criticized by his uncle Trevrizent, Arthur himself expresses no particular regret at his cousin the Red Knight's death. Where in Chrétien's *Conte del Graal* the Red Knight was both a menace to the court and unrelated to Arthur, Wolfram incorporates him into the kinship in a problematic relationship to the king. Karl Bertau notes the potential rivalry between cousins:

> Mutterbrüder sind sozusage 'positive Väter', deren Söhne hingengen sind besonders 'negative Brüder'. Denn der 'sun' hat etwa in seinen Erbansprüchen die Rivalität des 'neven' seines Vaters zu fürchten'.[110]

---

in Arthurian Romance', *Arthurian Literature* 25 (2008), 43–65 (pp. 62–4).

[106] *Alliterative Morte Arthure* in *King Arthur's Death*, ed. L. D. Benson (Exeter: Exeter University Press, 1986), line 3776; death of Gawain, lines 3840–73. Despite the reference to the 'false fostered child', it is not clear that the *Alliterative Morte* tradition identifies Mordred as Arthur's son.

[107] See Walter Delabar, *Erkantiu sippe unt hoch Geselleschaft: Studien zur Funktion des Verwandschaftsverbandes in Wolframs von Eschenbachs* Parzival (Göppingen, 1990), pp. 237–77.

[108] Compare the conflict between the grandsons of Sturla Þórðarson of Hvammr discussed in chapter two.

[109] Wolfram von Eschenbach, *Parzival*, ed. Lachmann, III: 145–6; see also Delabar, *Erkantiu sippe*, pp. 75–132.

[110] K. Bertau, 'Versuch über Verhaltenssemantik von Verwandten im "Parzival"', in K. Bertau, *Wolfram von Eschenbach: Neun Versuche über Subjektivität und Ursprünglichkeii in der Geschichte* (München, 1983), pp. 190–240 (p. 222).

('Mother's brothers are, so to speak, "positive fathers", their sons on the other hand are especially "negative brothers". For in his demand for his inheritance the "son" has to some extent to fear the rivalry of his father's "nephew"').

The closeness of the original sister-son bond is likely to dissipate in succeeding generations and thus cousins find themselves in conflict.

Conclusion

Affines and siblings, brothers and sisters-in-law, wives and husbands all replay the sibling tensions and sibling loyalties of their primary families in their new relationships. Different affinal-sibling patterns emerge in medieval narratives, closely correlating with the age and genre of the texts in which they appear. In heroic and epic material, sisters and wives who are exchanged to ensure peace find themselves at the centre of the alliances' collapse, as innocent or deliberate instigators of breakdown, or as victims of male power-strategies. In other genres, particularly narratives set in urban contexts, continuing closeness after marriage can safeguard a sister's position; her brothers have oversight over the functioning of the marriage and they can act to head off public scandal and private unhappiness. Brothers-in-law, uninhibited by shared childhood and blood, turn readily to murder to recalibrate power differentials between families, while sisters-in-law deploy the most intimate of female secrets in their struggles for supremacy. The worst facets of sisterly and brotherly relationships are played out at an affinal level; men become sexual predators with regard to their wives' sisters or their brothers' wives, and women become embroiled in rivalries which make public intimate, often sexual, secrets. Not all affinal relationships are negative; marriage alliances hold and children are born, recasting siblings in new role as uncles and aunts. These new affective bonds offer hope for future generations, a hope often cruelly dashed in feud contexts, but which flowered in the legend-traditions of great European kings and their sister-sons.

The primary affinal relationship is entered into for reasons of expediency. Sisters are married for political or social gain to men whom their brothers need, but may not necessarily like. Among foster- or sworn-brothers, the men's relationship is primary: the sister or another woman is exchanged only to seal a pre-existing homosocial tie. How fictive siblings negotiate the tensions of siblinghood, whether the willingly contracted sworn-brother bond or the more problematic foster-bond is explored in the next chapter.

8

'Trewethes togider that gun plight': Fictive Siblings

Introduction

Brothers' quest for differentiation leads them to carve out different roles within the family structure and, as chapter two argued, they often thrive best when keeping each other at arm's length. Although brothers-in-law are chosen, rather than acquired by accident of blood, strategic considerations often operate to bring a socially acceptable but not necessarily emotionally congenial affine into the sibling cohort. Nevertheless, although 'the sibling self is the social self', as Juliet Mitchell avers, a friend differs from a brother in crucial ways.[1] In romance especially, when the young man sets out into the world he frequently looks for someone who is like him, but who is not involved in the complex rivalries of the sibling group. Thus he often chooses for himself a kind of double, a sworn-brother who functions as a second self. Driven by an 'urge towards similitude . . . the impulse to pattern the self on the other, and thus generalize "sameness" at the expense of "difference"', as Sarah Kay observes, released from the sibling pressure to differentiate himself from a brother and from the competition for parental affection and inheritance, the young man seeks someone who is just like him.[2] Unlike the twins discussed in chapters two and three, such fictive brothers are often physically similar, even identical to one another. Their external resemblance figures an inner similitude which demands that the men spend their lives together, while, on the level of plot, it frequently facilitates the substitution of one fictive brother for the other.

The most important model for male friendship available to medieval authors was the Ciceronian ideal of *amicitia*, dominant in monastic and intellectual contexts. Cicero insisted that, 'nisi in bonis amicitiam esse non posse' ('friendship cannot exist except among good men'), and that the highest form of friendship, closely allied to virtue, was not driven by hopes of advantage, but by natural inclination: 'a natura . . . potius quam ab indigentia orta amicitia' ('friendship springs rather from nature than from need').[3] Friendship is thus, inevitably,

---

[1] Mitchell, *Siblings*, pp. 36–7.
[2] Kay, *The Chansons de Geste*, p. 145; see also A. Bray, *The Friend* (Chicago, 2003), ch. 1.
[3] All quotations from Marcus Tullius Cicero, *Laelius de amicitia*, ed. C. F. W. Müller (Leipzig, 1884); English translation from *De amicitia*, ed. and trans. W. A. Falconer,

predicated on similarities: 'Verum enim amicum qui intuetur, tamquam exemplar aliquod intuetur sui' ('Again, he who looks upon a true friend, looks, as it were, upon a sort of image of himself').[4] This need not always entail equivalence in terms of social status, for the powerful friend can help the other to rise. Cicero's authoritative discussion chimed with biblical models in medieval thinking about male affective bonds: the friendship of David and Jonathan, between an erstwhile shepherd-boy and a king's son, was frequently adduced as exemplary.[5]

Sworn-brotherhood seems to have been a distinctively Germanic social institution in origin, but later-medieval exploration of the relationship expands into a range of contexts and genres.[6] It occurs in epic, in *chansons de geste* and – predominantly – in romance, its various inflections often genre-dependent. In contradistinction to the 'ennobling love' discussed by C. Stephen Jaeger, and posited within the Ciceronian model, sworn-brotherhood tends to be contracted between parties who are broadly equal; marked disparity in rank and possessions may be a precursor of relationship breakdown.[7] The sworn-brother bond is often doubled by the brother-in-law bond; the *amicitia* between the men is sealed by the giving of a sister. How far homosociality might shade into the homoerotic in the texts considered in this chapter is a moot point; while sworn-brothers do not engage in erotic activity with one another, their mediation of their relationship through one or more women is often problematic, and sometimes markedly 'queer'.[8] Mimetic desire, in Girard's terms, often occurs within both sworn-brother and foster-brother relationships; sworn-brothers generally find strategies which negotiate the complexities of such triangulations, but foster-brother bonds often founder on sexual rivalry.[9]

Loeb Classical Library XX (Cambridge MA, 1923). Cited from Corpus Scriptorum Latinorum; http://www.forumromanum.org/literature/cicero/amic.html#18 and http://penelope.uchicago.edu/Thayer/E/Roman/Texts/Cicero/Laelius_de_Amicitia/home.html. Here quotations from 5.18 and 8.27

[4] Cicero, *Laelius de amicitia*, 7. 23.
[5] See generally on friendship, R. Hyatte, *The Arts of Friendship: The Idealization of Friendship in Medieval and Early Renaissance Literature* (Leiden, 1994), ch. 1 and B. P. McGuire, *Friendship and Community: The Monastic Experience 350–1250* (Kalamazoo, 1988). For David and Jonathan, see P. Dronke, *Poetic Individuality in the Middle Ages: New Departures in Poetry, 1000–1150* (Oxford, 1970), p. 116. See I Samuel 18, where David and Jonathan meet and II Samuel 1 for David's planctus over the dead Jonathan, whose 'love . . . was wonderful, passing the love of women'.
[6] We saw in chapter one an early attestation to sworn-brotherhood in the case of Ealdred and Carl in early-eleventh-century Northumbria. See above, pp. 43–4.
[7] C. S. Jaeger, *Ennobling Love: In Search of a Lost Sensitivity* (Philadelphia, 1999); on the importance of equality between sworn-brothers, see M. Ailes, 'The Medieval Male Couple and the Language of Homosociality', in *Masculinity in Medieval Europe*, ed. D. M. Hadley (London, 1999), pp. 214–37 (p. 221), and in particular the *chanson de geste* of *Daurel et Beton*, discussed below.
[8] See C. Dinshaw, *Getting Medieval*; David Clark explores homosociality and homoerotics in English early-medieval literature in *Between Medieval Men: Male Friendship and Desire in Early Medieval English Literature* (Oxford, 2009).
[9] Girard, *Violence and the Sacred*, pp. 152–78.

Friends bound together by oaths in willingly contracted adult relationships are usually distinguished from foster-brothers who, raised together, do not necessarily escape the tensions of the sibling bond, and do not conform to the general taboo on fratricide: foster-brother conflict is a strong narrative motif where fostering is a prominent social institution. Less frequently encountered in medieval literature are foster-sisters. These women sometimes appear as their foster-brothers' first sexual partner; since they often come from lower social strata they may make unsuitable wives. More rarely, and predominantly in romance, foster cross-sibs succeed in marrying one another, often in the face of opposition from other members of the kin-group. This chapter begins by exploring narratives about foster-brothers, then compares and contrasts the tensions and affections of the sworn-brother relationship, before concluding with an examination of the fortunes of foster-sisters.

The Foster-Brother

Foster-brothers are usually reared together from a very young age, sometimes under a formal legally recognized fostering arrangement, frequent in Iceland and Ireland (see ch. 1, p. 42), sometimes under a less-formal system, as where children are near neighbours and play together in their early years.[10] The close bonds forged by childhood companionship, often reinforced by adults who comment on the boys' affection, differentiates this type of relationship from sworn-brotherhood contracted between men who meet for the first time in young adulthood. Foster-brothers too may swear a formal acknowledgement of their quasi-sibling relationship when they reach the age of reason. In the late Icelandic *fornaldarsaga Hjálmþés saga ok Ǫlvis*, two young foster-brothers, sons of a king and a *jarl* ('earl'), fight each other to a draw in a tournament; the *jarl* demands that they both immediately swear to their foster-brotherhood, 'svá at ykkart vinfengi haldist' ('so that your friendship will last').[11] The earl fears that their childhood affection for one another will founder on rivalry for honour if they do not formalize their obligation to one another. The typical story-patterns in foster-brother narratives polarize around extremes of love and loyalty, and of sudden accesses of extraordinary rage and hatred, very much as in sibling narratives. The Faithless Foster-Brother is a characteristic 'type motif' frequent in medieval Irish and Icelandic narrative; themes of treachery and quasi-incestuous adultery are often explored in such tales.[12]

[10] A. Hansen, 'Representations of Children in Early Icelandic Society' (unpublished PhD. thesis, University of Sydney, 2006), pp. 164–72; see also Hansen, 'Fosterage and Dependency'. See also Parkes, 'Fosterage, Kinship, and Legend'.
[11] *Hjálmþés saga ok Ǫlvis*, in *FSN*, IV: 178–243 (p. 181).
[12] See Motif P273.2 in I. M. Boberg, *Motif-Index of Early Icelandic Literature*, Bibliotheca Arnamagnea 27 (Copenhagen, 1966) and T. P. Cross, *Motif-Index of Early Irish Literature* (Bloomington, 1952).

Fictive Siblings

Medieval Scandinavia made detailed legal provision for fostering. A child would go to live with another family usually of equal status, sometimes indeed with his uncle, from a very young age, and thus would develop strong affective bonds with his foster-parents and siblings who might often be his cousins.[13] Once adult egos are at stake, whether the foster-brothers are racked by sexual jealousy, or competing for authority over a ship's crew, or whether deeper-seated feelings of inferiority and rivalry are involved, in the *Íslendingasögur* the foster-brother relationship sometimes ends with one brother murdering the other. That, as noted earlier, the topos of fratricide is absent in the *Íslendingasögur* may suggest a compensating interest in the rivalrous tensions of the foster-brother bond.[14] Foster-brother murder is strongly deplored; the killer's reputation will suffer if he himself survives the conflict. In *Njáls saga*, as W. I. Miller observes, the reputation of the otherwise well-respected Ásgrímr Elliða-Grímsson was permanently damaged after he killed his foster-brother Gaukr Trandilsson á Stǫng.[15] The circumstances under which this killing occurred were recorded in a saga which has not survived, and thus remain mysterious.

In *Víga-Glúms saga*, two young boys, cousins, are fostered by their grandmother.[16] Arngrímr and Steinólfr are six and four respectively when their grandmother asks a travelling wise-woman about their futures, 'ok spá vel' ('and prophesy well'), she urges.[17] Oddbjǫrg, the seeress, is at first evasive and equivocal, but when provoked by her hostess she admits that she foresees them killing one another, 'þeir munu banaspjót eptir berask' ('later they will bear a death-spear against one another'). As adults the cousins choose separate paths: one farms and one trades. Sexual jealousy precipitates a crisis between them; Arngrímr comes to believe (wrongly in the view of the community) that Steinólfr spends too much time talking to Arngrímr's wife when he comes home from his voyages, and their social relationship is suspended.[18] Later, in an attempt at reconciliation, Steinólfr lodges with Arngrímr once again. Steinólfr refuses an invitation to go with his foster-brother to the nearest port, preferring to stay at home. Arngrímr returns early from the trip; finding his

---

[13] See Hansen, 'Representations of Children', pp. 164–72; Hansen, 'Fosterage and Dependency', pp. 73–81. Vengeance for the foster-brother was considered in law as equivalent to vengeance for the brother by blood: see *Grágás: Codex Regius*, ed. T. Finsen (Copenhagen, 1852), § 90, *Grágás, efter det Arnamagnæanske haandskrift nr. 334 fol., Staðarhólsbók*, ed. T. Finsen (Copenhagen, 1879) § 293 and *Laws of Early Iceland: Grágás, the Codex Regius of Grágás with Material from Other Manuscripts*, ed. A. Dennis, P. Foote and R. Perkins, 2 vols (Winnipeg, 1980–2000), p. 154 ff. For more on the legal status and distinctions of fostering in Iceland, see Miller, 'Choosing the Avenger'.

[14] Miller, *Bloodtaking and Peacemaking*, p. 160.

[15] *Njáls saga*, ed. Einar Ólafur Sveinsson, pp. 72, 371; Miller, *Bloodtaking and Peacemaking*, p. 347, n. 35.

[16] *Víga-Glúms saga*, ed. G. Turville-Petre (Oxford, 1940), p. 21; *Viga-Glums saga*, trans. J. McKinnell (Edinburgh, 1987), pp. 78–80.

[17] *Víga-Glúms saga*, ed. Turville-Petre, p. 21; *Viga-Glums saga*, trans. McKinnell, p. 80.

[18] *Víga-Glúms saga*, ed. Turville-Petre, p. 33; *Viga-Glums saga*, trans. McKinnell, pp. 100–1.

foster-brother mending a little box that belongs to Þórdís, his wife, Arngrímr kills him. Þórdís divorces Arngrímr immediately, prophesies that her former husband will not live long and, no doubt coincidentally, later marries Ásgrímr Elliða-Grímsson, the chieftain whose reputation was tainted by foster-brother killing in *Njáls saga*.[19]

The murder leads to political disquiet in the neighbourhood; an expedition to declare Steinólfr an outlaw (and thus legitimately killed) ends with a pitched battle in which Arngrímr dies. The battle is highly significant in terms of the strategic balance of the district and the subsequent fates of its major figures: the narrative of the foster-brothers is evidently intrinsic to the saga's plot. Although Oddbjǫrg's prophecy is not literally fulfilled, Steinólfr's killing is indeed indirectly responsible for Arngrímr's death. Mutual killing often is difficult to stage within the realist mode of the sagas; the surprise attack by the jealous husband makes it impossible for Steinólfr to defend himself, but Arngrímr and Steinólfr's deaths are causally linked through their divergent alliances with the power factions of the Eyjafjǫrðr valley.

The motif of the murderous foster-brothers is also found in *Fóstbrœðra saga*, probably borrowed from *Víga-Glúms saga*. In this episode, the two boys Eyjólfr and Þorgeirr are brought up together by a widow and they love each other dearly. An old woman in the household prophesies that their affection will not last: 'svá vel sem nú er með ykkr, þá munu þit verst skilja ykkart vinfengi' ('however well you are getting along now, your friendship will end in the worst way').[20] Later in the saga the two foster-brothers, now trading-partners, sail back to Iceland from Norway in bad weather, arriving home late in the season. Despite surviving the perilous sea-crossing, the foster-brothers fall out over where to land. Eyjólfr wants to land immediately when they enter the fjord, Þorgeirr wants to sail further in, closer to where he lives. Exhausted by the journey, the crew vote for immediate landing. Conflict is averted, but during the winter the seeress who had prophesied about them dies; on his way home from her burial Eyjólfr travels past the farm where Þorgeirr is staying. Þorgeirr rushes out to attack his foster-brother; each kills the other and they are buried together. The seeress's prophecy sets up the audience's anticipation of the killings to come; command over the boat and status in the eyes of the crew are the issues at stake. The mutual killing demanded by the prophecy (and the archetype) is made possible by the circumstances of the confrontation: the fight is sought by both parties. Eyjólfr's journey past the farm is a deliberate provocation, for he could have taken a different route home, while Þorgeirr is on the watch for him, anticipating that he will have attended the funeral.[21]

In this saga the apparently incidental history of these two foster-brothers

---

[19] *Víga-Glúms saga*, ed. Turville-Petre, pp. 34–5; *Víga-Glums saga*, trans. McKinnell, pp. 102–3.

[20] *Fóstbrœðra saga* in *Vestfirðinga sögur*, ed. Björn K. Þórólfsson and Guðni Jónsson, ÍF 6 (Reykjavík, 1943), p. 197.

[21] Ibid., pp. 215–16.

is thematically linked to the main plot.[22] The chief foster-brother protagonists of *Fóstbrœðra saga*, Þorgeirr Hávarsson and Þormóðr Kolbrúnarskald grow up together and become sworn-brothers, initiating a formal contract in adulthood.[23] Thereafter, while behaving in ways often considered anti-social by the communities within which they live, they remain comrades through various adventures. As Jenny Jochens notes, since Þormóðr is a poet and seducer, and Þorgeirr is neither given to composing verse nor has any time for women, there is no cause for rivalry in the usual arenas of competition between Icelandic males.[24] There comes a point, however, relatively early in the saga, when Þorgeirr begins to wonder which of the two is stronger, 'hvárr okkarr myndi af ǫðrum bera, ef vit reyndim með okkr?' ('which of us would overcome the other if we tried our strength against each other?')[25] Once the question of comparison has arisen, Þormóðr concludes that their competition will escalate into rivalry and, likely, a fatal quarrel, that their 'friendship will end in the worst way', as the seeress prophesied of the saga's other two foster-brothers. Although Þorgeirr tries to retract his question, it is too late: Þormóðr decrees that they must now go their separate ways. In one version of the saga, Þorgeirr now challenges Þormóðr to ride his horse over a cliff into a snow-drift, a feat which Þormóðr sensibly refuses to attempt. Þorgeirr then kills an innocent passer-by who fails to answer a question that he had not heard. Þorgeirr's exaggeratedly violent reaction suggests that he is acting out the emotional trauma of the coming separation, but it also bears out Þormóðr's realization that his dangerous, even psychotic, companion could turn on him at any moment. The wiser of the two, Þormóðr consequently terminates their companionship, though their emotional bond does not cease with their separation. As Rolf Heller suggests, the other Þorgeirr, discussed above, represents a reduced version of Þorgeirr Hávarsson; the quarrel between the minor saga characters about the landing place is 'im Kleinen eine Frage nach dem Mächtigeren, die zur Entzweiung zwischen den Ziehbrüdern führt' (in little, a question about who is more powerful, that which leads to the separation between the foster-brothers).[26] Jochens concludes, 'it is only by dint of eschewing proximity that Þormóðr and Þorgeirr avoid rivalry in their private world and prolong their friendship to the end of their lives'.[27]

When Þorgeirr is killed in the service of saint Óláfr, the king of Norway, Þormóðr is devastated. He composes a long memorial poem which commemorates his

---

[22] Jónas Kristjánsson, 'Fóstbræðravíg', in *Einarsbók: Afmæliskveðja til Einars Ól. Sveinssonar*, ed. 'some friends' (Reykjavík, 1969), pp. 196–204.
[23] *Fóstbrœðra saga*, ed. Björn K. Þórólfsson and Guðni Jónsson, p. 125. Compare the similar ceremony described in *Gísla saga* and discussed in chapter seven above.
[24] J. Jochens, 'Representations of Skalds in the Sagas 2: Gender Relations', in *Skaldsagas*, ed. Poole, pp. 309–32.
[25] *Fóstbrœðra saga*, ed. Björn K. Þórólfsson and Guðni Jónsson, p. 151.
[26] See Rolf Heller, 'Fóstbrœðra saga und Víga-Glúms saga', *Acta Philologica Scandinavica* 31 (1976), 44–57 (p. 56). Compare *The Sagas of Kormák and the Sworn-Brothers*, trans. L. M. Hollander (Princeton, 1949), pp. 76–7.
[27] Jochens, 'Representations', p. 326.

friend's many feats. Þormóðr's account here of his rift with Þorgeirr is at variance with the prose tradition: the verse blames slander put about by deceitful people for causing strife between them.[28] Þormóðr's vengeance for his foster-brother leads him into dangerous adventures in Greenland, but he succeeds in taking exhaustive revenge on all those involved in Þorgeirr's death, and he too loses his life in the saint-king's service at the battle of Stiklastaðir (1030). Þormóðr instinctively recognized that, even though complementarity had been achieved within the foster-brother dyad, Þorgeirr had not learned to deal effectively with quasi-sibling rivalry by the time that the separation crisis occurred. Þormóðr's decisive abandonment of his foster-brother averts the threat of reciprocal killing; yet powerful emotional ties remain in force. While Þormóðr's poetry offers one plausible social motivation for the friendship's breakdown, the prose evolves a psychological explanation which meshes with the minor foster-brother episode of Þorgeirr and Eyjólfr and with the archetypal saga-pattern of foster-brother murder.

Laxdœla saga offers a nuanced and poignant treatment of two foster-brother cousins who grow up together; the relationship foregrounds the saga's unusual interest in emotion and its modes of expression.[29] Óláfr pá ('peacock') fosters his half-brother Þorleikr's son, in order to assuage Þorleikr's annoyance that his illegitimate half-brother should have inherited from their father. Bolli Þorleiksson thus grows up with Kjartan Óláfsson. Kjartan is outstanding in every respect, while Bolli 'gekk næst Kjartani um allar íþróttir ok atgørvi . . . Þeir unnusk mikit fóstbrœðr' ('was almost as good as Kjartan in all kinds of skills and attributes . . . The foster-brothers loved each other very much').[30] Bolli's slight but marked inferiority with respect to Kjartan's accomplishments will fuel the tragedy. Þuríðr, Kjartan's sister, also loves Bolli dearly: 'hon unni honum eigi minna en brœðrum sínum' ('she loved him no less than her brothers') and she gives him the accursed sword Fótbítr, which she had stolen from her former husband.[31] While the foster-brothers are in Norway, Kjartan wins the favour of King Óláfr Tryggvason. Bolli quietly resents the king for displacing him in Kjartan's affections, a reaction depicted with psychological astuteness.

Bolli's subsequent marriage to Guðrún Ósvífrsdóttir, with whom Kjartan had an understanding, fatally damages the friends' relationship; 'mimetic desire' sunders the bond and produces a monstrous doubling that can only end in quasi-fratricide. Kjartan's unhappiness when he finally returns to Iceland and

---

[28] P. M. Sørenson, 'The Prosimetrum Form 1: Verses as the Voice of the Past', in *Skaldsagas*, ed. Poole, pp.172–90 (p. 176).

[29] Suzanne Kramarz-Bein rightly identifies *Laxdœla saga* as the most 'modern' of the sagas, emphasizing its deployment of 'einer Art "neuen Innerlichkeit", einem neuen Umgang mit Gefühlen und inneren Befindlichkeiten' ('a kind of 'new interiority', a new treatment of feelings and internal sensitivities'); 'Modernität der *Laxdœla saga*', pp. 421–2.

[30] *Laxdœla saga*, ed. Einar Ólafur Sveinsson, p. 77.

[31] Ibid., p. 83. See also chapter three for Þuríðr's comforting of Kjartan when he loses Guðrún.

finds that his foster-brother has married the woman he expected to wed was discussed in chapter three (p. 87–8). Tensions escalate between the households of Guðrún and Bolli, and Kjartan and his wife Hrefna, until finally Guðrún succeeds in stirring up her brothers and the reluctant Bolli to ambush Kjartan. Kjartan repeatedly provokes Bolli in the fight: terming him 'frændi' ('kinsman') he taunts him with their sundered relationship. Finally, Bolli draws Fótbítr and deals Kjartan his death-wound; he dies in Bolli's arms. Kjartan's father Óláfr refrains from revenge and restrains Kjartan's brothers from pursuing Bolli. But once Óláfr is dead Kjartan's brothers go after Bolli, their erstwhile foster-brother. In his last stand Bolli echoes Kjartan's final words to him; calling his foster-brother's brothers his 'brothers', he urges them to attack in the hope of hastening his fate.

Laxdœla saga's portrait of the foster-brother relationship is the most psychologically intimate of the foster- or sworn-brother relationships in the *Íslendingasögur*. Margaret A. Madelung observes how frequently the saga narrator asserts the young men's love for one another: 'the establishment of such togetherness makes the final rift all the deeper. The love and friendship they originally had for one another was not enough to prevent Bolli from sensing his subordinate position.'[32] The marriage precipitates the crisis in the relationship, but the saga is more interested in exploring Guðrún's lingering regret for the match she might have had and her corrosive envy of Kjartan's wife Hrefna than in Bolli's anxious attempts to avert the inevitable showdown. The saga's unusual focus on Guðrún as its central figure, from the moment that she makes her first appearance, diminishes some of the tragedy of the rift between the two foster-brothers. Their alienation from one another is not – as in the case of the brothers in *Víga-Glúms saga* – straightforwardly caused by sexual jealousy over Guðrún; rather it begins with the loosening of the homosocial ties between Kjartan and Bolli when the charismatic King Óláfr enters the scene. It is intensified by Bolli's politicized realization that, in becoming the king's man, Kjartan has compromised his Icelandic identity – and his claim on Iceland's most outstanding woman. Yet Bolli cannot break with Kjartan; he follows him into the Christian religion and he cannot bring himself to sever the relationship between their households, neither before nor after Kjartan's marriage. Even in their dying moments, Kjartan and Bolli acknowledge their emotional history, their profound ties to one another and to their family.

These Icelandic foster-brother narratives share the preoccupations of the fraternal tales discussed in chapters two and four. The usual fraternal jealousies – those stemming from inequalities in political, entrepreneurial or sexual power – also cause trouble between foster-brothers; these inequalities are the more difficult to resolve because fosterlings perceive that they *should* broadly be equal, free from the hierarchy imposed by birth order. Sibling quarrels can be settled through the father or elder brother's authority, but discord between friends is less amenable to regulation by the family. The attempt of one foster-brother to

---

[32] A. M. A. Madelung, *The Laxdœla Saga: Its Structural Patterns* (Chapel Hill NC, 1972), p. 76.

dominate, or to wrest dominance from, the other, often triggered by the most trivial of disagreements, precipitates catastrophe, except where, as in *Fóstbrœðra saga*, the wiser fosterling anticipates and heads off the crisis.

Apart from Irish heroic legend, which reflects the importance of the fostering custom in medieval Ireland, other European literatures recount few tales of foster-brothers. In the French *Mort Artu* (and the Post-Vulgate *Mort*), Mordred kills his foster-brother Sagremor just before he advances against his father; this escalation from regular combat to kin-murder anticipates his ultimate crime of parricide.[33] Mordred's slaying aligns him with Judas Iscariot who, also incestuously born, murders his foster-brother as a prelude to slaying his unrecognized father.[34] In his *Historia regum Britanniae*, Geoffrey of Monmouth depicts Cadwallo, the British king of Gwynedd, and the Anglo-Saxon Edwin of Northumbria as foster-brothers. Edwin is born at the court of Gwynedd where his mother has sought refuge after being exiled by her husband. The two boys are fostered at the court of Salomon of Brittany. On the death of their fathers they return to Britain, 'eam amicitiam quam prius patres illorum exercere coeperunt' ('renewing with each other the friendship which their fathers had enjoyed earlier on').[35] But when Cadwallo refuses to cede Northumbria to Edwin, Edwin rebels and drives him into exile in Ireland. Cadwallo eventually succeeds in assassinating the wizard whose magic keeps Edwin in power, and with the help of his nephew Brian (a more reliable ally than his foster-brother), he is able to defeat and kill Edwin in battle. Cadwallo reigns for forty-eight years and dies of old age. Contemporary historical sources, whether in Anglo-Saxon England or in Wales, know nothing of the kings' joint fostering.[36] The later development of this tradition, which was known to Reginald of Durham as well as to Geoffrey, partly grows out of the certainty that Edwin spent his youth in exile, away from the Northumbria ruled by King Æthelbald. That the Norman historians should envisage Cadwallo and Edwin as two foster-brothers, united not by blood but by shared history, who cannot come to terms over power-sharing and regional autonomy, underlines the strength of the warring foster-brothers topos, and by underscoring the illegitimacy of Anglo-Saxon claims to the British throne, they make a strategic intervention in Angevin political discourse.

---

[33] *La Mort le Roi Artu*, ed. Frappier, pp. 244–5; *L-G*, IV: 354; Mordred's fostering with Sagramor, *La Suite du Roman de Merlin*, ed. Roussineau, I: 59; *L-G*, IV: 384.
[34] As narrated in the *Legenda aurea*, Iacopo da Varazze, *Legenda aurea*, xlv, ed. G.P. Maggioni, 2 vols., 2nd edn (Florence, 1998), vol. 1, p. 279; *The Golden Legend*, trans. W. G. Ryan (Princeton and Oxford, 2012), pp. 167–9. See Archibald, *Incest and the Medieval Imagination*, pp. 108–9; 208–9.
[35] Geoffrey of Monmouth, *The History of the Kings of Britain*, ed. Wright, trans. Reeve, XI.190–201, pp. 262–77 (pp. 262–3).
[36] See *DNB*, s.v. 'Edwin', 'Cadwallon ap Cadfan'.

The Sworn-Brother

The widespread medieval tale of the loving foster- and sworn-brother pair, Amicus and Amelius, is first mentioned in 1090 by Ralph Tortarius, a monk at the abbey of Fleury, who notes that it was a tale 'popular amongst the Gauls and Saxons'.[37] The story was translated into a number of vernaculars. My discussion here focuses on *Amis and Amiloun*, the Middle English version; its earliest preserved manuscript dates from around 1330.[38] Amis and Amiloun are the sons of two barons who live close to one another in Lombardy. Born on the same day, they are so similar that not even their parents could tell them apart. 'By using folk magic (simultaneous conception and birth) and the rhetorical device of treating their childhoods as one, the English redactor prepares the audience subliminally for the unlikely coincidence of looks, and even makes it seem natural and plausible', notes Kathryn Hume.[39] As young men the foster-brothers seek service at the duke's court, where they formalize their affection by swearing a mutual oath:

> That, bothe bi day and bi night,
> In wele and wo, in wrong and right,
> That thai schuld frely fond [strive]
> To hold togider at everi nede,
> In word, in werk, in wille, in dede.[40]

The provisions of the oath, in particular standing by one another in wrong as well as in right, will be severely tested. Amiloun substitutes for his friend in a judicial combat, precipitated by the revelations of a jealous steward (Amis's 'monstrous double').[41] Amis cannot fight on his own behalf as he is forsworn in the matter of his concealed sexual relationship with the duke's daughter. Amiloun's punishment for his corruption of the trial process – leprosy – is cured when Amis sacrifices his children to give his friend a bath of their blood.[42] Since Amiloun's marriage has broken down, he spends the rest of his life with Amis, Amis's wife Belissent and their miraculously restored children. Finally the sworn-brothers enter a monastery, die on the same day and are buried together.

---

[37] For a translation of the Latin version see *Medieval Hagiography: An Anthology*, ed. T. Head (New York and London, 2001), pp. 441–58.
[38] *Amis and Amiloun*, in *Of Love and Chivalry: An Anthology of Middle English Romance*, ed. J. Fellows (London, 1993), pp. 73–145.
[39] *Amis and Amiloun*, ed. Fellows, line 51. See K. Hume, '"Amis and Amiloun" and the Aesthetics of Middle English Romance', *Studies in Philology* 70 (1973), 19–41 (p. 22). Cf. J. C. Ford, 'Contrasting the Identical: Differentiation of the "Indistinguishable" Characters of *Amis and Amiloun*', *Neophilologus* 86 (2002), 311–23.
[40] *Amis and Amiloun*, ed. Fellows, lines 148–53.
[41] Kay, *The Chansons de Geste*, pp. 153–5.
[42] Thus aligning him with Christ and suggesting that his debt to God is paid: Hume, '"Amis and Amiloun"', p. 29.

In the Latin version, more closely affiliated to hagiography, the relationship of the two friends is held up as entirely admirable. Amelius is saintly, while Amicus's wife learns of her children's killing only after their resurrection and the healing miracles. The primary bond of loyalty in this version is sworn-brotherhood: all other ties are unquestioningly subordinated to it. The vernacular versions, in contrast, align themselves more closely with family-oriented, secular values; the sworn-brothers' understanding of their oath as trumping all other relationships, both human and divine, becomes problematic. Amiloun's wife sharply reprimands her husband for impersonating Amis in the combat, 'With wrong and michel unright / Thou slough ther a gentil knight', while an angel warns him of the consequences of swearing deceptive oaths.[43] Amiloun's marriage fails, for his wife will not stand by the marriage vow's promise of constancy 'in wele and for woo' (echoed in the brothers' mutual oath) when he falls ill, while Amis and Belissent joyfully welcome the leper into their home.[44] Belissent's consciousness that her original seduction of Amis is more than a little to blame for Amiloun's plight modifies her reaction to the news that Amis has killed their children. Various moral dilemmas: Amis's loyalty to the duke and to his future wife, Amiloun's eschewing of truthfulness to save his friend's reputation and life, Belissent's pursuit of Amis, Amiloun's wife's uncharitable behaviour, and Amis's murder of his innocent children, with its overtones of the story of Abraham and Isaac, are all weighed against the sworn-brothers' original promise. Although the poem ends by praising their 'trewth and godhede' which has brought them 'the blisse of heven ... to mede', the poem's audience may draw different conclusions as to what kinds of oath should be sworn and how they should be kept.[45] The poem's revitalized model of sworn-brotherhood would prove highly productive in medieval romance across Europe, establishing a secular and vernacular alternative to the classical ideal of Ciceronian *amicitia*, the predominant model for monastic and intellectual close male friendships in Latin writings.[46]

Another romance of sworn-brothers, the late English *Eger and Grime*, takes up *Amis and Amiloun*'s interchangeability trope and uses it both to explore the loyalty entailed by homosocial bonds and to challenge the strict notions of chivalric success in force at the court where they both serve.[47] Two young

---

[43] *Amis and Amiloun*, ed. Fellows, lines 1492–3.
[44] Ibid., lines 11; 149; 155; 296; 372; 1469
[45] Ibid., lines 2494–5.
[46] See Hyatte, *The Arts of Friendship*, ch. 1, and McGuire, *Friendship and Community*, in particular the Introduction.
[47] *Eger and Grime* is referred to in the fifteenth century and was probably composed around 1450, but no medieval manuscripts have survived. It is preserved in the Percy folio (London, British Library, MS Additional 27879) and in three seventeenth- and early-eighteenth-century editions. The Huntington print, used along with the Percy Folio in Caldwell's edition, dates from 1687. See Cooper, *The English Romance in Time*, p. 416. See also p. 82 for Cooper's discussion of the uncanny doublings in *Eger and Grime*.

knights swear brotherhood with one another: 'these Knights Sir Egar & Sir Grime, / they were fellowes good & fine; / they were nothing sib of blood, / but they were sworne Bretheren good'.[48] Eger is a younger son and therefore poor, while Grime has better prospects. Winglaine, the daughter of the earl whom the two knights serve, falls in love with Eger although his poverty makes the match unlikely.[49] Having ventured out to win honour, Eger returns home in a sorry state; he was defeated in battle with a (probably otherworld) champion, the terrifying Gray-Steel, who has severed one of his fingers. Eger's life was saved by lady Loosepine, who nursed him speedily back to health with the aid of magic. Eger is reluctant to tell Winglaine that he has been disgraced; rightly so, for when she overhears Eger's narrative to Grime, she rejects her former beloved. Grime mourns for his friend's plight, 'as any sister, or as brother', and then offers to recuperate his friend's honour by seeking out Graysteel while wearing Eger's armour.[50] Grime's victory over Graysteel wins him Loosepine's love. Eger appropriates Graysteel's horse and golden accoutrements, won for him by Grime, in order to ride publicly into the court and claim to have killed his former foe. Eger gets away with this imposture; after punishing Winglaine for her fickleness, he eventually agrees to marry her, while Grime weds Loosepine.

Eger and Grime makes creative use of a number of the tropes associated with the sworn-brother narrative as exemplified by *Amis and Amiloun*. Sexual intrigue, eavesdropping, substitution for one sworn-brother by another, deception in a matter of honour, and the fickleness of women are all redeployed here. Winglaine combines the roles of the desirable woman who outranks her suitor and the changeable lover, ready to call off her wedding when Eger fails against Graysteel, despite his many other honourable exploits and the regard in which her parents have come to hold him. Like Amiloun's wife, she is punished for her lack of kindness towards the suffering hero, but only briefly, for she remains too good a match to forgo. Her eavesdropping on Eger's story, like that of the false steward in the earlier poem, complicates the love-relationship between one of the heroes and his lady. Eger and Grime are not exactly identical in appearance; Grime is able to masquerade as his friend when leaving and returning to the earl's court only by wearing borrowed armour. The romance makes witty play with the interchangeability motif, for Loosepine immediately sees through Grime's disguise when she pulls off his glove after the battle and notes that, unlike Eger, he has a full complement of fingers. In the Percy version, Grime's victory over

---

[48] *Eger and Grime*, ed. J. R. Caldwell, Harvard Studies in Comparative Literature IX (Cambridge MA, 1933), lines 43–6.
[49] The differential inheritance expectations between the sworn-brothers is also present in *Amis and Amiloun*, where, as Françoise Le Saux notes, Amiloun inherits from his father while Amis makes a hypergamic marriage with the duke's daughter. F. Le Saux, 'From *Ami* to *Amys*: Translation and Adaptation in the Middle English *Amys and Amylion*', in *The Formation of Culture in Medieval Britain: Celtic, Latin and Norman Influences on English Music, Literature, History and Art*, ed. F. Le Saux (Lampeter, 1995), pp. 111–27 (p. 118).
[50] *Eger and Grime*, ed. Caldwell, line 537.

Graysteel remains secret from Winglaine and her kindred, even after his younger brother Pallias has been married off to Graysteel's daughter. In the Huntington print, confession and penance brings a different kind of resolution. After Grime dies, Eger acknowledges who really killed Graysteel and Grime gains deserved, if posthumous, glory. Winglaine then deserts her husband, while Eger makes amends for his deception by going on crusade, returning when his wife is dead to marry Loosepine. Crucially, the sworn-brothers' substitution neither involves formal oath-taking nor judicial combat, while Grime's important role in avenging their own kin-losses at Graysteel's hands is finally made clear to his wife and her family. Any tension between affective quasi-fraternal bonds and the heroes' concealment of the truth is recast as a pragmatic strategy: Eger's considerable heroic value must be theatrically restaged in order to persuade his lady to keep her promises to him, and the imposture is consequently treated as the less reprehensible by the romance's poets. Nevertheless, the Huntington text recognizes a problematic moral dimension to the narrative; as Amis atones by sacrificing his children, Eger too must pay his debt to God, through confession and taking the Cross.

Sworn-brother stories often feature one brother risking his life for the other at the narrative climax, and, just as Eger and Grime conspire to mislead Winglaine, the tales frequently involve the deception of a woman and her family. In a *Decameron* Tale (X.8) set in classical times, a Roman gentleman sends his son Titus to study in Athens.[51] He lodges with a friend of his father's and becomes a fictive brother to the Greek's son, Gisippus:

> una fratellanza e una amicizia sí grande ne nacque tra loro, che mai poi da altro caso che da morte non fu separata: niun di loro aveva né ben né riposo se non tanto quanto erano insieme.
>
> ('such a great brotherhood and friendship grew up between them, that no other case than death would separate them: neither of them felt happy or relaxed unless they were in one another's company.')[52]

Gisippus intends to marry, but when Titus meets his friend's fiancée, he falls desperately in love with her. Once Gisippus weds Sofronia, Titus substitutes for him in the bridal bed; the giving of consent, exchange of rings and consummation in the darkness results in a legal marriage, even though Sofronia remains unaware that the bed-trick has taken place – and indeed is recurring on a nightly basis. Eventually Titus has to return to Rome, so he confesses the stratagem; arguing that 'il legame dell'amistà troppo piú stringa che quel del sangue o del parentado' ('the laws of friendship [are] much stronger than those of blood or of

---

[51] *Decameron* X.3; trans. Waldman, pp. 635–51. The tale has an important analogue in Lydgate's *Fabula Duorum Mercatorum*, and is also retold in Sir Thomas Elyot's 1537 work, *The Gouernor* 2.12, a source for Shakespeare's *Two Gentlemen of Verona*.
[52] *Decameron* X.8, 007.

kinship').[53] His high social standing and rhetorical skill persuade Sofronia and her family to accept the *fait accompli*, but the unfortunate Gisippus is shunned for his part in the deception.[54] At the story's conclusion Titus is able to save his friend's life in a Roman court by claiming falsely that he himself committed the murder with which Gisippus is charged and for which the penalty is crucifixion. The real murderer, moved by the friends' mutual loyalty, confesses and the emperor, also moved, pardons all three of them. The sworn-brothers' nobility, as in the ending of Chaucer's 'Franklin's Tale', triggers equally generous and forgiving behaviour on the part of the magistrate and emperor. Gisippus is taken into Titus's household where Sofronia, at last forgiving, 'il ricevette come fratello' ('received him as a brother').[55] Now Gisippus marries Titus's sister and the two couples live together until death finally separates them. Boccaccio's narrator, Filomena, laments that such friendship is rarely to be seen nowadays: although men have hordes of acquaintances, none would be ready to give up his life, indeed to be crucified, for the love of another.[56]

The sworn-brother theme here harnesses the pull of heterosexual love, masculine readiness to deceive an innocent woman and willingness to die in self-sacrifice for the friend, while physical identicality is reduced to a mere bed-trick.[57] Sofronia makes a virtue of necessity ('fatta della necessità vertù') and reconciles herself to the change of spouse.[58] In Lydgate's analogue, the *Fabula Duorum Mercatorum*, Egypt's fiancée blandly puts up with the trade and lives happily with the substitute husband; here there 'is not the slightest hint at any ethical complications'.[59] Interchangeability, as we have seen, produces considerable anxiety in sibling stories; how far, and under what circumstances can one man really be accepted as the same as another? Titus's rhetoric works to challenge this notion: he asserts Gisippus's wisdom in ceding Sofronia to him, emphasizing his own still gentler birth and the advantages accruing both to the woman and her family. Mimetic desire is managed through renunciation; this in turn short-circuits the metamorphosis of the sworn-brothers into monstrous doubles. In Chaucer's 'Knight's Tale', in contrast, the rivalry of the scarcely distinguishable Palemon and Arcite can only be resolved through the elimination of one sworn-brother. That it is Saturn's fury that brings Arcite down and not the hand of his sworn-brother and that they are reconciled at Arcite's death-

---

[53] *Decameron* X.8, 62.
[54] See Jill Mann's discussion of Titus's arguments in *Feminizing Chaucer* (Cambridge, 2002), p. 164.
[55] *Decameron* X.8, 1087; trans. Waldman, p. 650.
[56] For a full discussion of Titus and Gisippus's *amistà* see Hyatte, *The Arts of Friendship*, pp. 145–61.
[57] Doniger, *The Bedtrick*, especially pp. 216–19.
[58] *Decameron* X.8.89.
[59] R. Stretter, 'Rewriting Perfect Friendship in Chaucer's *Knight's Tale* and Lydgate's *Fabula Duorum Mercatorum*', *Chaucer Review* 37 (2003), 234–52 (pp. 247–8). Stretter argues that, as a monastic writer, Lydgate shapes his version of the story with reference to the monastic ideal of *amicitia* and in conscious distinction to Chaucer's sworn-brothers in 'The Knight's Tale'.

bed, serves to facilitate Emelye's eventual transition between the two men.[60]

Romance understands that chivalry is fundamentally predicated on homosociality, but also that homosocial ties must be be guaranteed by heteronormative marriage arrangments. Otherwise, as Carolyn Dinshaw notes, 'the homosexual potential of bonds between men . . . imperil[s] heterosexual fulfilment.'[61] Sworn-brother relations look, and perhaps are, intrinsically queer; Wendy Doniger adduces the communicating bedrooms of Titus and Gisippus to support her observation that 'the underlying tension between love (lust) for the male friend's girl and love (ostensibly affection, but perhaps also lust) for the male friend pervades this corpus'.[62] Social sworn-brotherhood 'was less explicitly non-sexual than medieval *amicitia*'; in contrast to the monastery where heteronormative relationships are absent, the presence of women in these tales allows the men to express their love more openly.[63] Thus, although the sworn-brothers prove their heterosexuality through marriage (and in the case of Amis, fathering children), the real emotional power of the tales remains 'between men'.[64]

In *Karlamagnús saga*, Rollant and Oliver first meet when ranged on different sides; they are on the verge of fighting in single combat. Oliver's uncle prudently advises him to withdraw from the contest, to become Rollant's friend and to marry his sister Adein to him. The two young men agree to this proposal, and, in the king's presence,

> kystu báðir hann (*sc.* Karlamagnús) ok sórust síðan í brœðralag. Rollant sór ok Adeini, at hann skyldi hana eiga at konu, ef guð gæfi honum líf til.

> ('they both kissed him (*sc.* Karlamagnús) and afterwards swore brotherhood to one another. Rollant also swore to Adein, that he would have her as his wife if God granted him life.')[65]

The Norse text may well be drawing on a sworn-brother relationship originating in its lost French sources, but this understanding of the relationship also chimes strongly with Norse literary tradition. That Rollant should become doubly bound to his friend by betrothal to his sister is, as in *Gísla saga*, a means of strengthening the fictive fraternal bond through an affinal connection.[66] The offer of a sister also obviates sexual rivalry over the woman whose function is to triangulate the sworn-brother bond. Consequently, when the sworn-brothers fall out at Roncevalles, when Rollant finally agrees to blow his olifant to summon

---

[60] Geoffrey Chaucer, 'The Knight's Tale', in *The Riverside Chaucer*, ed. Benson.
[61] Dinshaw, *Getting Medieval*, p. 130.
[62] Doniger, *The Bedtrick*, p. 216.
[63] Stretter, 'Rewriting Perfect Friendship', p. 252, n. 25.
[64] E. K. Sedgwick, *Between Men: English Literature and Male Homosocial Desire* (New York, 1985).
[65] *Karlamagnús saga ok kappa hans*, ed. Unger, pp. 38–9. The spelling of Adein/Auða's name varies throughout the saga.
[66] As discussed in chapter seven.

Fictive Siblings

Charlemagne's reinforcements, Oliver replies in fury, 'Eigi skal þat at mínu ráði, ok þat veit ek vist, ef ek fynda Auðu systur mína, at þú skyldir aldri síðan hvíla á millum armleggja henni' ('Don't do that on my account, and this I know for certain, if I see my sister Auða, you will never afterwards sleep in her arms').[67] Here the saga draws directly on the *Chanson de Roland*: 'Par ceste meie barbe, / Se puis vëeir ma gente sorur Alde, / Ne jerriiez jamais entre sa brace!'('By this beard of mine if it's granted to me to see my noble sister Alde, you will never lie in her arms!').[68] Marianne Ailes notes, 'if we see tenderness in this relationship, it also contains violence – at least of word. When they quarrel it is with virulence.'[69] The sworn-brothers do indeed quarrel like blood-siblings at this moment, yet Rollant's determination to seek vengeance for Oliver as a real brother would – and with the same kinds of oscillation between rage and love – suggests that the sworn-brother bond also comprehends and negotiates the same kinds of ambivalences as real brotherhood. The heteronormative invocation of Auða / Alde at the height of the argument defuses the danger that the homosocial will shade into the homoerotic, but the implication remains that Auða substitutes for her brother as erotic object; it is significant that the sworn-brothers perish before the relationship can be consummated. Alde/Auða herself dies of grief when she learns of Rollant's death.

These two sworn-brothers die fighting side-by-side. Others are not so fortunate, for when two warriors are not linked by kinship they may find themselves on opposing sides in battle. So two of the mightiest heroes of Ireland, Cú Chulainn and Fer Diad, despite an apparently loving shared history, are driven to fight against one another in one of the climactic battles of the *Táin Bó Cúailnge*, recounted in the *Comrac Fir Diad*.[70] Cú Chulainn's opponent, Queen Medb, and her advisors decide to send against him Fer Diad, 'the horn-skinned warrior from Irrus Domann . . . Cúchulain's own ardent and adored foster-brother'.[71] Fer Diad and Cú Chulainn are in fact sworn-brothers, rather than boys who were raised together; they were fellow-students of war with the Scottish warrior-woman Scáthach, and thus Fer Diad knows all the techniques which Cú Chulainn mastered there. Fer Diad does not possess the *gae bolga*, Cú Chulainn's magic torpedo-like spear, but because he has impermeable skin, Medb's councillors think that this will not matter.

---

[67] *Karlamagnús saga*, ed. Unger, p. 517.
[68] *Chanson de Roland*, ed. and trans. J. Dufournet (Paris, 1993), st. 130, lines 1719–21.
[69] Ailes, 'The Medieval Male', p. 219. See also S. Gaunt, *Gender and Genre in Medieval French Literature* (Cambridge, 1995), p. 37: 'It is as if Oliver is always a *potential* enemy to Roland, always a *potential* threat. Their companionship always contains its own *potential* disintegration' (italics in original).
[70] For discussion of the debates over the relative dating of the material in the *Táin*, and of the different recensions and manuscripts, see R. Ó hUiginn, 'The Background and Development of *Táin Bó Cúailnge*', in *Aspects of the Táin*, ed. J. P. Mallory (Belfast, 1992), pp. 29–67. For the complex foster-relationships of Cú Chulainn, both vertical and lateral, see Ó Cathasaigh, 'The Sister's Son', and Parkes, 'Fosterage, Kinship, and Legend', pp. 598–603.
[71] *The Táin*, trans. Kinsella, pp. 168–205.

At first Fer Diad refuses the fight, but when Medb claims untruthfully that Cú Chulainn has disparaged Fer Diad's warrior skills and courage, he falls for her stratagem and agrees to attack his sworn-brother. Cú Chulainn's foster-father Fergus mac Roich warns him who his next opponent is. '"I swear I don't want this meeting," Cúchulain said. "Not because I fear him, but because I love him so much"'.[72] When the two heroes meet in the middle of the ford, Cú Chulainn urges his foster-brother to go home, while Fer Diad reminds Cú Chulainn that when they were Scáthach's students, young Cú Chulainn had served him, 'you fixed my spears and made my bed', a reminder which evokes mutual care-taking rather than Cú's junior status. In his formal verse challenge, Cú Chulainn tempers his words with regret, 'My bosom friend and heart's blood / dear above all, I am going to miss you'. Fer Diad rejects the appeal, 'Forget that we were foster-brothers'.[73] After four days of battle, they are still evenly matched. When Fer Diad stabs Cú Chulainn in the breast with his sword, Cú Chulainn calls for the *gae bolga*. It enters Fer Diad's body through the anus where he is unprotected by his horn-skin and he falls and dies in Cú Chulainn's arms. Traumatized, Cú Chulainn mourns his lost friendship and his dead friend: 'When we were away with Scáthach / learning victory overseas, / it seemed our friendship would remain / unbroken till the day of doom'.[74]

Fer Diad in fact is an eleventh-century addition to the roll-call of warriors in the *Táin*; he does not exist outside the first and second recensions of the text. He is modelled on Ferbaeth and Lóch, earlier combatants against Cú Chulainn, also sworn-brothers and fellow-students of Scáthach. Little is made of the sworn-bond in these earlier episodes and both men quickly fall to Cú Chulainn. In the *Comrac Fir Diad*, the bond between the men is significantly elaborated both in the prose and in the poetry. As Cú Chulainn gazes on his dead friend's body, he expresses both erotic appreciation of his beauty and a tender recollection of their youth in which they shared the same bed.[75] The emotional centre of the episode, and perhaps of this recension of the *Táin*, is in Cú Chulainn's lyrical and highly charged lament for his foster-brother, a man bound to him through sharing extreme experiences in battle: 'Fast friends, forest-companions, / we made one bed and slept one sleep'.[76] His lament harks back, as Ann Dooley notes, to an 'Edenic space of heroic innocence' in which

[72] Ibid., p. 173.
[73] Ibid., p. 186.
[74] Ibid., p. 200.
[75] S. Sheehan, 'Fer Diad De-flowered: Homoerotics and Masculinity in Comrac Fir Diad', in *Ulidia 2: Proceedings of the Second International Conference on the Ulster Cycle of Tales, Maynooth 24–27 June 2005*, ed. R. Ó hUiginn and B. Ó Catháin (Maigh Nuad, 2009), pp. 54–65.
[76] *Táin*, trans. Kinsella, p. 186. Cú Chulainn's tropes are drawn from the language of female mourning, specifically those laments attributed to Cú Chulainn's wife Emer at his death; the language of lament may be gendered female in eleventh-century Ireland. The converse of the situation in Anglo-Saxon England where the laments ascribed to female speakers, such as *The Wife's Lament*, draw on the language of lord-retainer relationships for their emotional effects.

'the heroic twins... with a gendered identity unproblematically bivalent, could enact without anxiety games of mutual deference, heroic play, and heroic love.'[77] The erotic dimension to sworn-brotherhood is foregrounded in this episode; the relationship has been re-imagined, possibly under the influence of classical models (the heroes of the Trojan War were well known in medieval Ireland), or the powerful same-sex friendships warned against in Irish monastic literature.[78] The elaboration of the sworn-brothers' confrontation and the strikingly erotic language of Cú Chulainn's laments suggest that eleventh-century Irish poets were interested in exploring the emotional possibilities of the bond between fellow-warriors, sworn to one another.

The heterosexual allure of Medb's daughter Finnabair, promised to Fer Diad, and her mother's cynical lie that Cú doubted his foster-brother's courage, combine to destroy the homosocial bond. Other primary concomitants of honour culture contribute to Fer Diad's decision: the promise of material reward, the acquisition of reputation, the avoidance of shame, and clan loyalty. Medb and her counsellors argue that, as the son of a king of Connacht, Fer Diad's group-identity is shared with Cú Chulainn's opponents, not with the Ulstermen whose interests Cú is defending.

With the tragic exception of Cú and Fer Diad, the sworn-brothers discussed here found ways to manage incipient rivalries. Their careers end with a rough equality of social status; the triangulation demanded by heterosexual love, including the mimetic desire of one brother for the other's woman, is resolved through self-sacrifice or serial marriage. Yet, despite the best intentions of the men involved, foster- or sworn-brotherhood cannot efface or undo profound inequalities. While the status difference between Amiloun and Amis, and Eger and Grime is significant – Amis's advancement depends on the duke's daughter, Eger is a younger brother with reduced prospects – the divergence in their resources is not particularly marked.

In the probably twelfth-century Occitan romance *Daurel et Beton*, Boves is duke of Antona, while count Gui possesses only a single castle.[79] Boves asks his friend to swear *companhia* ('sworn-brotherhood'), but, as the poet quickly reveals, 'l'us es fizels amicx et l'audre mescrezens' ('one is a faithful friend and the other a traitor'); the disparity in social standing also proves to be a moral disparity.[80] Their fantasy of homosocial unity is maintained for ten years until Boves marries Charlemagne's sister Ermenjart. The introduction of a woman

---

[77] A. Dooley, *Playing the Hero: Reading the Irish Saga* Táin Bó Cúailgne (Toronto, 2006), p. 168.

[78] Dooley, *Playing the Hero*, p. 167; on Trojan comparisons see ÓhUiginn 'The Background and Development', pp. 36–41; on monastic homosociality, see Sheehan, 'Fer Diad De-flowered', pp. 58–9.

[79] *A Critical Edition of the Old Provençal Epic* Daurel et Beton, ed. A. S. Kimmel (Chapel Hill NC, 1971).

[80] F. E. Sinclair, 'The Power of the Gift: Desire and Substitution in *Daurel et Beton*', *Modern Language Review* 99 (2004), 902–219 (p. 903). Cf. also M. Ailes, 'The Medieval Male Couple', p. 291; *Daurel et Beton*, ed. Kimmel, line 30.

into the economy of gift-exchange and mutual obligation disrupts the strong homosocial bonds of feudal service and sworn-brotherly love. Boves's desire for Ermenjart triggers instant mimetic desire in Gui, transforming him covertly into his *companh*'s monstrous double.[81] Gui's attraction to Ermenjart emerges as a symptom of his suppressed rivalrous feelings about his *companh* Boves; 'Rejecting the homosocial bond in favour of heterosexual desire, Gui betrays the masculine brotherhood', comments Sarah Kay.[82] Social ambition is also a powerful component of Gui's desire; he envies the affinal relationship with the emperor which Ermenjart brings to Boves.

On the journey home from the wedding, Gui draws Boves's attention to the new dynamic by asking if he is willing to share his bride as he shares his other possessions; Boves responds jokingly that Gui will have to pray for his death. Eventually after the couple have a son, Gui does indeed murder his *companh*, disguising the deed as a hunting accident. The dying Boves, tendering his forgiveness and offering his heart for Gui to devour, is transformed into a sacrificial victim.[83] Although Ermenjart refuses to accept Gui's account of the 'accident', Gui bribes the emperor, who awards him both Boves's fief and his widow. Ermenjart strongly objects, commenting ironically on the questionable nobility of her brother, 'Que per aver de sa sor fai mercatz' ('who makes a commodity of his sister').[84] The rest of the romance hinges on the fate of Beton, the young son of Boves and Ermenjart, who is protected from his murderous stepfather by Daurel the *jongleur*. Beton grows up in exile; he finally reclaims his fief, rescues his mother and executes all the traitors. The only manuscript breaks off just as the young man is demanding redress from his uncle.

Gui's desire for Ermenjart catalyses the rupture of the *companhia* bond, along with all that possession of the emperor's sister signifies: Charlemagne's favour, and Boves's lands and fief.[85] Also significant, more markedly than in the other sworn-brother stories discussed, is the huge disparity in wealth and status which creates tension between the sworn-brothers; notions of exchange and reciprocity are thrown out of kilter. For Finn Sinclair, what motivates Gui is the hatred of Cain for Abel, the envy which demands the 'fulfilment of a fundamental lack'.[86] Some critics have seen unconscious homoerotic desire present in Gui's conflicted feelings towards his friend: the triangulation of the sworn-brother relationship as precipitating a sexual crisis.[87] Boves's quixotic

---

[81] Kay, *The Chansons de Geste*, pp. 155–7.
[82] Kay, *The Chansons de Geste*, p. 155; Girard, *Violence and the Sacred*, pp. 152–78.
[83] Boves hopes that Gui will ingest love for his little son Daurel if he consumes his heart. See Sinclair, 'The Power of the Gift', p. 910.
[84] *Daurel et Beton*, ed. Kimmel, line 623; lines 639–41. See also Gaunt, *Gender and Genre*, pp. 66–70 on Ermenjart's role as 'diagnostic'; the role of women in *Daurel* is to offer 'surrogate voices for critical impulses within the genre', p. 69.
[85] See Sinclair, 'The Power of the Gift'.
[86] Ibid., p. 906.
[87] S. López Martínez-Morás and G. Pérez Barcala, 'Femmes et espace dans *Daurel et Beton*', *Revue des langues romanes* 104 (2000), 317–36 (p. 319), and J.-C. Huchet, 'Du père

Fictive Siblings

choice of a *companh* who is nowhere near his equal indeed suggests a powerful unacknowledged attraction to his vassal. All the ambivalences capable of destroying the relationship of actual brothers are compounded in this story: economic envy, discrepant political power and mimetic heterosexual desire combine to turn this sworn-brother romance into tragedy.

The Loving Foster-Sister

The loving inseparability of Amis and Amiloun is troped by their physical identicality. So, too, Floire and Blancheflor, the passionate fosterlings whose romance was widely translated across medieval literatures, share a powerful physical resemblance: 'de biauté s'entresambloient', symbolizing that they are destined for one another.[88] Born on the same day, to a Muslim queen and a captive Christian lady-in-waiting, Floire and Blancheflor are reared together. They do not, however, share a wet-nurse, a distinction ascribed to their religious difference. Milk siblings were widely believed to form quasi-sibling bonds; for same-sex siblings the tie was conducive to loyalty and life-long affection, but for cross-sex milk-siblings, the relationship could offer an impediment to marriage.[89] Once weaned, however, the fosterlings share their meals and sleep in the same bed: 'en un lit . . . [elle] les couçoit', circumstances which, as we have seen, are conducive to incest in siblings, but which here encourage the fosterlings' devotion to one another.[90]

Floire's parents, who disapprove of his love for the child of a Christian prisoner, sell Blancheflor to merchants and she is trafficked into the harem of the Emir of Babylon. Floire's quest for his lost love is made considerably easier when other characters know to direct him on Blancheflor's track precisely because he looks so much like her. 'Thou art ilich here of alle thinge / Of semblant . . ., / But thou art a man and she is a maide', notes, in the Middle English version, the lady of the house where both Floris and Blauncheflor stay before they embark ship.[91] Reunited, the lovers make an erotic paradise of Blancheflor's chamber, abandoning all thoughts of escape. When the Emir, surprised by Blancheflor's failure to appear for handmaiden duties, enters the chamber accompanied

---

en littérature', in *Le Moyen Âge dans la modernité: mélanges offerts à Roger Dragonetti*, ed. J. R. Scheidegger (Paris, 1996), pp. 281–98 (p. 283).

[88] *Le Conte de Floire et Blancheflor*, ed. J.-L. Leclanche (Paris, 1980), line 224, p. 24. See also N. J. Lacy, 'The Flowering (and Misreading) of Romance: *Floire et Blancheflor*', *South Central Review* (1992), 19–26 (p. 20).

[89] This is still the case in island Greece, for example; see M. E. Kenna, *Greek Island Life. Fieldwork on Anafi* (Amsterdam, 2001), p. 89, cited from Parkes, 'Fosterage, Kinship, and Legend', p. 591. Parkes notes the continuing significance of milk-kinship in contemporary Islamic societies. See also the discussion of Cú Cuchullain and Derbforgaill below.

[90] *Le Conte de Floire*, ed. Laclanche, line 195.

[91] *Floris and Blancheflour*, ed. E. Kooper (Kalamazoo, 2006), lines 419–21.

by his chamberlain (in the Old Norse version, a squire), they discover the extraordinarily identical couple asleep in one another's arms. Their different genders are revealed by exposing their breasts; the squire seeks to mitigate the Emir's wrath by suggesting, 'Mun hann ekki vera bróðir hennar?' ('Might he not be her brother?') and thus prevents them from being slain immediately.[92] The young people's evident devotion to one another impresses the Emir's barons and finally moves the Emir himself to spare their lives. Floire is baptized and marries Blancheflor; they succeed to Floire's father's kingdom, release her mother from servitude and marry her to a duke.

Differences of status (although Blancheflor's parents are of chivalric rank the child is illegitimate) and of religion matter little to these foster-siblings; their shared childhood intimacy and their similarity of appearance signal that they are intended by fate for one another. Dating from around 1150 in French, the romance is a very early indicator of a nascent understanding of noble marriage as – ideally – involving romantic love and sexual desire, resulting from freely given consent, and encouraging mutual respect and companionability between husband and wife. So, for example, Flores demands that Blaunchefloure be allowed to study alongside him: '"Ne shal not Blancheflour lerne with me? / Ne can y noght to scole goon / Without Blaunchefloure"'; after five years they know 'inowgh . . . of Latyne / And wel wryte on parchemyn'.[93] Flores's insistence points up the realization that educational parity might contribute to a successful marriage; female literacy was becoming desirable for a noble wife who might need to oversee the administration of her husband's estates in his absence.[94]

Although *Floire et Blancheflor* focuses on Floire's feelings for his playmate, other cross-sex foster-sibling tales explore female desire. The French-derived werewolf romance, *William of Palerne*, dating in English probably from the mid-fourteenth century, hinges on the love of Melior, daughter of the emperor of Rome for the foundling William. He is really the king of Apulia's son, saved from his murderous uncle by a werewolf (son of the king of Spain and bewitched by his stepmother). Melior argues long with herself about the wisdom of loving her foster-brother because of his beauty: 'what? fy! schold i a fundeling . for his fairenesse tak? / nay, my wille wol nouȝt a-sent to my wicked hert'.[95] Melior's feelings intensify, and she confides her feelings in her friend Alexandrine, imploring her aid, for, she claims, unless 'ich haue bote of mi bale . . . I am ded as dore-nail'.[96] Alexandrine's magical knowledge allows her to send William a dream in which his foster-sister confesses her love for him and William realizes that he reciprocates it. Alexandrine enables the pair to confess their love to one another, although they must survive many tribulations before they marry.

---

[92] *Flóres saga ok Blankiflúr*, ed. E. Kölbing (Halle a. S, 1896), p. 68.
[93] *Floris and Blancheflour*, ed. Kooper, lines 18–20; lines 33–4.
[94] See C. Larrington, *Women and Writing in Medieval Europe* (London and New York, 1995), pp. 190–2, for a summary of secular women's education.
[95] *William of Palerne*, ed. W. W. Skeat, EETS ES 1 (London, 1867), lines 481–2.
[96] Ibid., lines 627–8.

Fictive Siblings

When William finally succeeds the emperor, he marries his sister Florence to the now disenchanted werewolf Alphons of Spain, while faithful Alexandrine weds Florence's disappointed suitor, Alphons's brother Braundinis. Once the barrier of disparate social rank is removed, the central match can proceed; as in the story of Kudrun (see chapter seven) new alliances are fostered through marriages involving sibling pairs. The contrast between *Floire et Blancheflor*'s acceptance of the social gulf between its two protagonists (although Floire is somewhat handicapped by his pagan beliefs) and *William of Palerne*'s insistence that the foundling must be revealed as royally born marks a change between the twelfth and fourteenth centuries; later romances problematize the possibility of love between those of different social rank, as fosterlings often are.

Expression of desire, even the offering of mild encouragement, on the part of a noble young woman to her potential suitor is culturally problematic. The Knight of the Tour-Landry relates, as a warning to his daughters, his own experience of a young woman who destroyed her prospects of becoming his fiancée by her over-boldness; he strongly deprecates her mild flirtatiousness.[97] Desire is risky then, and women's desire doubly so: Melior's psychologized exploration of her feelings for her foster-brother takes anxious account of his unknown birth; she also fears that he may not reciprocate her feelings, or might think she is mocking him by professing her love. The foster-sister romance is one of the few generic situations in which a woman can express her desire for a young man without fear of immodesty.[98] The familiarity of the beloved, the intimacy and affection which grows up between the young people, as well as William's nascent chivalric reputation, encourage Melior to voice her feelings. Alexandrine's intervention allows the lovers decently to declare themselves to one another; the romance thus takes a sympathetic view of the desiring female while acquitting her of the charge of immodesty.

While fostering could create propitious conditions for a strong, companionable marriage, the proposition that a young man could marry his foster-sister is not always well received. In the French romance *Richars li Biaus*, the hero is illegitimate, begotten through the deflowering of an inebriated princess by a young nobleman.[99] The resulting child is exposed by his royal grandfather, but rescued and fostered by a kindly count. When the countess proposes marrying the clearly well-born young man to their daughter, Richars realizes that his sister is not his sister; hence he must have a family elsewhere. Departing to discover his origins and identity, Richars reunites his parents and succeeds in making a rather better match, winning the hand of the daughter of the king of Montorgueuil and thereby attaining the royal status he could previously claim only through illegitimate and female descent. As noted in chapter six, the discovery that one's

---

[97] Caxton, *The Book of the Knight of the Tower*, ed. Offord, pp. 27–8; cf. Larrington, *Women and Writing*, pp. 30–1.
[98] Compare the *Lai d'Aubépine* in *Lais féeriques des XIIe et XIIIe siècles*, ed. and trans. A. Micha (Paris, 1998), pp. 224–51.
[99] *Richars li Biaus: roman du XIIIe siècle*, ed. A. J. Holden (Paris, 1983).

sister is not in fact a blood-relation is potentially exciting for a young man, but the dispelling of the incest-taboo does not encourage Richars's sexual desire to flourish at the expense of his social ambition. Suggesting that a woman to whom one has easy, unsupervised access may in fact be a potential sexual partner — the converse of the accidental incestuous encounter — could be highly unsettling, but, in this romance whose 'textual economy . . . illlustrates a shift in courtly values from the aristocracy to the bourgeoisie', Richars successfully 'speculates in order to accumulate', cutting his ties with his foster-family after his foster-father has knighted him and given him some useful cash in order to further his social aspirations.[100]

Other southern European romances suggest that fosterling-love can prosper when doubts about social rank are set at rest. In *Decameron* II.8, the count of Antwerp, disguised as a poor man and fleeing the calumnies of the queen of France, is forced to leave his two children to be fostered in different households in Britain.[101] Both children marry within their foster-families. Giannetta's foster-brother Giachetto is permitted to marry his foster-sister only when he succumbs to love-sickness for her and his life is in danger. Brother Perotto, fostered with a field-marshal's family, distinguishes himself in arms. When plague carries off almost all his foster-family, the field-marshal's daughter and heiress becomes free to marry the now well-regarded young man. Finally the queen of France confesses her sins against the count on her deathbed; her son, now king, seeks to make reparation. The count reveals his true identity and that of his children to the two brothers-in-law, Giachetto and Perotto. Giachetto claims the compensation offered by the king of France in lieu of his wife's dowry, and the count and his children are restored to their former rank. As usual when the narrative is triggered by calumny, it takes a generation for the slandered innocent to be vindicated; fortunately the romances between the fosterlings have restored the children's social rank in advance of their father's long-delayed revelation.

This tale is unusual in that the love-sick Giachetto is permitted to marry his beloved long before her true identity is revealed. Giannetta's refusal to countenance any sexual relationship outside marriage, and Giachetto's disgust at his mother's proposal that he should simply seduce his foster-sister makes possible the match. Perotto is able to advance his fortunes and achieve high social rank partly on his own merits, and partly through the social dislocation brought about by the Black Death; it is less likely that Perotto's foster-father would have countenanced the youth's marriage to his daughter, but the orphaned girl can choose for herself. The revelation of his noble parentage is less important to Perotto, the self-made man, than to his sister who can now refute the slurs of her parents-in-law and secure her dowry for her staunchly loving husband. The erotic attraction between the young people is vindicated by the revelation of the unknown child's true rank, but as in *Richars*, the disparity in economic

[100] See C. Jewers, 'C'est li chevaliers au Poisson: *Richars li biaus* as a Model of Speculative Chivalry', *French Studies* 61 (2007), 261–79 (pp. 262 and 261).
[101] Giovanni Boccaccio, *Decameron* II.8.

standing must also be addressed. Thus the tale pragmatically rewards Giachotto for his love and respect for his future wife with the eventual payment of dowry he had been willing to forgo.[102]

In Saxo's *Historia Danorum*, more than one foster-sister falls in love with her foster-brother. Nanna, daughter of King Gevar, falls in love with her highly talented foster-brother Høther and he with her.[103] But Nanna has excited the desire of Balder, the half-supernatural son of Odin, who has seen her bathing; the rivalry of the two heroes eventually brings about the death first of Balder, then of Høther at the hands of Balder's brother, Bo.[104] Elsewhere in Saxo, the hero's first sexual relationship is with a young woman he has known from childhood; often the woman makes the first overtures. Gram, son of Skjǫld, the progenitor of the Skjǫldung dynasty, 'educatoris sui Roari filiam coaevam sibi collactaneamque, quo maiorem incunabilis gratiam referret, uxorem ascivit' ('to show a fuller gratitude for his fostering ... took to wife his teacher Roar's daughter, who was of the same age and had been nourished at the same breast').[105] The foster-sister, a *collactanea* or milk-sister, is only temporarily suitable as a partner; she is soon married off to Bess, a close associate of Gram, when a better match becomes possible for the prince. As implied in the tale of Floire and Blancheflor above, a *collactanea* would likely have been subject to certain taboos; the sharing of milk creates a fictive relationship which intersects with incest prohibitions.

Gram's sons are fostered by giants; one, Hadingus, is cajoled by his giant foster-sister Harthgrepa into a sexual relationship after she reminds him that he was obliged to her for the gift of his first rattle.[106] Harthgrepa accompanies her fosterling-lover back to Denmark and helps him during a supernatural attack. Her fellow-giants regard her as having betrayed her race through her sexual relationship with the human hero and kill her, conveniently freeing Hadingus to wed a human princess. Early experimental liaisons with the foster-sister tend not to last, for the hero's future lies beyond his childhood home and so the first sexual partner is abandoned in favour of an exogamic, more socially advantageous alliance. Showing exceptional solidarity with her foster-brother, Amleth's nameless foster-sister has a consensual and rather acrobatic sexual encounter (apparently not their first) with Amleth when he is pretending to be insane.[107] Amleth's enemies have calculated that willingness to have sex would prove that Amleth is not mad at all. By dint of sending a horsefly with a straw tucked under its tail towards Amleth, his foster-brother alerts him to treachery. Amleth's metaphorical cast of mind allows him to intuit the hidden

---

[102] Compare *Decameron* V.7 in which a fosterling romance resulting in pregnancy eschews a tragic ending borrowed from the story of Canace and Machaire by the revelation that the slave-born father of the child is the kidnapped son of an Armenian noble.
[103] Saxo, *GD*, III; Saxo, *HD*, pp. 69–75.
[104] See chapter two, pp. 108–9 for other mythic reflexes of the story.
[105] Saxo, *GD* I.4.1; Saxo, *HD*, p. 16.
[106] Saxo, *GD* I.5.1–6.6 ; Saxo, *HD*, pp. 21–4.
[107] Saxo, *GD* III.6.10–11; Saxo, *HD*, pp. 85–6. The foster-sister is of course the model for Ophelia.

import, so he carries his foster-sister off to a private place where they can have intercourse unwitnessed. He also contrives to complete the sexual encounter while resting on a colt's foot, a cock's comb and a piece of roof. When he later recounts this circumstance it is thought to be confirmatory evidence of his madness. Amleth begs his foster-sister to keep his secret; although the sexual liaison does not continue both foster-siblings remain loyal to him in his vendetta against his uncle.

The similarities between the foster-sister, the *collactanea* and the blood-sister, and the implications of the *collactanea* bond as creating a potential sexual taboo, underlie a story about Cú Chulainn, likely dating from the tenth century.[108] The hero is able to escape an obligation to Derbforgaill, the daughter of Ruad, king of Norway (Lochlann) by initiating a fictive sibling relationship with her. In one version of *Tochmarc Emire*, Cú Chulainn rescues Derbforgaill from being sacrificed by the Fomori, a tribe of otherworld beings.[109] Ruad offers Cú Chulainn his daughter, but he puts off the matter. A year later he and his friend Lugaid are walking by the sea when two birds fly up. Cú Chulainn aims a stone from his sling at one of the birds and hits it; the injured creature reveals herself to be Derbforgaill, come with her handmaid in bird-form to seek him. Cú Chulainn sucks the stone and a surrounding clot of blood out of the wound, and swiftly declares that because he has drunk the girl's blood he cannot marry her. Instead, she may wed his companion, Lugaid, sometime represented as his foster-son, and Derbforgaill consents.[110]

Cú's apparently healing action – undoing a wound which he himself inflicted – seems to induct Derbforgaill into a taboo relationship. Ingridsdotter discusses the connections between blood and incest, but comes to no definite conclusion about how the blood-sucking might render Derbforgaill unmarriageable. Since medieval physiological theory holds that milk is transformed blood, a process which only women can effect, Cú's drinking of Derbforgaill's blood transforms her into a milk-sister; that she could be converted into a *blood*-sibling, analogous to a blood-brother, seems ruled out by the failure to *exchange* substances.[111] The milk relationship, which as Parkes shows, converts men into fictive brothers in early Ireland, probably entails an incest prohibition between cross-sex milk-sibs.[112] Cú Chulainn's quick thinking neatly reverses the loving foster-sister motif; it releases him from an undesired relationship with Derbforgaill without offending her father.

---

[108] See the review of dating evidence in K. Ingridsdotter, '*Aided Debforgaill*: A Critical Edition with Introduction, Translation and Textual Notes', Ph.D. dissertation, Celtic Section, University of Uppsala, June 2009, pp. 64–7.

[109] The tale is recounted in two texts: *Aided Derbforgaill* and *Tochmarc Emire*. C. Marstrander, 'The Deaths of Lugaid and Derbforgaill', *Ériu* 5 (1911), 201–18; *Tochmarc Emire* in *Compert Con Culainn*, ed. van Hamel, ¶ 84; K. Meyer, trans. 'The Wooing of Emer', *Archaeological Review* 1 (1888), 68–75; 150–5; 231–5; 298–307 (pp. 304–5).

[110] Ingridsdotter, *Aided Debforgaill*, pp. 22–4.

[111] J. C. Hodges, 'The Blood Covenant among the Celts', *Revue celtique* 44 (1927), 109–53.

[112] Parkes, 'Fosterage, Kinship, and Legend'.

Conclusion

For nuanced exploration of the complexities of sameness and difference, of identity, homosocial bonding and erotic love between equals, genres such as romance and saga turn to narratives of the fictive sibling. The genres probe some of the tensions of family dynamics by displacing them into relationships with fictive brothers. Foster-brothers are as capable – because of the quasi-sibling ambivalences generated through their shared childhoods – as full or half brothers, of astonishing rivalry and hatred, as well as powerful loyalty, imitating the extremes of siblinghood in their behavioural and emotional interaction. Foster-brother resentment flares up in moments of adult fury; their ingratitude becomes a folk-tale stereotype, suggesting a folk-psychological recognition of a strongly sibling-inflected rage. As with other tales of fraternal rage, sexual jealousy, envy of power or wealth, or the most trivial of slights, can catalyse the sundering of the foster-relationship.

Sworn-brother ties seem more durable; the adult decision to enter into or redefine the relationship on a formal basis enables the forging of powerful homosocial obligations, and the affective bond is underpinned by a publicly taken oath. Although it is tested by the heteronormative demands of marriage and children, the sworn-brother relationship is consistently imagined as outweighing other obligations. Lasting sworn-brother love requires roughly equal social status, or at least no larger a discrepancy in fortune than might characterize real brothers. Where the disparity is too great, the relationship can break down, rupture once again precipitated by sexual jealousy or envy. The triangulation of the sworn-brother bond through the heterosexual imperative can stir Girard's 'mimetic desire', potentially turning the sworn-brothers into 'monstrous doubles', unless the situation is resolved through renunciation, reciprocal sacrifice, or the doubling of the desired object so that both men can have the woman they want. The queer potential of the sworn-brother relationship is either earthed by the heteronormative, or is erased through violence on the beloved's body, whether at the sworn-brother's hand or executed by another agent. Whether or not it is triangulated by a woman, the sworn-brother bond offers a freely negotiated lateral relationship that generally circumvents the ingrained tensions and obligations of siblinghood.

Cross-sex foster siblings bring acknowledged sexual possibilities, whether reciprocated or not, to their relationships as young adults. If the difficulties of disparate rank or religious affiliation can be overcome, successful marriage follows. But if the disparity is too great, foster-sister desire will not translate into marriage, though an unofficial sexual liaison may be embarked upon. The canny hero knows that he can do better for himself through an exo- and hypergamic alliance, rather than contenting himself with an available girl within his family. Saxo's Danish heroes nevertheless take the sexual and emotional loyalty of their foster-sisters for granted and they are useful allies in their foster-brother's struggles for self-determination.

Fosterling stories are staples of societies where fostering is an important social practice, in Iceland and the Celtic countries, and they offer good opportunities to reflect on quasi-fraternal relations; other cultures and other genres focus rather on sworn-brother relations as representative of male friendship bonds and as models for ideal fraternity. All adults have to negotiate their peer relations, to weigh them against all kinds of other demands on a man's loyalty, even those made by God. Yet the relationship is an enduringly successful one: the stories considered in this chapter indicate how fictive siblings are integrated into a complete ethic of social and emotional lateral relationships in the medieval imagination.

CONCLUSION

Unofficial, popular or folk theories of sibling psychologies and how these relate to children and to adults have become assimilated into our thinking about family relationships in the West in the twenty-first century. Although Freud sheered away from close analysis of the sibling bond, he formulated the insight that, in the case of siblings: 'an intimate friend and a hostile enemy' 'come together in a single individual'.[1] Freud's observation lacks nuance of course; he takes little account of how sibling relationships are conditioned by gender, by birth order, and by varying socio-historical factors, but his identification of the ambivalences of siblinghood is acute. Psychologists, particularly those who have conducted lifespan investigations into sibling relationships, have thickened and complicated our perceptions of sibling, affine and fictive sibling relationships. The work of developmental and cross-cultural psychologists, along with the close focus Juliet Mitchell brings to her psychoanalytical framing of sibling questions, has provided new theoretical bases for considering the relationship, even if the outcome of these analyses is generally to confirm the unofficial beliefs we hold about the bond. We recognize these ambivalences from our own childhood sibling experiences, and that these formative experiences inflect our relationships with our peers, with our friends, and, very particularly, with our in-laws.

But can we project modern sibling theory back a millennium to explain the sibling dynamics in medieval culture? I argue that the answer is a qualified yes. Siblings are born into a family usually consisting of two parents, and although medieval families were prone to disruption – through high mortality rates for parents and children, through the acquisition of half-, step-, adopted and foster-sibs – so too are modern Western families, through separation, divorce, remarriage, fostering, adoption and other, less formal, processes. The historical realities for siblings between 500 and 1500 were extremely various, as various as those today, but the essential parameters of brothers' and sisters' feelings for one another: of love, of hatred, of loyalty and rivalry remain unchanged.

The social conditions under which those dynamics find particular expression were of course very different in the medieval period. Children lost their parents and siblings very young, they might be forced into the labour market while not yet adolescent, or be trained up for particular vocations with little consultation as to individual wishes. Young men and women might find themselves obliged to marry spouses whom they had not chosen for themselves – or be forbidden, or unable, to marry at all. Some siblings would expect a sizeable portion of parental assets as dowry or inheritance, others would get nothing. Distance and communications difficulties would separate some brothers and sisters,

---

[1] Freud, *On the Interpretation of Dreams*, p. 483.

while others would find that their siblings were too close for comfort, living in the same house, or just around the corner. Concepts of gender and social rank, the significance of country of birth and residence, the impact of different legal systems, and the century in which people lived all had very distinct effects on lateral relationships. Chapter one laid out, over a broad geographical area and long time-span, some of the highly varied facets of siblinghood as lived experience, showing how, in their investigations of sibling micro-narratives, historians are drilling down into the implications of brother–sister and affinal interactions.

Exploration of sibling themes across the many kinds of writing from medieval Europe, from Spain to Iceland, from Constantinople to Ireland, confirm the intuition that sibling dynamics remain broadly constant. They are, fundamentally, as the mother quoted by Judy Dunn observed, 'all about love and hate', whether the love that drives a brother to the ends of the known world to avenge his half-brother, or the hatred that causes a sister to thrust a flaming brand into her brother's mouth to see if he is dead yet.[2] Nevertheless, sibling behaviours, interactions, and sibling emotion are of course inflected, even produced, by circumstance and context. Sibling crises, giving rise to dramatic or emblematic situations, show a surprising continuity with the crisis points for brothers and sisters in modern families. Sibling marriage – how much do the parents give the child when it weds? How does the new spouse get on with the family? The parents' death – who inherits? How is the estate apportioned? What are the prospects for the younger children? Siblings' children – how do uncles and aunts relate to their maternal and paternal nephews and nieces? All these questions are as current today as they were in the medieval period. Anxieties about interchangeability and loss of identity, familiar to therapists and psychoanalysts, underpin medieval texts, while strategies to achieve differentiation and individuality play out across different medieval genres. Although, as Juliet Mitchell suggests, siblings may be 'the personnel of postmodernism with its focus on sameness and difference, its concern with time present rather than time past', that very focus on sameness and difference is a constant in the constitution of sibling identity and the catalyst for sibling dramas in medieval as in modern narratives.[3]

Love and loyalty are the most highly esteemed sibling emotions in the medieval imagination. The texts interrogated in this book have unpacked how brothers, in particular, must learn to manage their rivalry, to avoid competing directly for thrones, estates, businesses, and wives. Taking separate paths, developing identities which complement one another sustains a fraternity best. Sisters are also highly supportive of one another, though their usual fate, to marry and to move to a new household, lessens the possibility of conflict, except at the crisis point of finding a husband. Sisters, particularly older ones, nurture and care for their brothers, pursuing vengeance for them and zealously

[2] Dunn and Kendrick, ed., *Siblings*, p. 208
[3] Mitchell, *Siblings*, p. 31.

maintaining their reputations, wielding a post-mortem power over their brothers which they could not exercise in life. Brothers' concern for sisters tends to be subordinated to larger questions of family honour and advantage, rather than taking account of the woman's own happiness or sense of agency. The absolute importance of homosocial ties relegates women's subjectivities to an inferior status.

'Waxing and waning, the relationship between siblings peaks at times of stress and change', note Banks and Kahn.[4] Conflict, rivalry and hatred are exacerbated when there is a clear sense of unjust parental favouritism, or where resources are scarce. When there is only one throne, one suitor, or, curiously, one mule-bridle, the less-favoured brother or sister acts out the rage and hostility always inherent in the relationship. And the brother who de-identifies, who rejects the values of the fraternal cohort to go his own way, is likely to face extreme hostility, to become the 'monstrous double' who must be eliminated. Sisters will fall out, like their brothers, when sexual rivalry, social status or material possessions are at stake; rivalry over their children's prospects is also a key domain in sisterly conflict. Incest occurs relatively infrequently in medieval literature, though the circumstances in which it occurs square to some degree with the warnings of contemporary moralists. Insufficient parental discipline, or being orphaned and thrown together under traumatic circumstances, can be triggers for deliberate incest, usually initiated by the brother. Casual sexual encounters outside but not too far from the home produce inadvertent incest, as the returning brother, glorying in his new adult status, proves unable to manage re-assimilation into a changed family group. If the incest can be concealed and its product incorporated into the kindred as a sister-son, the child may be heroic and remarkable – though he will not produce children of his own. There is no future in his line, for an ancestor born from incest is not a desirable one.

When the sibling marries, the opportunity for recalibrating lateral relationships to include the affines can produce strong alliances, successful unions, and children who seal the connection between the families. More often in literary texts, however, brothers and brothers-in-law act out the fratricidal fantasies which are powerfully tabooed in medieval culture. Homosocial bonds are forged and broken; sisters and sisters-in-law are both victims and villains, offering an alternative perspective on, a counter-narrative to, epic and courtly versions of masculinity. Such sibling complexities can be eschewed in favour of the sworn-brother, freely chosen, a kind of brother whose similarity does not disturb his friend's sense of identity, and who is not a rival for parental resources. The emotional primacy of the homosocial bond is foregrounded in these narratives; the introduction of a woman as the guarantor of heteronormative desire in the men complicates the main relationship. Ceding the woman to the sworn-brother, marrying his sister, but remaining faithful to him until death separates the companions demonstrates one way of escaping fraternal obligations and rivalries: by finding a better-than-brother and cleaving to him. The foster-sibling

[4] Bank and Kahn, *The Sibling Bond*, p. 16.

is poised on a dangerous borderline between sameness and difference; a rival, a potential lover, a loyal friend, or a murderer, the fosterling relationship magnifies many of the tensions inherent in the sibling bond.

Sibling tales have proved how good they are to think with. Beyond their supple evocations of family dynamics in myriad forms, they invite exploration of larger themes. The systemic nature of feud, the toll exacted by vengeance cultures; definitions of sexual honour; thinking about love and desire, crucial questions which map gender relations; the equitable or efficient transmission of resources across generations; nascent ideas about commonality, democracy, political authority and its exercise: all these questions have been foregrounded in the sibling stories considered in this book.

BIBLIOGRAPHY

Primary Texts

Abelard, Peter, *Ethics*, ed. and trans. D. Luscombe (Oxford, 1971)
'*Aided Debforgaill*: A Critical Edition with Introduction, Translation and Textual Notes', K. Ingridsdotter, Ph.D. dissertation, Celtic Section, University of Uppsala, 2009
Aided Debforgaill, in 'The Deaths of Lugaid and Derbforgaill', ed. C. Marstrander, *Ériu* 5 (1911), 201–18
Aided Óenfir Aífe, in *Compert Con Culainn*, ed. A. G. van Hamel, pp. 9–15
'La mort du fils unique d'Aífe', trans. C.-J. Guyonvarc'h, *Ogam* 9 (1957), 115–21
'Amicus and Amelius', in *Medieval Hagiography: An Anthology*, ed. T. Head (New York and London, 2001)
'Amis and Amiloun', in *Of Love and Chivalry: An Anthology of Middle English Romance*, ed. J. Fellows (London, 1993), pp. 73–145
Aquinas, Thomas, *Summa Theologiae*: http://www.corpusthomisticum.org/iopera.html
Aquinas, Thomas, *Summa Theologiae*, trans.: http://www.newadvent.org/summa/
Asser, *Alfred the Great: Asser's Life of King Alfred and Other Contemporary Sources*, ed. and trans. S. Keynes and M. Lapidge (Harmondsworth, 1984)
Augustine, *De civitate Dei*: http://www.thelatinlibrary.com/august/html
Ásmundar saga kappabana, in *FSN*, ed. Guðni Jónsson, I: 383–408
Bede, *Bede's Ecclesiastical History of the English People*, ed. and trans. B. Colgrave and R. A. B. Mynors (Oxford, 1969)
Klaeber's Beowulf and the Fight at Finnesburh, ed. R. D. Fulk, R. Bjork and J. D. Niles (Toronto, 2008)
Benoît de Ste Maure, *Roman de Thèbes*, 2 vols, ed. L. Constans (Paris, 1890)
Bevers saga, ed. C. Sanders (Reykjavík, 2001)
Bevis of Hamptoun, in *Four Romances of England*, ed. R. B. Herzman, G. Drake and E. Salisbury (Kalamazoo, 1999)
Boccaccio, Giovanni, *Decameron*, (based on V. Branca's 1992 edition): http://www.brown.edu/Departments/Italian_Studies/dweb/texts/
——, *Decameron*, trans. G. Waldman (Oxford, 1993)
'Branwen uerch Lyr', in *Pedeir Keinc y Mabinogi*, ed. Williams, pp. 29–48
'Branwen, daughter of Llŷr', in *The Mabinogi*, trans. Ford, pp. 57–72
Brennu-Njáls saga, ed. Einar Ólafur Sveinsson, ÍF 12 (Reykjavík, 1954)
Caesarius of Heisterbach, *The Dialogue on Miracles*, ed. H. von E. Scott and C. C. S. Bland, 2 vols (London, 1929)
Caxton, William, *The Book of the Knight of the Tower*, ed. M. Y. Offord, EETS ss 2 (Oxford, 1971)
La Chanson de Roland, ed. and trans. J. Dufournet (Paris, 1993)

Chaucer, Geoffrey, *The Canterbury Tales*, in *The Riverside Chaucer*, ed. L. D. Benson (Oxford, 1988)
The Chester Mystery Cycle, ed. R. M. Lumiansky and D. Mills, 2 vols, EETS ss 3, 9 (Oxford, 1974, repr. 1986)
Chrétien de Troyes, *Romans*, gen. ed. M. Zink (Paris, 1994)
——, *Le Conte del Graal*, ed. C. Méla, in *Romans*, gen. ed. Zink
——, *Perceval: The Story of the Grail*, in *Arthurian Romances*, trans. D. D. R. Owen (London, 1993)
——, *Le Chevalier au Lion*, ed. D. Hult, in *Romans*, gen. ed. Zink
——, *Philomena*, ed. C. de Boer, trans. O. Collet, in *Romans*, gen. ed. Zink
Cicero, Marcus Tullius, *Laelius de amicitia*, ed. C. F. W. Müller (Leipzig, 1884)
——, *De amicitia*, ed. and trans. W. A. Falconer, Loeb Classical Library XX (Cambridge MA, 1923)
Compert Con Culainn and other stories, ed. A.G. van Hamel, Mediaeval and Modern Irish Series, III (Dublin, 1933)
'La conception de Cúchulainn', trans. C.-J. Guyonvarc'h, *Ogam* 17 (1965), pp. 363–91
Coudrette, *Le roman de Mélusine ou Histoire de Lusignan*, ed. E. Roach (Paris, 1982)
——, *Le roman de Mélusine*, trans. L. Harf-Lancner (Paris, 1993)
Die Crescentialegende in der deutschen Dichtung des Mittelalters, ed. K. Baasch (Stuttgart, 1968)
Dante Alighieri, *Commedia*: http://www.danteonline.it/italiano/opere.asp?idope=1&idlang=OR
Dante, *L'Inferno*, ed. and trans. J. D. Sinclair (New York, 1939, repr. 1981)
A Critical Edition of the Old Provençal Epic Daurel et Beton, ed. A. S. Kimmel (Chapel Hill NC, 1971)
'De Obsessione Dunelmi', in Symeonis Monachi, *Opera Omnia*, ed. T. Arnold, Rolls Series 75, 2 vols (London, 1882–5), I, 215–20
Dictionary of Medieval Latin from British Sources (Oxford, 1975–2013)
Edda: Die Lieder des Codex Regius, ed. G. Neckel and H. Kuhn, 4th edn (Heidelberg, 1962)
The Poetic Edda: Volume I, Heroic Poems, ed. U. Dronke (Oxford, 1969)
The Poetic Edda, trans. C. Larrington (Oxford, 2014)
Eger and Grime, ed. J. R. Caldwell. Harvard Studies in Comparative Literature IX (Cambridge MA, 1933)
Egils saga Skalla-Grímssonar, ed. Sigurður Nordal, ÍF 2 (Reykjavík, 1933)
Egils saga, trans. C. Fell (London, 1993)
English and Scottish Popular Ballads, ed. F. J. Child, 5 vols (New York, 1884)
Erec: Roman arthurien en prose, ed. C. Pickford, 2nd edn (Geneva and Paris, 1968)
Eyrbyggja saga, ed. Matthías Þorðarson, ÍF 4 (Reykjavík, 1935)
Felix's Life of Saint Guthlac, ed. and trans. B. Colgrave (Cambridge, 1985)
Le Conte de Floire et Blancheflor, ed. J.-L. Leclanche (Paris, 1980)
Florence de Rome: chanson d'aventure du premier quart du XIIIe siècle, ed. A. Wallensköld, 2 vols, SATF (Paris, 1907–9)
Le Bone Florence of Rome, ed. C. F. Heffernan (Manchester, 1976)
Flóres saga ok Blankiflúr, ed. E. Kölbing (Halle a. S, 1896)
Floris and Blancheflour, ed. E. Kooper (Kalamazoo, 2006)
La Folie Lancelot: A Hitherto Unidentifed Portion of the Suite de Merlin Contained in MSS B. N. fr. 112 and 12599, ed. F. Bogdanow, Beihefte zur Zeitschrift für romanische Philologie 109 (Tübingen, 1965)

Bibliography

Fornaldarsögur Norðurlanda, ed. Guðni Jónsson, 4 vols (Reykjavík, 1954)
Fóstbrœðra saga, in *Vestfirðinga sögur*, ed. Björn K. Þórólfsson and Guðni Jónsson, ÍF 6 (Reykjavík, 1953)
The Sagas of Kormák and the Sworn-Brothers, trans. L. M. Hollander (Princeton, 1949)
Freud, Sigmund, *On the Interpretation of Dreams*, trans. J. Strachey, Standard Edition vols 4 and 5 (London, 1953)
The Complete Letters of Sigmund Freud to Wilhelm Fliess 1887–1904, ed. and trans. J. F. Masson (Cambridge MA, 1985)
Froissart, Jean, *Chronicles*, trans. G. Brereton (Harmondsworth, 1978)
The Tale of Gamelyn, in *Robin Hood and Other Outlaw Tales*, ed. S. Knight and T. H. Ohlgren (Kalamazoo, 1997)
Geoffrey of Monmouth, *The History of the Kings of Britain: An Edition and Translation of* De gestis Britonum, ed. N. Wright, trans. M. D. Reeve (Woodbridge, 2007)
——, *Vita Merlini / Life of Merlin*, ed. and trans. B. Clarke (Cardiff, 1973)
Gerald of Wales, *Opera*, ed. J. S. Brewer, J. F. Dimock *et al.*, 8 vols, *Topographia Hibernica*, III, ed. J. F. Dimock (London, 1867)
Gesta Romanorum: or Entertaining Moral Stories, trans. C. Swann (London, 1824)
Early English Versions of the Gesta Romanorum, ed. S. J. H. Herrtage (London, 1879), http://name.umdl.umich.edu/Grom.
Giovanni di Pagolo Morelli, *Ricordi*, in *Mercanti scrittori*, ed. V. Branca (Milan, 1986)
Gísla saga Súrssonar, in *Vestfirðinga sögur*, ed. Björn K. Þórólfsson and Guðni Jónsson, ÍF 7 (Reykjavík, 1953)
Gower, John, *Confessio Amantis*, ed. R. A. Peck *et al.*, 3 vols (Kalamazoo, 2003)
Gregory of Tours, *Life of the Fathers*, trans. E. James, 2nd edn (Liverpool, 1991)
Grettis saga Ásmundarsonar, Bandamanna saga, Odds Þáttr Ófeigssonar, ed. Guðni Jónsson, ÍF 7 (Reykjavík, 1936)
Grimm, J. and W., *Kinder- und Hausmärchen: Jubiläums-Ausgabe*, 3 vols, ed. H. Rölleke (Stuttgart, 1982)
The Complete Fairy Tales of the Brothers Grimm, 3rd edn, trans. J. Zipes (New York, Toronto, London, 1992)
Grágás efter det Arnamagnæanske haandskrift nr. 334 fol., Staðarhólsbók, ed. T. Finsen (Copenhagen, 1879)
Laws of Early Iceland: Grágás, the Codex Regius of Grágás with Material from Other Manuscripts, ed. A. Dennis, P. Foote and R. Perkins, 2 vols (Winnipeg, 1980–2000)
Guibert de Nogent, *Autobiographie*, ed. and trans. E. R. Labande (Paris, 1981)
The Guthlac Poems of the Exeter Book, ed. J. Roberts (Oxford, 1979)
Hartmann von Aue, *Gregorius, Der Arme Heinrich und Iwein*, ed. and trans. V. Mertens (Frankfurt-am-Main, 2004)
——, *Arthurian Romances, Tales and Lyric Poetry: The Complete Works of Hartmann von Aue*, trans. F. Tobin, K. Vivian, and R. Lawson (University Park PA, 2001)
——, *German Romance III: Iwein, or The Knight with the Lion*, ed. and trans. C. Edwards (Cambridge, 2007)
Harðar saga ok Holmverja, ed. Þorhallur Vilmundarson and Bjarni Vilhjálmsson, ÍF 13 (Reykjavík, 1991)
Haukdœla þáttr, in *Sturlunga saga*, ed. Jón Jóhannesson *et al.*, I, 61–3
Heinrich von dem Türlin, *Diu Crône: Mittelhochdeutsche Leseausgabe*, ed. G. Felder (Berlin and Boston, 2012)
——, *The Crown*, trans. J. W. Thomas (Lincoln NE and London, 1989)

Heldris de Cornouailles, *Silence: A Thirteenth-Century French Romance*, ed. and trans. S. Roche-Mahdi (East Lansing MI, 1992)
Hjálmpés saga ok Ǫlvis, in *FSN*, IV: 178–243
Hrólfs saga Gautrekssonar, in *FSN*, IV: 51–176
Hrólfs saga kraka in *FSN*, I: 1–105
The Saga of Hrolf Kraki, trans. J. Byock (London, 1998)
Index exemplorum, ed. F. C. Tubach (Helsinki, 1969)
Ívens saga, ed. and trans. M. Kalinke, in *Norse Romance II: The Knights of the Round Table*, ed. M. Kalinke (Cambridge, 1999)
Jean d'Arras, *Mélusine. Roman du XIVe siècle*, ed. L. Stouff (Geneva, repr. 1974)
——, *Melusine; or, the Noble History of Lusignan*, trans. D. Maddox and S. Sturm-Maddox (University Park PA, 2012)
'The Jeaste of Sir Gawain', in *Sir Gawain: Eleven Romances and Tales*, ed. T. Hahn (Kalamazoo, 1995)
Deutsche Kaiserchronik eines Regensburger Geistlichen, ed. E. Schröder (Hannover, 1892), http://etext.lib.virginia.edu/cgi-local/german/frames.pl?file=kchr.xml
Kalevala: http://runeberg.org/kalevala/
The Kalevala, trans. F. P. Magoun jr (Cambridge MA, 1969)
Karlamagnús saga ok kappa hans: Fortællinger om keiser Karl Magnus og kappa hans, ed. C. R. Unger (Christiania [Oslo], 1860)
Karlamagnús saga: The Saga of Charlemagne and his Heroes, trans. C. B. Hieatt, 3 vols (Toronto, 1975–80)
Kempe, Margery, *The Book of Margery Kempe*, ed. B. Windeatt (Harlow, 2000)
King Arthur's Death: The Middle English Stanzaic Morte Arthur and Alliterative Morte Arthure, ed. L. D. Benson, rev. E. E. Foster (Kalamazoo, 1994)
Kudrun, ed. R. Wisniewski, 2nd edn (Stuttgart, 1969)
Kudrun, trans. and intro. B. Murdoch (London, 1987)
Lancelot: roman en prose du XIIIe siècle, ed. A. Micha, 8 vols (Geneva, 1978–82)
Lancelot-Grail: The Old French Arthurian Vulgate and Post-Vulgate in Translation, ed. N. J. Lacy et al., 5 vols (New York, 1993–6)
Laxdœla saga, ed. Einar Ólafur Sveinsson, ÍF 5 (Reykjavík, 1934)
Iacopo da Varazze, *Legenda aurea*, xlv, ed. G.P. Maggioni, 2 vols., 2nd edn (Florence, 1998)
The Golden Legend, trans. W. G. Ryan (Princeton and Oxford, 2012)
Lydgate, John, *Fall of Princes*, ed. H. Bergen, 4 vols, EETS ES 121–4 (London, 1924–7)
——, *Siege of Thebes* 2 vols, ed. A. Erdman and E. Ekwall, EETS ES 108, 125 (London, 1930)
——, *The Siege of Thebes*, ed. R. R. Edwards (Kalamazoo, 2001)
The Mabinogi and Other Medieval Welsh Texts, trans. P. K. Ford (Berkeley and Los Angeles, 1977)
Mandeville's Travels, ed. M. Seymour (Oxford, 1967)
Malory, Sir Thomas, *Le Morte Darthur*, ed. P. J. C. Field, 2 vols, Arthurian Studies 80 (Cambridge, 2013)
Marie de France, *Lais*, ed. and trans. A. Micha (Paris, 1994)
——, *The Lais of Marie de France*, trans. G. Burgess and K. Busby (Harmondsworth, 1999)
'Math uab Mathonwy', in *Pedeir Keinc y Mabinogi*, ed. Williams, pp. 67–92
'Math, son of Mathonwy', in *The Mabinogi*, trans. Ford, pp. 89–110.
Matthew Paris, *Chronica majora*, ed. H. R. Luard, 7 vols (London, 1872–3)

Bibliography

Melusine, part I: Text, Notes and Commentary, ed. A. K. Donald, EETS ES 68 (Oxford, 1895; repr. 2010)
The Middle English Breton Lays, ed. A. Laskaya and E. Salisbury (Kalamazoo, 1995)
Mirk, John, *Instructions for Parish Priests*, ed. G. Kristensson, Lund Studies in English (Lund, 1974)
La Mort le Roi Artu: roman du XIIIe siècle, ed. J. Frappier (Geneva, 1964)
La Mule sans Frein, in *Two Old French Gauvain Romances*, ed. R. C. Johnston and D. D. R. Owen (Edinburgh and London, 1972)
Das Nibelungenlied (Bibliotheca Augustana), ed. H. Reichert, based on the edition of Karl Bartsch (Leipzig, 1870–8): http://www.hs-augsburg.de/~harsch/germanica/Chronologie/12Jh/Nibelungen/nib_intr.html
The Nibelungenlied: The Lay of the Nibelungs, trans. C. Edwards (Oxford, 2010)
Norton, Thomas and Thomas Sackville, *Gorboduc* in *Minor Elizabethan Drama, Vol I, Pre-Shakespearean Tragedies* (Letchworth, 1910, repr. 1959)
Ovid, *Heroides and Amores*, ed. and trans. G. Showerman, Loeb Classical Library 41 (London, 1931)
Oxford Dictionary of National Biography online resource: http://www.oxforddnb.com
Paston Letters and Papers of the fifteenth century, ed. N. Davis, 2 vols (Oxford, 1971–6)
Patrologia Latina database, online resource: http://www.pld.chadwyck.com
Pedeir Keinc y Mabinogi, ed. I. Williams (Cardiff, 1930)
Poems of Wisdom and Learning in Old English, ed. T. A. Shippey (Cambridge and Totowa NJ, 1976)
Prose Roman de Thèbes, in M. Lynde-Recchia, *Prose, Verse, and Truth-Telling in the Thirteenth Century: An Essay on Form and Function in Selected Texts, Accompanied by an Edition of the* Prose Thèbes *as found in the* Histoire ancienne jusqu'à César (Lexington KY, 2000)
'Lai d'Aubépine', in *Lais fériques des XIIe et XIIIe siècles*, ed. and trans. A. Micha (Paris, 1998), pp. 224–51
'Lai le Fraine', in *The Middle English Breton Lay*, ed. A. Laskaya and E. Salisbury (Kalamazoo, 1995)
La Queste del Saint Graal, ed. A. Pauphilet (Paris, 1975)
La Quête du Saint Graal, ed. F. Bogdanow (Paris, 2006)
The Quest of the Holy Grail, trans. P. Matarasso (Harmondsworth, 1969)
La version Post-Vulgate de la Queste del Saint Graal *et de la* Mort Artu: *Troisième partie du Roman du Graal*, ed. F. Bogdanow, 4 vols (Paris, 1991–2000)
Richars li Biaus: roman du XIIIe siècle, ed. A. J. Holden (Paris, 1983)
Romancero tradicional de las lenguas hispánicas, ed. R. Menéndez Pidal *et al.*, 2 vols (Madrid, 1963)
Saxo Grammaticus, *Historia Danorum*: http://www2.kb.dk/elib/lit/dan/saxo/
——, *History of the Danes* ed. H. Ellis-Davidson, trans. P. Fisher (Cambridge, 1998)
Sir Gawain and the Green Knight, ed. J. R. R. Tolkien and E. V. Gordon, 2nd edn, rev. N. Davis (Oxford, 1967)
Snorri Sturluson, *Heimskringla*, ed. Bjarni Aðalbjarnarson, ÍF 26–8, 3 vols (Reykjavík, 1941–51)
——, *Edda: Skáldskaparmál: Introduction, Text and Notes*, ed. A. Faulkes (London, 1998)
——, *Edda*, trans. A. Faulkes (London, 1987)
Sólarljóð, ed. C. Larrington and P. Robinson, in *Poetry on Christian Subjects*, 2 vols, Skaldic Poetry of the Scandinavian Middle Ages 7, gen. ed. M. Clunies Ross, I (Turnhout, 2007)

Statius, *Thebaid: Books 1–7*, ed. D. R. Shackleton Bailey (Cambridge MA and London, 2003)
Sturla Þórðarson, *Hákonar saga Hákonarsonar*, in *Det Arnamagnæanske håndskrift 81A fol.: Skálholtsbók yngsta*, ed. A. Kjaer and L. Holm-Olsen (Oslo, 1926–86)
Sturlunga saga, ed. Jón Jóhannesson, Magnús Finnbogason and Kristján Eldjarn, 3 vols (Reykjavík, 1946)
Sturlunga saga, trans. J. H. McGrew and R. G. Thomas, 2 vols (New York, 1970–4)
La Suite du Roman de Merlin, ed. G. Roussineau, 2 vols (Geneva, 1996)
Táin Bó Cualaigne, ed. P. Ó Fiannachta (Dublin, 1966)
The Tain, trans. T. Kinsella (Oxford, 1969)
Thietmar von Merseburg, *Die Chronik des Bischofs Thietmar von Merseburg und ihre Korveier Überarbeitung. Thietmari Merseburgensis episcopi chronicon*, ed. R. Holtzmann, MGH, Scriptores 6, Scriptores rerum Germanicarum, Nova Series 9 (Berlin, 1935)
——, *Ottonian Germany: The Chronicon of Thietmar of Merseburg*, trans. D. Warner (Manchester and New York, 2001)
Tochmarc Emire la Coinculaind, ed. K. Meyer, *Zeitschrift für celtische Philologie* 3 (1901), 229–63
'The Wooing of Emer', trans. K. Meyer, *Archaeological Review* 1 (1888), 68–75; 150–5; 231–5; 298–307
The Towneley Plays, ed. M. Stevens and A. C. Cawley, 2 vols, EETS ss 13–14 (Oxford, 1994)
Updike, John, *Gertrude and Claudius* (London, 2000)
Valentine and Orson, trans. H. Watson, ed. A. Dickson EETS os 204 (London, 1937)
Vita Anstrudis abb. Laudunensis, MGH, SS rerum Merovingiae 6, ed. B. Krusch and W. Levison (Hannover, 1913), pp. 66–78
'Life of Anstrude', in *Sainted Women of the Dark Ages*, trans. J. A. McNamara and J. Halborg with E. G. Whatley (Durham NC, 1992), pp. 289–303
Víga-Glúms saga, ed. G. Turville-Petre (Oxford, 1940)
Viga-Glums saga, trans. J. McKinnell (Edinburgh, 1987)
Vǫlsunga saga: The Saga of the Volsungs, ed. and trans. R. G. Finch (London, 1965)
The Vulgate Version of the Arthurian Romances, ed. H. O. Sommer, 8 vols (Washington DC, 1908–16)
William of Palerne, ed. W. W. Skeat, EETS es 1 (London, 1867)
Wolfram von Eschenbach, *Parzival*, ed. K. Lachmann, 6th edn (Berlin and New York, 1998)
——, *Parzival*, trans. C. Edwards, Arthurian Studies 56 (Cambridge, 2004)
——, *Willehalm*, http://www.hs-augsburg.de/~harsch/germanica/Chronologie/13Jh/Wolfram/wol_wio6.html
——, *Willehalm*, trans. M. M. Gibbs and S. M. Johnson (Harmondsworth, 1984)
Ywain and Gawain, ed. A. B. Freedman and N. T. Harrington, EETS os 254 (Oxford, 1964)
Þiðreks saga af Bern, ed. Guðni Jónsson, 2 vols (Reykjavík, 1951–4)
The Saga of Thidrek of Bern, trans. E. Haymes (New York and London, 1988)
Þórðar saga kakala, in *Sturlunga saga*, ed. Jón Jóhannesson *et al.*, II

Bibliography

Secondary Texts

Icelanders are alphabetized under first name.

Acker, P., and C. Larrington, ed., *Revisiting the Poetic Edda: Essays on Old Norse Heroic Legend* (New York and London, 2013)
Adler, A., *The Individual Psychology of Alfred Adler*, ed. H. L. Ansbacher and R. R. Ansbacher (New York, 1956)
Ailes, M., 'The Medieval Male Couple and the Language of Homosociality', in *Masculinity in Medieval Europe*, ed. D. M. Hadley (London, 1999)
Alexandre-Bidon, D., and D. Lett, *Children of the Middle Ages: Fifth–Fifteenth Centuries* (Notre Dame IN, 1999)
Allen, G., 'Sibling Solidarity', *Journal of Marriage and the Family* 39 (1977), 177–84
Apter, T., *The Sister Knot* (New York and London, 2007)
Archibald, E., 'Malory's Ideal of Fellowship', *Review of English Studies* 43 (1992), 311–28
——, '*Lai le Freine*: The Female Foundling and the Problem of Romance Genre', in *The Spirit of Medieval English Popular Romance*, ed. A. Putter and J. Gilbert (Harlow, 2000), pp. 39–55
——, *Incest and the Medieval Imagination* (Oxford, 2001)
——, 'Comedy and Tragedy in Some Arthurian Recognition Scenes', in *Comedy in Arthurian Literature*, ed. K. Busby and R. Dalrymple, Arthurian Literature 19 (Cambridge, 2003), 1–16
Armstrong, D., and K. Hodges, *Mapping Malory: Regional Identities and National Geographies in* Le Morte Darthur (New York, 2014)
Armstrong, G., 'Questions of Inheritance: *Le Chevalier au Lion* and *La Queste del Saint Graal*', in *Rereading Allegory: Essays in Memory of Daniel Poirion*, Yale French Studies 95 (1999), pp. 171–92
Arseneau, I., 'Gauvain et les métamorphoses de la merveille: déchéance d'un héros et déclin du surnaturel', in *Une étrange constance. Les motifs merveilleux dans la littérature d'expression française du Moyen Âge à nos jours*, ed. F. Gingras, Collections de la République des Lettres. Symposiums (Québec, 2006), pp. 91–106
Aurell, M., ed., *La parenté déchirée: les luttes intrafamiliales au Moyen Âge* (Turnhout, 2010)
——, 'Rompre la concorde familiale: typologie, imaginaire, questionnements', in *La parenté*, ed. Aurell, pp. 9–59
Balk, D., 'Adolescents' Grief Reactions and Self-Concept Perceptions Following Sibling Death', *Journal of Youth and Adolescence* 12 (1983), 137–61
Bank, S., and M. Kahn, 'Intense Sibling Loyalties', in *Sibling Relationships: Their Nature and Significance across the Lifespan*, ed. M. Lamb and B. Sutton-Smith (Hillsdale NJ and London, 1982), pp. 251–67
——, and M. Kahn, *The Sibling Bond* (New York, 1982)
Barbero, A., *Un santo in famiglia: vocazione religiosa e resistenze sociale nell'agiografia latine medievale* (Torino, 1991)
Batt, C., *Malory's* Morte Darthur: *Remaking Arthurian Tradition* (New York and Basingstoke, 2002)
Battles, D., *The Medieval Tradition of Thebes: History and Narrative in the OF 'Roman de Thèbes', Boccaccio, Chaucer, and Lydgate* (London and New York, 2004)

Baumgartner, E., 'Fiction and History: The Cypriot Episode in Jean d'Arras's *Mélusine*', in *Mélusine of Lusignan*, ed. Maddox and Sturm-Maddox, pp. 185–200

Beitscher, J., '"As the twig is bent ...": Children and their Parents in an Aristocratic Society', *Journal of Medieval History* 9 (1976), 181–91

Benton, J., *Self and Society in Medieval France: The Memoirs of Abbot Guibert of Nogent (1064?–c. 1125)* (New York, 1970)

Berman, C. H., *The Cistercian Evolution: The Invention of a Religious Order in Twelfth-Century France* (Philadelphia PA, 2000)

Bertau, K., 'Versuch über Verhaltenssemantik von Verwandten im "Parzival"', in K. Bertau, *Wolfram von Eschenbach: Neun Versuche über Subjektivität und Ursprünglichkeit in der Geschichte* (München, 1983), pp. 190–240

Black, N. B., *Medieval Narratives of Accused Queens* (Gainsville FL, 2003)

Blaess, M., 'Arthur's Sisters', *Bibliographic Bulletin of the International Arthurian Society* 8 (1956), 69–77

Bluestine, C., 'The Power of Blood in the Siete Infantes de Lara', *Hispanic Review* 50 (1982), 201–17

Boberg, I. M., *Motif-Index of Early Icelandic Literature*, Bibliotheca Arnamagnea 27 (Copenhagen, 1966)

Bogdanow, F., *The Romance of the Grail: A Study of the Structure and Genesis of a Thirteenth-Century Arthurian Prose Romance* (Manchester and New York, 1966)

Boquet, D., P. Nagy and L. Moulinier-Brogi, ed., *La chair des émotions*, *Médiévales* 61 (2011)

Bray, A., *The Friend* (Chicago, 2003)

Bresc, H., 'Europe: Town and Country (Thirteenth–Fifteenth Century)', in *A History of the Family*, ed. Burguière *et al.*, I, pp. 430–66

Brewster, P., *The Incest Theme in Folksong*, Folklore Fellowship Communications 212 (Helsinki, 1972)

Bruckner, M. T., '*Le Fresne*'s Model for Twinning in the *Lais* of Marie de France', *Modern Language Notes* 121 (2006), 946–60

Burguière, A. *et al.*, *A History of the Family*, 2 vols (Cambridge, 1996)

Burns, E. J., 'Raping Men: What's motherhood got to do with it?', in *Representing Rape*, ed. Robertson and Rose, pp. 127–60

Busby, K., 'Chrétien de Troyes English'd', *Neophilologus* 71 (1987), 596–613

Butler, J., *Gender Trouble: Feminism and the Subversion of Identity* (New York and London, 1999)

——, *Antigone's Claim: Kinship between Life and Death* (New York, 2000)

Burkert, W., *Homo Necans: The Anthropology of Ancient Greek Sacrificial Ritual and Myth*, trans. P. Bing (Berkeley CA, 1983)

Carrier, N., 'Patrimoine et conflits dans les familles paysannes des Alpes occidentales au temps du "remembrement lignager" (XIIIe–XVe siècles)', in *La parenté*, ed. Aurell, pp. 129–45

Cassagnes-Brouquet, S., and M. Yvernault, ed. *Frères et sœurs: les liens adelphiques dans l'Occident antique et médiéval* (Turnhout, 2007)

Certin, A.-M., 'Relations professionnelles et relations fraternelles d'après le journal de Lucas Rem, Marchand d'Augsbourg (1481–1542)', *Médiévales* 54 (2008), 83–98

Charles, M., 'Sibling Mysteries: Enactment of Unconscious Fears and Fantasies', *Psychoanalytic Review* 86 (1999), 877–901

Cherewatuk, K., 'Speculum Matris: Duoda's Manual', *Florilegium* 10 (1988–91), 49–64
——, *Marriage, Adultery and Inheritance in Malory's* Morte Darthur, Arthurian Studies 67 (Cambridge, 2006)
Cicirelli, V. G., 'Sibling Relationships in Adulthood: A Life Span Perspective', in *Aging in the 1980s*, ed. L. W. Poon (Washington DC, 1980), pp. 455–62
——, 'Feelings of Attachment to Siblings and Well-Being in Later Life', *Psychology and Aging* 4 (1989), 211–16
——, 'Sibling Relationships in Cross-Cultural Perspective', *Journal of Marriage and the Family* 56 (1994), 7–20
——, *Sibling Relationships across the Life-Span* (New York, 1995)
Ciklamini, M., 'The Combat between Two Half-Brothers: A Literary Study of the Motif in *Ásmundar saga kappabana* and *Saxonis Gesta Danorum*', *Neophilologus* 50.2 (1966), 269–79; concluded 50.3 (1966), 370–9
Clark, D., 'Undermining and En-gendering Vengeance: Distancing and Anti-Feminism in the Poetic Edda', *Scandinavian Studies* 77 (2005), 173–200
——, *Between Medieval Men: Male Friendship and Desire in Early Medieval English Literature* (Oxford, 2009)
Coles, P., *The Importance of Sibling Relationships in Psychoanalysis* (London, 2003)
——, ed., *Sibling Relationships* (London, 2006)
Cooper, E. H., *The English Romance in Time* (Oxford, 2004)
Conklin, G., 'Ingeborg of Denmark, Queen of France, 1193–1223', in *Queens and Queenship in Medieval Europe*, ed. A. J. Duggan (Woodbridge, 1997), pp. 39–52
Connidis, I. A., 'Siblings as Friends in Later Life', *American Behavioural Scientist*, 33 (1989), 81–93
——, 'Life Transitions and the Adult Sibling Tie', *Journal of Marriage and the Family* 54 (1992), 972–82
Cowell, A., *The Medieval Warrior Aristocracy: Gifts, Violence, Performance and the Sacred* (Cambridge, 2007)
Crouch, D., 'Marshal, William (I), Fourth Earl of Pembroke (c. 1146–1219)', *DNB*, Oxford University Press, 2004; online edn, May 2007 [http://ezproxy.ouls.ox.ac.uk:2117/view/article/18126]
Coulton, G. G., *The Medieval Village* (Cambridge, 1925, repr. 1989)
Cross, T. P., *Motif-Index of Early Irish Literature* (Bloomington IN, 1952)
Davidoff, L., 'The Sibling Relationship and Sibling Incest in Historical Context', in *Sibling Relationships*, ed. Coles, pp. 17–47
——. *Thicker than Water: Siblings and their Relations 1780–1920* (Oxford, 2012)
d'Avray, D. L., *Dissolving Royal Marriages: A Documentary History, 860–1600* (Cambridge, 2014)
Delabar, W., *Erkantiu sippe unt hoch Geselleschaft: Studien zur Funktion des Verwandschaftsverbandes in Wolframs von Eschenbach* Parzival (Göppingen, 1990)
Dinshaw, C., *Getting Medieval: Sexualities and Communities, Pre- and Postmodern* (Durham NC, and London, 1999)
Donnelly, C., 'Aristocratic Veneer and the Substance of Verbal Bonds in "The Weddynge of Sir Gawen and Dame Ragnell" and "Gamelyn"', *Studies in Philology* 94 (1997), 321–43
Doniger, W., *The Bedtrick: Tales of Sex and Masquerade* (Chicago, 2000)
Dooley, A., *Playing the Hero: Reading the Irish Saga Táin Bó Cúailgne* (Toronto, 2006)
Dronke, P., *Poetic Individuality in the Middle Ages: New Departures in Poetry, 1100–1150* (Oxford, 1970)

Drukker, T., 'Thirty-Three Murderous Sisters: A Pre-Trojan Foundation Myth in the Middle English Prose *Brut*', *Review of English Studies* 54 (2003), 449–63
Duby, G., *The Knight, the Lady and the Priest: The Making of Modern Marriage in Medieval France*, trans. B. Bray (Harmondsworth, 1985)
——, *William Marshal: The Flower of Chivalry*, trans. R. Howard (London, 1986)
Dunn, J., and C. Kendrick, *Siblings: Love, Envy and Understanding* (London, 1982)
Edwards, R., L. Hadfield, et al., *Who is a Sister and a Brother? Biological and Social Ties* (London, 2005)
Epstein, S., *Wills and Wealth in Medieval Genoa: 1150–1250* (Cambridge MA, 1984)
——, 'The Medieval Family: A Place of Refuge and Sorrow', in *Portraits of Medieval and Renaissance Living: Essays in Memory of David Herlihy*, ed. S. K. Cohn and S. Epstein (Ann Arbor MI, 1996), pp. 149–71
Finkelhor, D., 'Sex among Siblings: A Survey on Prevalence, Variety, and Effect', *Archives of Sexual Behavior* 9 (1980), 171–94
Finucane, R., *The Rescue of the Innocents: Endangered Children in Medieval Miracles* (Basingstoke, 1997)
Fletcher, R., *Bloodfeud: Murder and Revenge in Anglo-Saxon England* (Oxford, 2004)
Floyd, K., and M. C. Morr, 'Human Affection Exchange: VII. Affectionate Communication in the Sibling/Spouse/Sibling-in-Law Triad', *Communications Quarterly* 51 (2003), 247–61
Foot, S., *Monastic Life in Anglo-Saxon England, c. 600–900* (Cambridge, 2006)
Ford, J. C., 'Contrasting the Identical: Differentiation of the "Indistinguishable" Characters of *Amis and Amiloun*', *Neophilologus* 86 (2002), 311–23
Fossier, R., 'The Feudal Era (Eleventh–Thirteenth Century)', in *A History of the Family*, ed. Burguière et al., I, pp. 407–29
Frakes, J. C., *Brides and Doom: Gender, Property, and Power in Medieval German Women's Epic* (Philadelphia, 1994)
Frevert, U., *Emotions in History – Lost and Found* (Budapest and New York, 2011)
Furtado, A. L., 'The Questing Beast as Emblem of the Ruin of Logres in the "Post-Vulgate"', *Arthuriana* 9.3 (1999), 27–48
Gaunt, S., *Gender and Genre in Medieval French Literature* (Cambridge, 1995)
Gentry, F., 'Gahmuret and Herzeloyde: Gone but not Forgotten', in *A Companion to Wolfram's* Parzival, ed. W. Hasty (Columbia SC, 1999), pp. 3–11
Gibson, G. M., 'Scene and Obscene: Seeing and Performing Late Medieval Childbirth', *Journal of Medieval and Early Modern Studies* 29 (1999), 7–24
Girard, R., *Violence and the Sacred*, trans. P. Gregory (Baltimore and London, 1977)
Godelier, M., *Métamorphoses de la Parenté* (Paris, 2004)
Goering, J., 'Neckam, Alexander (1157–1217)', *DNB*, Oxford University Press, 2004 [http://ezproxy.ouls.ox.ac.uk:2117/view/article/19839]
Goetting, A., 'The Developmental Tasks of Siblingship over the Life Cycle', *Journal of Marriage and Family* 48 (1986), 703–14
Goldberg, P. J. P., *Women, Work and Life Cycle in a Medieval Economy: Women in York and Yorkshire c. 1300–1520* (Oxford, 1992)
——, *Women in England: c. 1275–1525: Documentary Sources* (Manchester and New York, 1995)
——, *Medieval England: A Social History 1250–1550* (London, 2004)
Goodich, M., 'Sexuality, Family, and the Supernatural in the Fourteenth Century', in *Medieval Families*, ed. Neel, pp. 302–28

Bibliography

Goody, J., 'Introduction', in *Family and Inheritance: Rural Society in Western Europe, 1200–1800*, ed. J. Goody, J. Thirsk and E. P. Thompson (Cambridge, 1978)

——, 'The Labyrinth of Kinship', *New Left Review* 36 (2005), 127–39

Gottzmann, C., "*Vǫlsunga saga*: Legendary History and Textual Analysis," in *Preprints of the 4th International Saga Conference* (Munich, 1979), I (articles individually paginated)

Gravdal, K., 'Confessing Incest: Legal Erasures and Literary Celebrations in Medieval France', in *Medieval Families*, ed. Neel, pp. 329–46

Greenberg, M., 'Post-adoption Reunion – Are We Entering Uncharted Territory?', *Adoption and Fostering* 17 (1993), 5–15

——, and R. Littlewood, 'Post-adoption Incest and Phenotypic Matching: Experience, Social Meanings and Biosocial Implications', *British Journal of Medical Psychology* 68 (1995), 29–44

Griffin, M., 'Writing out the Incest: Arthur, Charlemagne and the Spectre of Incest', *Neophilologus* 88 (2004), 499–519

Griffiths, F. J., 'Siblings and the Sexes within the Medieval Religious Life', *Church History* 77 (2008), 26–53

Guerin, M. V., 'The King's Sin: The Origins of the David-Arthur Parallel', in *The Passing of Arthur: New Essays in Arthurian Tradition*, ed. C. Baswell and W. Sharpe (New York, 1998), 15–30

Gwara, S., *Heroic Identity in the World of Beowulf* (Leiden and Boston, 2008)

Haas, L., 'Women and Childbearing in Medieval Florence', in *Medieval Family Roles: A Book of Essays*, ed. C. Jorgensen Itnyre (New York and London, 1996), pp. 87–99

Hadley, D., 'Introduction: Medieval Masculinities', in *Masculinity in Medieval Europe*, ed. D. M. Hadley (London, 1999), pp. 1–18.

Hafner, S., 'Charlemagne's Unspeakable Sin', *Modern Language Studies*, 32 (2002), 1–14

Hanawalt, B., *The Ties that Bound: Peasant Families in Medieval England* (New York and Oxford, 1986)

——, 'Medievalists and the Study of Childhood', *Speculum* 77 (2002), 440–60

Hansen, A., 'Representations of Children in Early Icelandic Society' (unpublished Ph.D. dissertation, University of Sydney, 2006)

——, 'Fosterage and Dependency in Medieval Iceland and its Significance in *Gísla saga*', in *Youth and Age*, ed. Lewis-Simpson, pp. 73–86

Harf-Lancner, L., *Les fées au Moyen Âge* (Paris, 1984)

Hatto, A. T., 'On the Excellence of the "Hildebrandslied": A Comparative Study in Dynamics', *Modern Language Review* 68 (1973), 820–38

Heinrichs, A., 'Die jüngere und die ältere Þóra: Form und Bedeutung einer Episode in *Haukdœla þáttr*', *Alvíssmál* 5 (1995), 3–28

Heller, R., 'Fóstbrœðra saga und Víga-Glúms saga', *Acta Philologica Scandinavica* 31 (1976), 44–57

Herlihy, D., *Medieval and Renaissance Pistoia: The Social History of an Italian Town, 1200–1430* (New Haven and London, 1967)

——, with C. Klapisch-Zuber, *Tuscans and their Families: A Study of the Florentine Catasto of 1427* (New Haven and London, 1985)

Hill, T. D., 'Hæðcyn, Herebeald, and Archery's Laws: *Beowulf* and the *Leges Henrici Primi*', *Medium Ævum* 81.2 (2012), 210–21

Higley, S. L., 'Dirty Magic: Seiðr, Science and the Parturating Man in Medieval Norse and Welsh Literature', *Essays in Medieval Studies* 11 (1994), 137–45

Hinshelwood, R. D., and G. Winship, 'Orestes and Democracy', in *Sibling Relations*, ed. Coles, pp. 75–96

Hodges, J. C., 'The Blood Covenant among the Celts', *Revue celtique* 44 (1927), 109–53

Hogan, P. C., *The Mind and its Stories* (Cambridge, 2009)

——, *What Literature Teaches us about Emotion* (Cambridge, 2011)

Hollis, S., *Anglo-Saxon Women and the Church: Sharing a Common Fate* (Woodbridge, 1992)

Holt, J. C., 'King John and Arthur of Brittany', *Nottingham Medieval Studies* 44 (2000), 82–103

Holtsmark, A., *Studies in the* Gísla saga, Studia Norvegica 6 (Oslo, 1951)

Howell, M., *Eleanor of Provence: Queenship in Thirteenth-Century England* (Oxford, 1998)

Huchet, J.-C., 'Du père en littérature', in *Le Moyen Âge dans la modernité: mélanges offerts à Roger Dragonetti*, ed. J. R. Scheidegger (Paris, 1996), pp. 281–98

Hughes, D. O., 'Domestic Ideals and Social Behavior: Evidence from Medieval Genoa', in *Medieval Families*, ed. Neel, pp. 124–56

Hume, K., '"Amis and Amiloun" and the Aesthetics of Middle English Romance', *Studies in Philology* 70 (1973), 19–41

Hyams, P., 'Feud and the State in Late Anglo-Saxon England', *Journal of British Studies* 40 (2001), 1–43

Hyatte, R., *The Arts of Friendship: The Idealization of Friendship in Medieval and Early Renaissance Literature* (Leiden, 1994)

Irigaray, L., *Speculum de l'autre femme* (Paris, 1974)

——, *Speculum of the Other Woman*, trans. G. Gill (Ithaca NY, 1985)

Jackson, M., 'Ambivalence and the Last-Born: Birth-Order Position in Convention and Myth', *Man* 13 (1978), 341–61

Jaeger, C. S., *The Origins of Courtliness – Civilizing Trends and the Formation of Courtly Ideals – 939–1210* (Philadelphia PA, 1985)

——, *Ennobling Love: In Search of a Lost Sensitivity* (Philadelphia PA, 1999)

Jarman, A. O. H., 'The Merlin Legend and the Tradition of Welsh Prophecy', in *The Arthur of the Welsh*, ed. R. Bromwich, A. O. H. Jarman and B. F. Roberts (Cardiff, 1991), pp. 117–45

Jeanne, C., 'Seules ou accompagnées? Les veuves parisiennes et leurs fratries à la fin du moyen âge', *Médiévales* 54 (2008), 69–81

Jewers, C., 'C'est li chevaliers au Poisson: *Richars li biaus* as a model of speculative chivalry', *French Studies* 61 (2007), 261–79

Jesch, J., 'Runic Inscriptions and the Vocabulary of Land, Lordship and Social Power in the Late Viking Age', in *Settlement and Lordship in Viking and Early Medieval Scandinavia*, ed. S. M. Sindbaek and B. Poulsen (Turnhout, 2011), pp. 31–44

Jillings, L., 'The Rival Sisters Dispute in *Diu Crône* and its French Antecedents', in *An Arthurian Tapestry: Essays in Memory of Lewis Thorpe*, ed. K. Varty (Glasgow, 1981), pp. 248–59

Jochens, J., 'The Politics of Reproduction: Medieval Norwegian Kingship', *American Historical Review* 92 (1987), 327–49

——, *Old Norse Images of Women* (Philadelphia, 1996)

——, 'Representations of Skalds in the Sagas 2: Gender Relations', in *Skaldsagas*, ed. Poole, pp. 309–32

Jóhanna Katrín Friðriksdóttir, *Women in Old Norse Literature: Bodies, Words and Power* (New York and London, 2013)

Bibliography

Jóhanna Katrín Friðriksdóttir, '"Gerðit hon . . . sem konor aðrar": Women and Subversion in Eddic Heroic Poetry', in *Revisiting the Poetic Edda*, ed. Acker and Larrington, pp. 117–35

Johnson, C., and D. W. Sabean, ed., *Sibling Relations and the Transformations of European Kinship 1300–1900* (Oxford and New York, 2011)

Johnson, C., 'Marriage Agreements from Twelfth-Century Southern France', in *To Have and to Hold*, ed. Reynolds and Witte jr, pp. 215–59

Johnson, L., 'Return to Albion', *Arthurian Literature* 13 (1995), 19–40

Jónas Kristjánsson, 'Fóstbræðravíg', in *Einarsbók: Afmæliskveðja til Einars Ól. Sveinssonar*, ed. 'some friends' (Reykjavík, 1969), pp. 196–204

Jones, N. A., 'The Daughter's Text and the Thread of Lineage in the Old French *Philomena*', in *Representing Rape in Medieval and Early Modern Literature*, ed. E. Robertson and C. M. Rose (New York, 2001), pp. 161–87

Jonin, P., 'Aspects de la vie sociale au XIIe siècle dans *Yvain*', *L'information littéraire* 16 (1964), 47–54

Jurasinski, S., *Ancient Privileges:* Beowulf, *Law and the Making of Germanic Antiquity* (Morganstown WV, 2006)

Kaeuper, R., 'A Historian's Reading of *The Tale of Gamelyn*', *Medium Ævum* 52 (1983), 51–62

Kalinke, M., *Bridal-Quest Romance in Medieval Iceland*, Islandica 46 (Ithaca NY, 1990)

——, ed., *The Arthur of the North* (Cardiff, 2011)

Karras, R. M., 'Invisible Women', *Medieval Feminist Forum* 39 (2005), 15–21

Kay, S., *The Chansons de Geste in the Age of Romance* (Oxford, 1995)

Kelly, H. A., *Love and Marriage in the Age of Chaucer* (Ithaca NY, 1975)

Kemp, S., and F. Hunt, 'Exploring the psychology of inheritances', *Zeitschrift für Sozialpsychologie* 32 (2001), 171–9

Kenna, M. E., *Greek Island Life. Fieldwork on Anafi* (Amsterdam, 2001)

Kennedy, E. D. 'Mordred's Sons', in *The Arthurian Way of Death*, ed. K. Cherewatuk and K. S. Whetter (Cambridge, 2009), pp. 33–49

Kermode, J., 'Sentiment and Survival: Family and Friends in Late Medieval English Towns', *Journal of Family History* 24 (1999), 5–18

Kinoshita, S., 'Heldris de Cornuälle's *Roman de Silence* and the Feudal Politics of Lineage', *Proceedings of Modern Languages Association* 110 (1995), 397–409

Klagsbrun, F., *Mixed Feelings: Love, Hate, Rivalry and Reconciliation between Brothers and Sisters* (New York, 1992)

Klapisch-Zuber, C., *Women, Family and Ritual in Renaissance Italy* (Chicago, 1987)

Knight, S., *Arthurian Literature* (Basingstoke, 1983)

Kooper, E., 'Multiple Births and Multiple Disaster: Twins in Medieval Literature', in *Conjunctures: Medieval Studies in Honor of Douglas Kelly*, ed. K. Busby and N. J. Lacy (Amsterdam, 1994), pp. 253–69

Kramarz-Bein, S., '"Modernität" der *Laxdæla saga*', in *Studien zum Altgermanischen: Festschrift für Heinrich Beck*, ed. H. Uecker (Berlin, 1994), pp. 421–42

Kullmann, D., *Verwandtschaft in epischer Dichtung. Untersuchungen zu den französischen chansons de geste und Romanen des 12. Jahrhunderts* (Tübingen, 1992)

Lacy, N.J., 'The Form of the Prose *Erec*', *Neuphilologische Mitteilungen* 85 (1984), 169–77

——, 'The Flowering (and Misreading) of Romance: *Floire et Blancheflor*', *South Central Review* (1992), 19–26

Lambert, P.-Y., 'Magie et pouvoir dans la quatrième branche du Mabinogi', *Studia Celtica* 28 (1994), 97–107

Laqueur, T., *Making Sex: Body and Gender from the Greeks to Freud* (Cambridge MA, 1992)
Larrington, C., *Women and Writing in Medieval Europe* (London and New York, 1995)
——, 'The Fairy Mistress: A Medieval Literary Fantasy', in *Writing and Fantasy*, ed. C. Sullivan and B. White (Harlow, 1999), pp. 32–47
——, 'Some Recent Developments in the Psychology of Emotion and their Relevance to the Study of the Medieval Period', *Early Medieval Europe* 10 (2001), 251–6
——, *King Arthur's Enchantresses: Morgan and her Sisters in Arthurian Tradition* (London, 2006)
——, 'Awkward Adolescents: Male Maturation in Norse Literature', in *Youth and Age*, ed. Lewis-Simpson, pp. 145–60
——, 'The Enchantress, the Knight and the Cleric: Authorial Surrogates in Arthurian Romance', *Arthurian Literature* 25 (2008), 43–65
——, 'Stjúpmœðrasögur and Sigurðr's Daughters', in *Á austrvega. Saga and East Scandinavia. Preprint Papers of The 14th International Saga Conference*, Uppsala, 9–15 August 2009, ed. A. Ney, H. Williams and F. Charpentier Ljungqvist, 2 vols (Gävle, 2009), II, pp. 568–75
——, 'Queens and Bodies: The Norwegian Translated *Lais* and Hákon IV's Kinswomen', *Journal of English and Germanic Philology* 108 (2009), 506–27
——, 'Sibling Relations in Malory's *Morte Darthur*', *Arthurian Literature* 28 (2011), 57–74
——, 'Sibling Drama: Laterality in the Heroic Poems of the Edda', in *Myth, Legends, and Heroes: Studies in Old Norse and Old English Literature in Honour of John McKinnell*, ed. D. Anlezark (Toronto, 2011), pp. 169–87
——, '*Vǫlsunga saga* and *Ragnars saga* and Romance in Old Norse: Revisiting the Relationship', in *The Legendary Sagas: Origins and Development*, ed. Ármann Jakobsson, A. Lassen and A. Ney (Reykjavík, 2012), pp. 251–70
——, '"I have long desired to cure you of old age": Sibling Drama in the Later Heroic Poems of the Edda', in *Revisiting the Poetic Edda*, ed. Acker and Larrington, pp. 140–56
——, 'New Thoughts on Old Wisdom: Norse Gnomic Poetry, the Narrative Turn and Situational Ethics' (forthcoming)
——, 'Mourning Gawein: Performing Grief in *Diu Crône*', in *Arthurian Emotion: Voice, Mind, Body*, ed. F. Brandsma, C. Larrington and C. Saunders (Cambridge, forthcoming)
Lathrop, T. A., *The Legend of the Siete Infantes de Lara* (Chapel Hill NC, 1972)
Lawson, M. K., 'Harthacnut (c. 1018–1042)', *DNB*: http://ezproxy.ouls.ox.ac.uk:2117/view/article/12252
Lecuppre, G., 'L'oncle usurpateur à la fin du Moyen Âge', in *La parenté*, ed. Aurell, pp. 147–56
Ledwige, F., 'Relations de famille dans la correspondance de Gerson', *Revue historique* 271 (1984), 3–23
Lee, T. R., J. A. Mancini and J. W. Maxwell, 'Sibling Relationships in Adulthood: Contact Patterns and Motivations', *Journal of Marriage and Family* 52 (1990), 431–40
Leleu, L., 'Frères et sœurs ennemis dans la Germanie du Xe siècle', *Médiévales* 54 (2008), 35–52
Lejeune, R., 'Le péché de Charlemagne et la Chanson de Roland', in *Studia Philologica: Homenaje ofrecido a Dámaso Alonso*, 3 vols (Madrid, 1961), II, 339–71

Bibliography

Lett, D., 'Adult Brothers and Juvenile Uncles: Generations and Age Differences in Families at the End of the Middle Ages', *History of the Family* 6 (2001), 391–400

——, ed. *Frères et sœurs – Ethnographie d'un lien de parenté, Médiévales* 54 (2008)

——, 'Les frères et les sœurs, "parents pauvres" de la parenté', *Médiévales* 54 (2008), 5–12

——, 'Liens adelphiques et endogamie géographique dans les Marches de la première moitié du XIVe siècle', *Médiévales* 54 (2008), 53–68

——, *Frères et sœurs: histoire d'un lien* (Paris, 2009)

Lévi-Strauss, C., *The Elementary Structures of Kinship*, trans. R. Harle Bell, J. R. von Sturmer, and R. Needham (London, 1969)

Lewin, E., ed., *Feminist Anthropology: A Reader* (Oxford, 2006)

Lewis-Simpson, S., ed., *Youth and Age in the Medieval North* (Leiden, 2008)

Lieberman, D., J. Tooby and L. Cosmides, 'Does Morality have a Biological Basis? An Empirical Test of the Factors Governing Moral Sentiments Relating to Incest', *Proceedings of the Royal Society: Biological Sciences* 270 (2003), 819–26

Lindow, J., *Murder and Vengeance among the Gods: Baldr in Scandinavian Mythology* (Helsinki, 1997)

Lofmark, C., *Rennewart in Wolfram's Willehalm: A Study of Wolfram von Eschenbach and his Sources* (Cambridge, 1972)

MacCannell, J. F., *The Regime of the Brother: After the Patriarchy* (London, 1991)

McConnell, W., *The Epic of Kudrun: A Critical Commentary*, GAG 463 (Göppingen, 1988)

McCracken, P., *The Curse of Eve, the Wound of the Hero: Blood, Gender, and Medieval Literature* (Philadelphia, 2003)

McFarlane, K., 'A Business Partnership in War and Administration, 1421–1445', *English Historical Review* 78 (1963), 290–310

McGuire, B. P., *Friendship and Community: The Monastic Experience 350–1250* (Kalamazoo, 1988)

——, 'Late Medieval Care and Control of Women: Jean Gerson and his Sisters', *Revue d'histoire ecclésiastique* 92 (1997), 5–37

——, 'Jean Gerson and the End of Spiritual Friendship: Dilemmas of Conscience', in *Friendship in Medieval Europe*, ed. J. Haseldine (Stroud, 1999), pp. 229–50

McLaughlin, M. M., 'Survivors and Surrogates: Children and Parents from the Ninth to the Thirteenth Centuries', in *Medieval Families*, ed. Neel, pp. 20–124

Macé, L., 'Les frères au sein du lignage : la logique du lien adelphique chez les seigneurs de Montepellier (XIe siècle)', in *Frères et sœurs*, ed. Cassagnes-Brouquet and Yvernault, pp. 127–36

Madelung, A. M. A., *The Laxdœla Saga: Its Structural Patterns* (Chapel Hill NC, 1972),

Maddox, D., *The Arthurian Romances of Chrétien de Troyes: Once and Future Fictions* (Cambridge, 1991)

——, and S. Sturm-Maddox, *Mélusine of Lusignan: Founding Fictions in Late Medieval France*, ed. D. Maddox and S. Sturm-Maddox (Athens GA and London, 1996)

Maillot, C., 'Bernard de Clairvaux et la fratrie recomposée', *Médiévales* 54 (2008), 13–34

Mann, J., '"Taking the Adventure": Malory and the *Suite du Merlin*', in *Aspects of Malory*, ed. T. Takamiya and D. Brewer, Arthurian Studies 1 (Cambridge, 1981), pp. 71–91

——, *Feminizing Chaucer* (Cambridge, 2002)

Marchand, J., 'Dhuoda: The Frankish Mother', in *Medieval Women Writers*, ed. K. M. Wilson (Manchester, 1984)

Marcus, M., 'Cross-Fertilizations: Folklore and Literature in *Decameron* 4.5', *Italica* 66.4 (1989), 383–98

Martineau, H., *Autobiography*, 3 vols (London, 1877)

Martinet, S., 'Le péché de Charlemagne, Gisèle, Roland et Ganelon', in *Amour, Mariage et Transgressions au Moyen Age*: Actes du Colloque des 24, 25, 26 et 27 mars 1983, ed. D. Buschinger and A. Crépin (Göppingen, 1984), pp. 9–16

Martínez-Morás, S. L., and G. P. Barcala, 'Femmes et espace dans *Daurel et Beton*', *Revue des langues romanes*, 104 (2000), 317–36

Mead, M., *Sex and Temperament in Three Primitive Societies* (New York, 1935)

Menéndez Pidal, R., *La leyenda de los Infantes de Lara*, 3rd edn (Madrid, 1971)

Miller, N. J., and N. Yavneh, ed., *Sibling Relations and Gender in the Early Modern World: Sisters, Brothers and Others* (Aldershot, 2006)

Miller, W. I., 'Choosing the Avenger: Some Aspects of the Bloodfeud in Medieval Iceland and England', *Law and History Review*, 1.2 (1983), 159–204

——, *Bloodtaking and Peacemaking: Feud, Law and Society in Saga Iceland* (Chicago, 1997)

Mitchell, J., *Mad Men and Medusas: Reclaiming Hysteria and the Effects of Sibling Relations on the Human Condition* (Harmondsworth, 2000)

——, *Siblings: Sex and Violence* (Cambridge, 2003)

Mitterauer, M., and R. Rieder, *The European Family: Patriarchy to Partnership from the Middle Ages to the Present* (Oxford, 1982)

Mock, D., *More than Kin and Less than Kind* (Cambridge MA, 2004)

Moi, T., 'The Missing Mother: The Oedipal Rivalries of René Girard', *Diacritics* 12 (1982), 21–31

Moore, H., *Feminism and Anthropology* (Cambridge, 1988)

Morgan, H. G., 'The Role of Morgan le Fay in Malory's *Morte D'Arthur*', *Southern Quarterly* 2 (1963–4), 150–68

Morley, E., 'The Influence of Sibling Relationships on Couple Choice and Development', in *Sibling Relationships*, ed. Coles, pp. 197–224.

Morris, C. J., *Marriage and Murder in Eleventh-Century Northumbria: A Study of De Obsessione Dunelmi* (York, 1992)

Morris, R., 'Uther and Ygerne: A Study in Uncourtly Love', *Arthurian Literature* 4 (1985), 70–92

Mosatche, H. S., E. M. Brady and M. R. Noberini, 'A Retrospective Lifetime Study of the Closest Sibling Relationship', *The Journal of Psychology* 113 (1983), 237–43

Moser, C. J., R. Jones et al., 'The Impact of the Sibling in Clinical Practice: Transference and Countertransference Dynamics', *Psychotherapy: Theory, Research, Practice, Training* 42 (2005), 267–78

Muir, L. R., 'The Questing Beast: Its Origin and Development', *Orpheus* 4 (1957), 24–32

Murdoch, B., *Gregorius: An Incestuous Saint in Medieval Europe and Beyond* (Oxford, 2012)

Nagle, B. R., 'Byblis and Myrrha: Two Incest Narratives in the "Metamorphoses"', *The Classical Journal* 79 (1983), 301–15

Nagy, P., and D. Boquet, ed., *Le sujet des émotions au moyen âge* (Paris, 2009)

Najemy, J., *A History of Florence, 1200–1575* (Oxford, 2006)

Bibliography

Neel, C., ed. *Medieval Families: Perspectives on Marriage, Household, and Children* (Toronto, 2004)

Nelson, J. L., 'Women at the Court of Charlemagne: A Case of Monstrous Regiment?', in *Medieval Queenship*, ed. J. C. Parsons (New York, 1993), pp. 43–62

Nichol, S. G., 'Melusine between Myth and History: Profile of a Female Demon', in *Mélusine of Lusignan*, ed. Maddox and Sturm-Maddox, pp. 137–64

Nitze, W. A., 'The Beste Glatissante in Arthurian Romance', *Zeitschrift für romanische Philologie* 56 (1936), 409–18

Nolan, M., 'Lydgate's Literary History: Chaucer, Gower, and Canacee', *Studies in the Age of Chaucer* 27 (2005), 59–92

Noltze, H., *Gahmurets Orientfahrt: Kommentar zum ersten Buch von Wolframs "Parzival"* (Würzburg, 1995)

Ó Cathasaigh, T., 'The Sister's Son in Early Irish Literature', *Peritia* 5 (1986), 128–60

Ó Concheanainn, T., 'A Connacht Medieval Literary Heritage: Text Derived from Cín Drommo Snechtain through Leabhar na hUidhre', *Cambridge Medieval Celtic Studies* 16 (1988), 1–40

——, 'The Textual Tradition of *Compert con Culainn*', *Essays in Honour of Brian Ó Cuív, Celtica* 21 (1990), 441–55

O'Donoghue, H., 'What has Baldr to do with Lamech? The Lethal Shot of a Blind Man in Old Norse Myth and Jewish Exegetical Traditions', *Medium Ævum* 72 (2003), 82–107

Ó hUiginn, R., 'The Background and Development of *Táin Bó Cúailgne*', in *Aspects of the Táin*, ed. J. P. Mallory (Belfast, 1992), pp. 29–67

Orchard, A., *A Critical Companion to* Beowulf (Cambridge, 2003)

Orme, N., *Medieval Children* (New Haven CN and London, 2001)

Ortner, S. B., 'Is Female to Male as Nature is to Culture?', in *Women, Culture and Society*, ed. M. Z. Rosaldo and L. Lamphere (Stanford CA, 1974), pp. 68–87

——, and H. Whitehead, ed, *Sexual Meanings: The Cultural Construction of Gender and Sexuality* (Cambridge, 1981)

——, 'Introduction: Accounting for Sexual Meanings', in *Sexual Meanings*, ed. Ortner and Whitehead, pp. 1–27

Owen, D. D. R., 'Paien de Maisières — A Joke that Went Wrong', *Forum for Modern Language Studies* 2 (1966), 192–6

——, 'Two More Romances by Chrétien de Troyes?', *Romania* 92 (1971), 246–60

Pafenberg, S. B., 'The Spindle and the Sword: Gender, Sex, and Heroism in the "Nibelungenlied" and the "Kudrun"', *Germanic Review* 70 (1995), 106–15

Pagels, E., *Adam, Eve and the Serpent* (Harmondsworth, 1990)

Parkes, P., 'Fosterage, Kinship, and Legend: When Milk was Thicker than Blood?', *Comparative Studies in Society and History* 46 (2004), 587–615

——, 'Celtic Fosterage: Adoptive Kinship and Clientage in Northwest Europe', *Comparative Studies in Society and History* 48 (2006), 359–95

Parsons, J. C., '"Que nos in infancia lactauit". The Impact of Childhood Caregivers on Plantagenet Family Relationships in the Thirteenth and Early Fourteenth Century', in *Women, Marriage, and Family in Medieval Christendom*, ed. Rousseau and Rosenthal, pp. 289–324

Pateman, C., *The Disorder of Women: Democracy, Feminism and Political Theory* (Cambridge, 1989)

Patterson, L., 'The "Parson's Tale" and the Quitting of the "Canterbury Tales"', *Traditio* 34 (1978), 331–80

Pedersen, F., 'Marriage Contracts and the Church Courts in Fourteenth-Century England', in *To Have and to Hold*, ed. Reynolds and Witte, jr (Cambridge, 2007), pp. 303–9

Pfouts, J. H., 'The Sibling Relationship: A Forgotten Dimension', *Social Work* 21 (1976), 200–4

Plomin, R., and D. Daniels, 'Why are Children in the Same Family so Different from One Another?', *International Journal of Epidemiology* 40.3 (2011), 563–82

Poole, R., ed., *Skaldsagas*, Ergänzungsbände zum Reallexikon der germanischen Altertumskunde 27 (Berlin and New York, 2001)

Quinn, J., 'The Endless Triangles of Eddic Tragedy: Reading *Oddrúnargrátr*', in *Studi anglo-norreni in onore di John S. McKinnell*, ed. M. E. Ruggerini (Cagliari, 2009), pp. 304–26

Quinones, R., *The Changes of Cain* (Princeton, 1991)

——, *Foundation Sacrifice in Dante's* Commedia (University Park PA, 1994)

Razi, Z., *Life, Marriage and Death in a Medieval Parish: Economy, Society, and Demography in Halesowen* (Cambridge, 1980)

Réal, I., *Vies de saints, vie de famille: représentation et système de la parenté dans le royaume mérovingien [481–751] d'après les sources hagiographiques* (Turnhout, 2001)

——, 'Représentations et pratiques des relations fraternelles dans la société franque du haut Moyen Age (VIe–IXe siècles)', in *Frères et sœurs*, ed. Cassagnes-Brouquet and Yvernault, pp. 73–93

Reinhard, B., 'Grendel and the Penitentials', *English Studies* 94.4 (2013), 371–85

Reiter, R. R., ed., *Toward an Anthropology of Women* (New York, 1975)

Reynolds, P. L., and J. Witte jr, ed., *To Have and to Hold: Marrying and its Documentation in Western Christendom, 400–1600* (Cambridge, 2007)

Rich, C. Y., 'Unferth and Cain's Envy', *South Central Bulletin* 33 (1973), 211–13

Robertson, E., and C. K. Rose, ed., *Representing Rape in Medieval and Early Modern Literature* (New York, 2001)

Rogers, M., and P. Tinagli, ed., *Women in Italy, 1350–1650: Ideals and Realities: A Sourcebook* (Manchester, 2005)

Roper, Michael, 'Slipping out of View: Subjectivity and Emotion in Gender History', *History Workshop Journal* 59 (2005), 57–72

Rosaldo, M. Z., and L. Lamphere, ed., *Woman, Culture and Society* (Stanford CA, 1974)

Rose, J., 'How do We Write about Honour Killing?', *London Review of Books*, 4 November 2009

Rosenthal, J., *Patriarchy and Families of Privilege in Fifteenth-Century England* (Philadelphia, 1991)

——, Rev. of J. C. Russell, *Medieval Demography: Essays by Josiah C. Russell*, with preface by D. Herlihy, *American Historical Review* 94 (1989), 741–2.

Rousseau, C., and J. Rosenthal, ed., *Women, Marriage, and Family in Medieval Christendom: Essays in Memory of Michael M. Sheehan C. S. N.* (Kalamazoo, 1998)

——, 'Kinship Ties, Behavioural Norms and Family Counselling', in *Women, Marriage, and Family in Medieval Christendom*, ed. Rousseau and Rosenthal, pp. 325–47

Rubin, G., 'The Traffic in Women: Notes on the "Political Economy" of Sex', in *Toward an Anthropology of Women*, ed. Reiter, 157–210

Russell, J. C., *Medieval Demography: Essays by Josiah C. Russell*, with preface by D. Herlihy (New York, 1987)

Rustin, M., 'Taking Account of Siblings – A View from Child Psychotherapy', *Journal of Child Psychotherapy* 33 (2007), 21–35

Sabean, D., 'Kinship and Property in Western Europe before 1800', in *Family and Inheritance: Rural Society in Western Europe*, ed. J. Goody et al. (Cambridge, 1976), pp. 96–111

Sanders, V., *The Brother–Sister Culture in Nineteenth-Century Literature: From Austen to Woolf* (Basingstoke, 2002)

Samples, S.,'The Rape of Ginover in Heinrich von dem Türlin's *Diu Crône*', in *Arthurian Romance and Gender: Selected Proceedings of the XVIIth International Arthurian Congress*, ed. F. Wolfzettel, Internationale Forschungen zur allgemeinen und vergleichenden Literaturwissenschaft 10 (Amsterdam, 1995), pp. 196–205

——, 'An Unlikely Hero: The Rapist-Knight Gasozein in *Diu Crône*', *Arthuriana* 22.4 (2012), 101–19

Saunders, C., *Magic and the Supernatural in Medieval English Romance* (Cambridge, 2010)

Le Saux, F., 'From Ami to Amys: Translation and Adaptation in the Middle English Amys and Amylion', in *The Formation of Culture in Medieval Britain: Celtic, Latin and Norman Influences on English Music, Literature, History and Art*, ed. F. Le Saux (Lampeter, 1995), pp. 111–27

Sawyer, B., *The Viking-Age Rune-Stones: Custom and Commemoration in Early Medieval Scandinavia* (Oxford, 2000)

Scala, E., 'Canacee and the Chaucer Canon: Incest and Other Unnarratables', *Chaucer Review* 30 (1995), 15–39

Schachter, F. et al., 'Sibling Deidentification', *Developmental Psychology* 12 (1976), 418–27

Schmidt-Wiegand, R., '"hantgemælde" Parzival 6, 19, Rechswort und Rechtssinn bei Wolfram von Eschenbach', in *Studien zu Wolfram von Eschenbach: Festschrift für Werner Schröder zum 75. Geburtstag*, ed. K. Gärtner and J. Heinzler (Tübingen, 1989), pp. 333–42

Schneider, D., 'Anglo-Saxon Women in the Religious Life: A Study of the Status and Position of Women in an Early Mediaeval Society' (unpublished Ph.D. dissertation, University of Cambridge, 1985)

Schulenburg, J. T., *Forgetful of their Sex: Female Sanctity and Society, ca. 500–1100* (Chicago and London, 1998)

Sedgwick, E. K., *Between Men: English Literature and Male Homosocial Desire* (New York, 1985)

Serp, C., 'Fratrie, fraternité et fratricide dans le cycle Lancelot-Graal', in *Frères et sœurs*, ed. Cassagnes-Brouquet and Yvernault, pp. 201–9

Serrano, R., 'No Place for a Lady in the "Song of Roland"', *Pacific Coast Philology* 27 (1992), 110–16

Sif Rikhardsdóttir, *Medieval Translations and Cultural Discourse; The Movement of Texts in England, France and Scandinavia* (Cambridge, 2012)

Sims-Williams, P., *Irish Influence on Medieval Welsh Literature* (Oxford, 2011)

Sinclair, F. E., 'The Power of the Gift: Desire and Substitution in *Daurel et Beton*', *Modern Language Review* 99 (2004), 902–219

Shahar, S., *Childhood in the Middle Ages* (London, 1990)

Sheehan, M. M., *Marriage, Family, and Law in Medieval Europe: Collected Studies*, ed. J. K. Farge (Cardiff, 1996)

Sheehan, S., 'Fer Diad De-flowered: Homoerotics and Masculinity in Comrac Fir Diad', in *Ulidia 2: Proceedings of the Second International Conference on the Ulster Cycle of Tales, Maynooth 24–27 June 2005*, ed. R. Ó hUiginn and Br. Ó Catháin (Maigh Nuad, 2009), pp. 54–65

Sherwin-White, S., 'Freud on Brothers and Sisters: A Neglected Topic', *Journal of Child Psychotherapy* 33 (2007), 4–20

Smith, R. M., 'Some Reflections on the Evidence for the Origins of the "European Marriage Pattern" in England', *The Sociological Review* 28 (1980), 74–112

——, 'Hypothèses sur la nuptialité en Angleterre aux XIIIe–XIVe siècles', *Annales: Histoire, Sciences Sociales* 38 (1983), 107–36

Smith, L. B., 'Fosterage, Adoption and God-Parenthood: Ritual and Fictive Kinship in Medieval Wales', *Welsh History Review* 16 (1992), 1–35

Sørensen, P. M., *The Unmanly Man: Concepts of Sexual Defamation in Early Northern Society*, trans. J. Turville-Petre (Odense, 1983)

——, 'Murder in Marital Bed: An Attempt at Understanding a Crucial Scene in *Gísla saga*', in *Structure and Meaning in Old Norse Literature*, ed. J. Lindow, L. Lönnroth and G. W. Weber, Viking Collection 3 (Odense, 1986), pp. 235–63

——, 'The Prosimetrum Form 1: Verses as the Voice of the Past', in *Skaldsagas*, ed. Poole, pp. 172–90

Spiegel, G. M., 'Maternity and Monstrosity: Reproductive Biology in the *Roman de Mélusine*', in *Mélusine of Lusignan*, ed. Maddox and Sturm-Maddox, pp. 100–24

Stafford, P., 'Sons and Mothers: Family Politics in the Early Middle Ages', in *Medieval Women*, ed. D. Baker (Oxford, 1978), pp. 79–100

——, *Queen, Concubines and Dowagers: The King's Wife in the Early Middle Ages* (London, 1983)

——, 'The King's Wife in Wessex, 800–1066', in *New Readings on Women in Old English Literature*, ed. H. Damico and A. Hennessy Olsen (Indianapolis IN, 1990), pp. 56–78

——, *Queen Emma and Queen Edith: Queenship and Women's Power in Eleventh-Century England* (Oxford, 1997)

Starkey, K., 'Performative Emotion and the Politics of Gender in the *Nibelungenlied*', in *Women and Medieval Epic: Gender, Genre and the Limits of Masculinity*, ed. S. Poor and J. K. Schulman (London and New York, 2007), pp. 253–71

Stenton, F. W., *Anglo-Saxon England* (Oxford, 1970)

Stretter, R., 'Rewriting Perfect Friendship in Chaucer's *Knight's Tale* and Lydgate's *Fabula Duorum Mercatorum*', *Chaucer Review* 37 (2003), 234–52

Sullivan III, C. W., 'Inheritance and Lordship in Math', in *The Mabinogi: A Book of Essays*, ed. C. W. Sullivan III (New York and London, 1996), pp. 347–66

Sulloway, F., *Born to Rebel* (London, 1996)

Sutton-Smith, B., and B. G. Rosenberg, *The Sibling* (New York, 1970)

Sweet, W., 'Lydgate and Scottish Lydgateans' (unpublished D.Phil. dissertation, University of Oxford, 2009)

Tatar, M., *The Hard Facts of the Grimms' Fairy Tales* (Princeton, 1987)

Taylor, J. H. M., 'Melusine's Progeny: Patterns and Perplexities', in *Melusine of Lusignan*, ed. Maddox and Sturm-Maddox, pp. 165–84

Tennant, E., 'Prescriptions and Performatives in Imagined Cultures: Gender Dynamics in *Nibelungenlied* Adventure 11', in *Mittelalter: Neue Wege durch einen alten Kontinent*, ed. J.-D. Müller and H. Wenzel (Stuttgart, 1999), pp. 273–316

Thomas, N., *Diu Crône and the Medieval Arthurian Cycle*, Arthurian Studies 50 (Cambridge, 2002)

Torfi Tulinius, *Skáldið í skriftinni: Snorri Sturluson og Egils saga* (Reykjavík, 2004)

Toubert, P., 'The Carolingian Moment (Eighth–Tenth Century)', in *A History of the Family*, ed. Burguière *et al.*, I, pp. 379–406

Tyler, E., 'Talking about History in Eleventh-Century England: The *Encomium Emmae* and the Court of Harthacnut', *Early Medieval Europe* 13 (2005), 359–83

Usher, J., 'Narrative and Descriptive Sequences in the Novella of Lisabetta and the Pot of Basil (*Decameron*, IV.5)', *Italian Studies* 38 (1983), 56–69

Uther, H.-J., *The Types of International Folktales: A Classification and Bibliography, Based on the System of Antti Aarne and Stith Thompson* (Helsinki, 2004).

Valente, C., 'Children of Revolt: Children's Lives in the Age of Simon de Montfort', in *Essays on Medieval Childhood*, ed. J. Rosenthal (Donington, 2007), pp. 91–107

Valente, R., 'Gwydion and Aranrhod: Crossing the Borders of Gender in Math', *Bulletin of the Board of Celtic Studies* 35 (1988), 1–9

Venarde, B. L., *Women's Monasticism and Medieval Society: Nunneries in France and England: 890–1215* (Ithaca NY, 1997)

Vésteinn Ólason, 'Morð í rekkju hjóna', in *Sagnaþing helgað Jónasi Kristjánssyni, sjötungum. 10 apríl 1994*, ed. Gísli Sigurðsson, Guðrún Kvaran and Sigurgeir Steingrímsson (Reykjavík, 1994), pp. 823–8

——, 'Gísli Súrsson – A Flawless or Flawed Hero?', in *Die Aktualität der Saga: Festschrift für Hans Schottmann*, ed. S. Toftgaard Andersen (Berlin and New York, 1999), pp. 163–75

Vial, C., 'Entre création et destruction: les liens adelphiques dans les récits arthuriens de langue anglaise', in *Frères et sœurs*, ed. Cassagnes-Brouquet and Yvernault, pp. 151–69

Vielhauer, I., *Bruder und Schwester: Untersuchungen und Betrachtungen zu einem Urmotiv zwischenmenschlicher Beziehung* (Bonn, 1979)

Vincent, N., 'Richard, First Earl of Cornwall and King of Germany (1209–1272)', *DNB*, [http://ezproxy.ouls.ox.ac.uk:2117/view/article/23501]

Waugh, S. L., *The Lordship of England: Royal Wardships and Marriages in English Society and Politics, 1217–1327* (Princeton, 1988)

Watson, P., *Ancient Stepmothers: Myth, Misogyny and Reality* (Leiden, 1995)

Welsh, A., 'Doubling and Incest in the Mabinogi, *Speculum* 65 (1990), 344–62

Weisner, T. S., 'Comparing Sibling Relationships Across Cultures', in *Sibling Interaction across Cultures; Theoretical and Methodological Issues*, ed. P. G. Zukow (New York, 1989), pp. 11–25

Wiehe, V. R., *Sibling Abuse: Hidden Physical, Emotional and Sexual Trauma*, 2nd edn (Thousand Oaks CA and London, 1997)

Wolf, A. P., *Sexual Attraction and Childhood Association: A Chinese Brief for Edward Westermarck* (Stanford CA, 1995)

Wolfzettel, F., 'Le *Roman d'Erec* en prose du XIIIe siècle: un anti-*Erec et Enide*?', in *The Legacy of Chrétien de Troyes*, ed. N. J. Lacy, D. Kelly and K. Busby, 2 vols (Amsterdam, 1988), II, pp. 215–28

Wyatt, D., *Slaves and Warriors in Medieval Britain and Ireland, 800–1200* (Leiden, 2009)

Yamamoto, D., *The Boundaries of the Human in Medieval English Literature* (Oxford, 2000)

Yoshimura, C. G., 'The Experience and Communication of Envy among Siblings, Siblings-in-Law, and Spouses', *Journal of Social and Personal Relationships* 27.8 (2010), 1075–88

Zecevic, N., 'Brotherly Love and Brotherly Service: On the Relationship between Carlo and Leonardo Tocco', in *Love, Marriage, and Family Ties in the Later Middle Ages*, ed. I. Davis, M. Müller, S. Jones (Turnhout, 2003), pp. 143–56

INDEX

Aaron 13
Abel 13, 16, 104–6, 114 n. 58, 128, 226
Abélard, Peter 89
Abraham 13, 218
Accolon of Gaul 148–9
Adam 14, 106, 155, 173 n. 81
Adein 222
adoption 1, 8, 18, 43, 163, 235
Adrastus, king of Argos 112–13
Ælred of Rievaulx 30
Æsa 72
Æthelbald, King 216
Æthelstan, King 55
affines 5, 11–12, 16, 32, 36, 39, 45, 53, 54, 57, 74, 81, 154, 161, 180, 181–207, 208, 222, 226, 235, 236, 237
Aglinde 177–8
Agnesa 160
Agravain 54, 66–7, 205
Ailes, Marianne 223
Alberto degli Alberti brothers 114
Albina 83–4
Albion, Albanie 84
Aldrian 204
Alexander, Emperor 147
Alexandrine 228–9
Álfr, legendary king of Sweden 122, 126–7, 196
Álfr, foe of Helgi 122
Alfred, King 25
Allen, Graham 8
Alliterative Morte Arthur 206
Almanzor 203
Alphons, of Spain 229
Alrekr 109, 122, 127
Alsace, kingdom of 53, 120
Alyze 89
Alþingi 192
Amanz, King, also known as Anyawse 136
Amelius 217–18

Amicus 217–18
Amiloun 217–19, 225, 227
Amis and Amiloun 217–19
Amis 217–20, 222, 225, 227
Amleth 121, 196–7, 231–2
Amnon 13, 31
Amurfina, Queen 137–8
Andreuccio 88–9, 161 n. 24
Andrew, duke of Hungary 33
Anfortas, Grail King 206
Anglo-Norman, Norman 61–2, 83–4, 216
Anglo-Saxon 30, 41, 43, 91–2, 107, 117, 183, 216, 224 n. 76
Anjou, Angevin 50–2, 63, 116, 216
Anna, king of East Anglia 37
Anstrude 90–2
Antigone, myth of 5, 113 n. 55
Antoine, son of Mélusine 53
Antonius 117
Antwerp, count of 230
Apter, Terri 81, 144
Apulia, king of 228
Aquinas, Thomas 174 n. 85
Aquitaine, duke of 173
Aranrhod 161–2, 168
Arapesh tribe, Samoa 12, 155
Archibald, Elizabeth 66 n. 97, 78, 155 n. 1, 161 n. 25, 167 n. 54, 173 n. 79, 175
Arcite 221
Argos 112–13
aristocracy 2, 3, 18, 21, 25, 31, 32–4, 52, 59, 74, 117, 125, 151, 154, 192, 230
Aristotle 48
Armenia, Armenian 53, 82 n. 34, 231 n. 102
Arngrímr 82 n. 34, 211–12
d'Arras, Jean 53 n. 36, 81, 82 n. 35, 119
Arriguccio 195
Arthgallo 59

261

Index

Arthur, King 43 n. 153, 53–4, 66–7, 70, 79–80, 94–6, 101, 129, 133–5, 137–8, 144–5, 148–50, 153, 163–7, 175, 205–6
Arthurian, romance 48, 53, 87, 94, 96, 98, 124–5, 129, 144, 146, 149–50, 153, 165, 166 n. 48, 169, 175–6, 205
Arthur, of Brittany 38
Ásgerðr 190–1
Ásgrímr Elliða-Grímsson 211–12
Asher, Martha 153
Ásmundar saga kappabana 71–2
Ásmundr 72, 109
Asser, King Alfred's biographer 25
Athens 198, 200, 220
Atli, brother of Grettir 46–7
Atli, king of the Huns 185, 187, 189, 191, 204
Auchinleck manuscript 62
Adein, Auða, Alde, Aude 222–3
Auðr 190–1
Augsburg 28
Augustine, saint 12, 155–6, 160
aunts 9, 82, 205, 207
Aurell, Martin 35, 38, 202
Austria, Austrian, Austro-Germany 28, 185, 201
Autobiographie, Guibert de Nogent 20 n. 12
Avalon 101, 149

Babylon or the Bonnie Banks o Fordie 159
Babylon, Emir of 227–8
Bademagu, King 95
Baldug, Baruch 52
Balan 69–70, 72, 125
Baldr, Balder 108, 231
Baldwin 90, 92
Balin 69–70, 72, 125
ballads 45, 72–3, 79, 87, 97, 109, 110, 121, 141–2, 143, 159, 169, 172, 175, 179, 192, 200
Ban, King 71
Banin 54
Bank, Stephen and Michael Kahn 7, 19, 23, 29 n. 72, 39, 47–8, 68, 69 n. 110, 76, 96 n. 97, 101, 119, 127, 132, 147 n. 75, 156, 176 n. 99, 178, 237
Bárðr 85 n. 43

La Bataille Loquifer 101
La Batârd de Bouillon 101
Beatrice 24
Becket, Thomas 24
Bede 36–7, 59, 117 n. 69
Beitscher, Jane 27, 38
Béla III, king of Hungary 33
Belinus 58
Belisent, sister of Karlamagnús 164
Belissent 81, n. 31, 147, 217–18
Bendigeidfran, king of Britain, 'Bran the Blessed' 193–4
Benedict of Nursia 29–30
Benedictine Revival 30
Benedictines 30, 38
Benjie 99
Beowulf 106–8, 183–4, 203
Beowulf 107–8, 183, 192
Bera, mother of Bǫðvarr bjarki 63
Bera, wife of Álfr 122
Berenger, Raymond (Ramondo Beringhiere) 32
Bergþóra 56, 65
Bernard, son of Dhuoda 25
Bernard of Clairvaux, Saint 30, 118
Bernard of Munster 192
Bertau, Karl 206
Berthe 145 n. 64
Bertholai 144
Bess 231
Beton 226
Bevers saga 62
Bevis of Hampton 62, 115
Bevis of Hamptoun 62
birth-order 56, 73
Bjarkamál 64
Bjǫrn, of Norway 63
Black Death 45, 230
Black Knight 50
Black, Nancy 197
Blaess, Madeleine 205
Blancheflor, Blaunacheflour 227–8, 231
Bo 231
Boccaccio, Giovanni 2, 15, 34, 76 n. 1, 112 n. 49, 113, 195, 221
Bǫðvarr bjarki 63–4, 78 n. 11, 82, 148
Boeve de Hamtoun 62
Bohemia 53
Bolli Þorleiksson 87, 214–15

The Bonny Hind 159, 171
Borghildr 169
Bǫrkr 190
Bors, Bo(o)rs 53, 67, 70–1, 125, 136
bourgeoisie 25, 52, 192, 195, 230
Boves, duke of Antona 112 n. 48, 225–6
Bravalla, battle of 203
Brian 216
Bricriu 163
Britain, British Isles 42, 56, 58–9, 73, 83–4, 101, 116, 129, 149, 193–4, 216, 230
Bran de Lis, Brandles 98
Branwen 193–4, 203
Branwen uerch Lyr 193–4
Braundinis 229
Bray, Alan 44
Brennius 58
bride-price 6, 19
Brittany 38, 165, 216
Brother Willie 97, 110
brothers 6, 11, 15, 18–40, 44–5, 46–75, 85–103, 104–27, 145–54, 155–80, 181–207, 237
Brown Robyn 171–2
Brown Robyn's Confession 171–2
Bruni 203
Brut, Prose 83
Brutus 84
Brynhildr, Prünhilt 143, 185–9, 200–1
Burns, E. Jane 199
Butler, Judith 96, 153, 167, 194
Byblis 176 n. 98
Byzantium, emperor of 29

Cadwallo 216
Caesarius of Heisterbach 31, 117–18, 129, 192
Cain 13, 16, 104–7, 108 n. 27, 110–11, 114, 119–21, 128, 226
Camelot, Karidol 95–6, 136–9, 205
Canace, Canacis 174–5, 231 n. 102
Canigou, Mount, in Roussillon 82
Canons of Theodore 26
Canterbury, archbishop of 38
Capetian monarchs 38
Carl, sworn-brother of Ealdred 43–4
Carmelide 144

Carolingian 17, 25, 32
Carrier, Nicolas 27–8
Cathay, kingdom of 49
Celestine III 36
Celtic 42, 162 n. 30, 168, 234
Cenwalh of Wessex 36
Chanson de Roland 165, 223
Chansons de geste 101, 209
Charlemagne, Karlamagnús 33 n. 95, 145 n. 64, 164–6, 168, 172, 205, 222–3, 225–6
Charles IV, king of France 146–7 n. 70
Charles Martel•29, 165 n. 41
Charles de Valois 38
Chaucer, Geoffrey 14, 113, 174 n. 86, 221
Chester, play of Cain and Abel 105–6, 119
Chiel Wyet 120–1
Chrétien de Troyes 97, 131, 133–6, 138, 153, 198, 206
Christ, Jesus 13, 96, 105, 106, 166, 204 n. 96, 217 n. 42
Christianity, Christian 13–14, 33, 37, 40, 57, 67–8, 71, 77, 82, 89, 95–6, 104, 106, 215, 227
Christine de Pizan 196
Christina of Markyate 30
chronicle 35, 58, 73–4, 83, 111
Cicero, Marcus Tullius 208–9, 218
Cicirelli, Victor 11, 48, 132, 139, 184 n. 15
Circe 176
Clauditte 131–2
Claudius 198 n. 74
Clement of Alexandria 14
Codre, le 78–9
Coles, Prophecy 88, 170
Colgrevaunce, Sir 125
Compert con Culainn 162
complementarity 7, 8, 11, 19, 29, 45, 73, 119, 127–8, 214, 236
Comrac Fir Diad 223–4
Conchobar 162–3, 168
Condwiramurs 63
Connacht 225
Connidis, Ingrid 10
Constantinople, emperor of, archbishop of 64–5, 140, 147, 197, 236

Continuations of Perceval 98
Corbenic 96
Coriolanus 58
Coudrette 82 n. 35, 119
counter-identification 8, 119, 122, 127, 129
cousins 15, 32, 53, 83, 145, 206–7, 211, 214
Creon 113
Crescentia-legend 196–7
cross-sex relationships 5, 14, 75, 85–103, 145–54, 179, 227–8, 232, 233
The Cruel Brother 171, 192
Cú Chulainn 157, 162–3, 167, 169, 204, 223–5, 232
Cundrie 70–1
Cupid 174, 176, 179
Cyprus 53

Dagr 184
Damian, Peter 19–21, 42
Dante Alighieri 32, 113–14
Daurel 226
Daurel et Beton 112 n. 48, 209 n. 7, 225–6
David, King 13, 31, 209
Davidoff, Leonore 1–2, 77
David's, Saint, the see of 38
Death-Song, of Hildebrand 72
Deichtine, Deichtire 162–4, 168
deidentification 7–8, 31, 50, 53, 120 n. 81, 128–30, 237
Denmark, Danish, Danes 36, 47, 63, 72, 107, 115, 116 n. 64, 121, 148, 183–4, 202–3, 231, 233
Derbforgaill 227 n. 89, 232
Dhuoda 25
Dietrich, twin brothers 196
differentiation 2, 5, 6–9, 22, 45–50, 60, 63, 64, 73, 75–7, 82, 85, 102, 104–5, 119, 144, 182, 207–8, 210, 236
Dinshaw, Carolyn 170 n. 64, 222
disloyalty 13, 184, 186, 191, 198
Doniger, Wendy 166 n. 48, 222
Dooley, Ann 224–5
Dowries Given by the Emperor to his Two Daughters 141
dowry 6, 11, 17, 19, 34–5, 78–9, 87, 126, 138–9, 141, 182, 230–1, 235,

Dunn, Judy 7, 236
Dylan, sea-god 161

Ealdred 43–4, 209 n. 6
Ebroin 92
Edward II 44, 146–7 n. 70
Edward the Confessor 41
Edwin, of Northumbria 216
Efnisien 193–4, 203
Eger 219–20, 225
Eger and Grime 218–20
Egidius, Saint (St Giles) 164
Egill Skallagrímsson 55
Egils saga 55–6, 60 n. 70
Egypt, Egyptian 155, 221
Eiríkr bloodaxe, King 55
Eiríkr, king of Sweden 109, 127
Ekbert, brother of Elisabeth of Schönau 30
elder brothers 10, 13, 25, 38, 49, 51–2, 53, 55–8, 61–2, 80, 72, 74, 104–6, 112, 118, 120–4, 215
elder sisters 32, 89, 130–43
Eleanor of Brittany 38
Eleanor of Provence 23, 32, 76 n. 3
Electra 83
The Elfin Knight 160
Elg-Fróði 63–4
Elidurus 59
Elisabeth of Schönau 30
Élisabeth, former sister-in-law of Humbeline 30
Emain Macha 163
Embrones, of Genoa 35–6, 183, 193
Emer 224 n. 76
Emere, prince of Hungary 197–8
Emma, of Normandy 41
Emelye 222
England, English 21, 22 n. 28, 23, 25, 27, 28, 32, 34 n. 101, 38, 40–3, 55, 57, 61–2, 66 n. 100, 70, 81, 84, 98, 105, 110, 115, 116 n. 66, 117, 124, 133–5, 190, 196–7, 209 n. 8, 216–18, 224 n. 76, 228 (See also 'Anglo-Saxon', 'Old English', 'Middle English')
Eolus 174–5
epic 45, 84, 89–90, 102, 112–13, 145–6, 185, 192, 201, 204, 207, 209, 237,
Epstein, Steven 183

Erec, Prose 151–3
Erec, son of Lac 151–4, 177–8
Ericus the Eloquent 47–9
Ermenjart, Charlemagne's sister 225–6
Erpr 100
Esau 13
Ethyocles, Eteocles 112–13, 114
Etzel 186, 189, 204
Eve 14, 155
The Exeter Maxims 104
Exodus, Book of 13
Eyjafjǫrðr, valley 212
Eyjólfr 212, 214
Eyrbyggja saga 190 n. 43
Eysteinn, King 126–7
exempla 14, 57–8, 67–8, 97, 117–18, 140–1, 192

Fabula Duorum Mercatorum 220 n. 51, 221
Fair Annie 79, 87, 123
Fair Annie, ballad 79
Faithless Foster-Brother, 'type motif' 210
fathers 4, 13, 15, 19, 20, 23–4, 30, 33–4, 36–9, 41, 46–8, 50, 56–7, 60, 63–5, 69, 71, 72, 74, 79, 83–5, 93–4, 98, 105–6, 108, 111, 115, 120–1, 124, 126, 130–1, 133, 134, 135, 137–8, 141, 144, 146, 151–2, 155, 158–9, 162–3, 165–9, 171–4, 176, 177, 193, 198, 204, 205, 214–16, 219, 232
fathers-in-law 62, 145, 146, 155
Feirefiz 70–1
Felix 91
Fengi 121
Fer Diad 223–5
Ferbaeth 224
Fergus mac Roich 224
Ferreux 116
fictive siblings 8, 16, 45, 66, 67, 83, 86, 94, 95, 96, 152, 185, 190, 207, 208–34
Fiers of Arramis 130
Filomena 221
Finland, Finnish 110, 158
Finn, of Frisia 183–4
Finnabair 225
Finnchoem 163
'Finnesburh Episode' (in *Beowulf*) 183

The Finnesburh Fragment 183
Finucane, Ronald 18–19, 24 n. 39
Fleury, abbey of 217
Fliess, Wilhelm 4
Floire, Flores, Floris 227–9, 231
Floire et Blancheflor 227–9
Florence, Florentine 15, 22–3, 37, 39
Florence de Rome, of Rome 196–8
Florence (de Rome) 196–8
Florence, sister of William of Palerne 229
Floris and Blancheflour 227–8
Flursensephin 130, 132
Foot, Sarah 117
Fóstbrœðra saga 212–14, 216
foster-brothers 42–3, 56, 87–8, 121, 124, 13, 166, 209–16, 217, 224, 228–9, 231, 233,
foster-sisters 56, 210, 227–32, 233
Fótbítr, sword 214–15
Frakes, Jerold C. 201–2
France, French 1, 17, 26–7, 29, 32, 34, 36, 42–3, 50, 52, 54, 61, 70, 74, 77, 78 n. 13, 87, 89, 101, 125 n. 102, 133–6, 144–7, 165, 196–8, 216, 222, 228–30
France, king of 230
France, queen of 230
Franks, Frank, Frankish 17, 33, 73, 90, 116–17
Frederick II, Emperor 160
Fresne, le 78
Freud, Sigmund, Freudian 1, 4, 192, 235
Frisia, Frisian 129, 164, 183–4
Fróði, brother of Halfdan 115
Frothi III, king of Denmark 47–8
Fromont 53, 118–19

Gabriel, angel 164
Gaheriet 66–7, 94, 205
Gaheris 54, 66, 81
Gahmuret, son of Gandin 50–3, 63, 70
Galahad 177
Galehault 145
Galoes, son of Gandin 50–2
Gamelyn 124
Gamelyn, Tale of 124
Gandin, king of Anjou 50
Ganelon 165

Ganieda 101
Gansguoter 137–8
Garcy, emperor of Constantinople 197
Gareth, Sir, Guerrhes 50, 54–5, 66–7, 70, 80–1, 125, 157, 160, 205
Gasozein de Dragoz 137–8, 150–1
Gaukr Trandilsson á Stǫng 211
Gaul, Gauls 58, 148, 217
Gautier de Coinci 196–7
Gautland 63, 168
Gaveston, Piers 44
Gawain, Gauvain, Gawein, Gawan 54–5, 66–7, 70, 94–8, 129–34, 136–9, 150, 153, 157, 160, 205–6
Genesis, Book of 13, 36, 104, 156
Genius 174
Genoa 35, 183
Geoffrey, son of Henry III 38
Geoffrey, of Monmouth 9 n. 42, 58–60, 84, 101, 109, 116, 205, 216
Geoffroy la Grand Dent 53, 118–20
Geordie 171
Gerald of Wales 38, 42–3
Gerald, David fitz 38
Gerlint 201
Germany, German, Germanic 19, 30, 47, 71, 107, 133, 137 n. 37, 173, 183–4, 192, 209
Gernot, Gernoz 189, 204 n. 99
Gerson, Jean 14, 31
Gerthruda 121
Gertrude 121–2, 198 n. 74
Gesta Romanorum 58, 141, 170–4, 178, 196, 198
Gevar, King 231
Giachetto 230–1
Giacomino 160
Giannetta 230
Giannole 160
Gilem 164–5, 168
Gilfaethwy 161–2
Ginglain 98
Giotto 40
Giovanni di Pagolo Morelli 39–40, 42
Girard, René 104, 120, 123, 182 n. 5, 188, 209, 213 n. 23, 233
Giselher, Gíslher 189, 204 n. 99
Gisippus 220–2
Gísla saga 85, 92 n. 81, 93 n. 83, 189–92, 222

Gísli Súrsson 85, 126 n. 108, 189–92
Gizurr Þorvaldsson, Earl 93, 143
Goetting, Ann 81
Goldberg, P. J. P. 21
Gonzalo Gonzales 200
Gonzalo Gustioz 204
Goody, Jack 12, 16
Gornemanz 206
Gotegrin 150–1
Gottzman, Carola 186
Gower, John 174–5
Grail 63, 71, 138, 175, 177, 206
Grail Castle 70–1, 96
Grail King 71, 175, 206
Grail Quest 70, 95, 125, 136
Gram 231
Des Granz Geanz 83
Gravdal, Kathryn 26, 179
Gray-Steel, Graysteel 219–20
Greece, Greek 113, 140, 155, 220, 227 n. 89
Green Knight 50
Greenland 214
Gregorius 162, 170, 173, 175, 177
Gregory the Great, Pope 29, 173
Gregory, monk-brother to Christina of Markyate 30
Gregory of Tours 59, 73, 116–17
Grendel 106, 111, 183
Grendel's mother 106
Grettir Ásmundarson 46–8, 64–5
Grettis saga 46–8, 64–5
Griffin, Miranda 165, 205
Griffiths, Fiona 30
Grime 219–20, 225
Grímr (Skalla-Grímr) 55
Grímr Njálsson 56–7, 65
Gringamour, Sir 80–1, 98
Guðmundr 169
Guðrún Ósvífrsdóttir 87, 214–15
Guðrún Gjúkadóttir, Kriemhilt, Grímhildr 99–100, 102, 143, 185–9, 191, 200, 204
Guðrúnarhvǫt 99 n. 110
Guenevere, Guenièvre, Ginover 66, 137–8, 144–5, 149–51, 167, 206
Guenièvre, False 144–6, 148, 154
Guerrhet 66–7
Gui, Count 225–6

Index

Guibert de Nogent 20, 43
Gunnarr, Gunther 185–9
Guthlac, saint 30, 91–2
Guttormr 188
Guy, son of Bevis 62
Guy, of Armenia 82 n. 34
Guyon de Lusignan, of Armenia 52–3, 82 n. 34
Gwern 193–4, 203, 204 n. 97
Gwydion 161–2
Gwynedd 162, 216
Gyburg, lady 89–90, 145–6, 157, 160

Hadingus 231
Hadubrand 71
Hæðcyn 108
Hagen von Troenich 186, 188–9, 204
Hákon IV, king of Norway 32–3, 87
Hákon jarl 56
Haldanus 72, 109
half-brothers 31, 41, 45, 47–9, 53, 54, 56, 64–5, 70–4, 88, 94, 100, 102, 109, 145, 148, 193 194, 214, 236,
Halfdan, king of Denmark 115
Hálfdan, husband of Steinvǫr 93–4
half-siblings 1, 8, 22, 31, 40–1, 48, 70, 72, 86, 89, 100, 168–9
half-sisters 31, 63, 88, 99–100, 140, 144–5, 148, 166, 193, 205
Hamðir 99–100
Hamðismál 99–100
Hanawalt, Barbara 17 n. 1, 21
Hans, Little 4
Hanunda 48
Harald Hilditǫnn (Battle-Tooth), king of Denmark 72, 202–3
Haraldr Fairhair, king of Norway 55
Haraldr harðráði 126 n. 109
Harðar saga 92–3
Harthacnut 41
Harthgrepa 231
Hartmann von Aue 134, 173–4
Hartmuot, of Normandy 201–2
Hassmyra, inscription 39
Hauksdæla þáttr 142–3
Hausbuch, Hausbücher 19, 28, 39
Hector de Mares, de Maris, Ector 53–4, 67, 71, 89 n. 63, 94
Heðinn 122–3, 143

Hegel, king of Ireland 201
Heiðarvíga saga 92 n. 81
Heinrich IV, Emperor 50 n. 19
Heinrich von den Türlin 130–1, 137–9
Heinrichs, Anne 143
Heldris de Cornouailles 135
Helgakviða Hjǫrvarðzsonar 122–3
Helgakviða Hundingsbana II 184
Helgi, king of Denmark 115
Helgi Hjǫrvarðsson 122–3, 143
Helgi Hundingsbani 169, 184
Helgi Njálsson 56–7, 65
Hélinas 81–2, 84
Heller, Rolf 213
Henry III, king of England 23, 32, 38
Henry V, king of England 44
Herebeald 108
Herlihy, David 17
Herwic of Zeeland, Herwig 201–2
Herzeloyde 70
Hildebrand, tradition 71, 107, 109
Hildebrandslied 71
Hildeburc 201–2
Hildeburh 183–4, 203
Hildegard of Bingen 30
Hildibrandr, Hildibrand, Hildebrand 48, 71–2, 109
Hildiger 71–2
Hill, Tom 107
Hinshelwood, Robert D. and Gary Winship 114
history 1, 3, 17–45
Hjálmþés saga ok Ǫlvis 210
Hjǫrvarðr 148
Hnæf 183, 203
Hodierna 43
Holmgautr, Hassmyra inscription 39
Holtsmark 191
Holy Land 82, 126, 172
hostility 4, 5, 6, 8, 16, 28, 36, 64, 104–28, 129–54, 183, 192, 237
Hǫðr 108–9
Hǫgni 188, 204
Hǫrðr 93
Hǫskuldr Þráinsson Hvítanessgóði 56, 57, 65 n. 96
Hǫskuldr Njálsson 56, 65
Hreðel 108
Hrefna 87–8, 215

Hróarr 115
Hróðny 65
Hrókr 115
Hrólfr, king of Denmark 63–4, 148
Hrólfs saga kraka 63–4, 115, 148
Hrothgar 106–7
Hugo, brother of Beatrice 24
Hugo, brother of Hildegard of Bingen 30
Humbeline, wife of St Bernard of Clairvaux 30
Hume, Kathryn 217
Hundingr, sons of 186
Hungary, duke of, king of 33, 197
Huns, Hunnish 48, 185, 204
Huntington, print 220
Hǫðr, Høther 108–9, 231

Iceland, Icelander, Icelandic 42, 46, 56–7, 59–60, 63, 65, 67–8, 71–2, 85, 87, 93–4, 109, 142–3, 184, 187, 189–92, 210, 211 n. 13, 212–15, 234, 236
Illugi 46–7, 64, 68
Ilmarinen 158
Imre, king of Hungary 33
Index Exemplorum 14 n. 63, 31 n. 83, 57, 97 n. 101, 129 n. 2
Indriði, husband of Þorbjǫrg 93
Ingeborg, queen of Denmark 36
Ingridsdotter, Kicki 232
inheritance 8, 16, 17, 19, 22, 26–9, 32, 34, 36, 38, 39, 41, 42, 45, 51–4, 58, 60, 61–4, 73, 74, 104, 110, 112, 114–17, 120, 124, 128, 129, 133–9, 141, 154, 187, 206, 207, 208, 235
Innocent III, Pope 33, 36
Ionákr 99
Ionian Islands 29
Ireland, Irish 42–3, 71, 157, 162, 193–4, 201, 203, 210, 216, 223, 224 n. 76, 225, 232, 236
Irigaray, Luce 5, 90, 92, 100
Irrus Domann 223
Isaac 13, 218
Isabella, queen of Edward II 147 n. 70
Ishmael 13
Íslendinga saga 59–60
Israel 13, 31 n. 84

Italy, Italian 11, 19, 23, 28, 34, 39, 58, 89, 160, 183, 194
Itys 199
Ívens saga 134
Iwein 134

Jacob 13
Jaeger, C. Stephen 209
jealousy 7, 56, 80, 120–3, 128, 139–45, 161, 171, 185, 186, 190–2, 200, 211–12, 215, 217, 223, 233
The Jeaste of Syr Gawain 98
Jenghiz, khan of Cathay 49, 58
Jocasta 113
Jochens, Jenny 213
Jock 159
John, Gospel of 13
John Cok 24
John, king of England 38, 39 n. 130
John of Lodi 19
John, Sir (*Tale of Gamelyn*) 124
John (*The Twa Brothers*) 110
John (*The Cruel Brother*) 171
Jonathan 13, 209
Jón Sigmundarson 142–3
Jóra 142–3
Jǫrmunrekkr, king of the Goths 99–100
Joseph 13
Josiane 62, 81 n. 31
Judas Iscariot 106, 119, 216

Die Kaiserchronik 196
Kalervo 110–11, 158
Kalevala 110–11, 158–9
Kardeiz 52 n. 31, 63
Kári Sǫlmundarson 47 n. 6, 56–7
Karlamagnús saga 164–6, 168, 204, 222–3
Karras, Ruth Mazo 40
Kay, Kei, Keu, foster-brother to King Arthur 43 n. 153, 136, 137,
Kay, Sarah 182, 197 n. 69, 208, 226
Kempe, Margery 22
Kermode, Jenny 40
The King's Dochter Lady Jean, 160
Kinoshita, Sharon 135
Kjartan Óláfsson 87–8, 214–15
Klagsbrun, Francine 22 n. 25, 29, 55 n. 46, 88, 139, 142, 147 n. 75, 181

Index

Klapisch-Zuber, Christiane 17
Knut, of Jutland 189 n. 40
Knut VI, king of Denmark 36
Kolbeinn Sighvatsson 60
Kolbeinn (*Gísla saga*) 85 n. 43
Kolbeinn ungi 93
Kudrun 201–2
Kudrûn 201–2, 229
Kullervo 111 n. 40, 158–9

Laban 13
Lablonde, Jeanne 37
Lacy, Norris 151–2, 153 n. 102
Lady Isabel and the Elf-Knight 160
Lady of the Lake 53, 148–9
Lady Maisry 120–1
Lambra, Doña 200–1
Lamorat 95
Lancelot, Launcelot, Sir 53–4, 61, 66–7, 71, 88–9 n. 63, 94, 144–5, 149, 151, 157, 166, 206
Latin 13, 83–4, 91, 99, 141, 217 n. 37, 218
Lavayne, sir 67
Lawson, M. K. 41
Laxdœla saga 87–8, 92 n. 81, 214–15
Lazarus 13
Leabhar na hUidre 163
Leah 13
Lecuppre, Gilles 38, 202 n. 92
Leigamur 130
Leir 9 n. 42, 116
Leodegrance 145
Leprous Lady 95–6
Lett, Didier 14–15, 17, 23, 25, 34
Lévi-Strauss, Claude 11–12, 15, 76, 155, 182 n. 5
lex Romana 18
Lindow, John 108–9
Lionel 53, 70–1, 125
Lizzie Wan 171
Lleu 162–3, 167
Lóch 224
Loherangrin 63
Loki 108
London 24, 44, 58, 166–7
Loosepine, lady 219–20
Lord Ingram 120–1, 123
Lord Ingram and Chiel Wyet 120–1

Lord Randal 159
Lord Thomas 79, 87
Lord Thomas and Fair Annet 87
Lot of Orkney, of Lothian 94, 166, 205
Louis IX, king of France and saint 24, 32
Louis, King (*Willehalm*) 145–6
love 3, 5–7, 13, 15, 16, 20, 25, 34, 35, 36, 41, 42, 44, 45, 46–75, 76–103, 120–1, 123, 125, 131–40, 141, 152, 154, 156, 160, 162, 164, 173–5, 176, 188, 190, 191, 199, 202, 209, 210, 212–15, 219, 221–5, 228–31, 233, 235–8
loyalty 7, 12–13, 16, 35, 38, 44, 45, 46–69, 70, 73–4, 75, 76–102, 107, 121, 124, 146, 149, 152, 156, 181, 184, 185, 188–91, 205, 206, 210, 218, 221, 225, 227, 233, 234, 235, 236, 17–18, 22
Lucette 37
Lucchesio of Poggibonsi, saint 28
Ludewic 201
Lugaid 232
Lugh 163, 168
Luke, Gospel of 13
Lydgate, John 112–13, 175, 221
Lyonet 70, 79–81
Lyonors 80–1, 98
Lýtingr 65–6

Mabinogion, Mabinogi tales 161–3, 193, 199, 203
MacCannell, Juliet Flower 6 n. 21, 74
Macé, Laurent 21
Machaire, Macharius 174, 231 n. 102
Maddox, Donald 53 n. 34, 53 n. 36, 134
Madelung, Margaret A. 215
Magnús, King, Saga of the Sons of 126–7
Maillezais, monastery of 118–20
Maledysant, Malydysaunt, Damesell 80 n. 20, 81
Malin 116
Malory, Sir Thomas 50, 54, 66–7, 69–70, 79–81, 83, 125, 136, 148–9, 157, 166–7
Mandeville, Sir John 49
Manfred, son of the lord of Tolentino 34
Märchen 63 n. 87, 86

Margaret 97
Marie de France 77, 87
Marjory 99
Marquet 24
Marrays, Annabile 37
Marrays, John 37
marriage 7, 9–12, 16, 23, 26, 32–7, 39, 41–3, 45, 48, 52, 53, 56, 57, 62, 65, 76–80, 83–4, 85, 88–90, 107, 113, 115, 119–20, 123, 126, 129–33, 139–45, 155–6, 181–207, 220–3, 229–31, 237
Marshal, John 24
Marshal, William 24–5
Martel, Charles, French king 29, 165 n. 41
Martha 13
Martineau, Harriet 154
Mary Magdalene 13
Math 161–2
Matholwch, king of Ireland 193–4, 204 n. 97
Matthew, Gospel of 15 n. 66,
McFarlane, Kenneth 44
Méa, sister of Giovanni di Pagolo Morelli 39–40
Mead, Margaret 12, 155
Medb, Queen 223–5
Melancolie 174
Melanippus 113
Melior 228–9
Mélior 82
Meljanz 131–3
Mélusine 31 n. 86, 53, 81–2, 84, 113, 115, 118–19
Mélusine, Histoire de, Roman de 29 n. 74, 52–3, 62, 81–2, 119
Mempricius 116
Menalippe, Menalippus 112–13
Meraugis 152
Merlin 69, 101, 125, 149, 166
Middle English 62, 78 n. 9, 83, 217, 227
Middle High German 184, 196 n. 66
Miles, son of Bevis 62
Miles, nephew of Willehalm 145
Miller, William 59, 65, 211
Minghino 160
Mirk, John 26, 169, 179
Mitchell, Juliet 4–6, 58, 61, 69 n. 109,
 69, 77, 85, 95 n. 91, 96, 102, 104, 120, 125, 145, 160, 170, 178, 181, 208, 235–6
Molyneux, Nicholas 44
monks 14 n. 63, 30, 31 n. 83, 35, 53, 118–20, 128, 150, 217
Montorgueuil, king of 229
Montpellier, lords of 21
Moors, Moorish 70, 201–4
Mordred 38, 54, 149 n. 82, 163, 165–7, 169, 171, 175, 197, 205–6, 216
Morgen, Morgan le Fay 101, 148–9, 164, 205
Morvidus 59
Moses 13
mothers 1, 4, 5, 7, 13, 19–26, 31, 34, 35, 36–8, 41, 43, 47, 48, 52, 58, 60–5, 78, 80, 81–2, 84, 88, 93, 99, 102, 106, 116, 129, 137, 142, 143, 146, 148, 149, 158–9, 162–3, 165, 169, 170–7, 184, 195, 199, 201, 203, 204, 225–6, 228, 230, 236
mothers-in-law 188
Mudarra 204
La Mule sans Frein 136, 138
Murdoch, Brian 173 n. 81, 201
Mylys (*Florence of Rome*) 197–8
Myrrha 176 n. 98

Nabor 177–8
Nabur, King 166
Najemy, John 37
Nanna 231
Neckham, Alexander 43
Das Nibelungenlied 181 n. 1, 185–9, 196, 201, 204
Nibelungs 204
Nisien 193
Njáll Þorgeirsson 56–7, 65
Njáls saga 47 n. 6, 55–7, 65–6, 92 n. 81, 211–12
Njálssons 56, 65, 67
nobility 23, 24, 27, 31, 33, 35, 38, 43, 44, 51, 53, 59, 61–2, 67, 68, 83–4, 114, 116–20, 126, 194
Noire Espine, lord of 133
Normandy 24, 41, 84, 201
Northumbria 44, 58, 115, 209 n. 6, 216
Norway, Norwegian 32–3, 48, 55–6,

63–4, 85, 87, 126–7, 142–3, 184, 212–14, 232
nuns 30

Obîe 131–3
Obîlot 131–3
Oddbjǫrg 211–12
Óðindísa, Hassmyra inscription 39
Óðinn, Odin, Odinic 108, 203, 231
Oedipus 4, 112, 167
Ohlgren, T. H. and S. Knight 124
Óláfr *pái* (peacock) 214–15
Óláfr the saint, king of Norway 213
Óláfr Tryggvason, King 214–15
old age 7, 9, 100–1
Old English 25, 47 n. 6, 91–2, 104–6, 107 n. 70
Old High German 71
Old Norse, Norse 15, 62, 85, 99, 108, 115, 122, 125, 133–4, 143, 164–5, 168, 184–6, 188–9, 222, 228
Oli 202–3
Oliver 222–3
Ophelia 231 n. 107
Órækja Snorrason 60
Orestes 83
Orians, King 166
Orkney 56, 66–7, 80–1, 94, 166, 169, 205
Orkney, earl of 56
Orkney, king of 80
Orkney, queen of 166, 169, 205
Ǫrlygsstaðir, battle of 60, 93 n. 84
Ormr Svínfellingr 143
Orson 61, 78 n. 11, 124, 145 n. 64–5, 147
Ortner, Sherry 12
Ortrûn 201–2
Ortwin 201–2
Orvendil 121–2
Osburh, King Alfred's mother 25
Ote, Sir 124
Ovid 13, 83 n. 38, 176, 198

Palamedes 175
Palemon 221
Palestine 82
Pallias 220
Pandion 198

parage 27, 124, 134–5
parents 2, 5, 7–9, 13, 17–26, 27–8, 45, 49, 62, 63, 81, 106, 119–20, 133, 139, 142, 158, 161, 171–2, 173, 175, 217, 219, 227–9, 235
Paris, Matthew 32
Parkes, Peter 42, 227 n. 89, 232
Patroclus, Saint, life of 117
Parzival 63, 70–1, 206
Paston, John II 25
Patrides, Sir 95
peasants 2, 11, 23, 27, 40, 44, 63, 74, 77, 80, 86, 110, 117, 128, 143, 153–4, 157, 172, 175, 181–3, 199, 214–15, 229, 233, 235
Pega 30, 91–2, 102
Pellehan, King 175
Pellinor, King 94, 175
Penda, king of Mercia 36
Pepin, King, Emperor 145 n. 64, 147, 151
Perceval 61, 94–6, 136 n. 32, 153
Percy, folio, version 218 n. 47, 219
Perotto 230
Persaunt of Inde, Sir 50
Peter, brother of Marquet 24
Peter of Wakefield 39 n. 130
Peveres, of Genoa 35–6, 183, 193
Pfouts, Jane H. 16
Philip Augustus, king of France 36
Philomena 198–9
Philomena 198–9
Poetic Edda 99 n. 110, 184
Polymyte 112–13
Polyneices 114
Porrex 116
Post-Vulgate Cycle 94, 96, 166–7, 169, 175, 178, 205
Post-Vulgate *Mort Artu* 216
Post-Vulgate *Queste del Saint Graal* 95–6, 100, 151, 153, 177
Post-Vulgate *Suite de Merlin* 67, 148–9, 164, 166
Présine 62 n. 83, 81–2
priests 13, 30, 120 n. 81, 125, 170, 172
primogeniture 10, 26–9, 31, 38, 41, 45, 49, 50–1, 59, 61–3, 64, 73–4, 114, 116, 121, 124, 133–5, 138–9
Progné 198–9

Proud Lady Margaret 97
Provence 21, 23, 32, 76 n. 3, 165
Prussia, Pruysse 40, 49
pseudo-history 33, 58, 60, 72, 73–4, 116, 123, 127, 147, 202
psychoanalytical theory 3, 4–6, 7, 16, 21, 55, 68, 128, 170, 181, 235–6
psychology 7–10, 16, 19, 21, 22, 29, 43, 47, 49, 56, 68
La Pucelle aux Petites Manches 131
Purgatory 43, 97

Quarrel of the Queens 196, 204
Quebeleplus 130–2
Queste del Saint Graal, La Quête du Saint Graal, La Queste de Saint Graal 94, 125 n. 102, 136, 141, 151, 167
Questing Beast 166–7, 175–6
Quinones, Ricardo 104, 111, 128
Quoikos 130–1

Rachel 13
ragna rǫk 15, 108–9
Raimondin 53, 82, 112 n. 48, 119
Rainouart 89
Randvér 99
Réal, Isabelle 17
Red Knight, Ither 50, 80, 206
Reginald, of Durham 216
Reinbald, the Frisian 164
Reinhard, Ben 107
Rem, Lucas 28
Renaud 53
Renfrei 164
Rennewart 89–90, 157, 160
Richard of Cornwall 32
Richard I 'Lionheart' 43
Richard III 38, 202 n. 92
Richars li Biaus 229–30
Richars 229–30
Ring 202–3
Roar 231
Robert 25
Roland, Rollant 164–5, 168, 169, 204–5, 222–3
Roller 47–9
romance 2, 27, 50–5, 61–3, 72–4, 79, 81–3, 97–9, 124–6, 129–39, 150, 157, 170, 173, 185, 197–9, 201, 204–7, 208, 209, 217–22, 229–31, 233
Rome, Roman 13, 18, 34, 44, 58, 114, 164, 172, 196–7, 220–1, 228
Romulus and Remus 13, 73
Roncesvalles 222
Ronsasvals, Provençal fragment 165
Roper, Michael 2
Rosenberg, B. G. 50
Rosenthal, Joel 21 n. 16, 28–9
Roucliff, Alice 37
Round Table 50, 54–5, 66–7, 80, 83, 94–6, 125, 149, 151–3, 206
Royns, king of North Wales 70
Ruad, king of Norway (Lochlann) 232
Rubin, Gayle 12, 35, 147 n. 72, 182
runestones, memorial 18, 39
Rupertsberg foundation 30
Russell, Josiah 21
Russia, Rossye 49, 71
Rørik 121

Sabean, David 26
saga 42, 45, 55–7, 59, 63, 64, 71–3, 74, 85, 87–8, 92–4, 99, 109, 157, 164–5, 189–92, 221–16,
Sagremor 166, 216
Salomon, of Brittany 216
same-sex relationships 5, 11, 49, 78, 102, 156, 181, 225, 227
Samples, Susann 150
Samuel, I, II, Book of 13, 31 n. 84, 209 n. 5
Sancha, Doña 200–1, 203–4
Saracens 145–6
Saturn 221
Sauve, Saint 28
Savoy 28
Sawyer, Birgit 39
Saxo Grammaticus 47, 71–2, 99 n. 110, 116 n. 64, 121, 154, 189 n. 40, 202–3, 231, 233
Saxons 217
Scotland, Scottish, Scots 56, 79, 223
Scandinavia 39, 42, 47, 63 n. 87, 71, 109, 127, 168, 183, 203, 211
Scáthach 223–4
Scholastica, Saint 29–30
Scylla 176
Serrano, Richard 165

Index

Sétanta 163
The Seven Sages 25
sexuality 2, 5, 101, 159, 160, 180
Sgoidamur 137–9, 151
Sheath and Knife 159, 171
Siete Infantes, los 200, 203–4
Los Siete Infantes de Lara 200–1, 203–4
Siggeir, king of Gautland 168
Sighvatr Sturluson 59–60, 93
Sigifridus, uncle of Thietmar of Merseburg 35
Sigmundr 168–9, 170 n. 67
Sigmundr Sigurðarson 204
Sigmundr, Hassmyra inscription 39
Signý 115, 168–9, 170 n. 67, 175
Signý (*Harðar saga*) 93 n. 82
Sigrún 184
Sigurðr, Sivrit, Sifrit, Sîfrît 99, 112 n. 48, 185–9, 196
Sigurðr Magnússon 126–7
Silence 135
Simon de Montfort 25
Sinclair, Finn 226
Sinfjǫtli 168–9, 171, 204
Sir Gawain and the Green Knight 205–6
sisters 5–6,12, 13–14, 29–31, 32 33–7, 39–40, 76–103, 129–54, 155–80, 181–200, 202–7
sisters-in-law 34, 143, 200–2, 207, 237
sister's sons 38, 83, 115, 162–9, 183, 193, 199, 202–7
Sivard 202
Sivrit, king of the Moors 201
Skarpheðinn Njálsson 56–7, 65
Skjǫld 231
Skuld 63–4, 148
Smith, Richard 22 n. 26
Snorri *góði* 191
Snorri Sturluson 55, 59–60, 108–9, 127
Sofronia 220–1
Sohrab-and-Rustum tale 69
Sólarljóð 67–8
Sophocles 113 n. 55
Sǫrli (*Sólarljóð*) 68
Sǫrli 99–100
Spain, Spanish 200, 204, 228–9, 236
Spiegel, Gabrielle 82
Spring of the Virgin 177–8
Stafford, Pauline 41, 197 n. 71

Stanzaic Morte Arthur 66 n. 100
Statius 112
Steinólfr 211–12
Steinvǫr 60 n. 72, 93–4
Stephen, King 24
stepbrothers 41
stepmothers 41, 47–8, 63, 169, 228
step-siblings 8, 40–1, 52
stepsisters 145
Stiklastaðir, battle of 214
Sturla Sighvatsson 60, 93 n. 84
Sturla Þórðarson of Hvammr 59–60, 206 n. 108
Sturlunga saga 93 n. 84, 142–3
substitutability 6, 128, 145, 154, 198, 217, 220–1
Sutton-Smith, Bruce 50
Svanhildr 99–100, 102
Sváva 122–3
Sweden, Swedish 39, 109, 122, 202
Sweet, Will 112
Sweet William 141
sworn brothers 43–4, 61, 79, 124, 161, 185–6, 190–1, 207, 208–9, 217–27, 233–4
Sørensen, Preben Meulengracht 190, 191 n. 47

Táin Bó Cualaigne, Táin Bó Cúailnge 157, 163, 223–4
Tereus, king of Thrace 198–9
Thamar 13, 31
Thebes 13, 112–14
Thèbes, Roman de 112–13
Theodoric 71
Theseus 113
Theuderic 92
Thietmar of Merseburg, *Chronicle of* 35, 38
Thomas, Lord 79, 87
Thrace 198, 200
Thurbrand 43
Titus 220–2
Tocco brothers, Carlo and Leonardo 29
Tochmarc Emire 232
Tolentino, lord of 34
Torfi Tulinius 55–6 n. 49, 60 n. 70
Tortarius, Ralph 217

La Tour-Landry, the knight of 31, 140, 150, 170, 229
Towneley, mystery cycle 106
Travels of John Mandeville 49
Trevrizent 206
triplets 61, 63–4, 82–4
Tristan 38, 65
Troy, Trojan 58, 84, 225
Tuscany 17, 114
The Twa Brothers 110, 141–2
The Twa Sisters 141–2
'Two Sisters' ballad motif 143
twins 60–3, 74, 78–9, 82, 124, 135, 162, 168, 170, 196, 208, 225, 222, 228
Tydeus 108, 112–13

Ugolino 113–14
Ulster, Ulstermen 157, 162–3, 225
ultimogeniture 22, 26, 28
uncles 9, 53, 108, 112, 115, 118, 137, 161, 207, 211, 236
Unferð 107
Untamo 110–11, 158–9
Updike, John 121, 198
Uppsala 122
Urian 52–3
Uriens 205
Urré 67
Uther Pendragon 206

Väinämöinen 158–9
Valentine 61, 78 n. 11, 124, 145 n. 64, 147
Valentine and Orson 61–3, 78 n. 11, 145 n. 64, 146–7, 151
Váli 109
Veláquez, Ruy 203–4
Vésteinn Ólason 192
Vésteinn Vésteinsson 189–91
La vie de saint Gilles 165 n. 41
Víga-Glúms saga 126 n. 106, 211–12, 215
Vígólfr 68
Viking 35, 39, 46
Vinheiðr, Brunanburh, battle of 55
Virgin Mary 172, 197
Vita Aegidii 165 n. 41
Vita Anstrudis 90–1
Vita Wulfstani 23
Vivianz 145–6

Vulgate Cycle 66, 166–7, 205
Vulgate *Estoire de Merlin* 166
Vulgate (Prose) *Lancelot* 144–5, 166
Vulgate *Merlin* 67, 205
Vulgate, *Mort Artu* 54, 66–7, 216
Vulgate *Queste del Saint Graal* 95
Vǫlsunga saga 99 n. 110, 168–9, 184–7, 204
Vǫlsungr 168
Vǫluspá 15, 108

Wales, Welsh 38, 42–3, 70, 161, 163, 192–4, 203, 216
Walter, of Norfolk 25
Waltheof, earl of Northumbria 44
Weisner, Thomas 10
Welser trading company 28
Wessex 36, 41
The Wife's Lament 224 n. 76
Willehalm 89, 145–6
William of Normandy 84
William of Palerne 228–9
William of Palerne 228–9
Winglaine 219–20
Winter, John 44
Wolfram von Eschenbach 50, 63, 70, 89, 131, 145, 157, 206
Wolfzettel, Friedrich 153
Worms, lord of 184–6
Wrath 174

Xanten 196

York 37
Young Benjie 99
younger brothers 10, 18, 23, 25–9, 32, 46, 48, 49, 51–3, 57–60, 63, 88–9, 110, 112, 115, 120, 121, 128, 133, 169, 220, 225
younger siblings 5, 11, 22, 28, 47, 55, 57, 58, 121, 132
younger sisters 10, 23, 32, 130–9, 140–3, 164, 173
Ymilia, lady of Tolentino 34
Yngling dynasty 109
Ynglingatal 109 n. 31
Yngvi 122, 126–7, 196
Ypomenés, King 170 n. 67, 175–6, 178
Yvain 94–6, 98, 133, 138, 148, 153, 205
Ywain and Gawain 134–5

Index

Þjóðólfr of Hvín 109 n. 31
Þiðrekr 204 n. 99
Þiðreks saga af Bern 184–6, 204
Þingvellir 142
Þóra, two sisters 142–3
Þorbjǫrg 93
Þorbjǫrn 85
Þorbjǫrn hook 46, 64
Þórdís Súrsdóttir 85, 93 n. 83, 189–91
Þórdís (*Víga-Glúms saga*) 212
Þórðar saga kakala 93
Þórðr kakali Sighvatsson 93–4
Þórðr Sturluson 59–60
Þorgeirr (*Víga-Glúms saga*) 212, 214

Þorgeirr Hávarsson 213–14
Þorgrímr 189–92
Þórhallr 56
Þórir hundsfótr 63–4
Þorkell Súrsson (brother of
  Gísli) 189–91
Þorleikr 214
Þormóðr Kolbrúnarskald 213–14
Þórólfr, brother of Egill 55–6
Þórólfr, brother of Grímr 55
Þorsteinn drómundr 48, 64–5
Þorvaldr Gizurarson 142–3
Þráinn Sigfússon 56–7, 65
Þuríðr 87–8, 214

www.ingramcontent.com/pod-product-compliance
Lightning Source LLC
Chambersburg PA
CBHW051605230426
43668CB00013B/1990